SHIKI TSUKAI

1

Story by To-ru Zekuu

Art by Yuna Takanagi

Translated and adapted by Mayumi Kobayashi

Lettered by North Market Street Graphics

Ballantine Books · New York

A Del Rey Trade Paperback Original

Shiki Tsukai volume 1 copyright © 2006 by To-ru Zekuu and Yuna Takanagi
English translation copyright © 2007 by To-ru Zekuu and Yuna Takanagi

Published in the United States by Del Rey Books, an imprint of The Random House Publishing Group, a division of Random House, Inc., New York.

DEL REY is a registered trademark and the Del Rey colophon is a trademark of Random House, Inc.

Publication rights arranged through Kodansha Ltd.

First published in Japan in 2006 by Kodansha Ltd., Tokyo

ISBN 978-0-345-49925-7

Printed in the United States of America

www.delreymanga.com

9 8 7 6 5 4 3 2 1

Translator and adaptor: Mayumi Kobayashi
Lettering: NMSG

Contents

Since *Shiki Tsukai* is about the seasons, calendars are very important to the story. Two types of calendars are referenced throughout this series. One is the Gregorian calendar, the familiar 12-month January-through-December system that is commonly used throughout the West and in many other parts of the world. But the lunisolar calendar—the one that was used in Japan until 1873, when Japan adopted the Gregorian calendar—is also referred to often. A lunisolar calendar is one that indicates both the moon phase and the time of the solar year.

Under the Gregorian calendar, in Japanese the months are literally called "first month (January)," "second month (February)," "third month (March)," etc.

But under the lunisolar calendar, each month has a name specifically tied to the seasons. They are as follows, with the names literally translated, and where the name is derived from.

January = *Mutsuki*, affection month. Family and friends get together to celebrate the New Year.

February = *Kisaragi*, layering clothes month. This month, wear layers for protection from cold.

March = *Yayoi*, new life month. Derived from spring.

April = *Uzuki*, Deutzias flower month. This month is when the Deutzias flowers bloom.

May = *Satsuki*, crop month. This is the best month to plant crops.

June = *Minazuki*, water month. End of the rainy season.

July = *Fumizuki*, letter month. Derived from the *Tanabata* holiday where you write a wish or a song on a piece of paper and hang it on bamboo.

August = *Hazuki*, leaf month. Month when the leaves fall.

September = *Nagazuki*, long month. The time of year when nights grow longer.

October = *Kannazuki*, God month. Gods gather in October for an annual meeting at the Izumo shrine.

November = *Shimotsuki*, frost month. The first frost of the winter.

December = *Shiwasu*, priest month. Priests are busy making end-of-year prayers and blessings.

The lunisolar calendar is also divided into 24 *sekki*. The 24 *sekki* are days that divide the lunisolar calendar into 24 equal sections and have special names to mark the change in seasons. The dates below are approximate and shift due to the differences in the lunisolar and Gregorian calendars.

Rishhun. February 4. First day of spring.

Usui. February 19.

Keichitsu. March 5.

Shunbun. March 20. Vernal equinox. Middle of spring.

Seimei. April 5.

Kokuu. April 20.

Rikka. May 5. First day of summer.

Shouman. May 21.

Boushu. June 6.

Geshi. June 21. Summer solstice. Middle of summer.

Shousho. July 7.

Taisho. July 23.

Rishuu. August 7. First day of autumn.

Shouho. August 23.

Hakuro. September 7.

Shuubun. September 23. Autumnal equinox. Middle of autumn.

Kanro. October 8.

Shoukou. October 23.

Rittou. November 7. First day of winter.

Shousetsu. November 22.

Taisetsu. December 7.

Touji. December 22. Winter solstice. Middle of winter.

Shoukan. January 5.

Daikan. January 20.

Honorifics Explained

Throughout the Del Rey Manga books, you will find Japanese honorifics left intact in the translations. For those not familiar with how the Japanese use honorifics and, more important, how they differ from American honorifics, we present this brief overview.

Politeness has always been a critical facet of Japanese culture. Ever since the feudal era, when Japan was a highly stratified society, use of honorifics—which can be defined as polite speech that indicates relationship or status—has played an essential role in the Japanese language. When addressing someone in Japanese, an honorific usually takes the form of a suffix attached to one's name (example: "Asuna-san"), is used as a title at the end of one's name, or appears in place of the name itself (example: "Negi-sensei," or simply "Sensei!").

Honorifics can be expressions of respect or endearment. In the context of manga and anime, honorifics give insight into the nature of the relationship between characters. Many English translations leave out these important honorifics, and therefore distort the feel of the original Japanese. Because Japanese honorifics contain nuances that English honorifics lack, it is our policy at Del Rey not to translate them. Here, instead, is a guide to some of the honorifics you may encounter in Del Rey Manga.

-san: This is the most common honorific, and is equivalent to Mr., Miss, Ms., or Mrs. It is the all-purpose honorific and can be used in any situation where politeness is required.

-sama: This is one level higher than "-san" and is used to confer great respect.

-dono: This comes from the word "tono" which means "lord." It is an even higher level than "-sama" and confers utmost respect.

-kun: This suffix is used at the end of boys' names to express familiarity or endearment. It is also sometimes used by men among friends, or when addressing someone younger or of a lower station.

-chan: This is used to express endearment, mostly toward girls. It is also used for little boys, pets, and even among lovers. It gives a sense of childish cuteness.

Bozu: This is an informal way to refer to a boy, similar to the English terms "kid" and "squirt."

Sempai/Senpai: This title suggests that the addressee is one's senior in a group or organization. It is most often used in a school setting, where underclassmen refer to their upperclassmen as "sempai." It can also be used in the workplace, such as when a newer employee addresses an employee who has seniority in the company.

Kohai: This is the opposite of "-sempai" and is used toward underclassmen in school or newcomers in the workplace. It connotes that the addressee is of a lower station.

Sensei: Literally meaning "one who has come before," this title is used for teachers, doctors, or masters of any profession or art.

[blank]: This is usually forgotten in these lists, but it is perhaps the most significant difference between Japanese and English. The lack of honorific means that the speaker has permission to address the person in a very intimate way. Usually, only family, spouses, or very close friends have this kind of permission. Known as *yobisute*, it can be gratifying when someone who has earned the intimacy starts to call one by one's name without an honorific. But when that intimacy hasn't been earned, it can be very insulting.

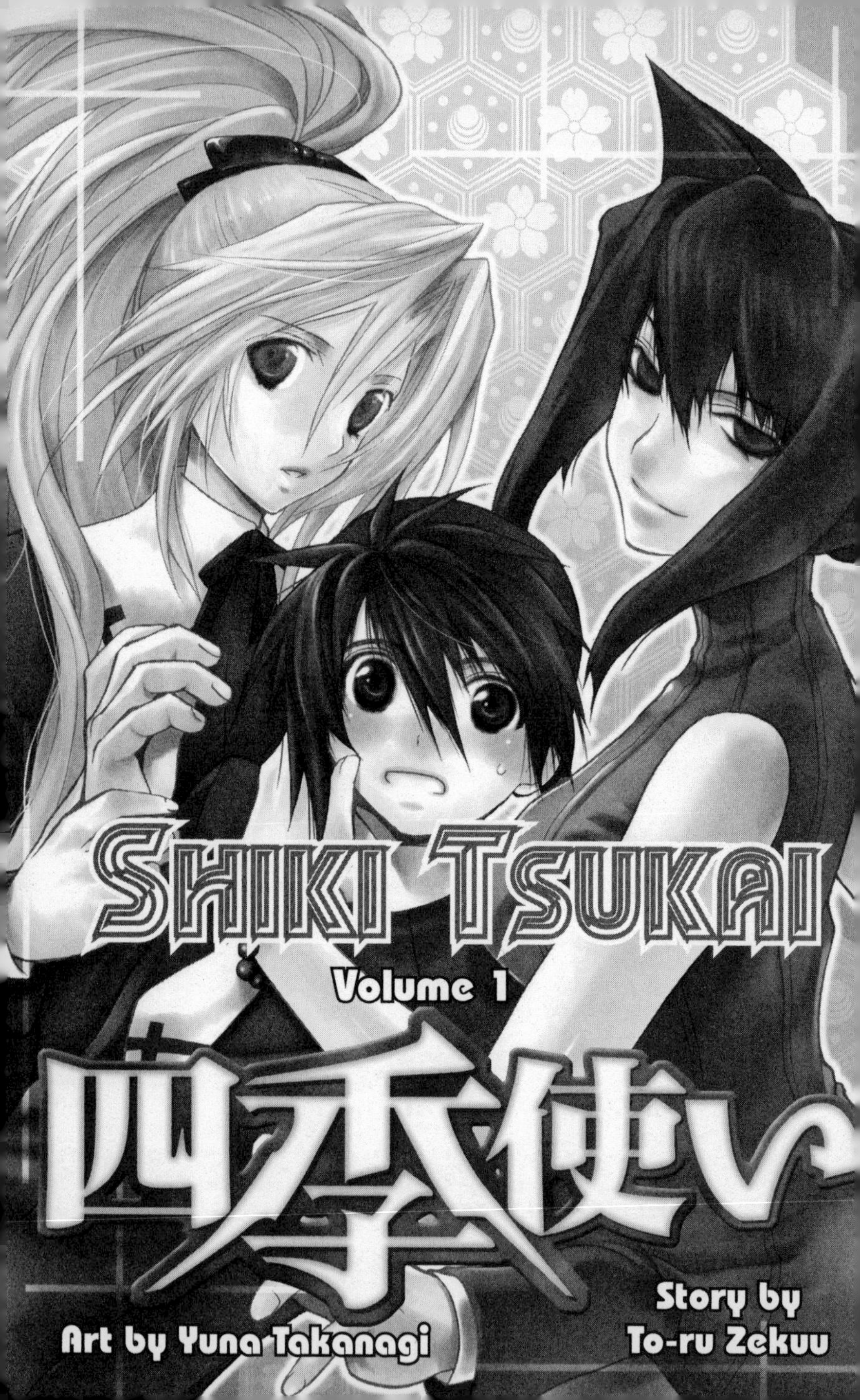
SHIKI TSUKAI
Volume 1
四季使い
Story by
To-ru Zekuu
Art by Yuna Takanagi

Table of Contents

SHIKI TSUKAI

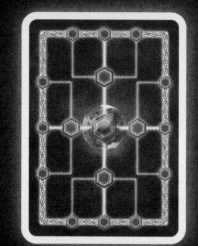

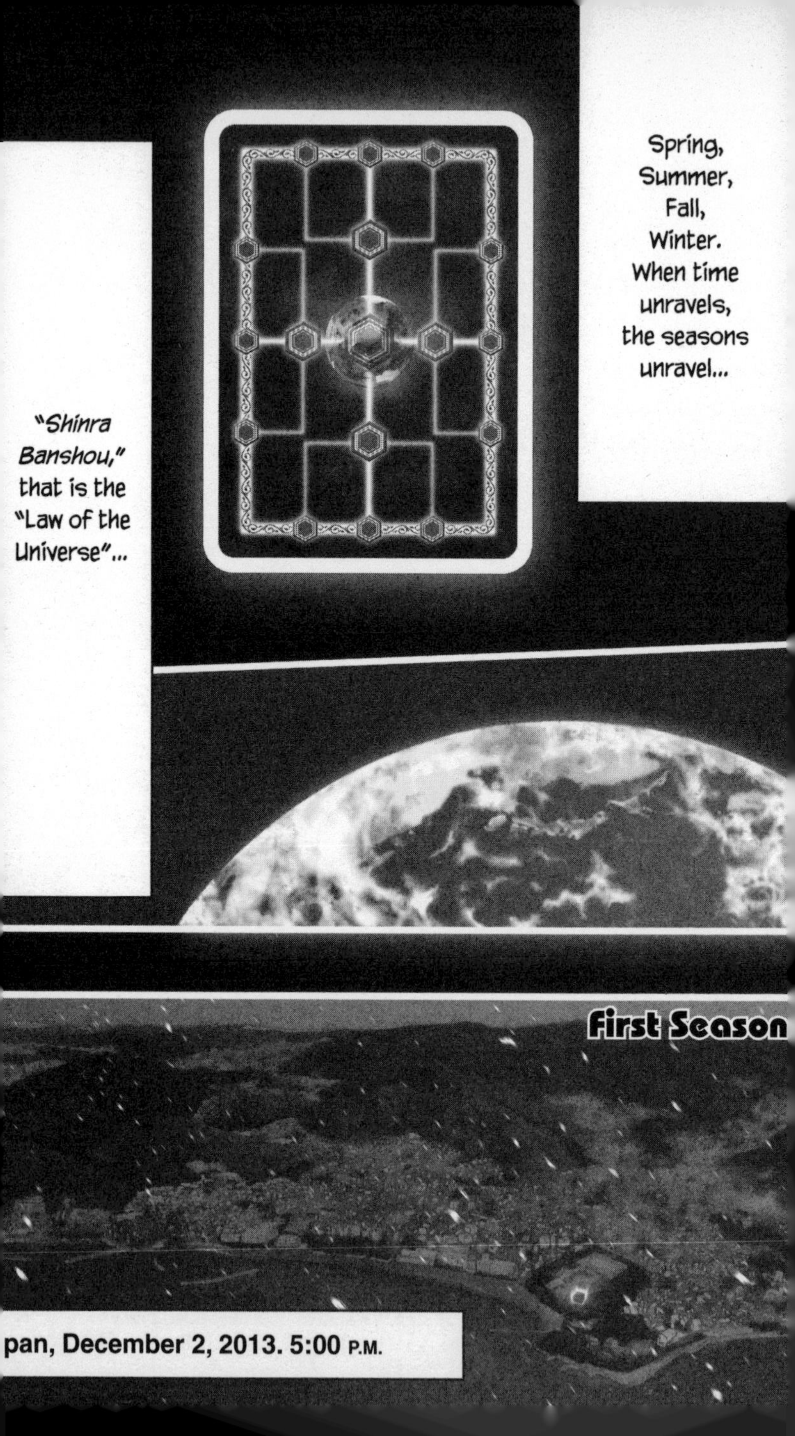

Spring,
Summer,
Fall,
Winter.
When time
unravels,
the seasons
unravel...

"*Shinra Banshou,*" that is the "Law of the Universe"...

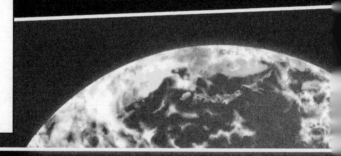

First Season

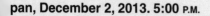

pan, December 2, 2013. 5:00 P.M.

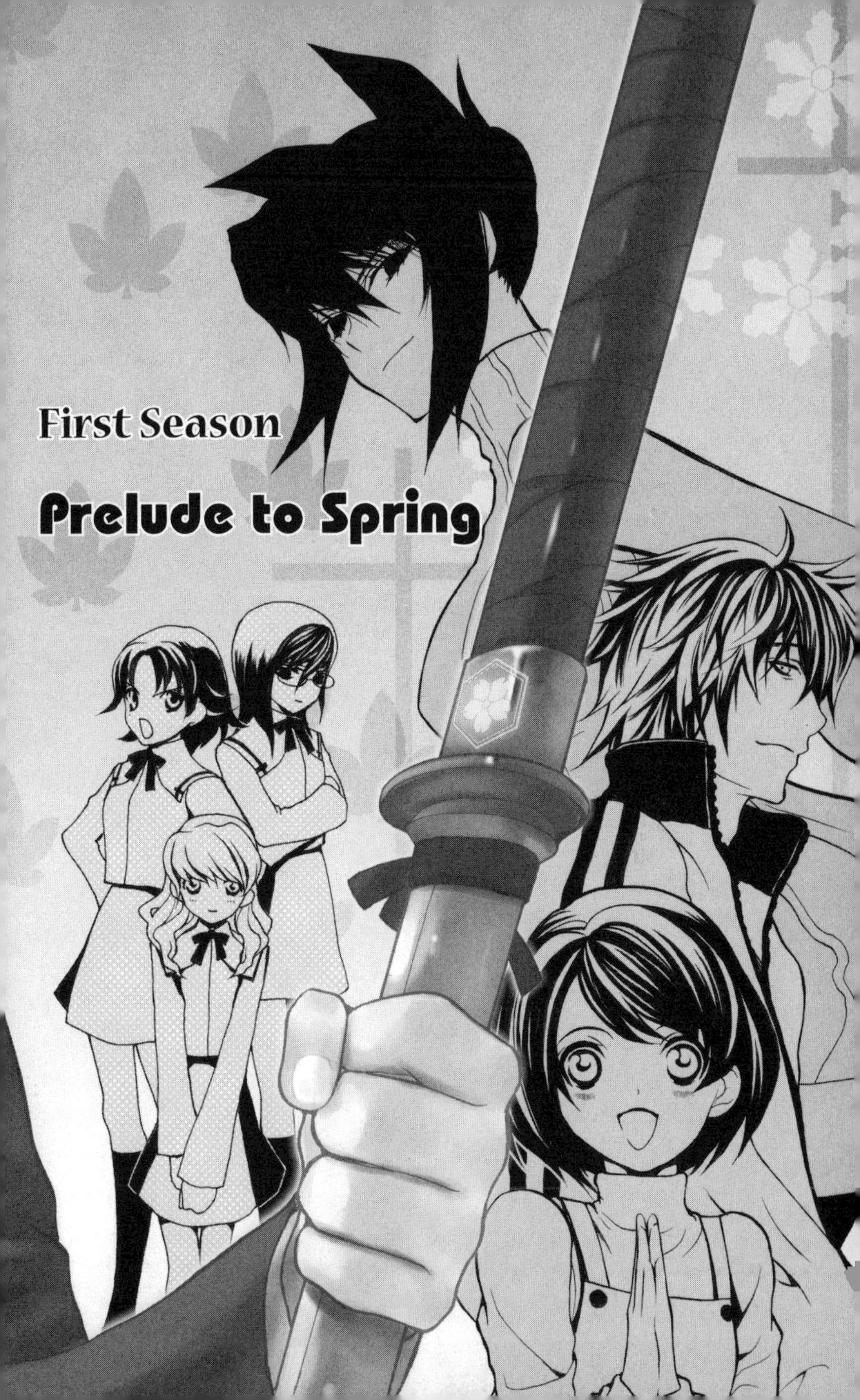
First Season
Prelude to Spring

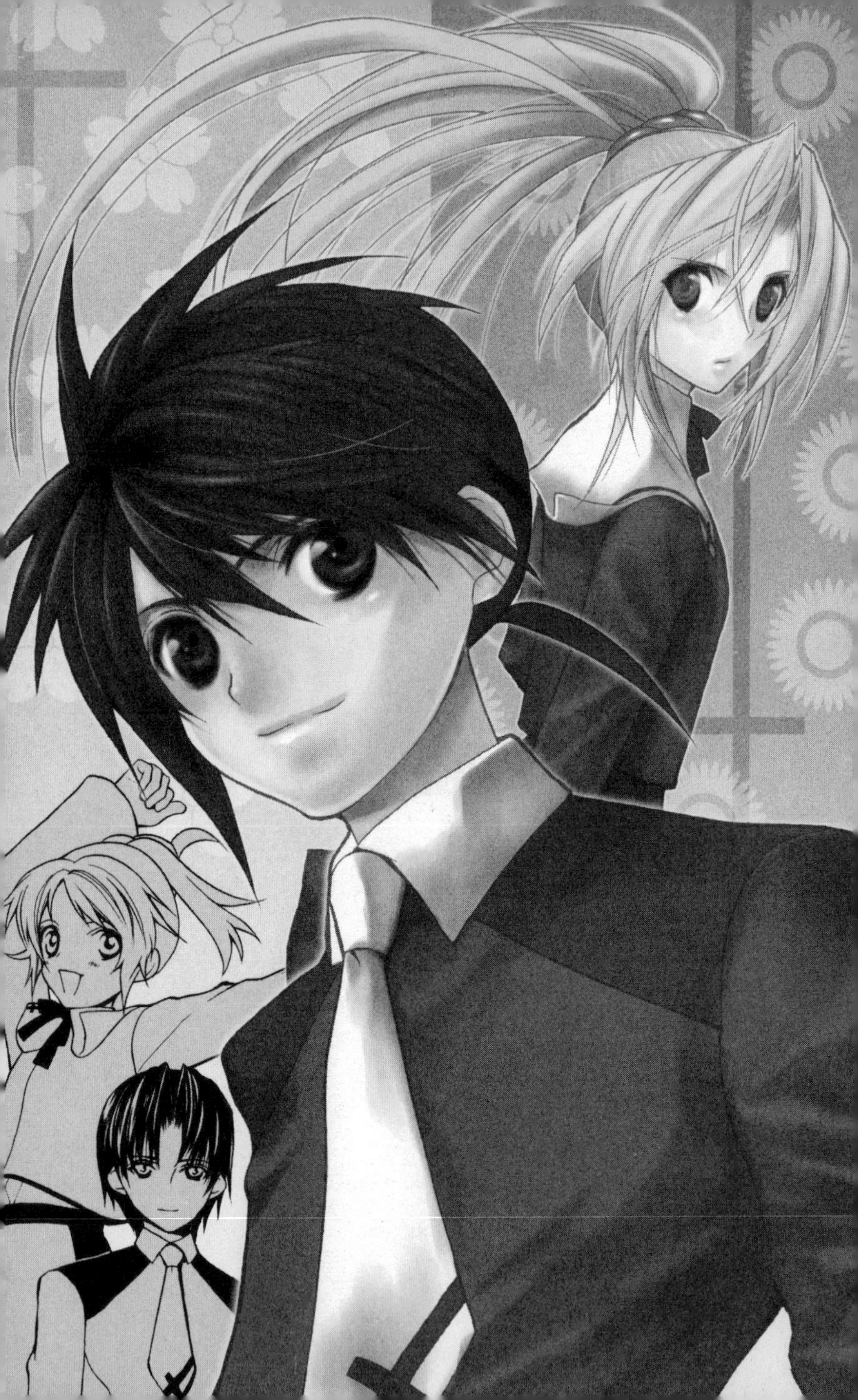

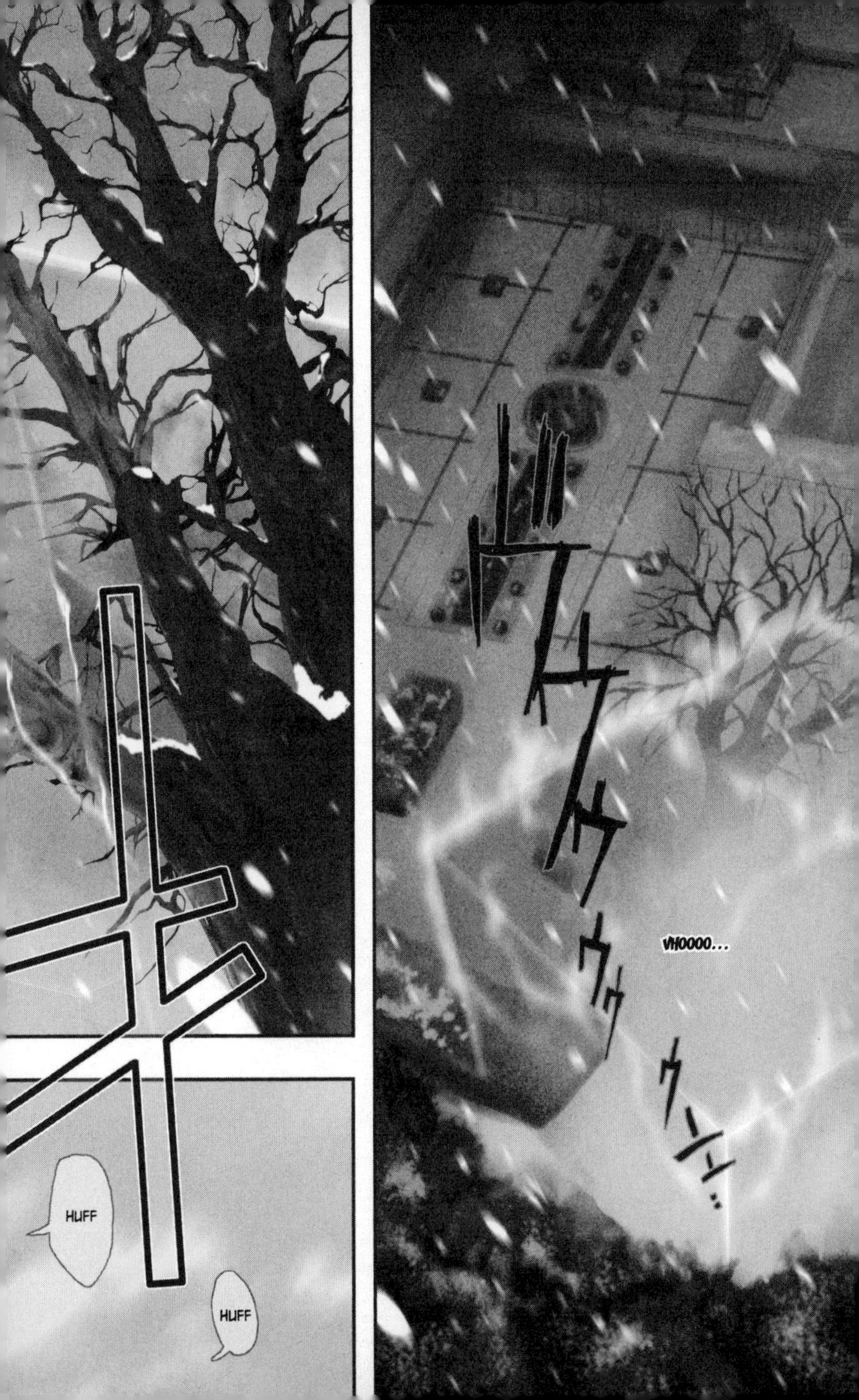
VHOOOO...
HUFF
HUFF

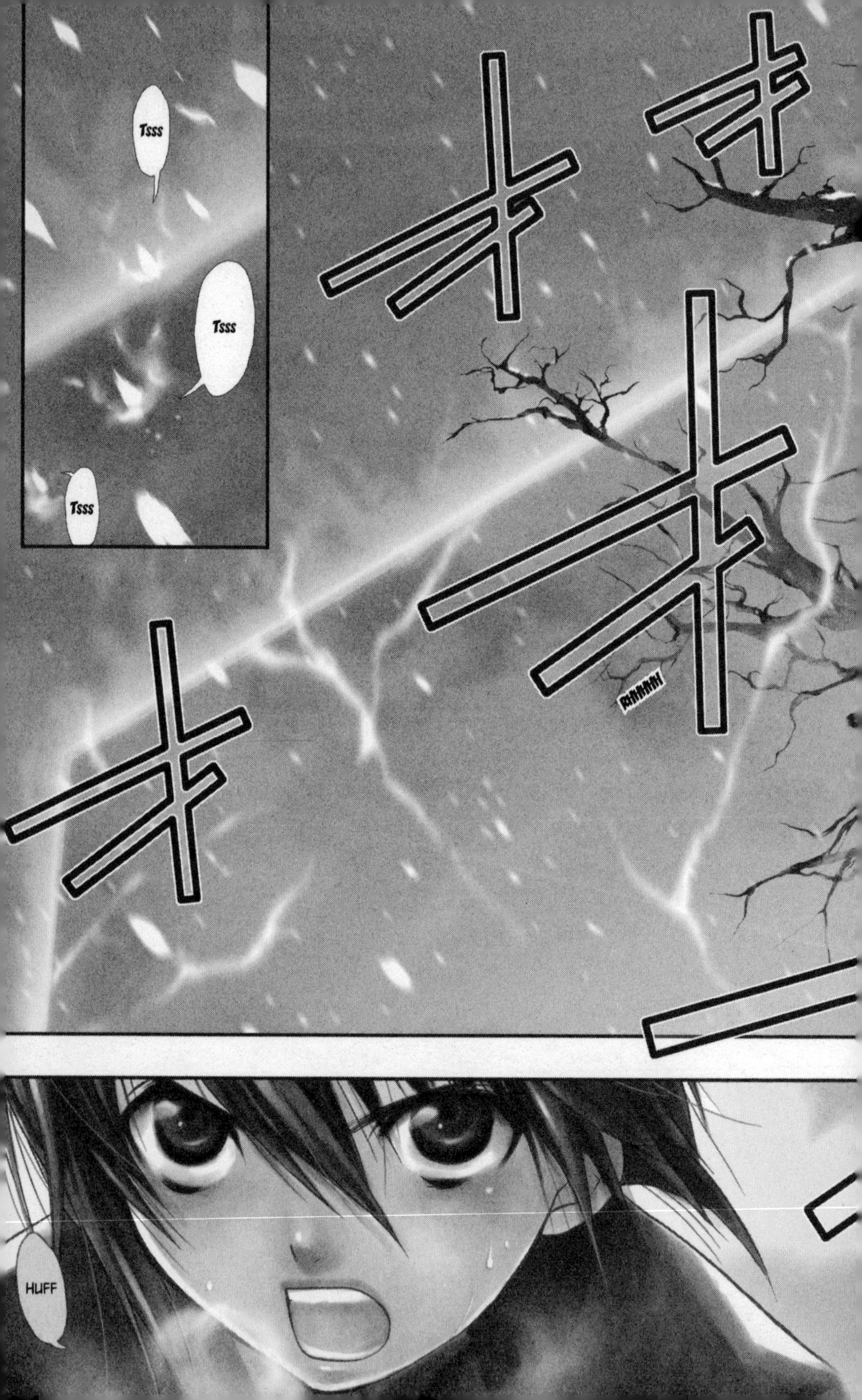
Tsss
Tsss
Tsss
HUFF

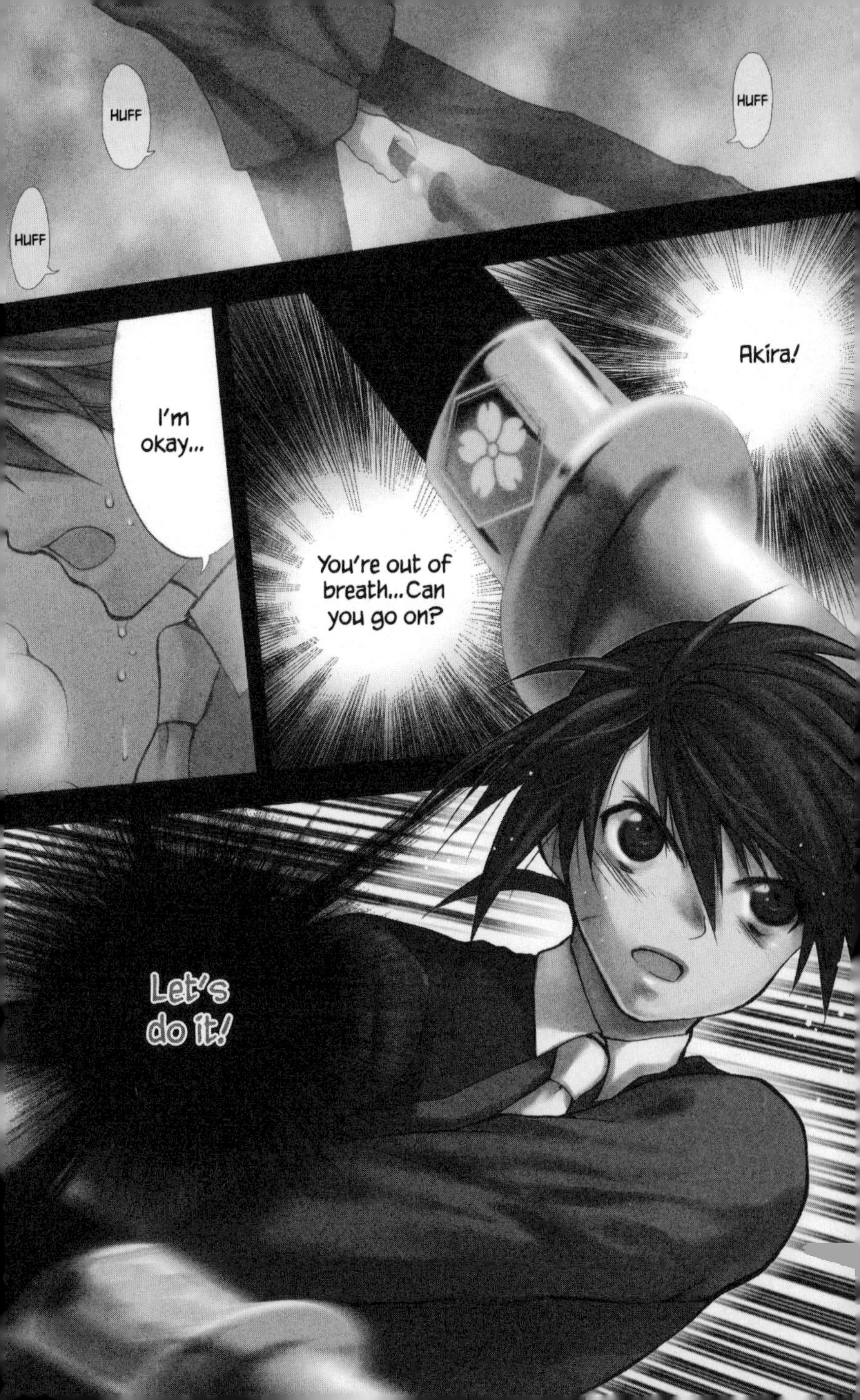
HUFF
HUFF
HUFF
Akira!
You're out of breath...Can you go on?
I'm okay...
Let's do it!

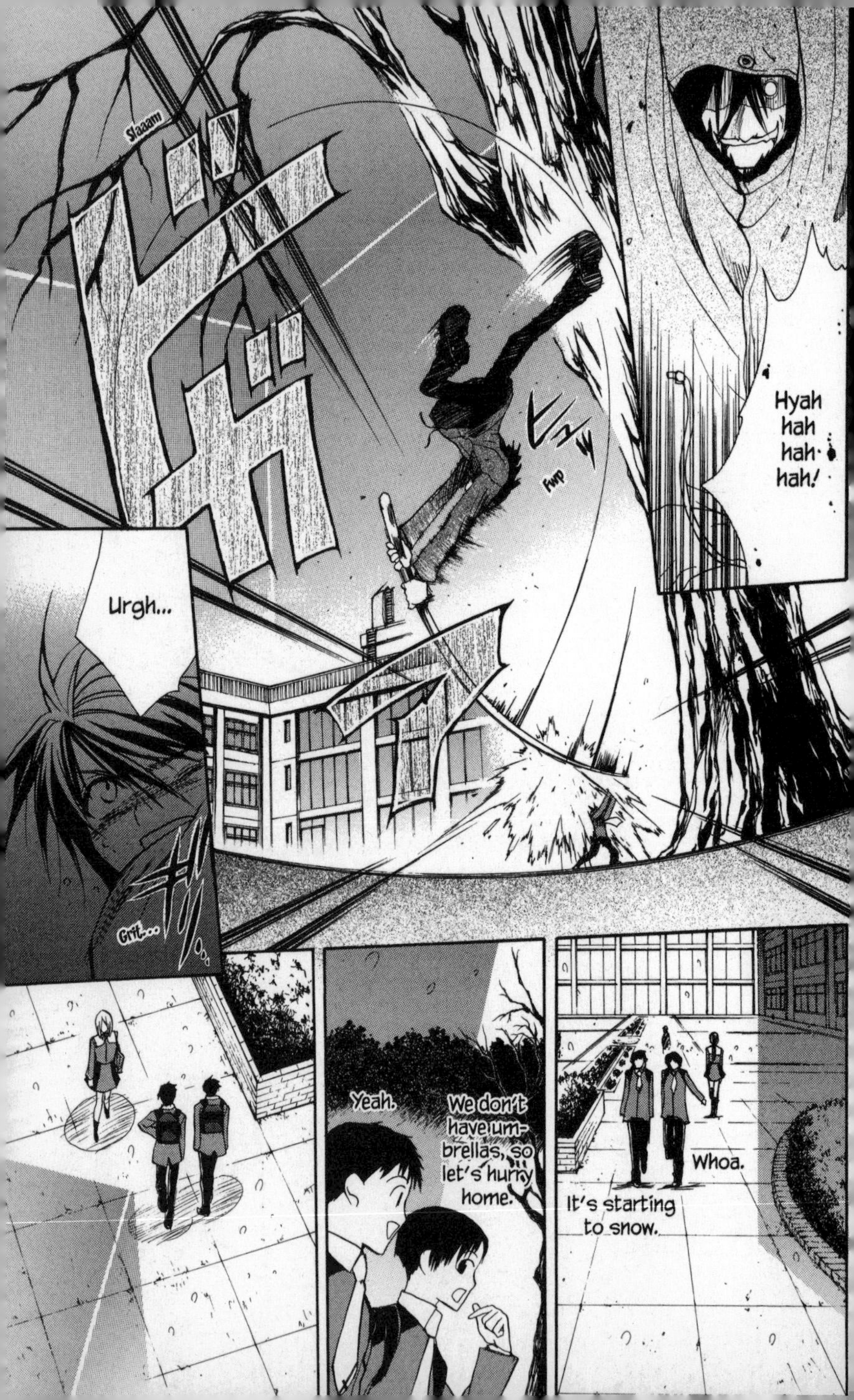
Hyah hah hah hah!
Slaaam
fwp
Urgh...
Grit...
Whoa.
It's starting to snow.
We don't have umbrellas, so let's hurry home.
Yeah.

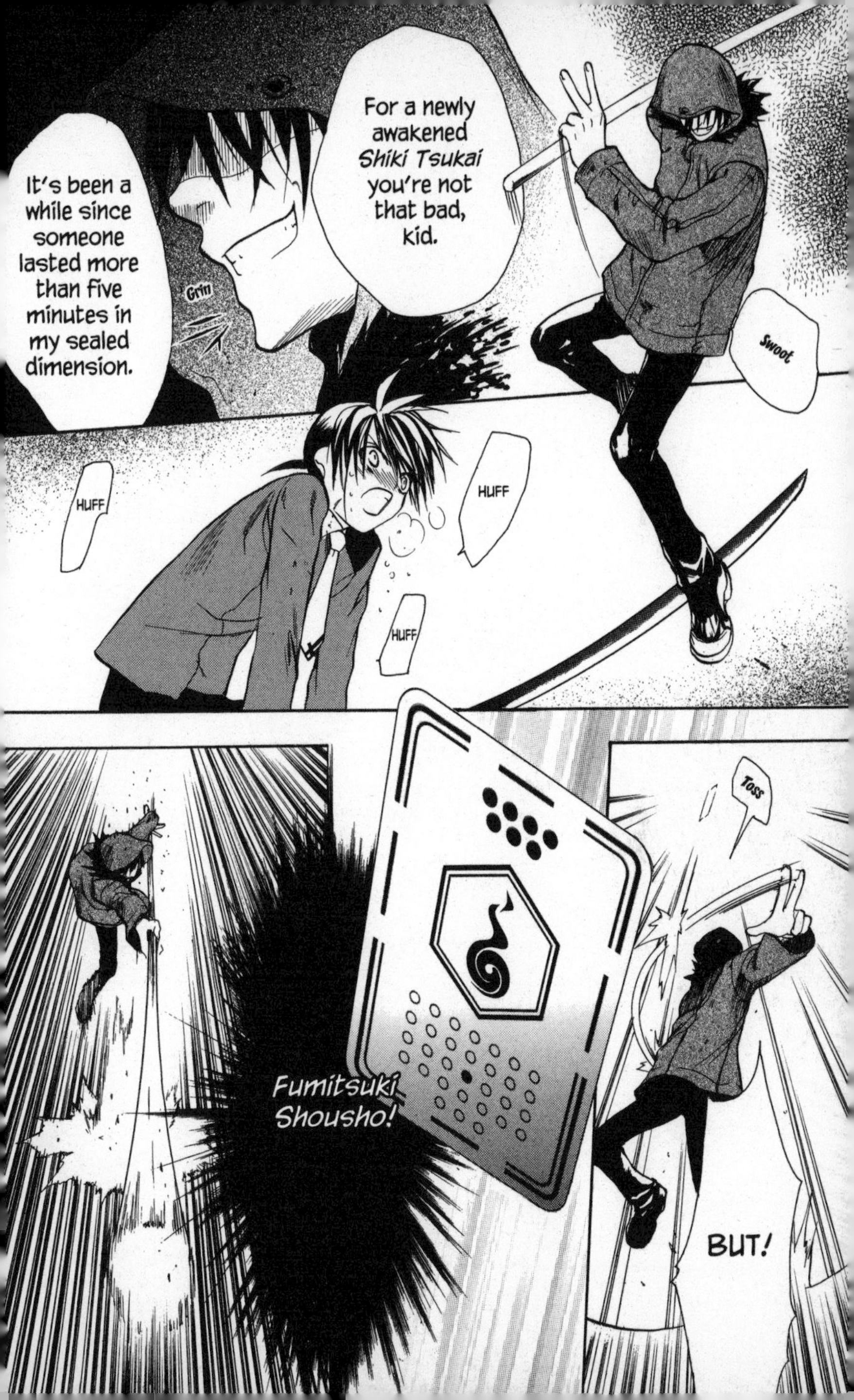
For a newly awakened *Shiki Tsukai* you're not that bad, kid.
It's been a while since someone lasted more than five minutes in my sealed dimension.
Grin
Swoot
HUFF
HUFF
HUFF
Toss
BUT!
Fumitsuki Shousho!

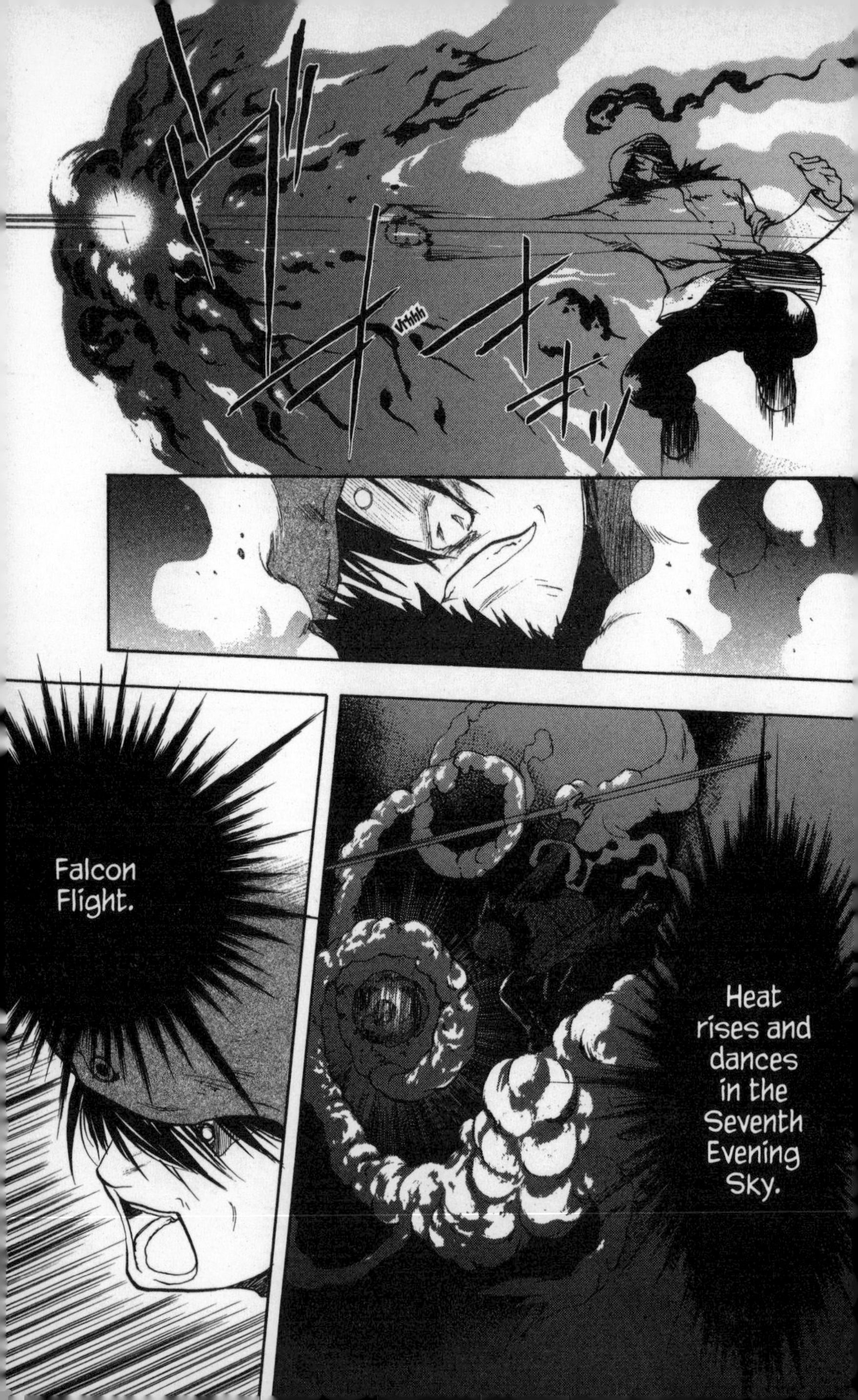
vrhhh
Heat rises and dances in the Seventh Evening Sky.
Falcon Flight.

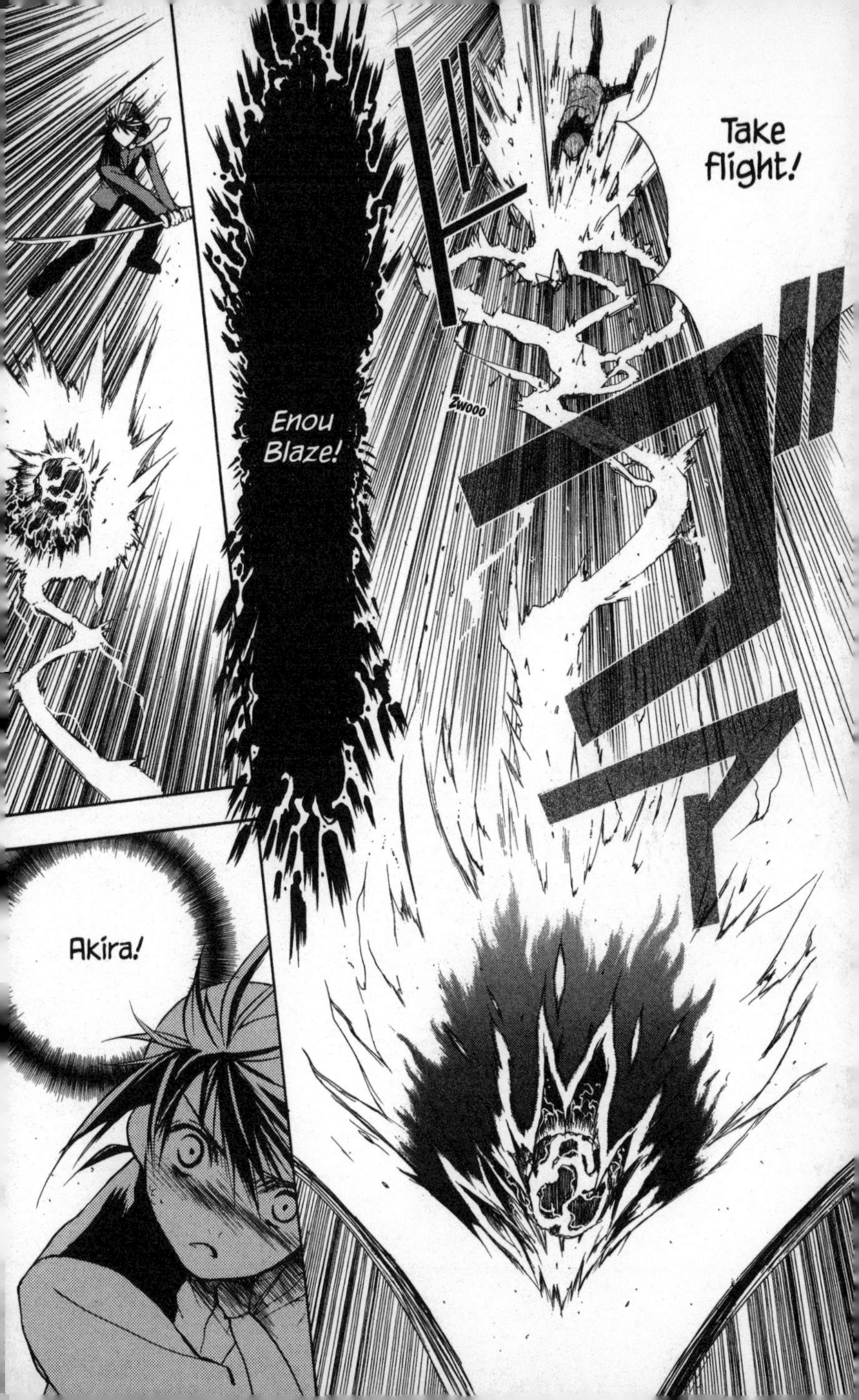
Take flight!
Zwooo
Enou Blaze!
Akira!

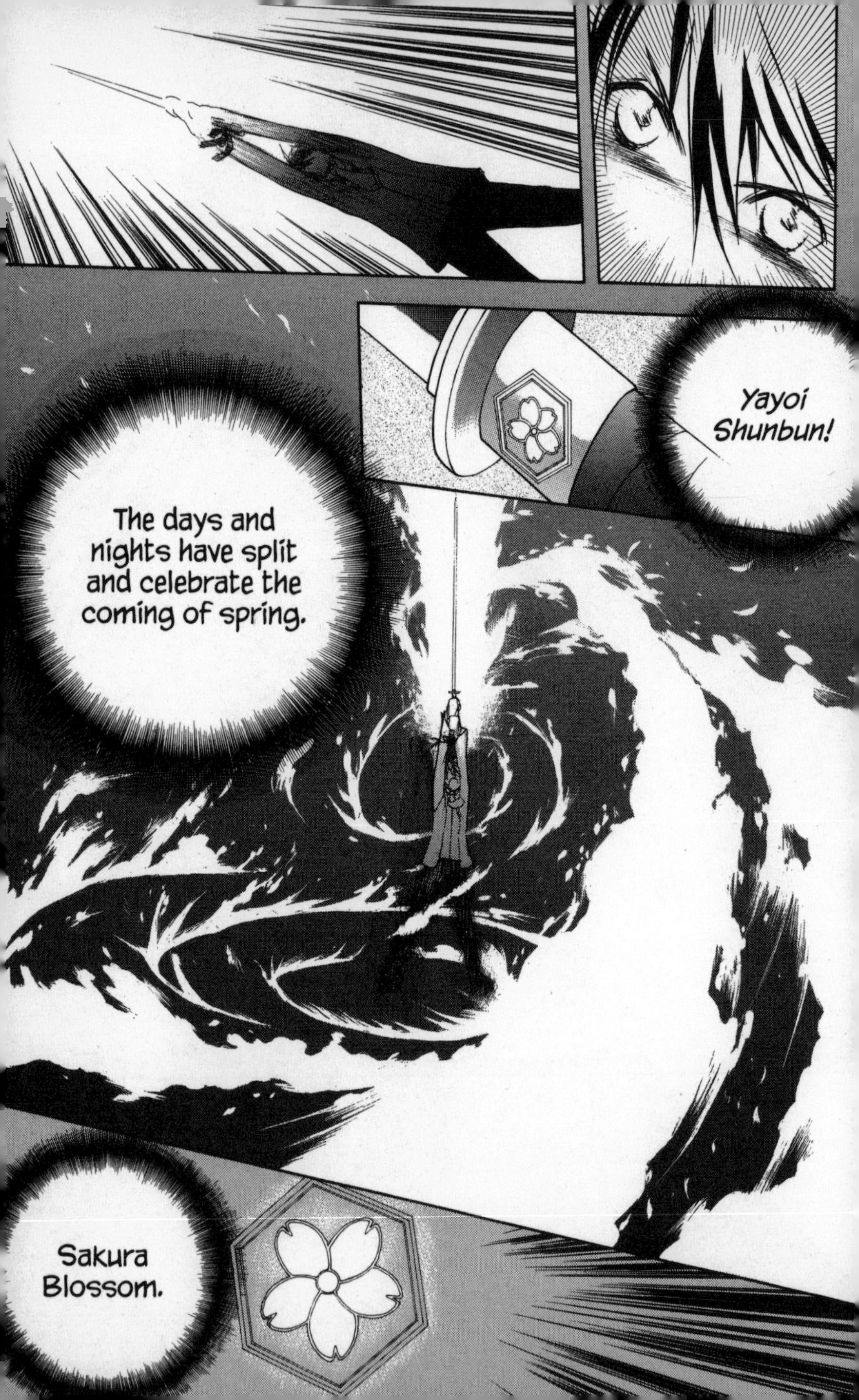
Yayoi Shunbun!
The days and nights have split and celebrate the coming of spring.
Sakura Blossom.

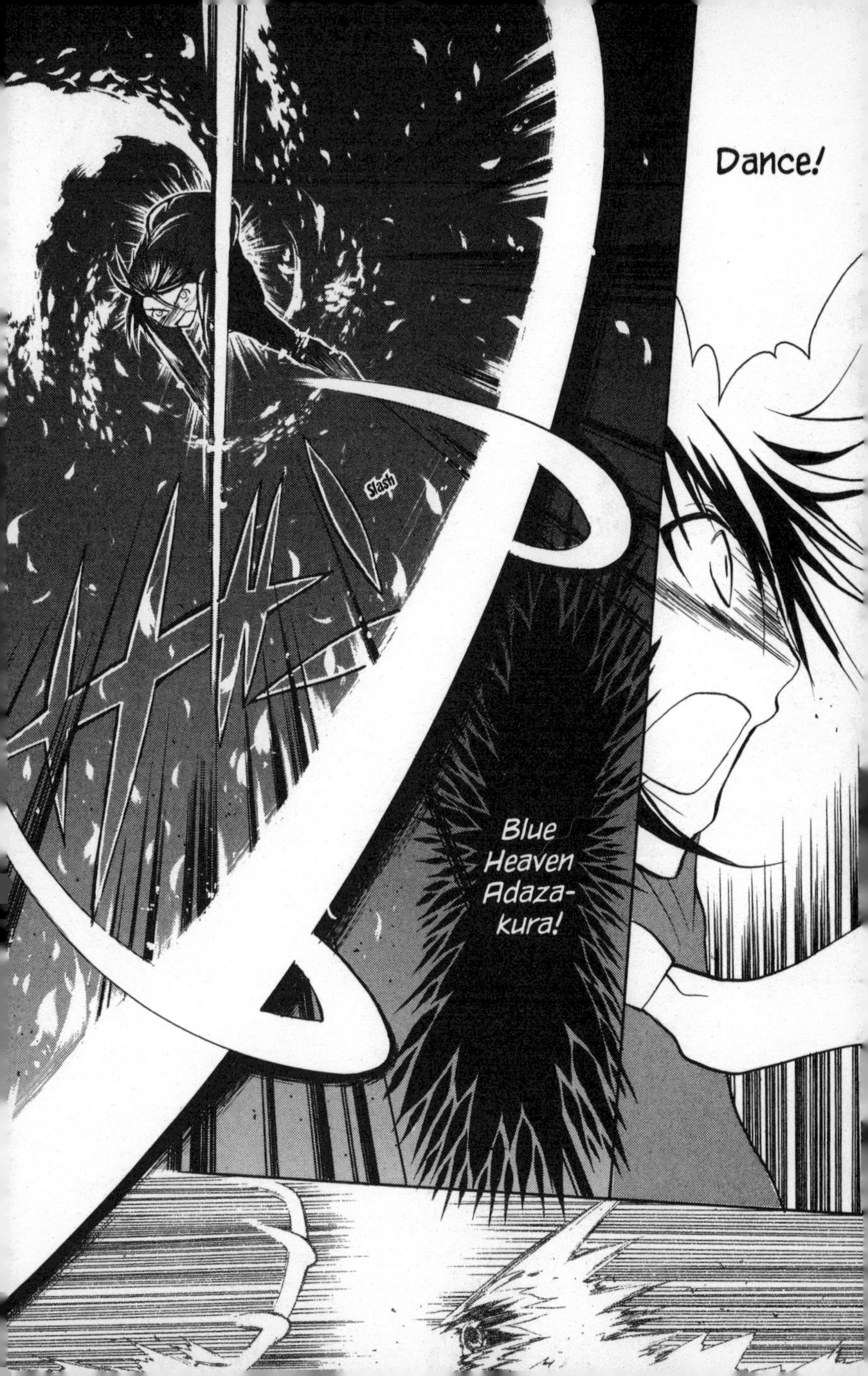
Dance!
Blue Heaven Adazakura!
Slash

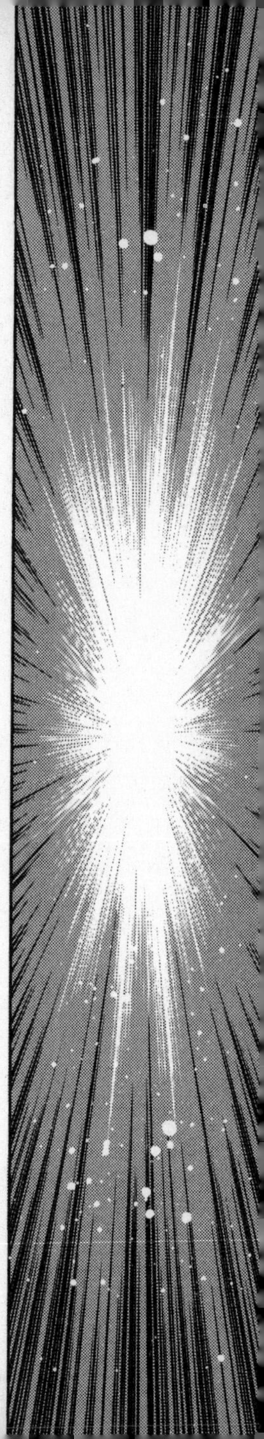

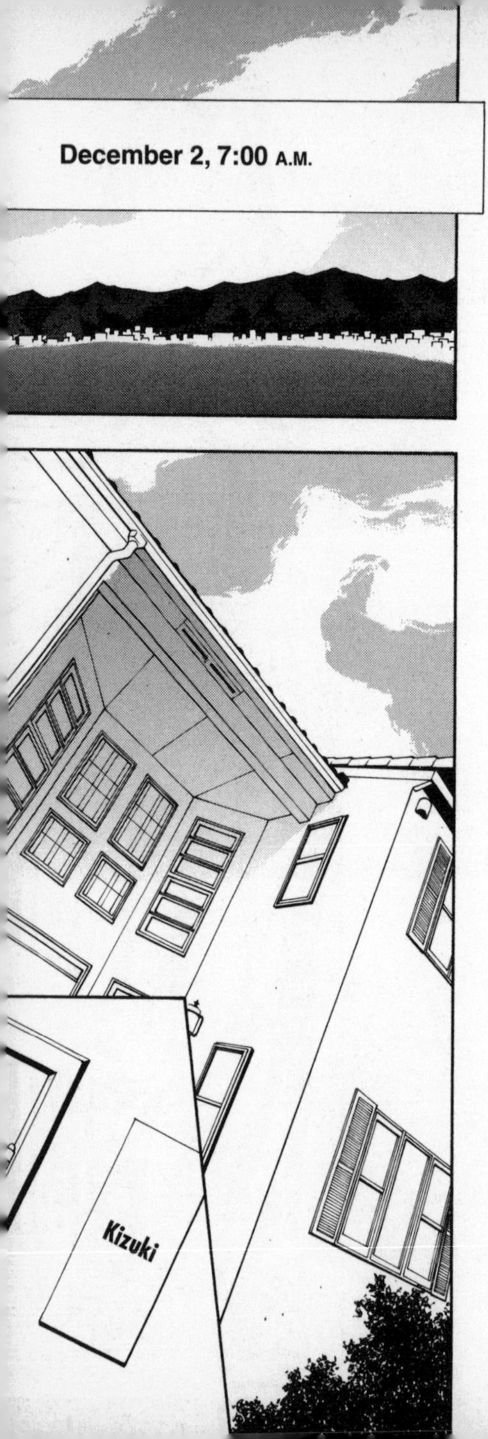
December 2, 7:00 A.M.
Kizuki

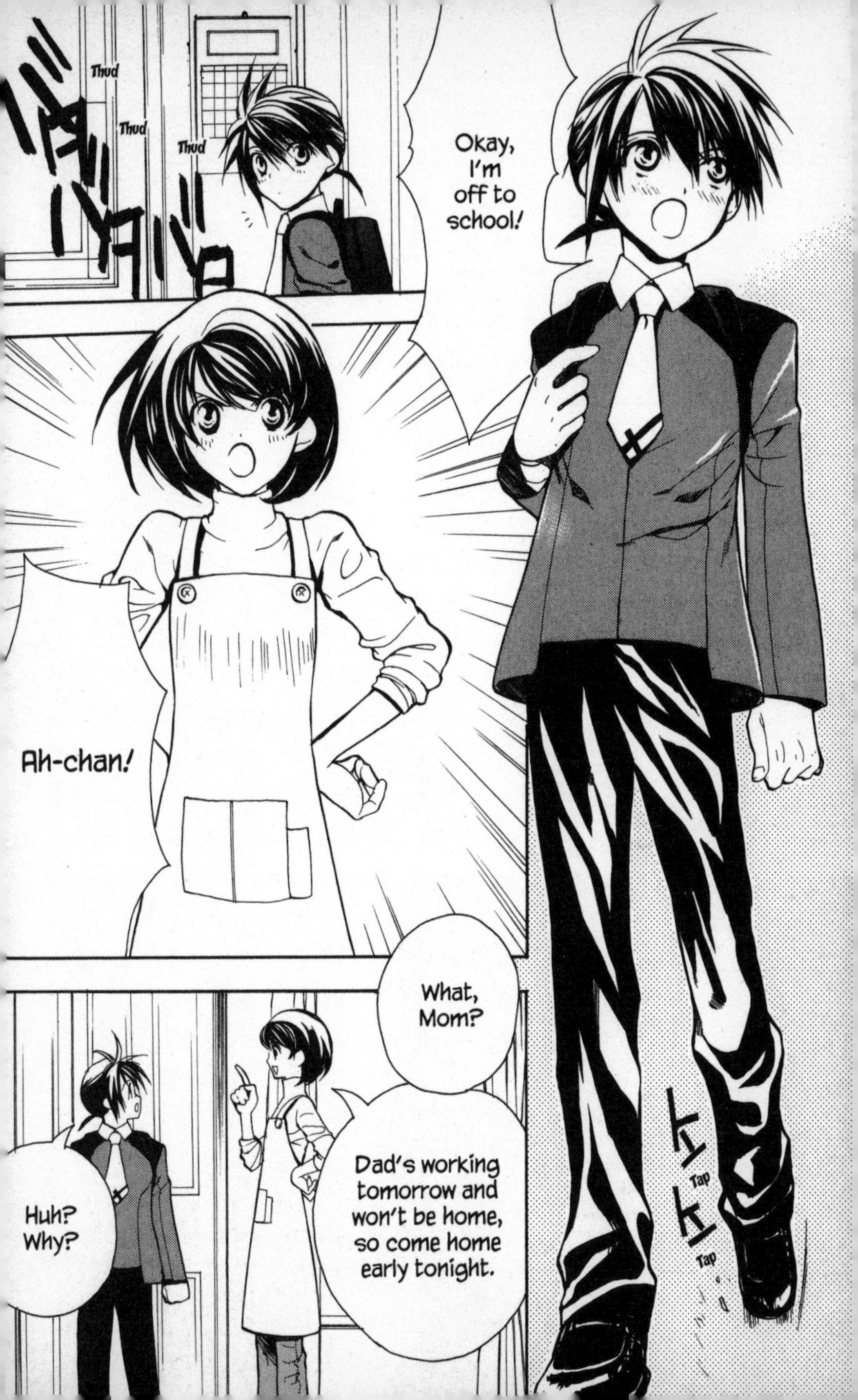
Okay, I'm off to school!
Tap
Tap
Thud
Thud
Thud
Ah-chan!
What, Mom?
Dad's working tomorrow and won't be home, so come home early tonight.
Huh? Why?

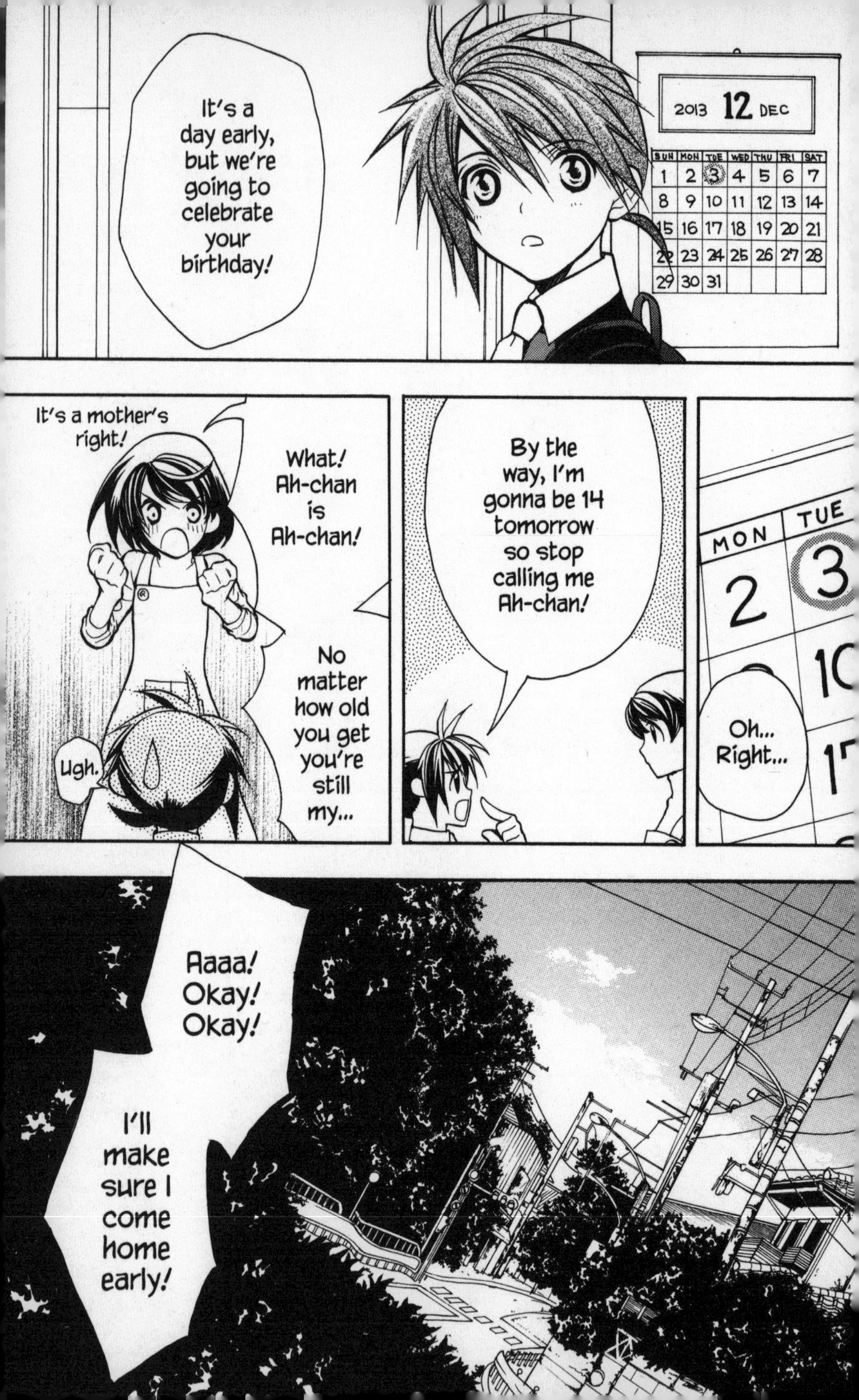
It's a day early, but we're going to celebrate your birthday!
2013 12 DEC
Oh... Right...
By the way, I'm gonna be 14 tomorrow so stop calling me Ah-chan!
What! Ah-chan is Ah-chan!
It's a mother's right!
No matter how old you get you're still my...
Ugh.
Aaaa! Okay! Okay!
I'll make sure I come home early!

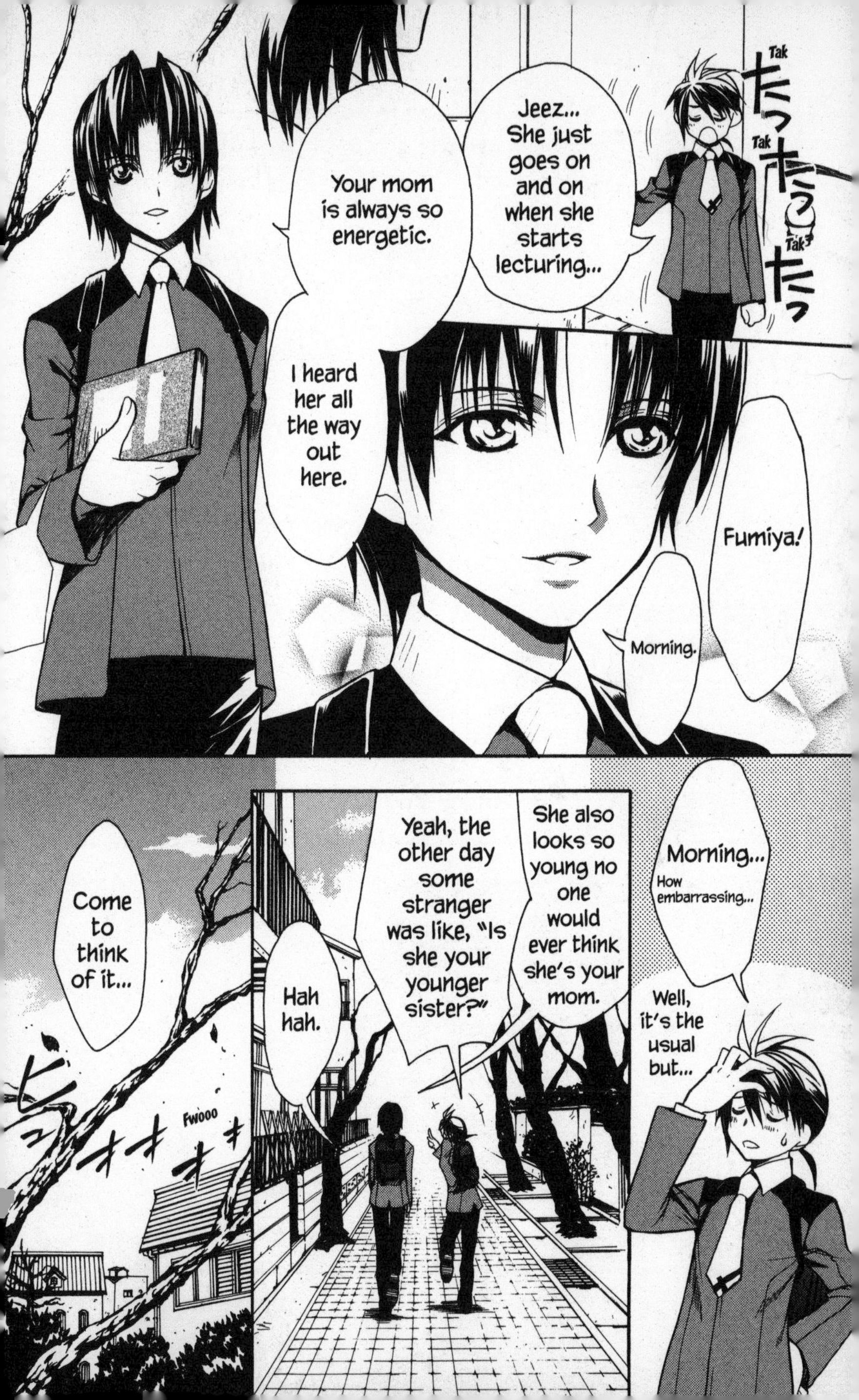
Tak Tak Tak
Fumiya!
Morning.
Your mom is always so energetic.
I heard her all the way out here.
Jeez... She just goes on and on when she starts lecturing...
Morning...
How embarrassing...
Well, it's the usual but...
She also looks so young no one would ever think she's your mom.
Yeah, the other day some stranger was like, "Is she your younger sister?"
Hah hah.
Come to think of it...
Fwooo

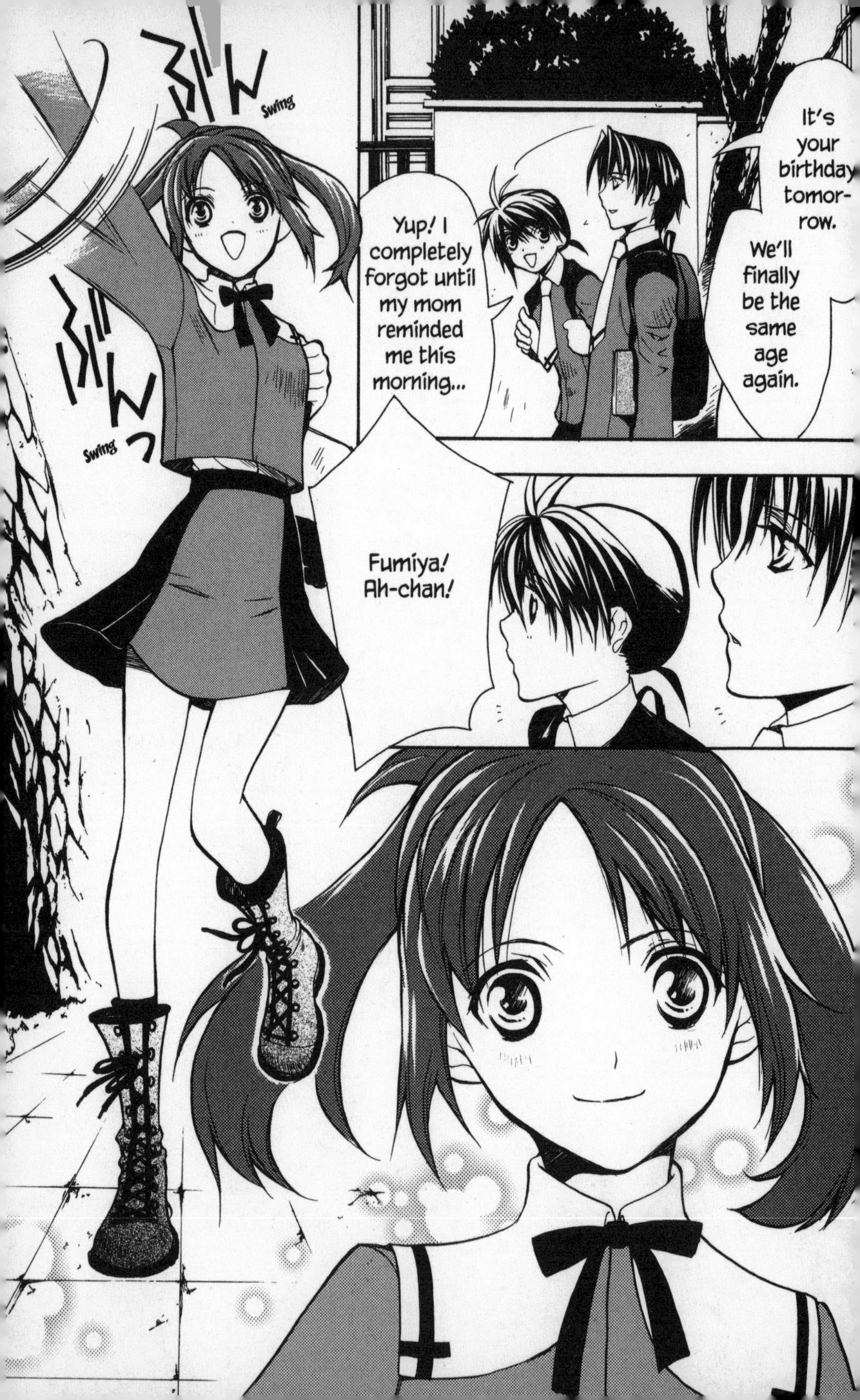
It's your birthday tomor-row. We'll finally be the same age again.
Yup! I completely forgot until my mom reminded me this morning...
Fumiya! Ah-chan!
ぶん
Swing
ぶんっ
Swing

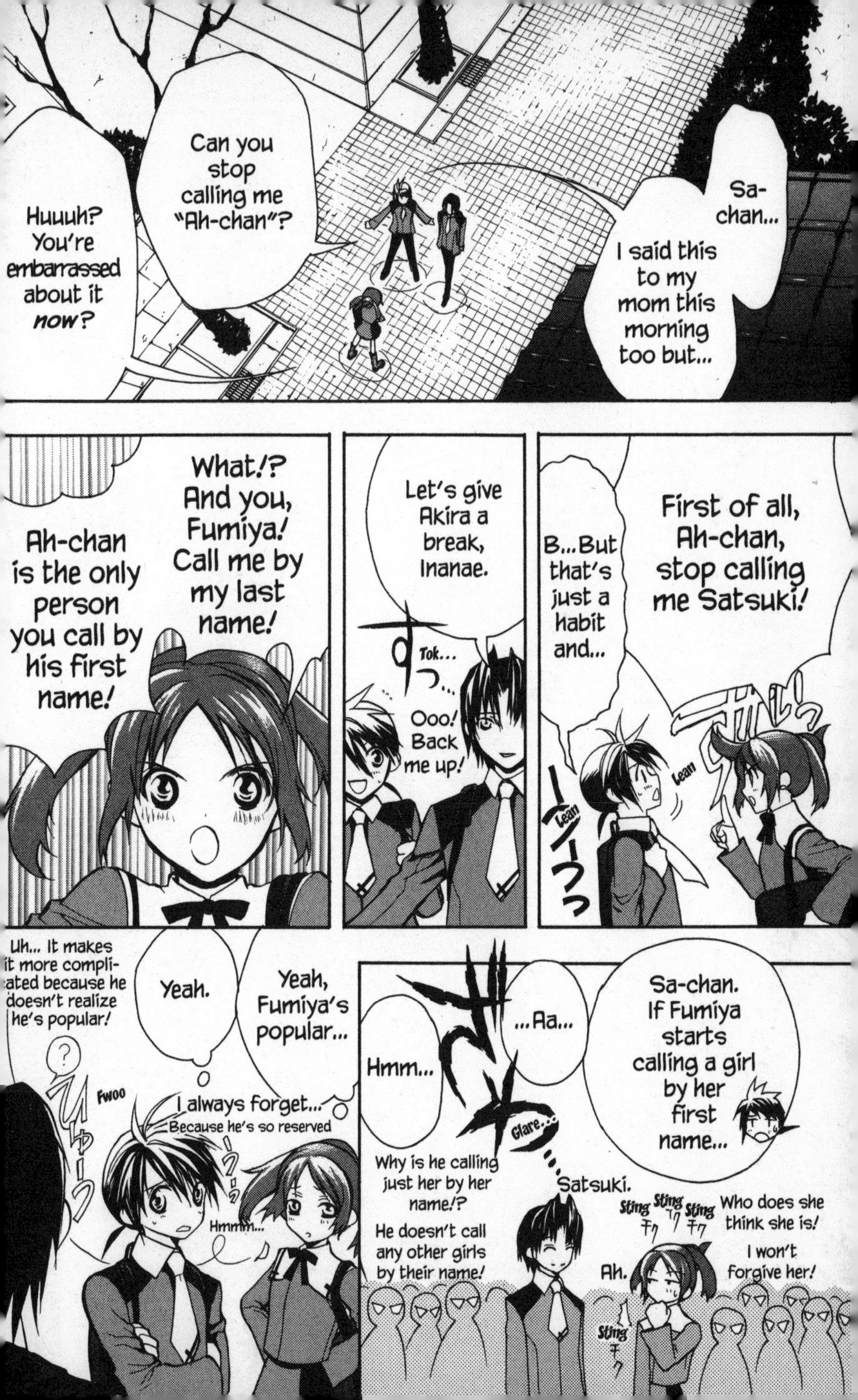
Sa-chan...
I said this to my mom this morning too but...
Can you stop calling me "Ah-chan"?
Huuuh? You're embarrassed about it *now*?
First of all, Ah-chan, stop calling me Satsuki!
B...But that's just a habit and...
Lean
Lean
Let's give Akira a break, Inanae.
Tok...
Ooo! Back me up!
What!? And you, Fumiya! Call me by my last name!
Ah-chan is the only person you call by his first name!
Sa-chan. If Fumiya starts calling a girl by her first name...
...Aa...
Hmm...
Glare...
Satsuki.
Who does she think she is!
I won't forgive her!
Sting Sting Sting
Ah.
Why is he calling just her by her name!?
He doesn't call any other girls by their name!
Sting
Yeah, Fumiya's popular...
Yeah.
Uh... It makes it more compli-cated because he doesn't realize he's popular!
I always forget...
Because he's so reserved
Hmmm...
Fwoo
?

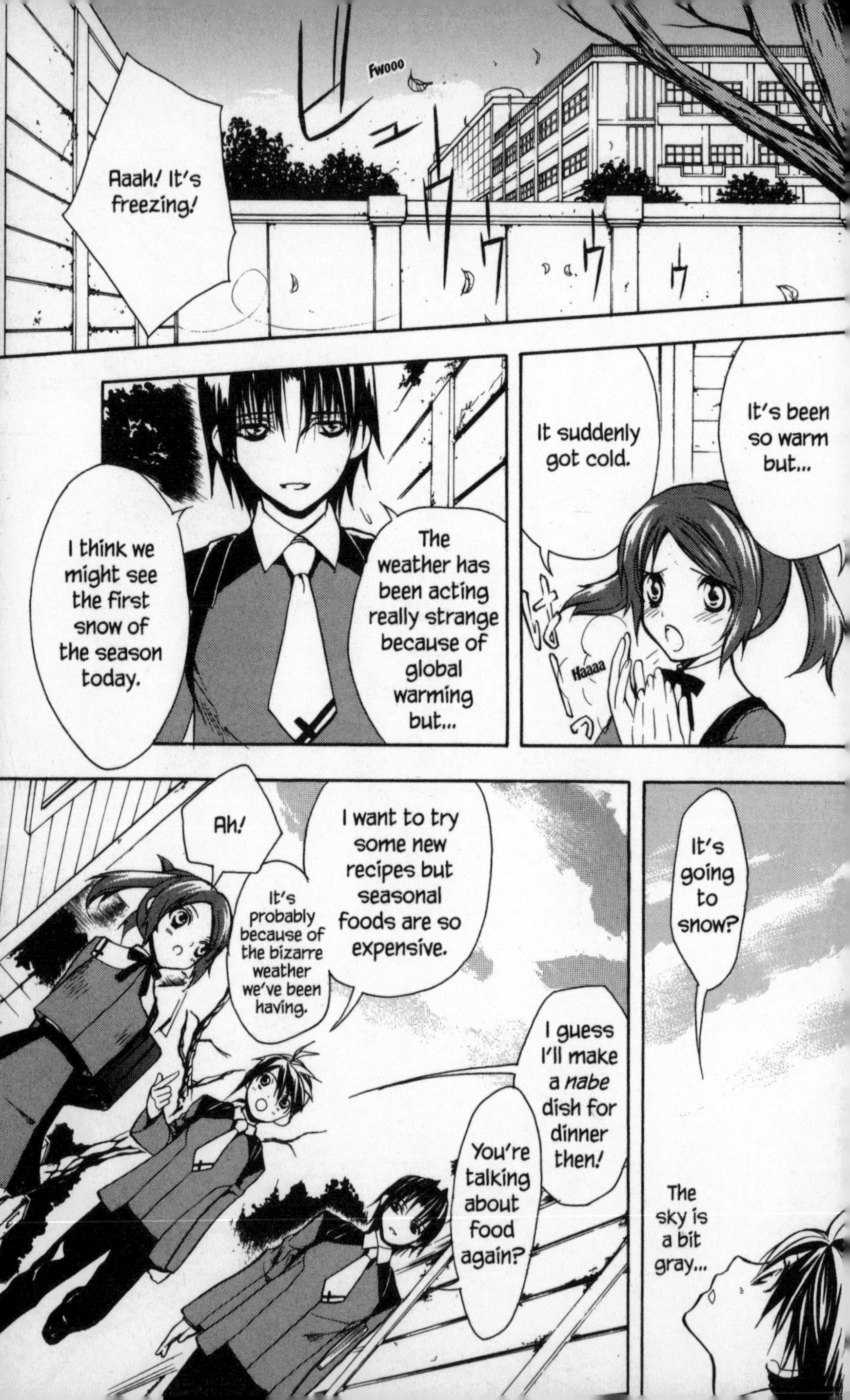

Fwooo
Aaah! It's freezing!
It's been so warm but...
It suddenly got cold.
Haaaa
The weather has been acting really strange because of global warming but...
I think we might see the first snow of the season today.
It's going to snow?
The sky is a bit gray...
I want to try some new recipes but seasonal foods are so expensive.
Ah!
It's probably because of the bizarre weather we've been having.
I guess I'll make a *nabe* dish for dinner then!
You're talking about food again?

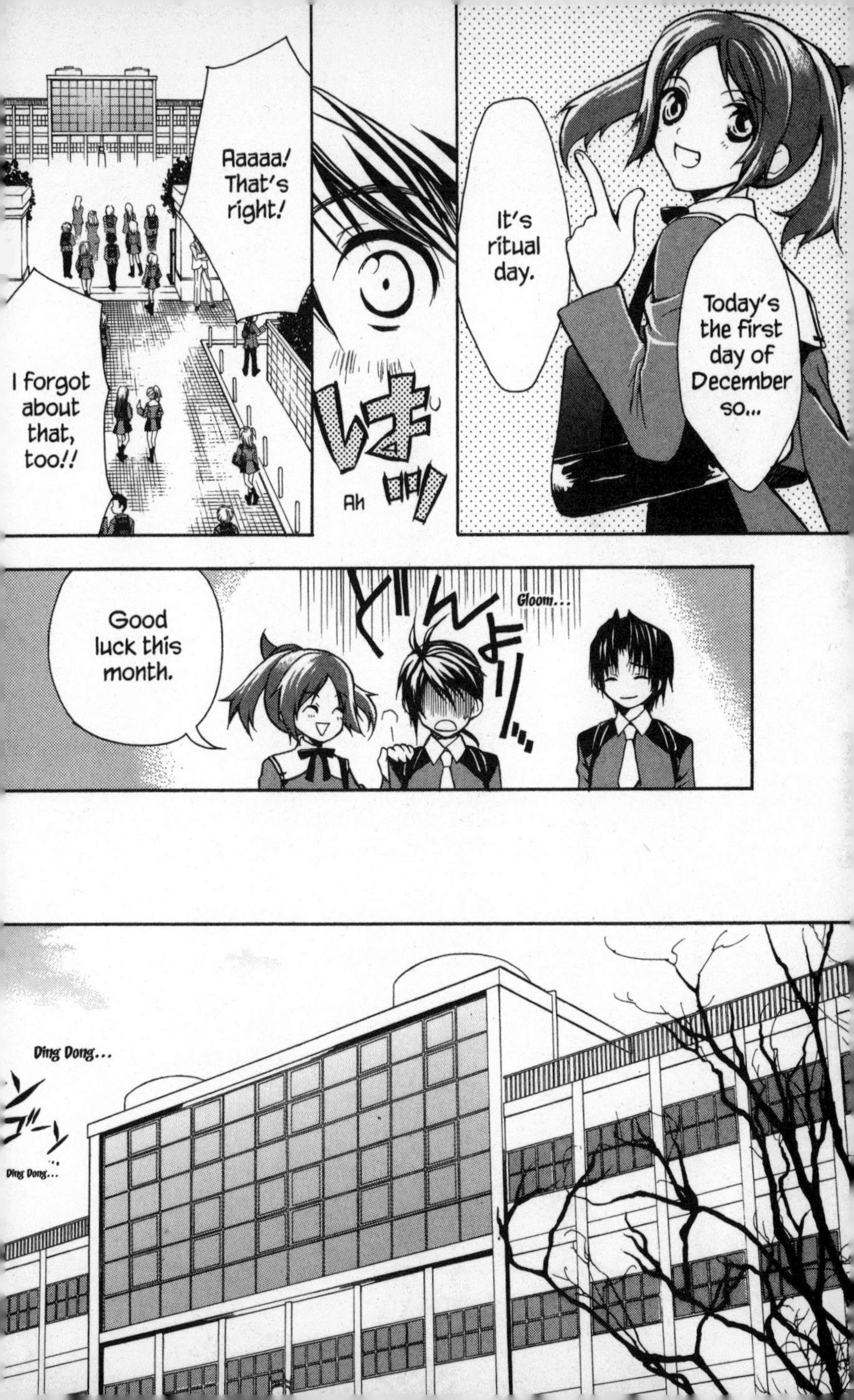
Today's the first day of December so...
It's ritual day.
Ah
Aaaaa! That's right!
I forgot about that, too!!
Gloom...
Good luck this month.
Ding Dong...
Ding Dong...

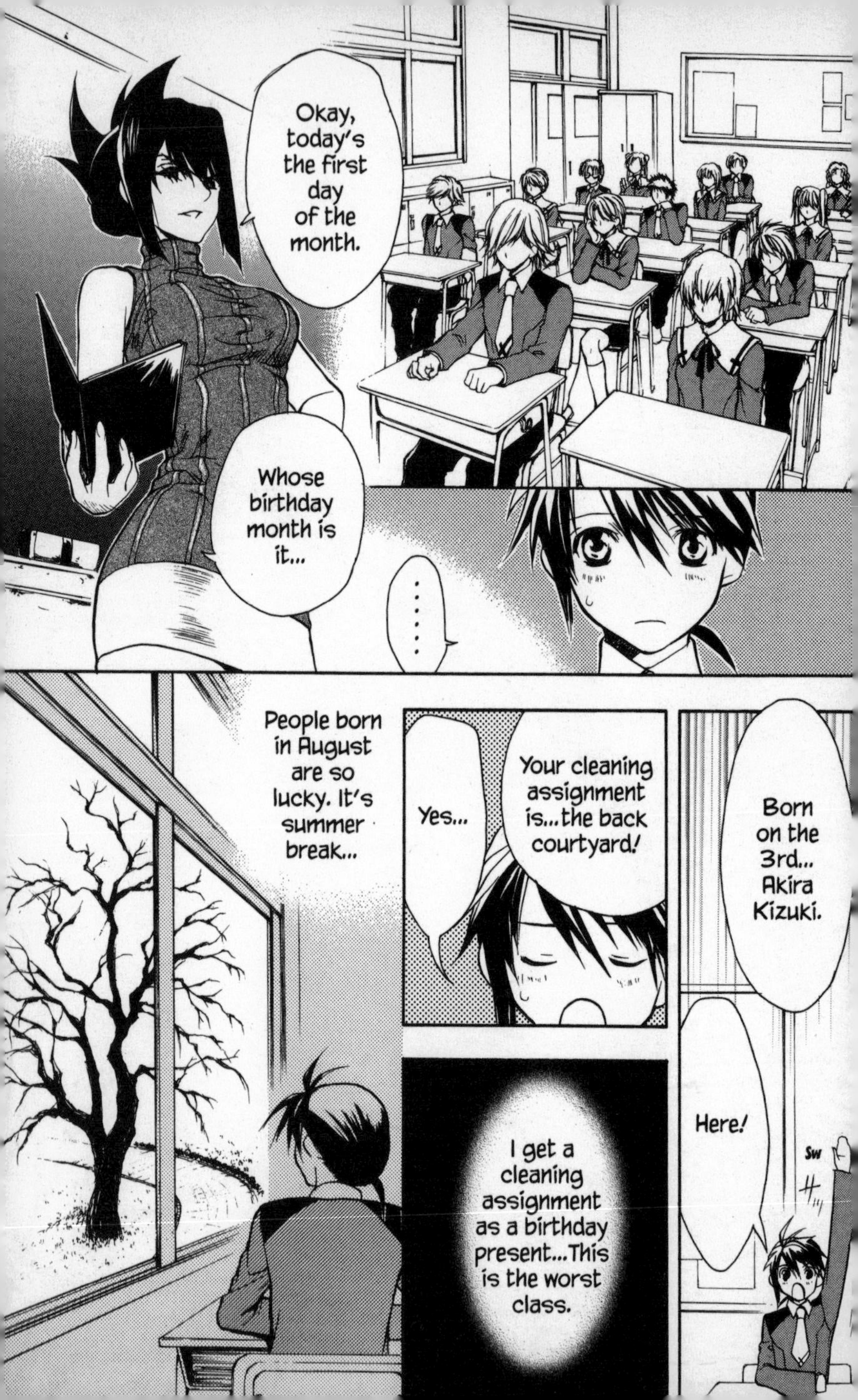

Okay, today's the first day of the month.
Whose birthday month is it...
......
Born on the 3rd... Akira Kizuki.
Here!
SW
Your cleaning assignment is...the back courtyard!
Yes...
I get a cleaning assignment as a birthday present...This is the worst class.
People born in August are so lucky. It's summer break...

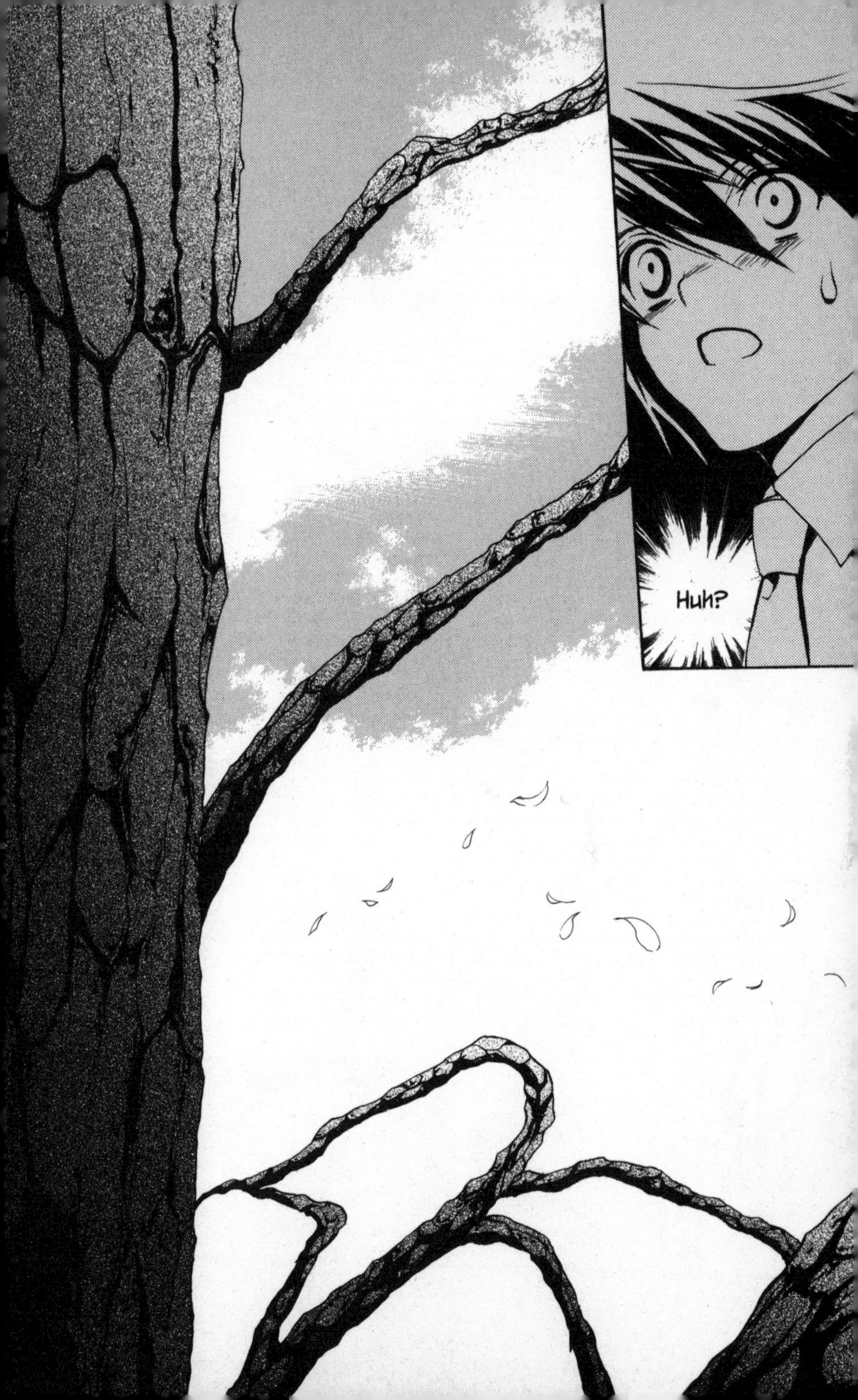
Huh?

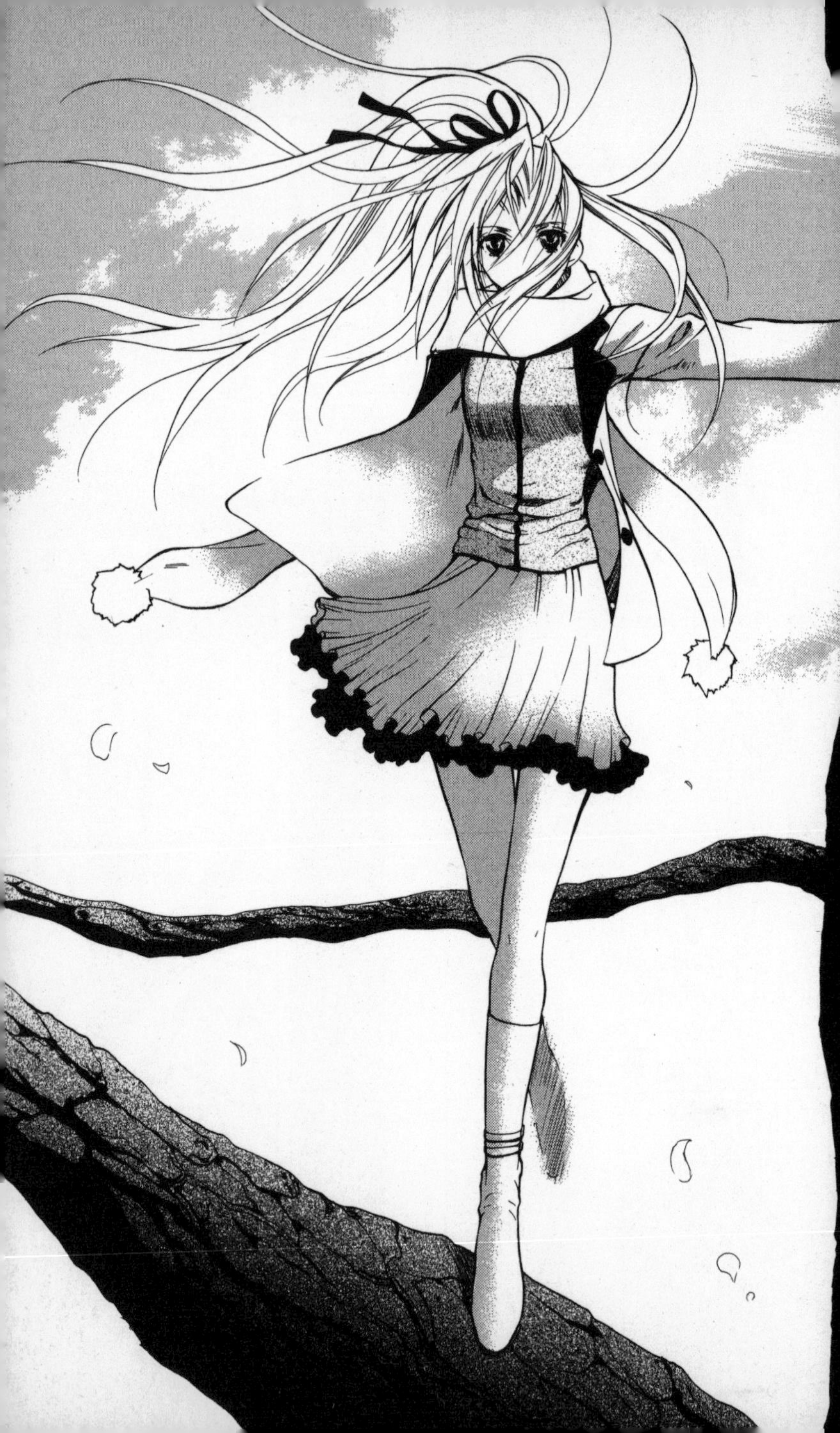

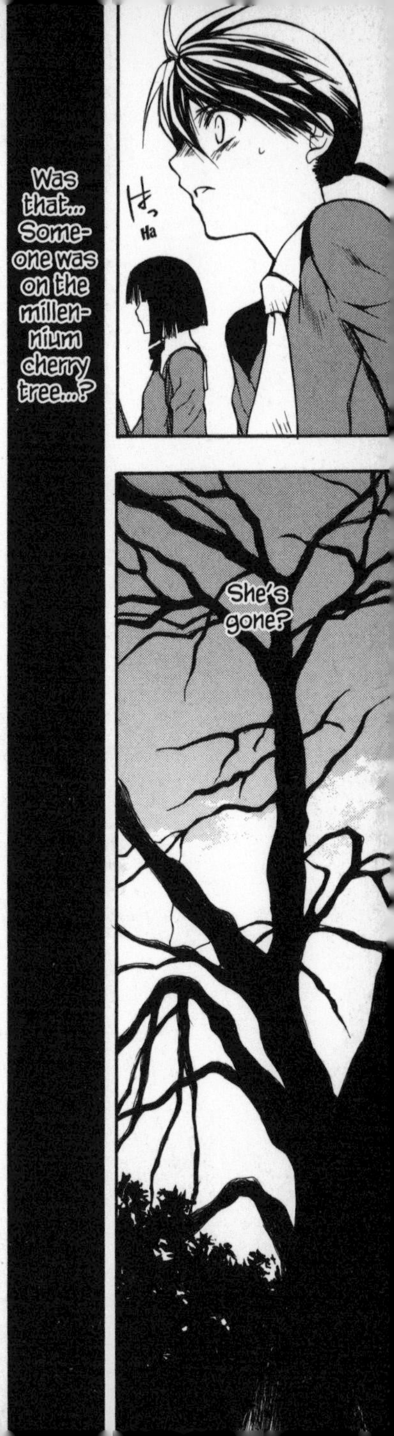
はっ
Ha
Was that... Someone was on the millennium cherry tree...?
She's gone?

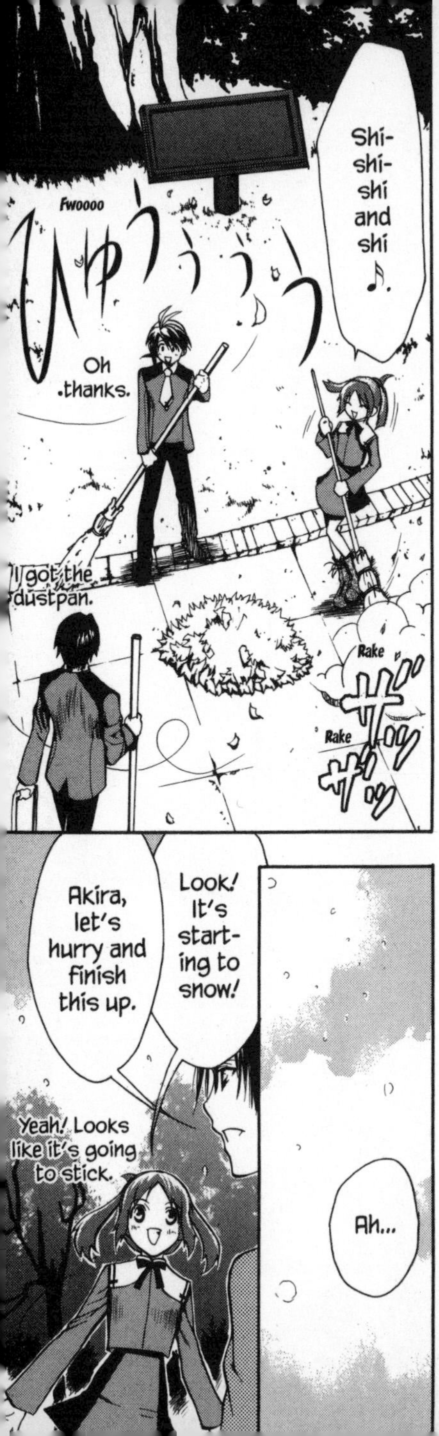
Shi-shi-shi and shi ♪.
ひゅうううう
Fwoooo
Oh .thanks.
I got the dustpan.
Rake
Rake
Ah...
Look! It's starting to snow!
Akira, let's hurry and finish this up.
Yeah! Looks like it's going to stick.

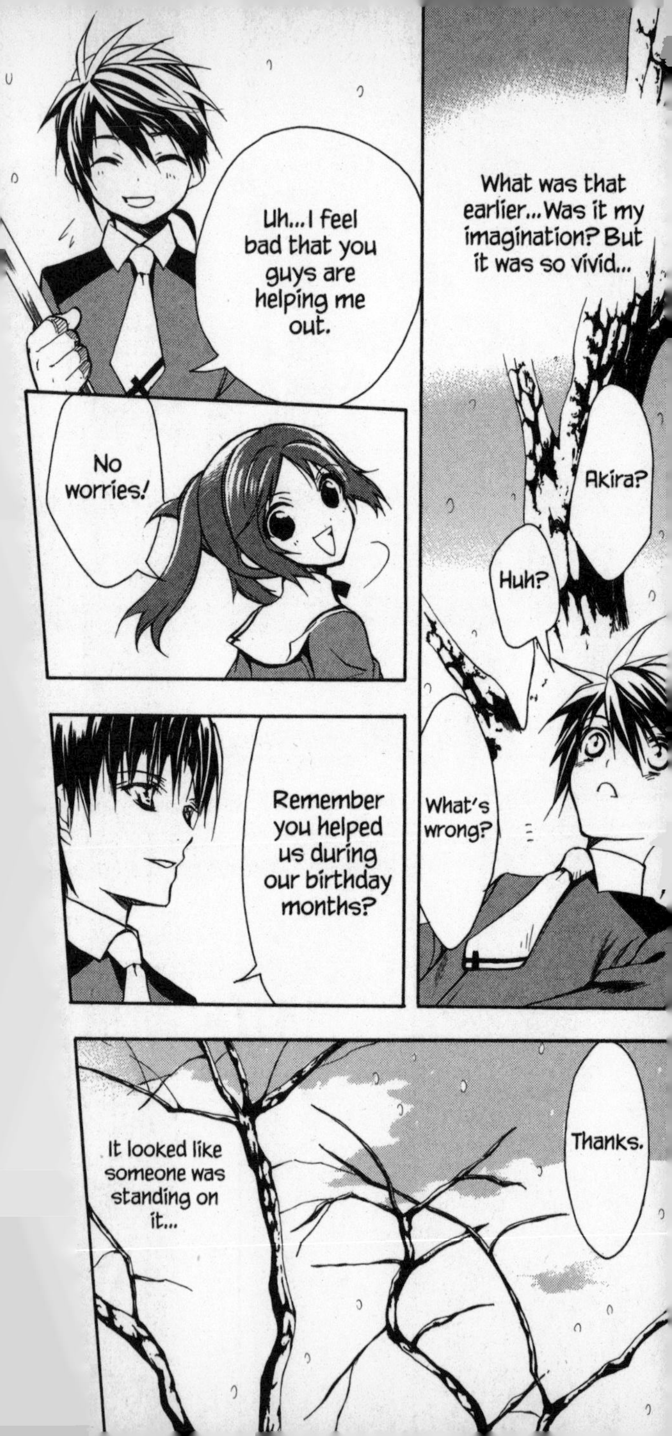
What was that earlier...Was it my imagination? But it was so vivid...
Akira?
Huh?
What's wrong?
Uh...I feel bad that you guys are helping me out.
No worries!
Remember you helped us during our birthday months?
Thanks.
It looked like someone was standing on it...

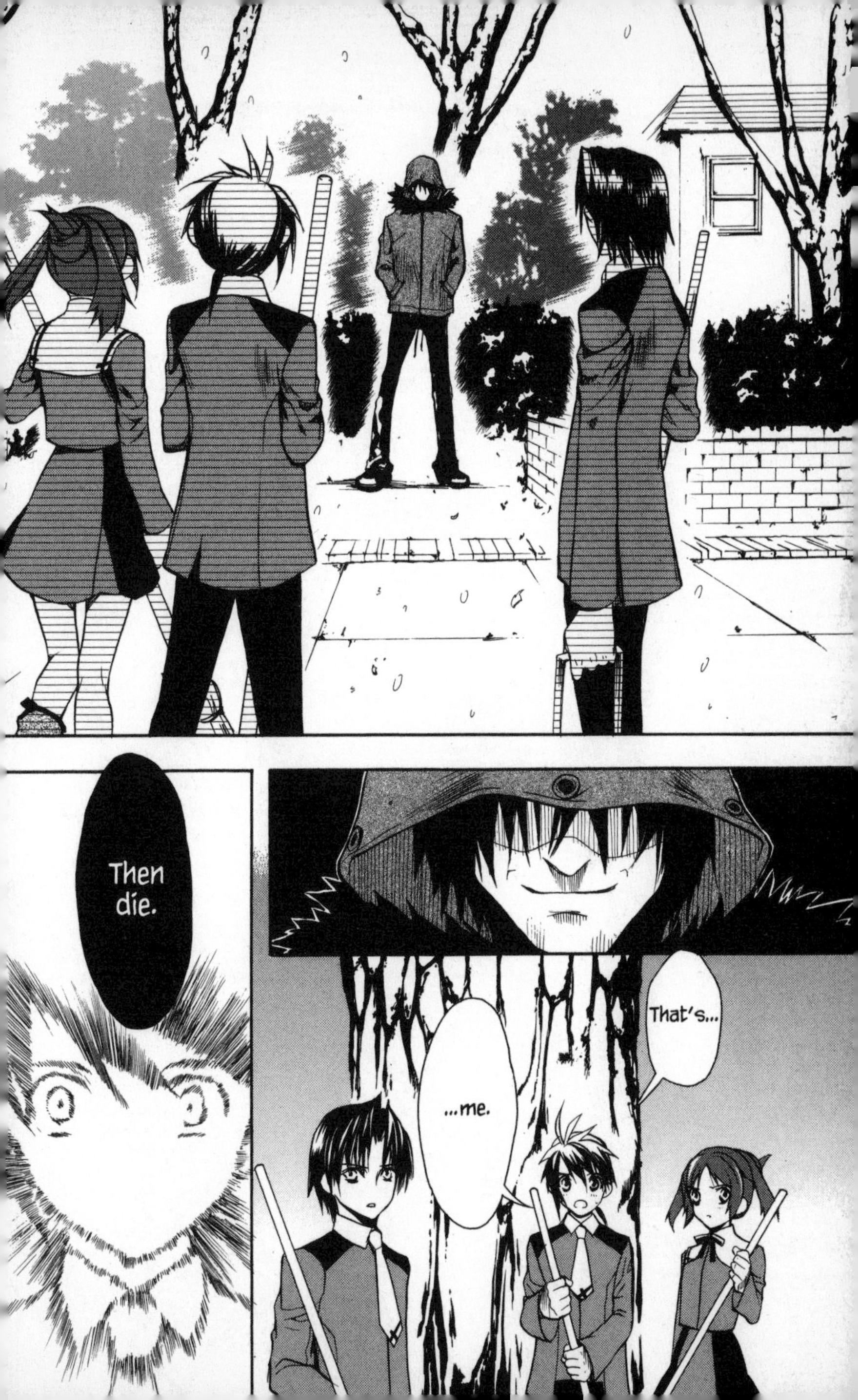
That's...
...me.
Then die.

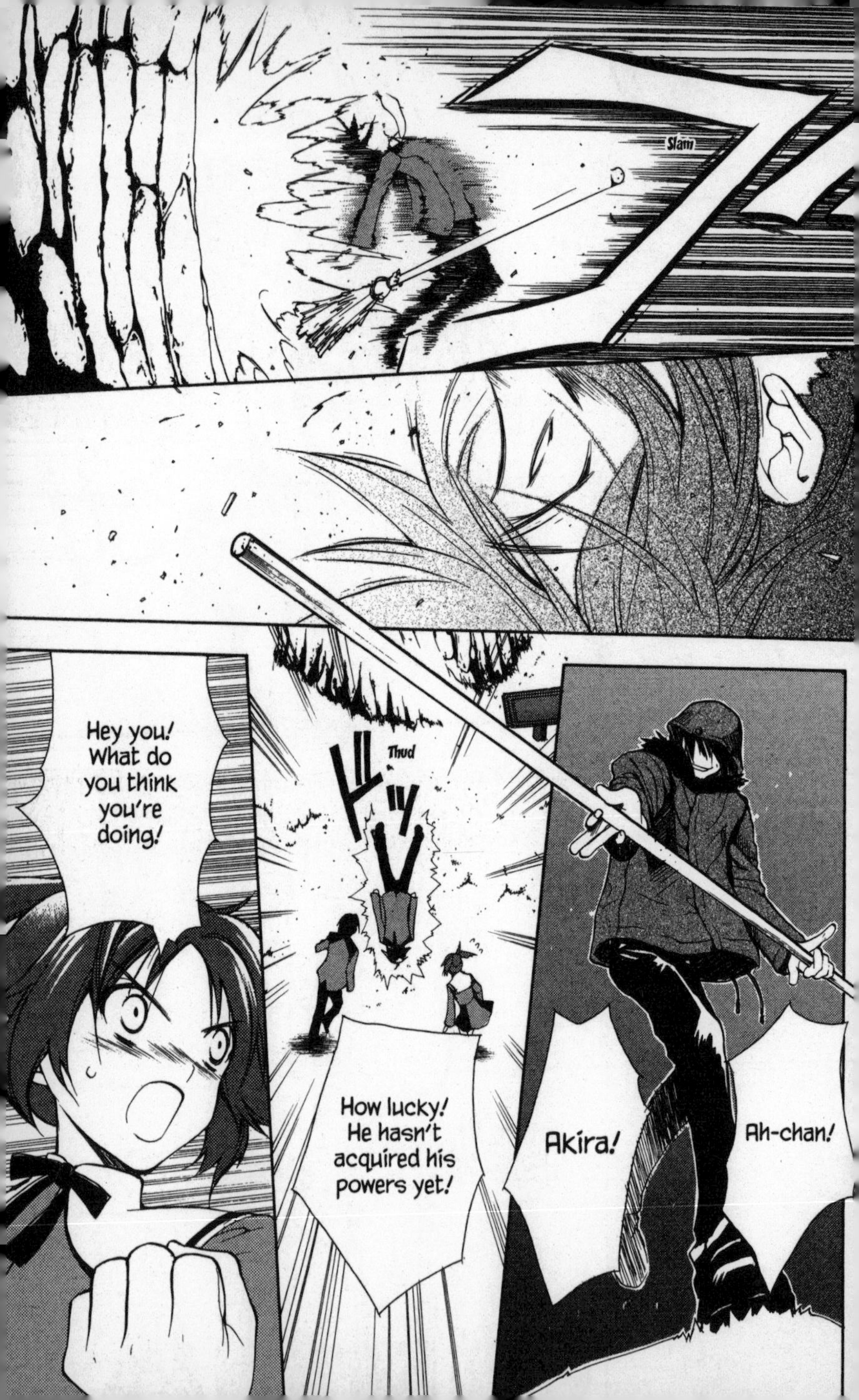
Slam
Ah-chan!
Akira!
ドッ
Thud
How lucky! He hasn't acquired his powers yet!
Hey you! What do you think you're doing!

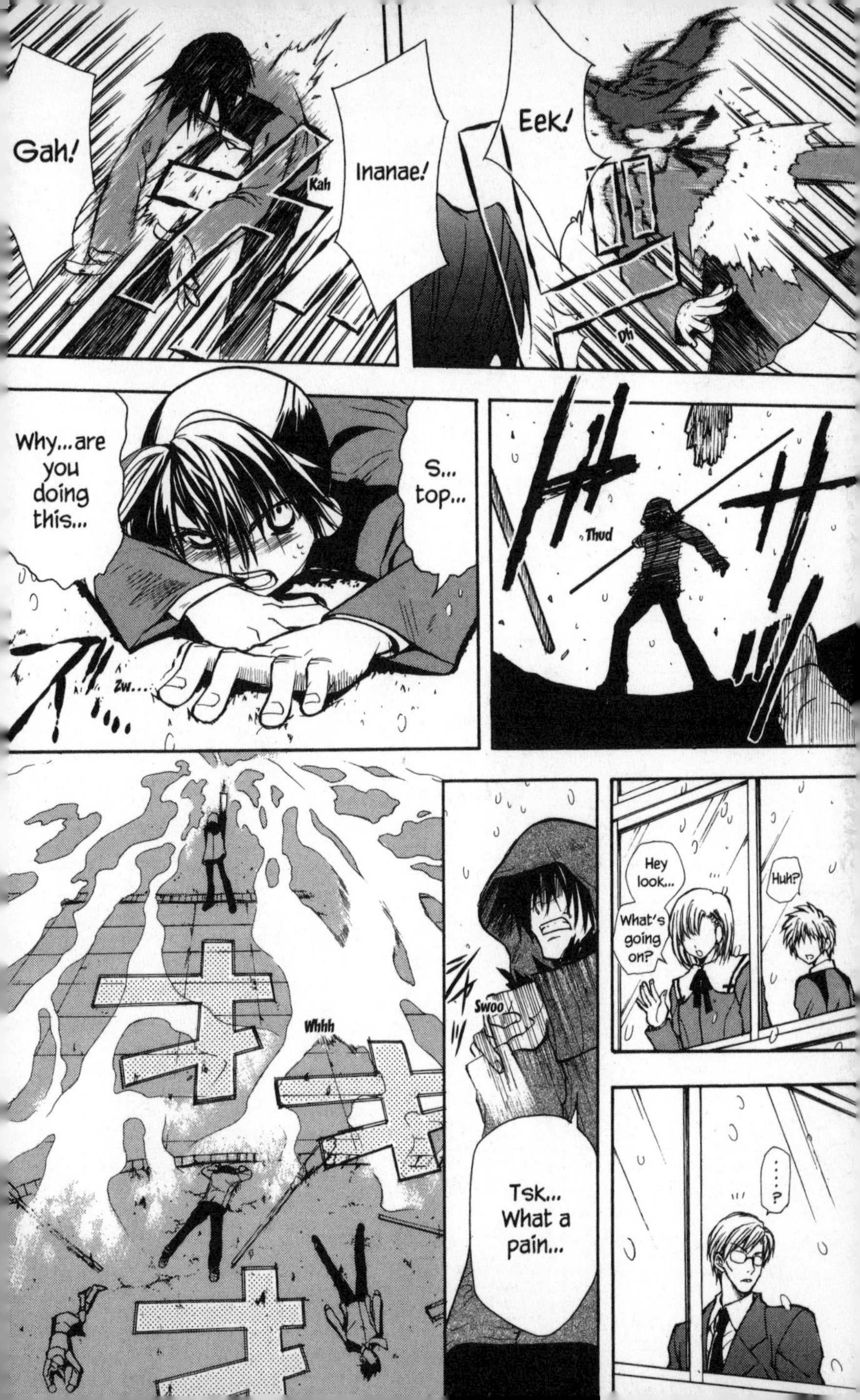
Eek!
Inanae!
Kah
Gah!
Dri
Thud
S... top...
Why...are you doing this...
Zw...
Huh?
Hey look...
What's going on?
...?
Swoo
Tsk... What a pain...
Whhh

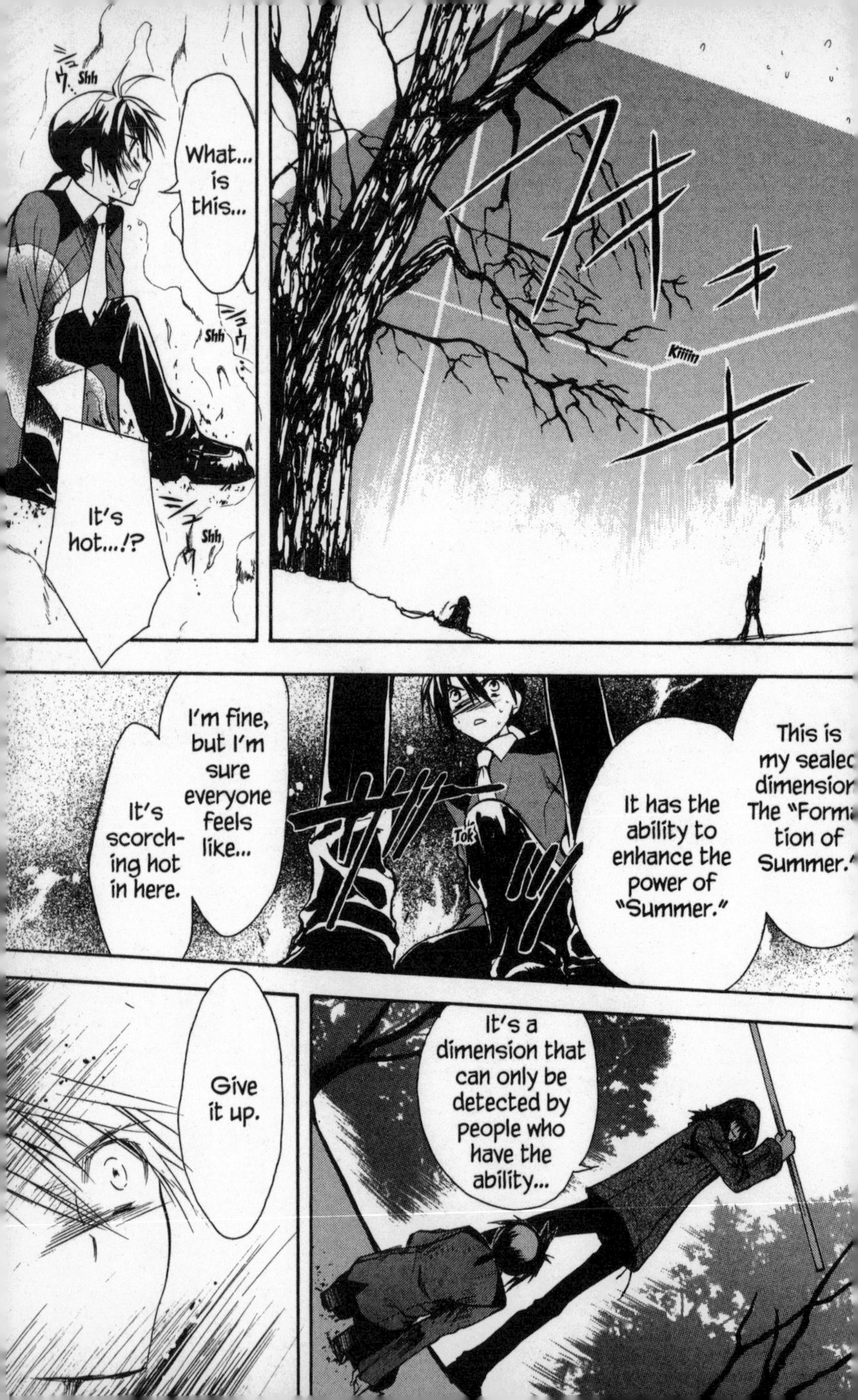
Kiiiin
Shh
What... is this...
Shh
It's hot...!?
Shh
This is my sealed dimension The "Formation of Summer."
It has the ability to enhance the power of "Summer."
Tok
I'm fine, but I'm sure everyone feels like...
It's scorching hot in here.
It's a dimension that can only be detected by people who have the ability...
Give it up.

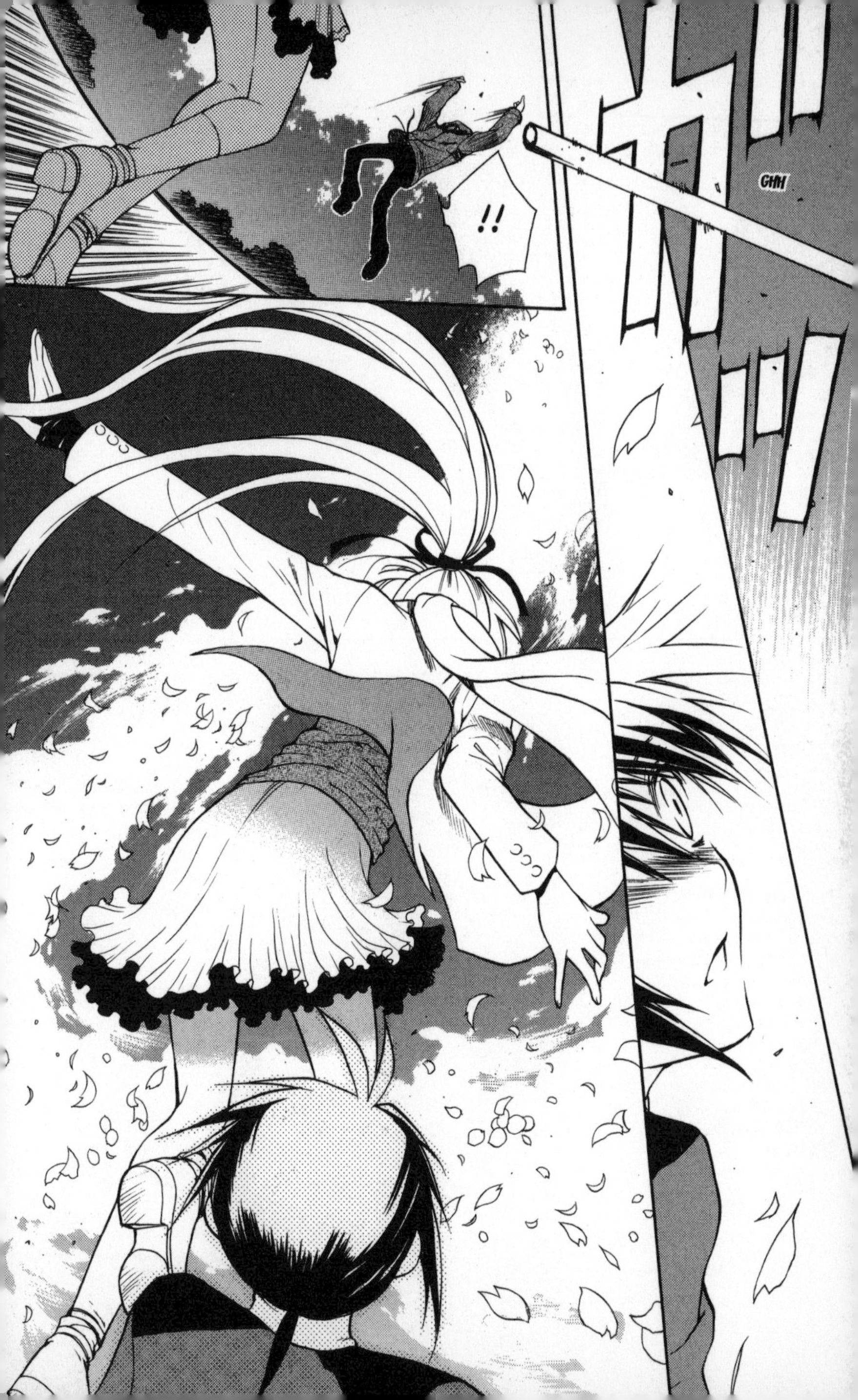
GHH
!!

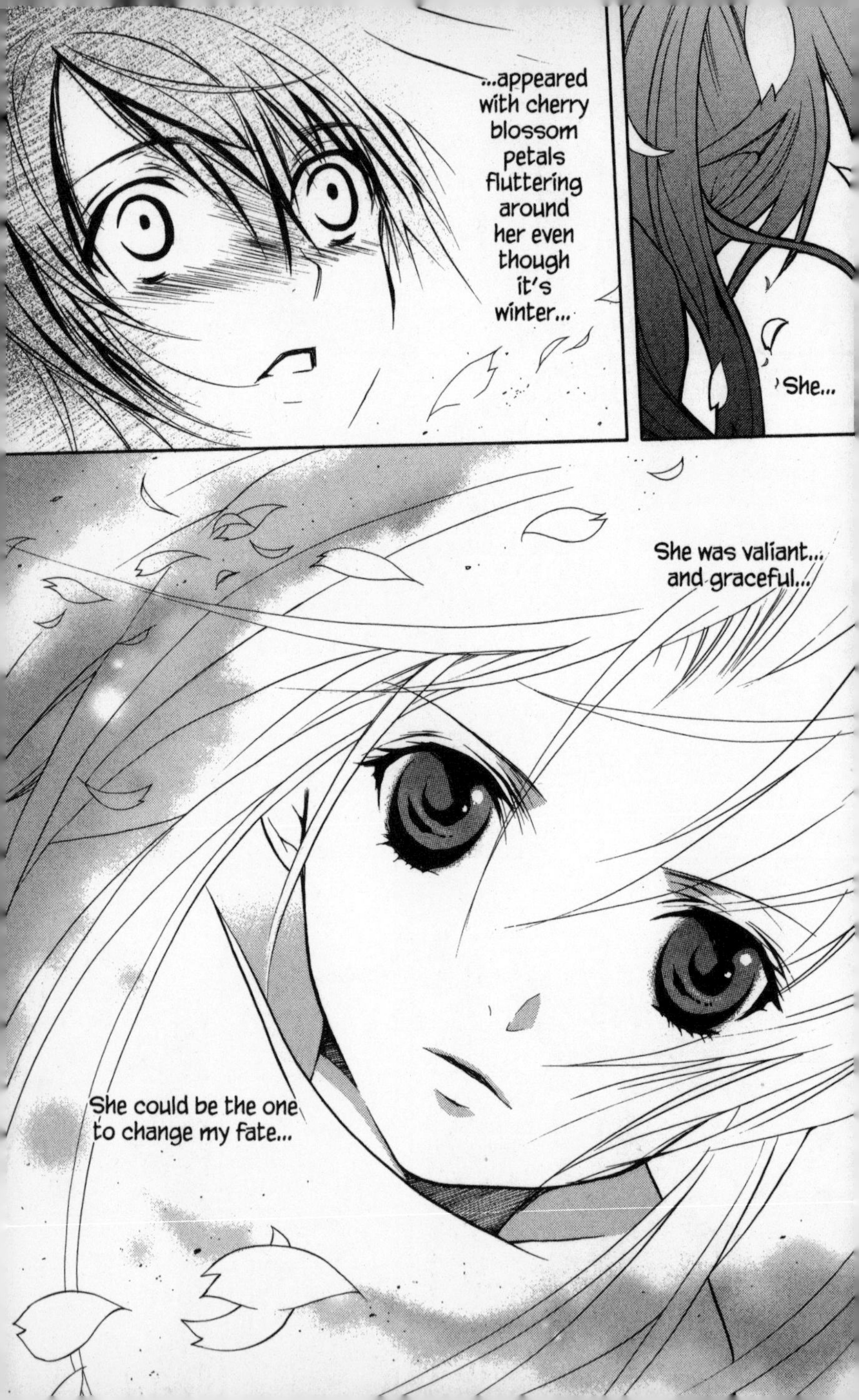
She...
...appeared with cherry blossom petals fluttering around her even though it's winter...
She was valiant... and graceful...
She could be the one to change my fate...

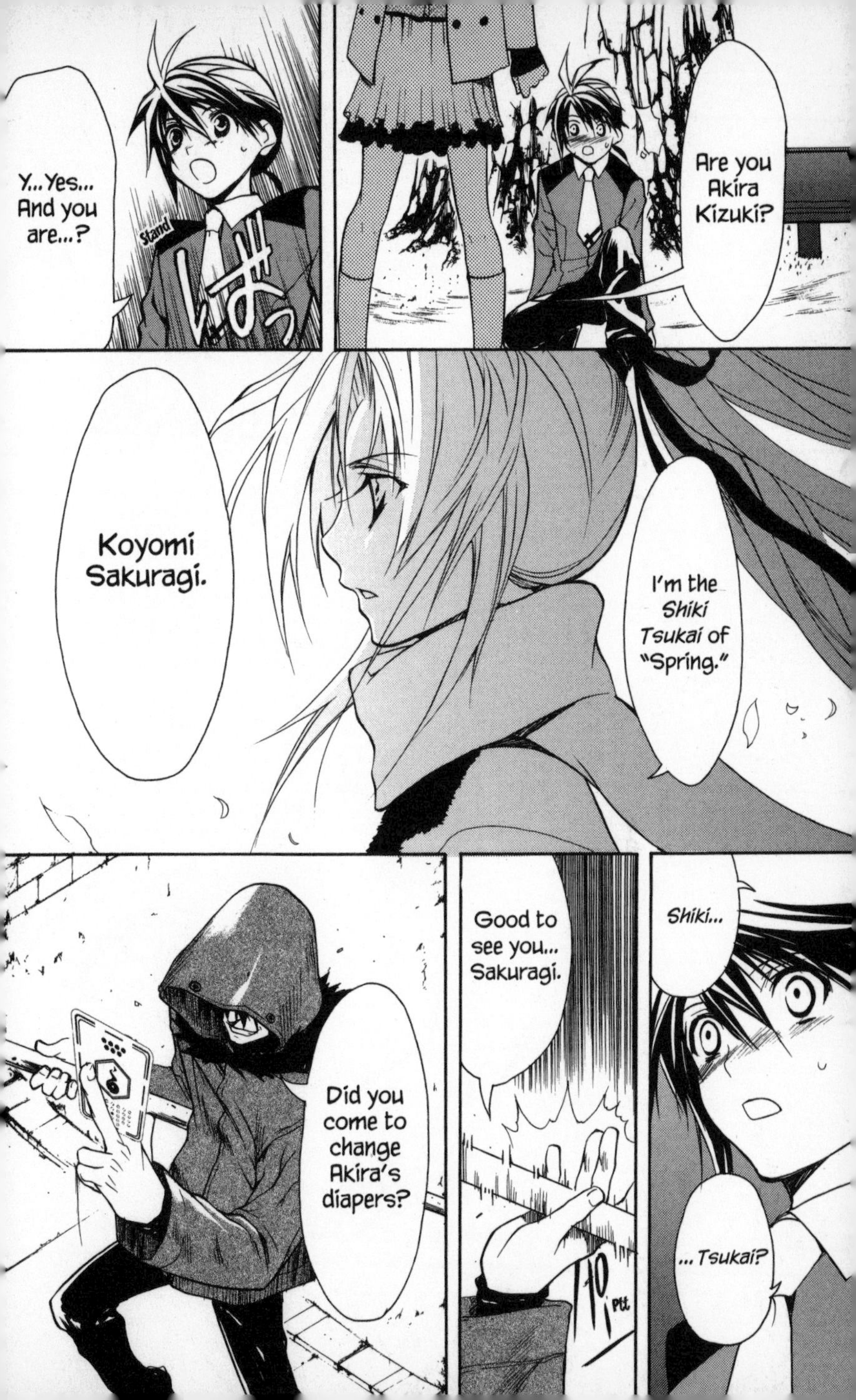
Are you Akira Kizuki?
Y... Yes... And you are...?
Stand
I'm the *Shiki Tsukai* of "Spring."
Koyomi Sakuragi.
Shiki...
...Tsukai?
Good to see you... Sakuragi.
Ptt
Did you come to change Akira's diapers?

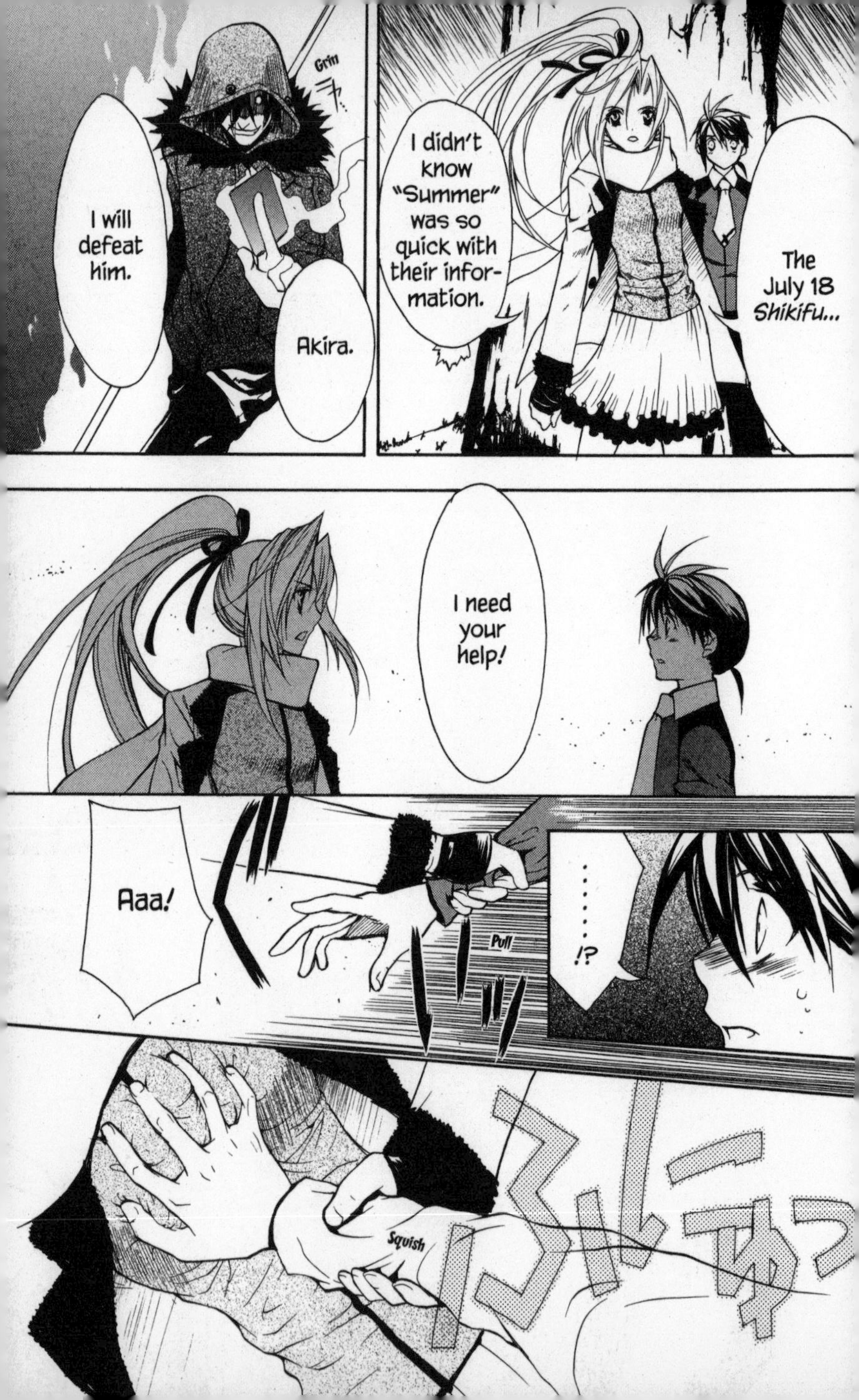
The July 18 Shikifu...
I didn't know "Summer" was so quick with their information.
Grin
Akira.
I will defeat him.
I need your help!
......
!?
Aaa!
Pull
Squish

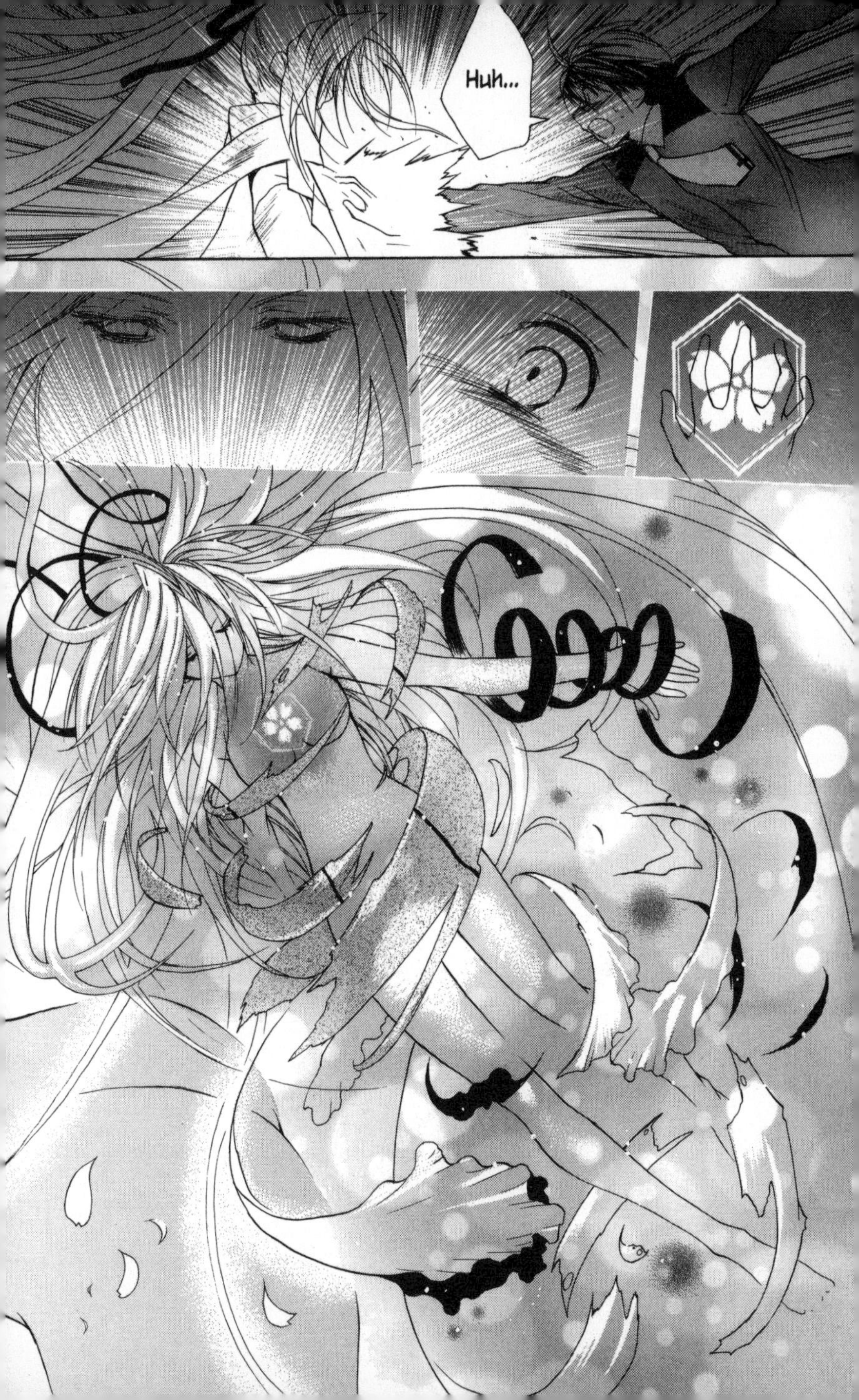
Huh...

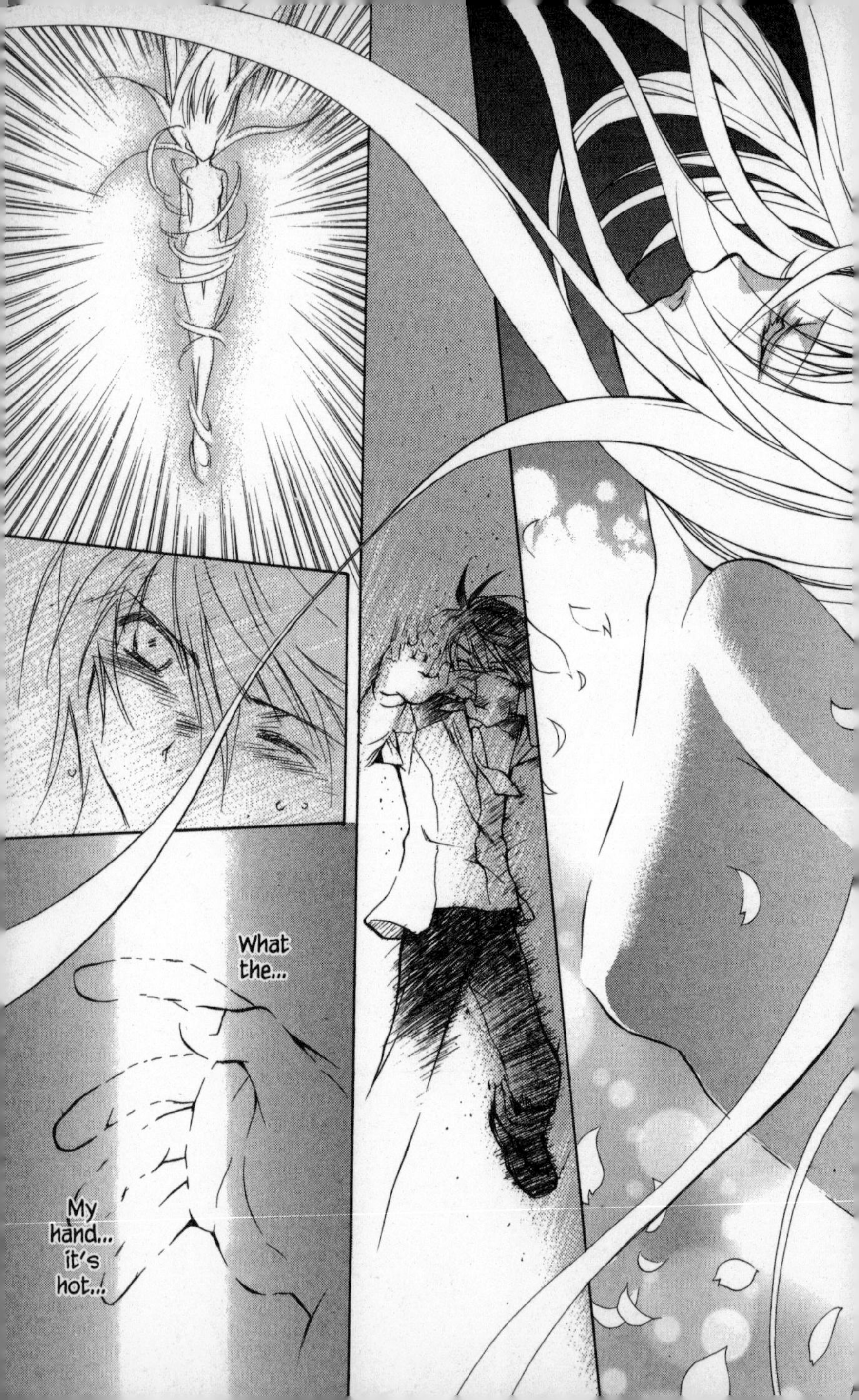
What the...
My hand... it's hot...

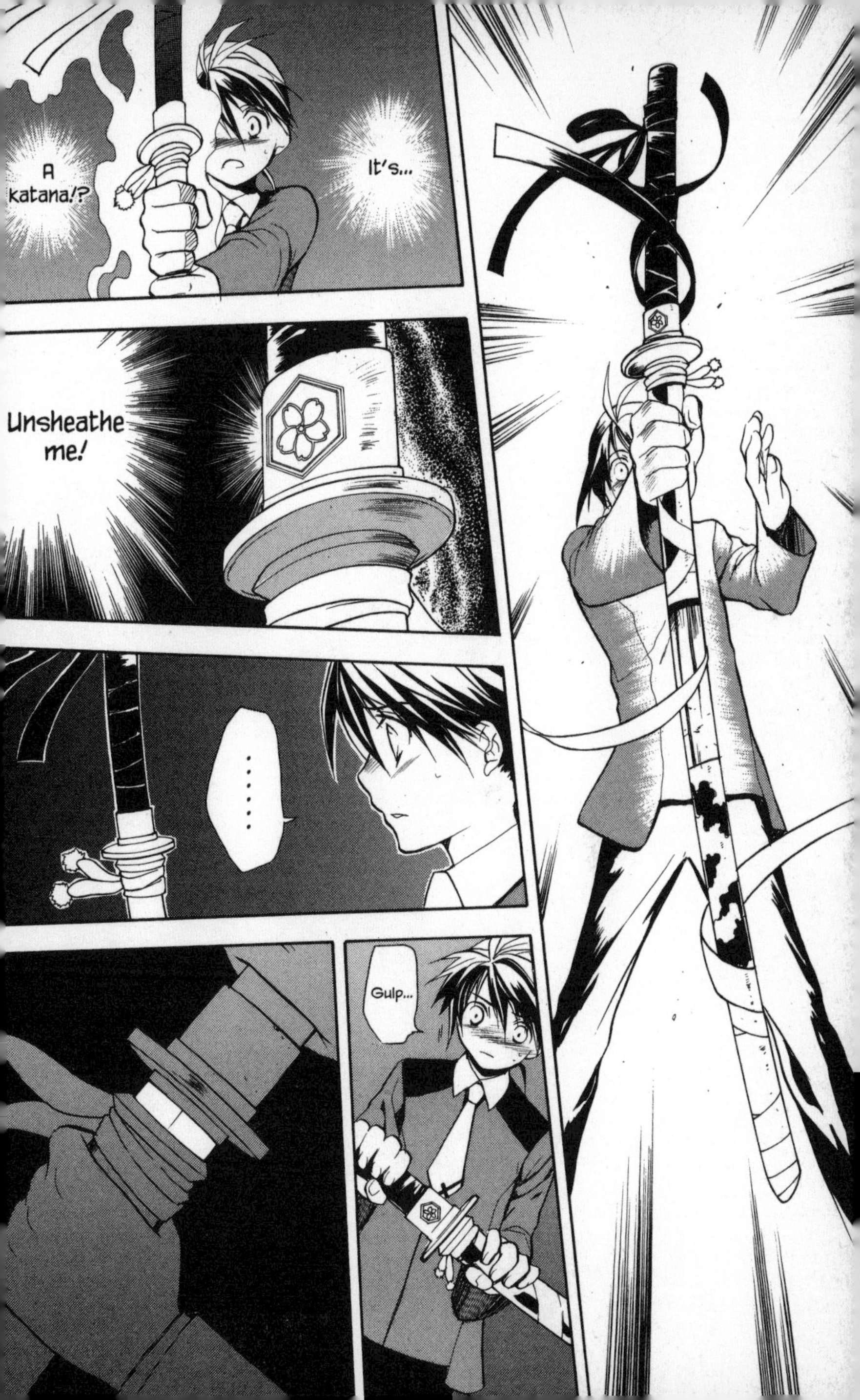
It's...
A katana!?
Unsheathe me!
......
Gulp...

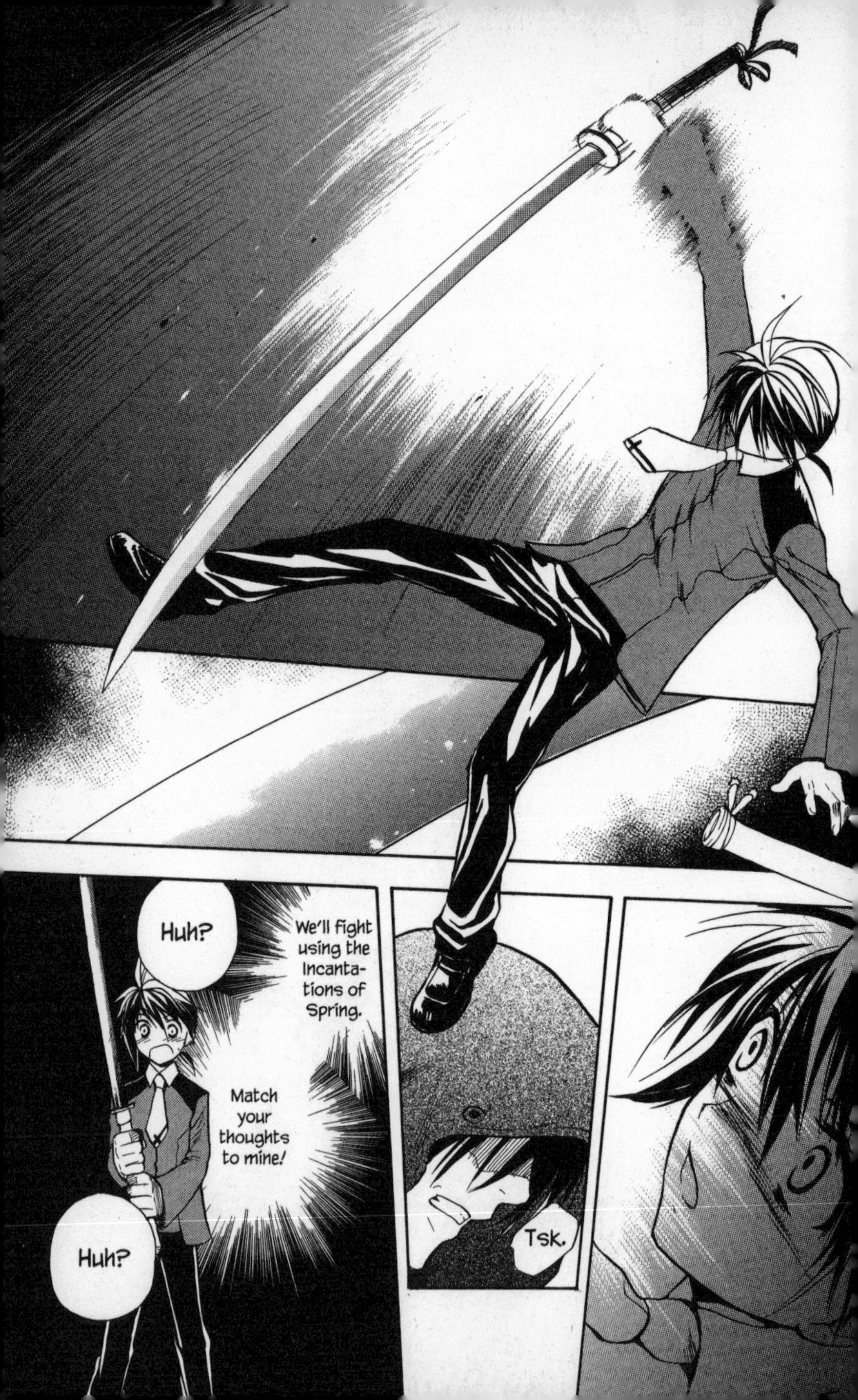
Tsk.
We'll fight using the Incantations of Spring.
Huh?
Match your thoughts to mine!
Huh?

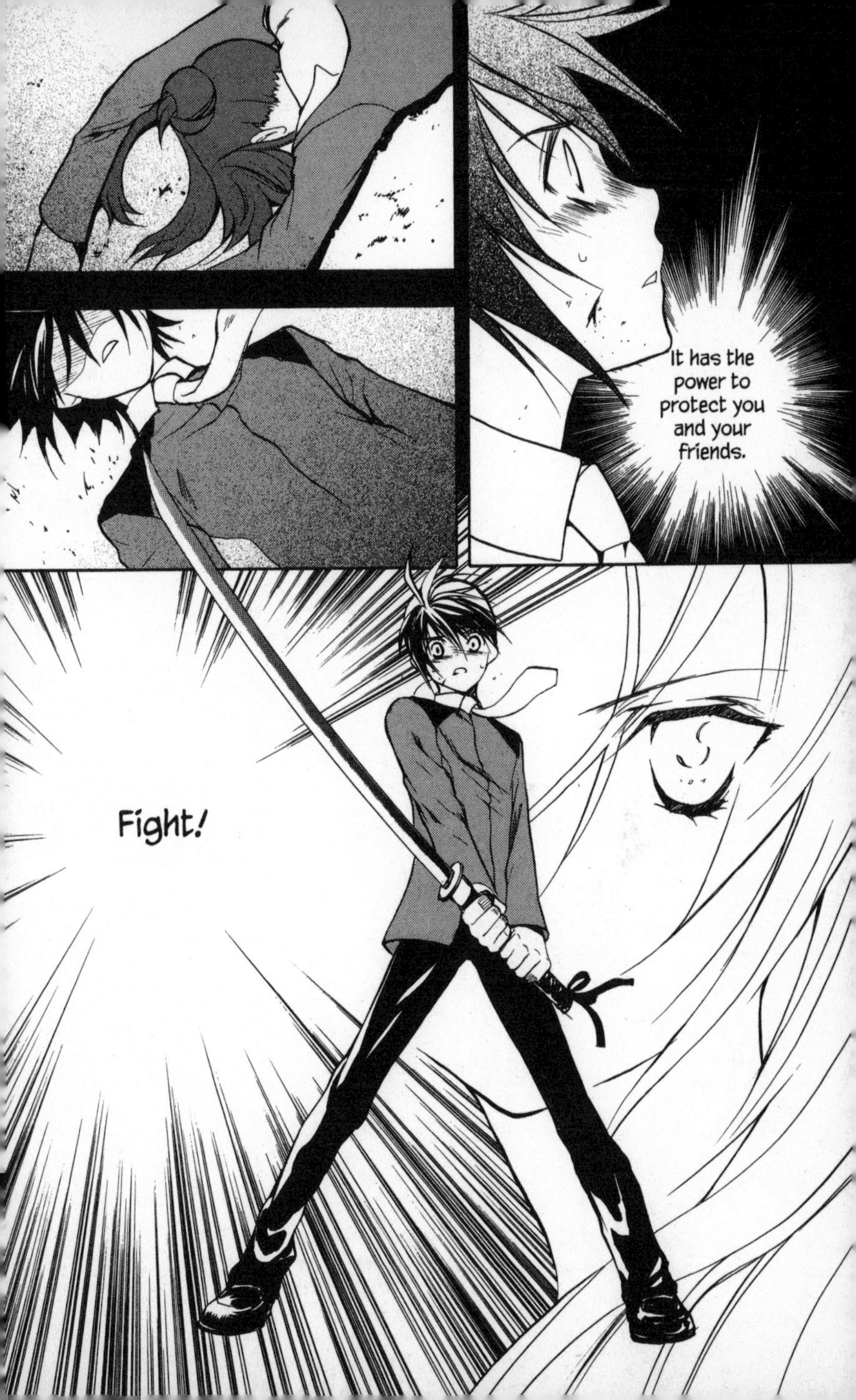
It has the power to protect you and your friends.
Fight!

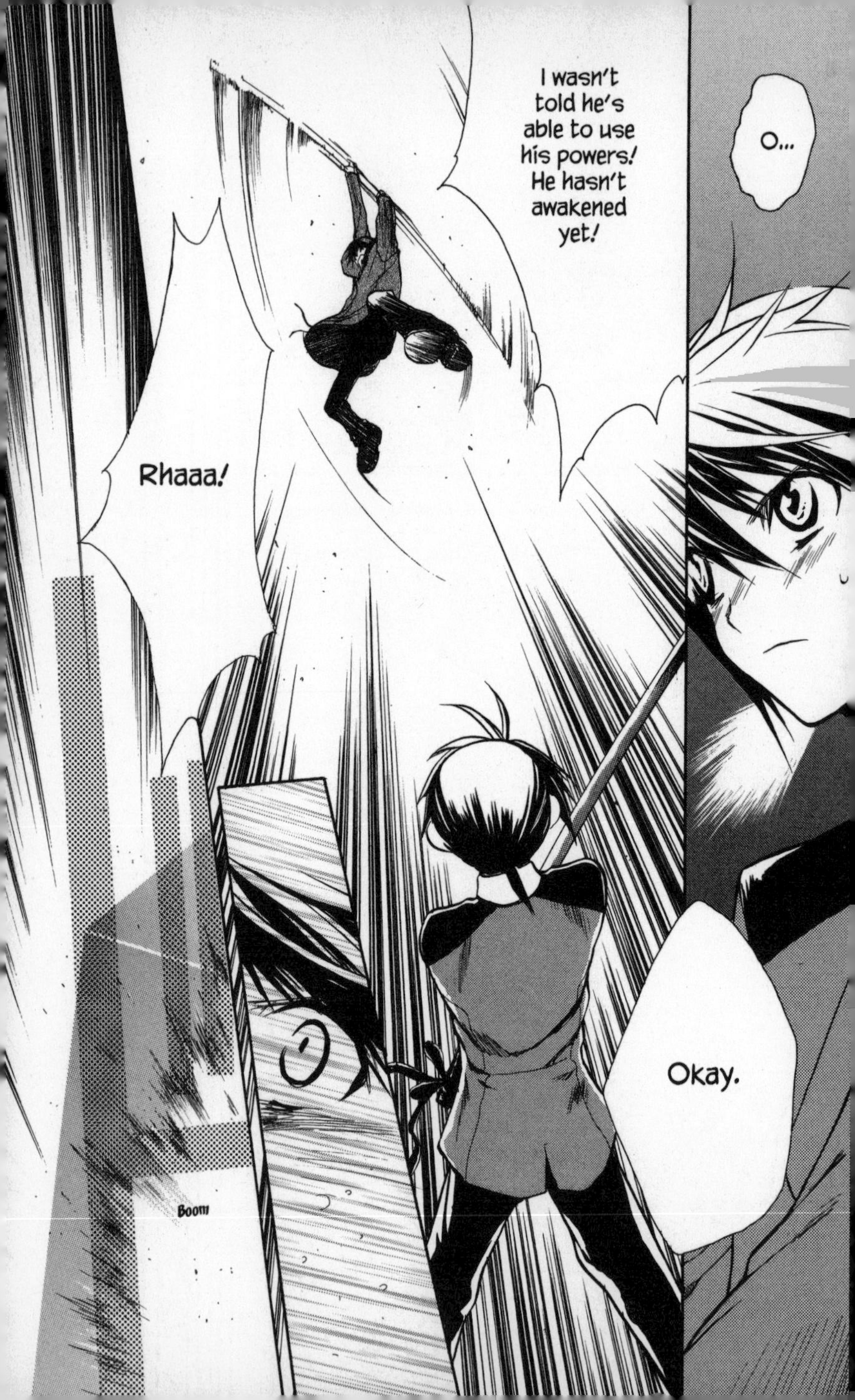
O...
Okay.
I wasn't told he's able to use his powers! He hasn't awakened yet!
Rhaaa!
Boom

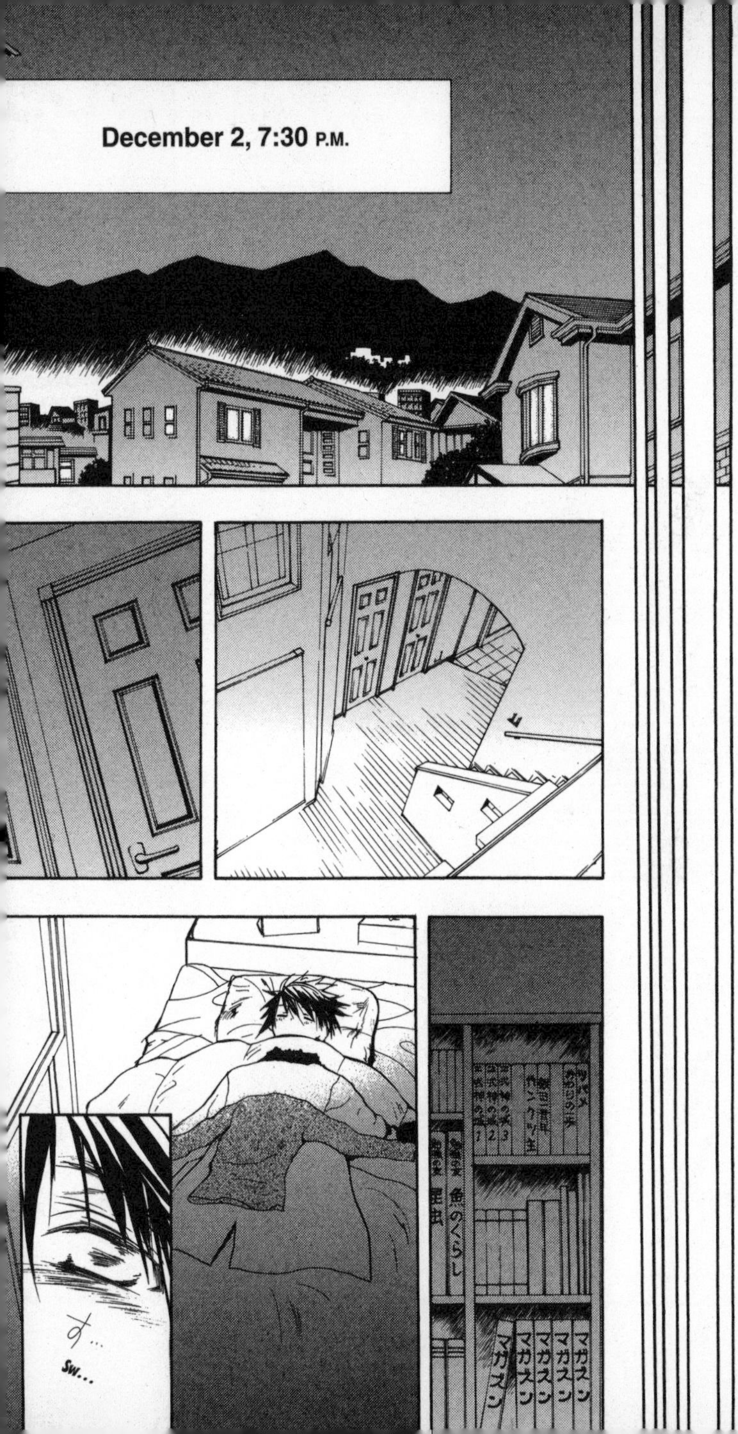
December 2, 7:30 P.M.
マガズン
マガズン
マガズン
マガズン
魚のくらし
昆虫
す…
Sw...

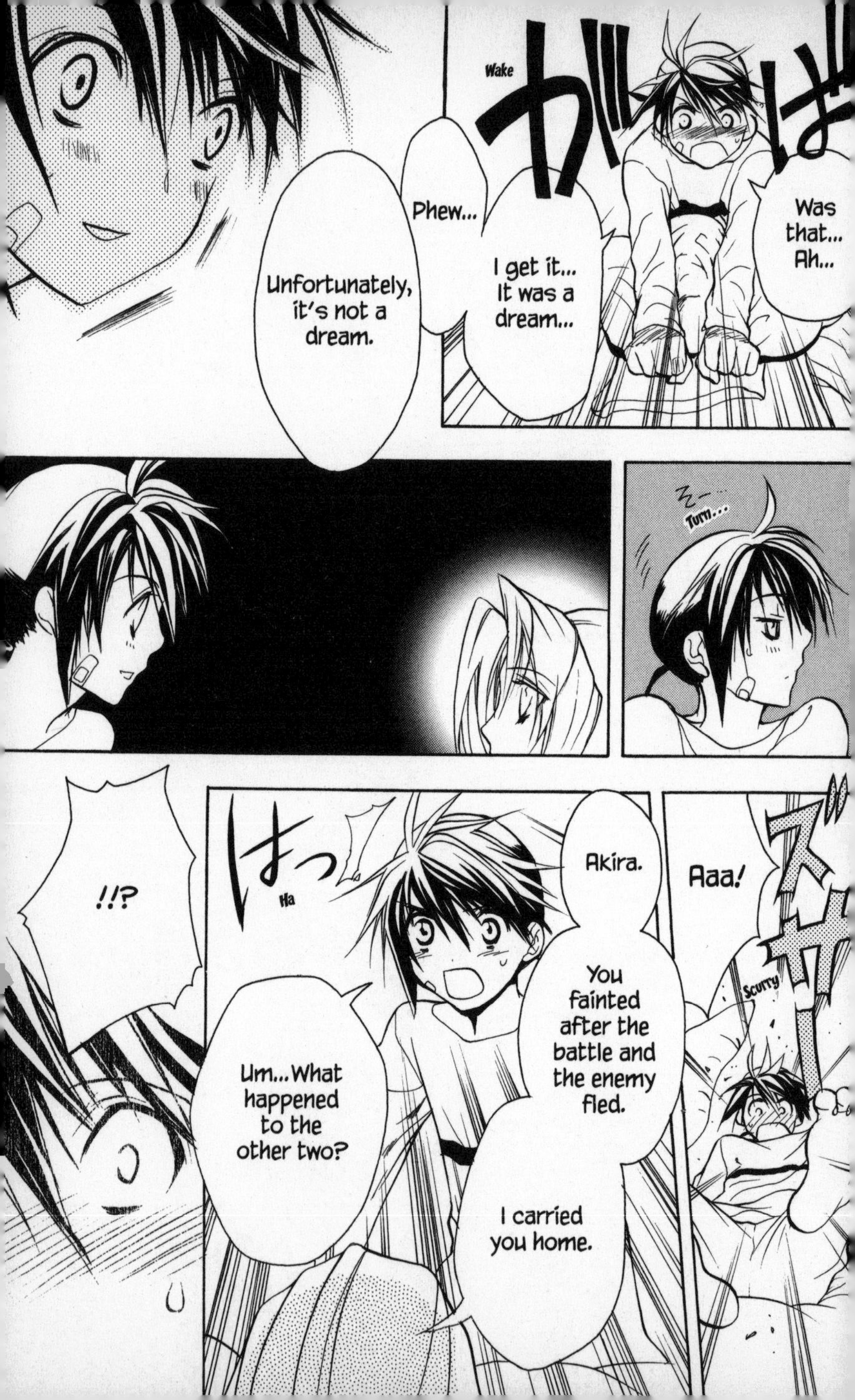
Wake
Was that... Ah...
I get it... It was a dream...
Phew...
Unfortunately, it's not a dream.
Turn...
Aaa!
Scurry
Akira.
You fainted after the battle and the enemy fled.
Ha
Um...What happened to the other two?
I carried you home.
!!?

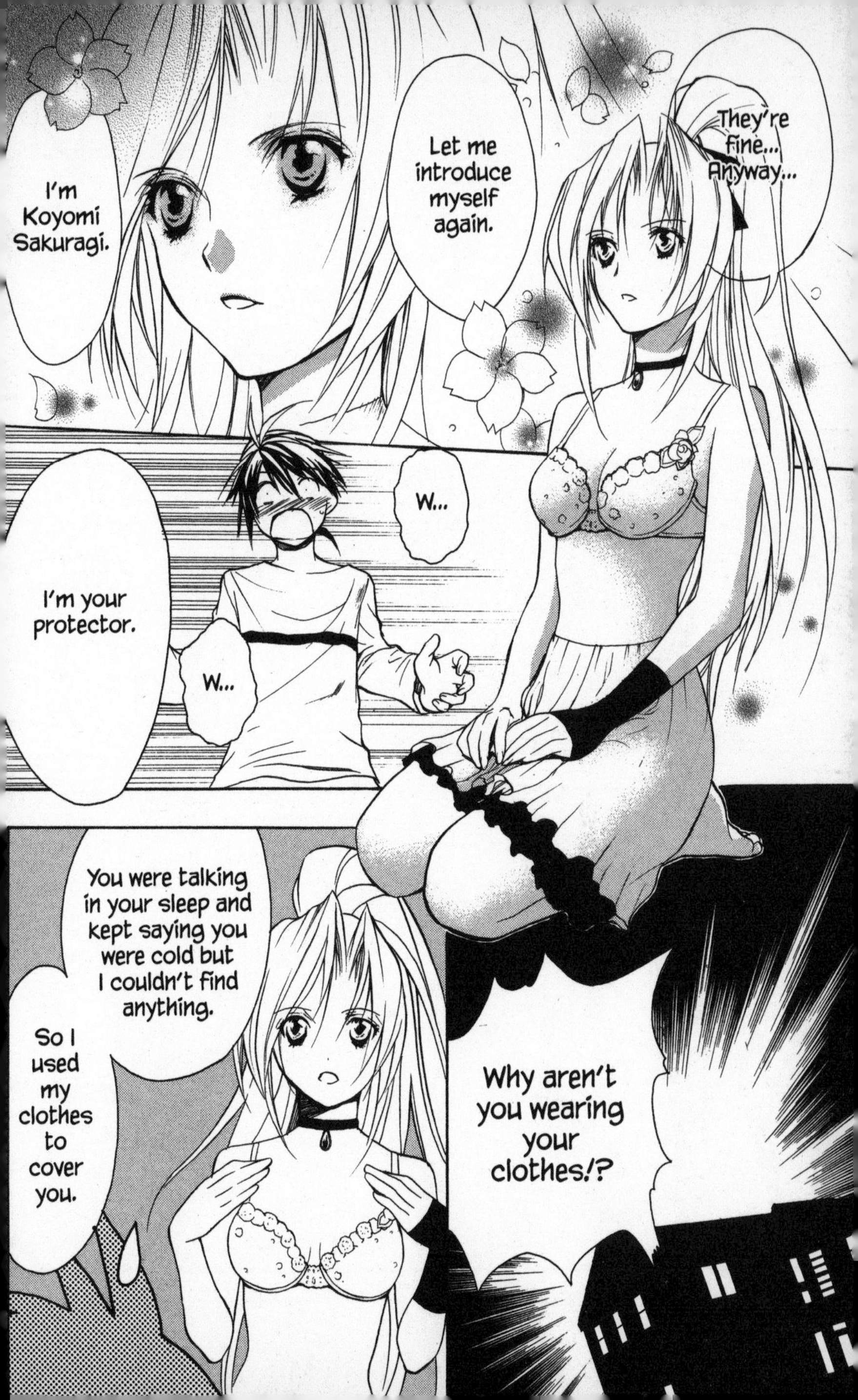
They're fine... Anyway...
Let me introduce myself again.
I'm Koyomi Sakuragi.
W...
I'm your protector.
W...
Why aren't you wearing your clothes!?
You were talking in your sleep and kept saying you were cold but I couldn't find anything.
So I used my clothes to cover you.

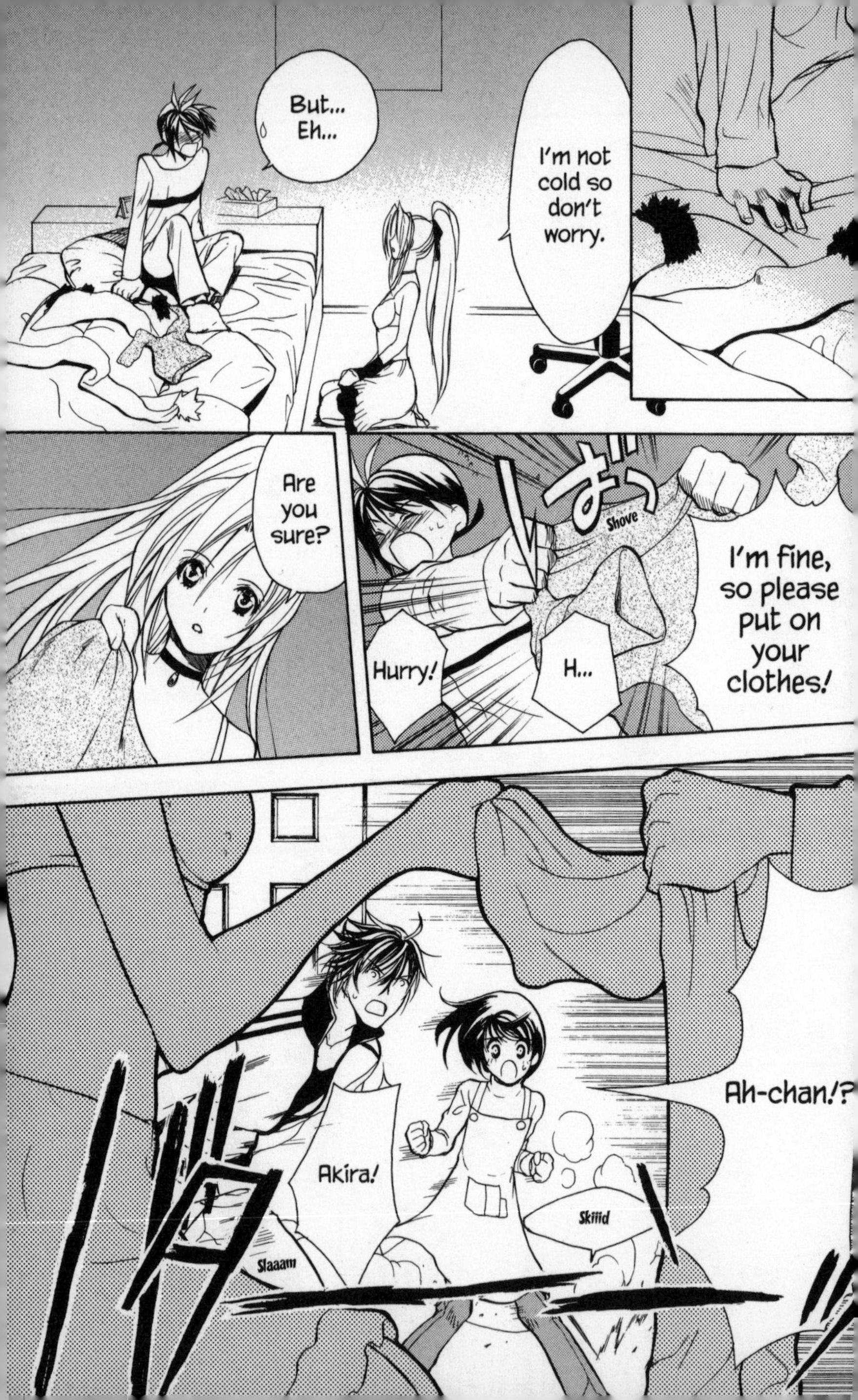
I'm not cold so don't worry.
But... Eh...
I'm fine, so please put on your clothes!
ずっ
Shove
H...
Hurry!
Are you sure?
Ah-chan!?
Skiiid
Akira!
Slaaam

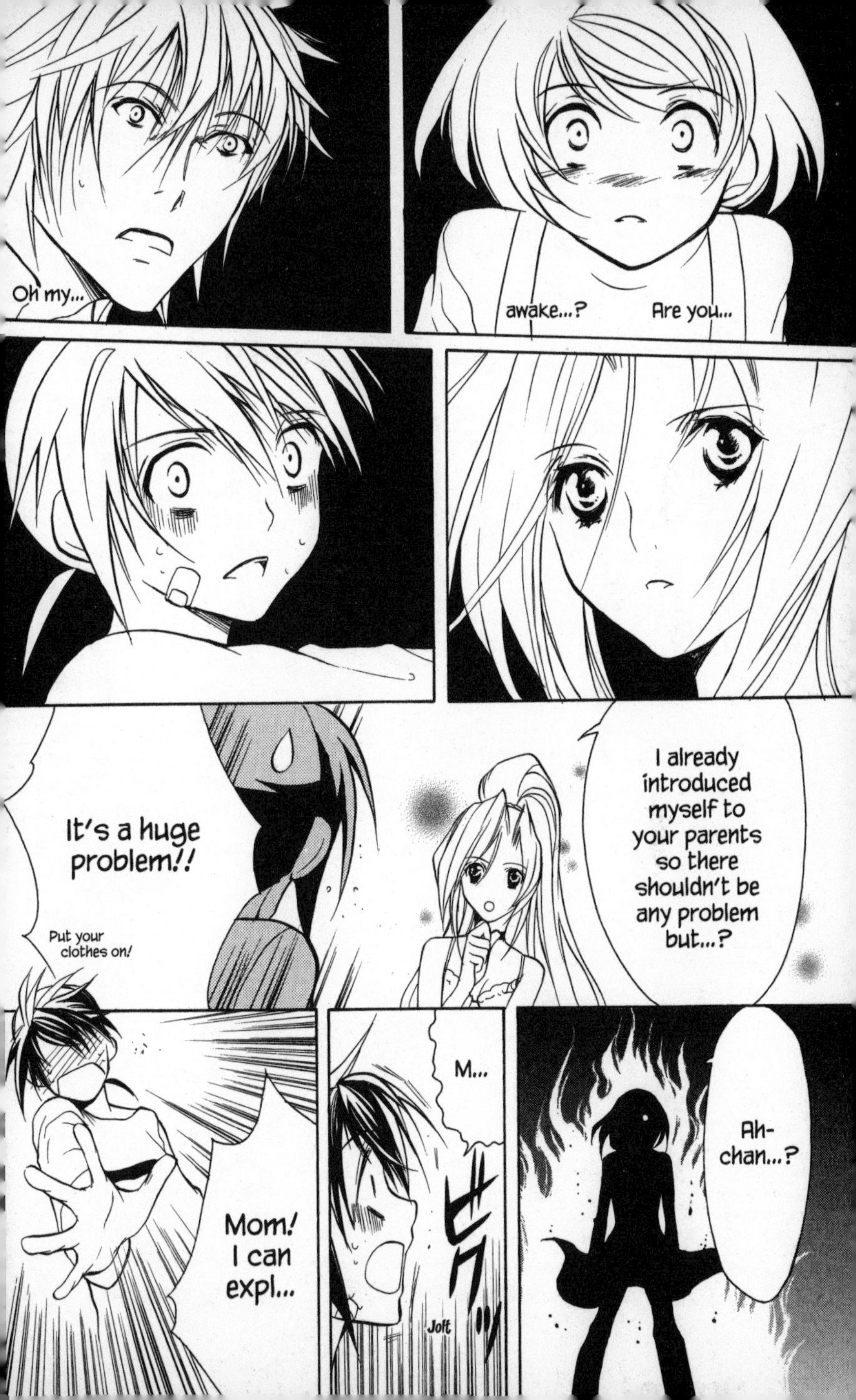
Are you...
awake...?
Oh my...
I already introduced myself to your parents so there shouldn't be any problem but...?
It's a huge problem!!
Put your clothes on!
Ah-chan...?
M...
Jolt
Mom! I can expl...

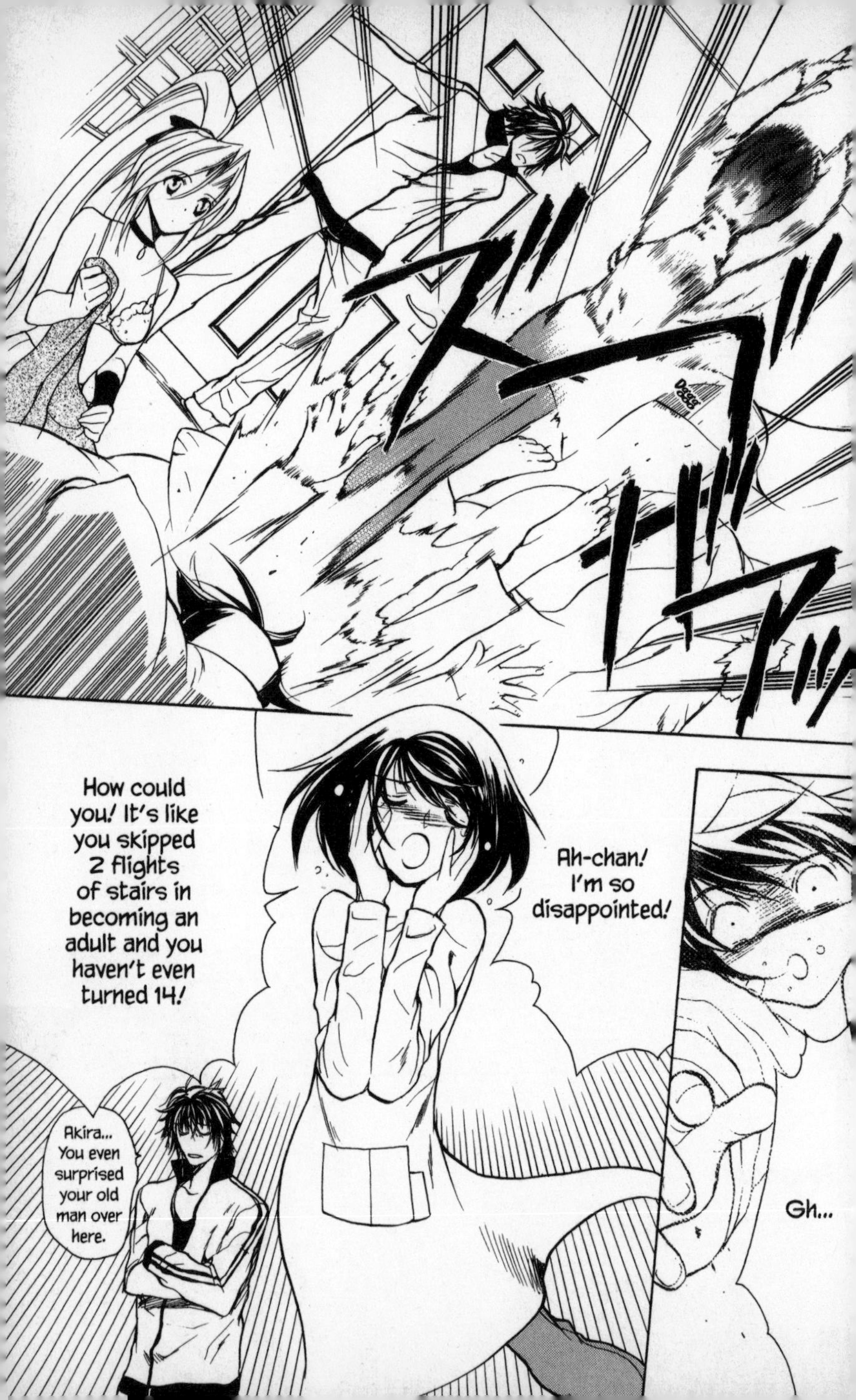
Gh...
Ah-chan! I'm so disappointed!
How could you! It's like you skipped 2 flights of stairs in becoming an adult and you haven't even turned 14!
Akira... You even surprised your old man over here.

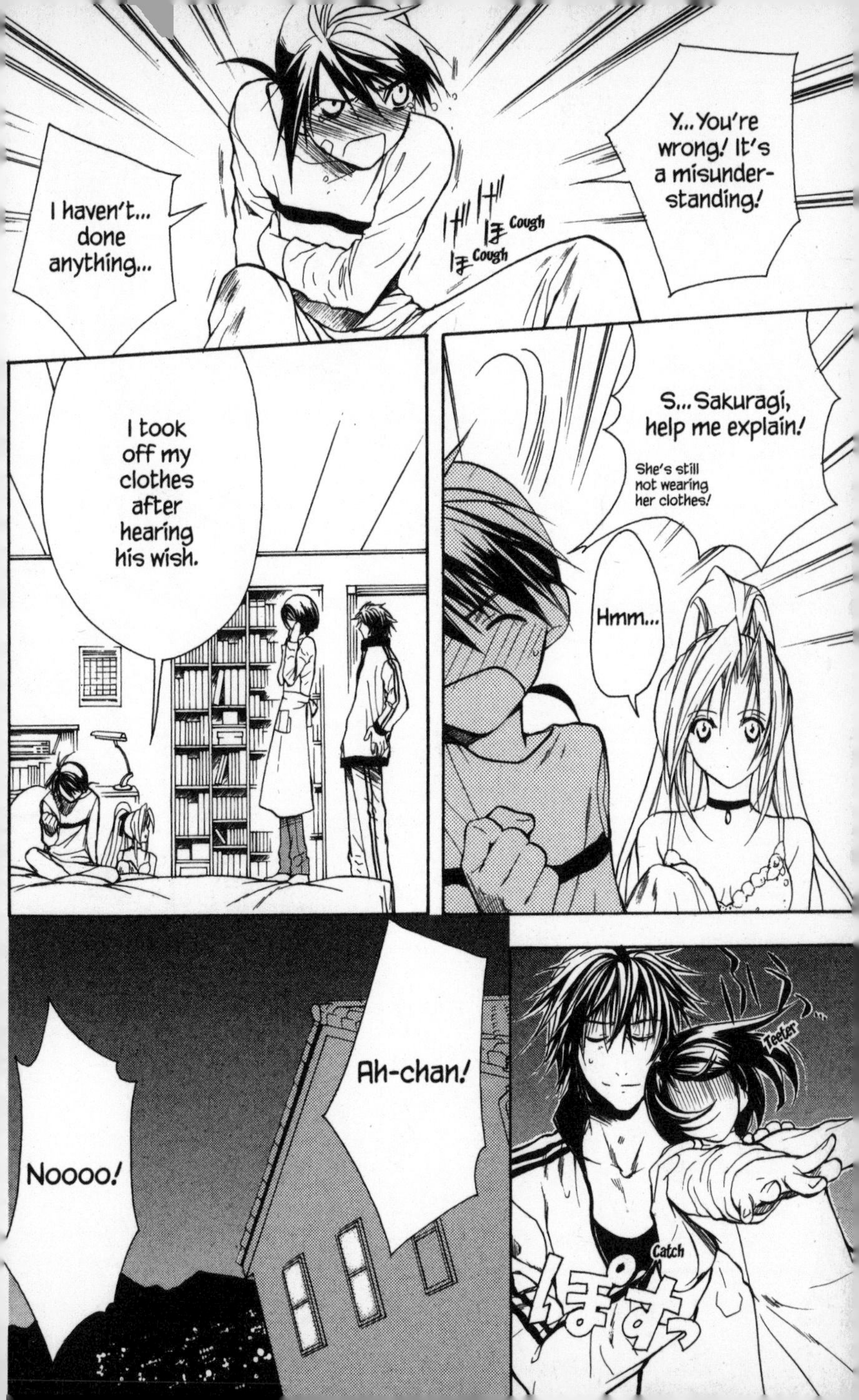
Y... You're wrong! It's a misunderstanding!
Cough
Cough
I haven't... done anything...
S... Sakuragi, help me explain!
She's still not wearing her clothes!
Hmm...
I took off my clothes after hearing his wish.
Teeter
Catch
ぽすっ
Ah-chan!
Noooo!

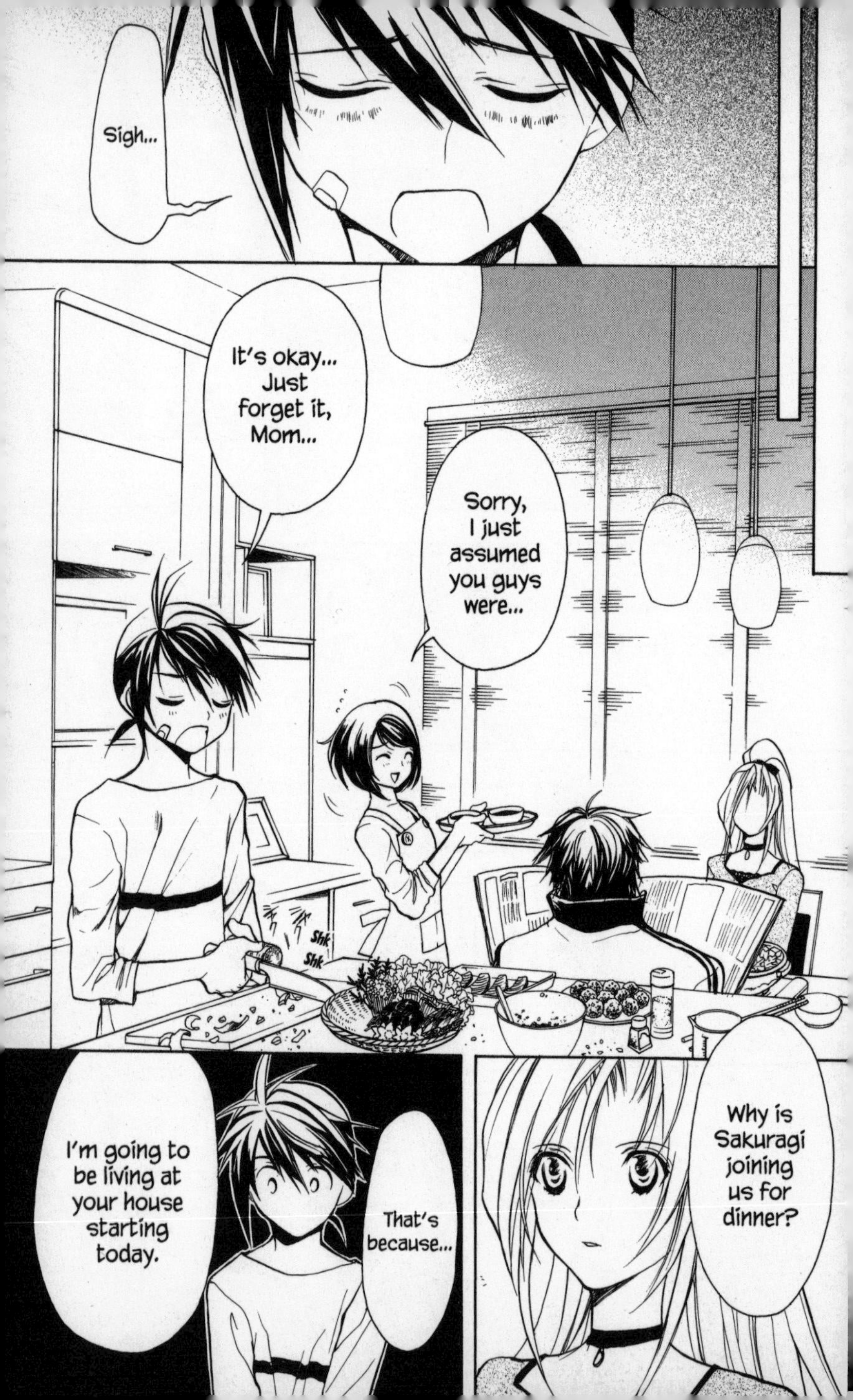
Sigh...
Sorry, I just assumed you guys were...
It's okay... Just forget it, Mom...
Shk
Shk
Why is Sakuragi joining us for dinner?
That's because...
I'm going to be living at your house starting today.

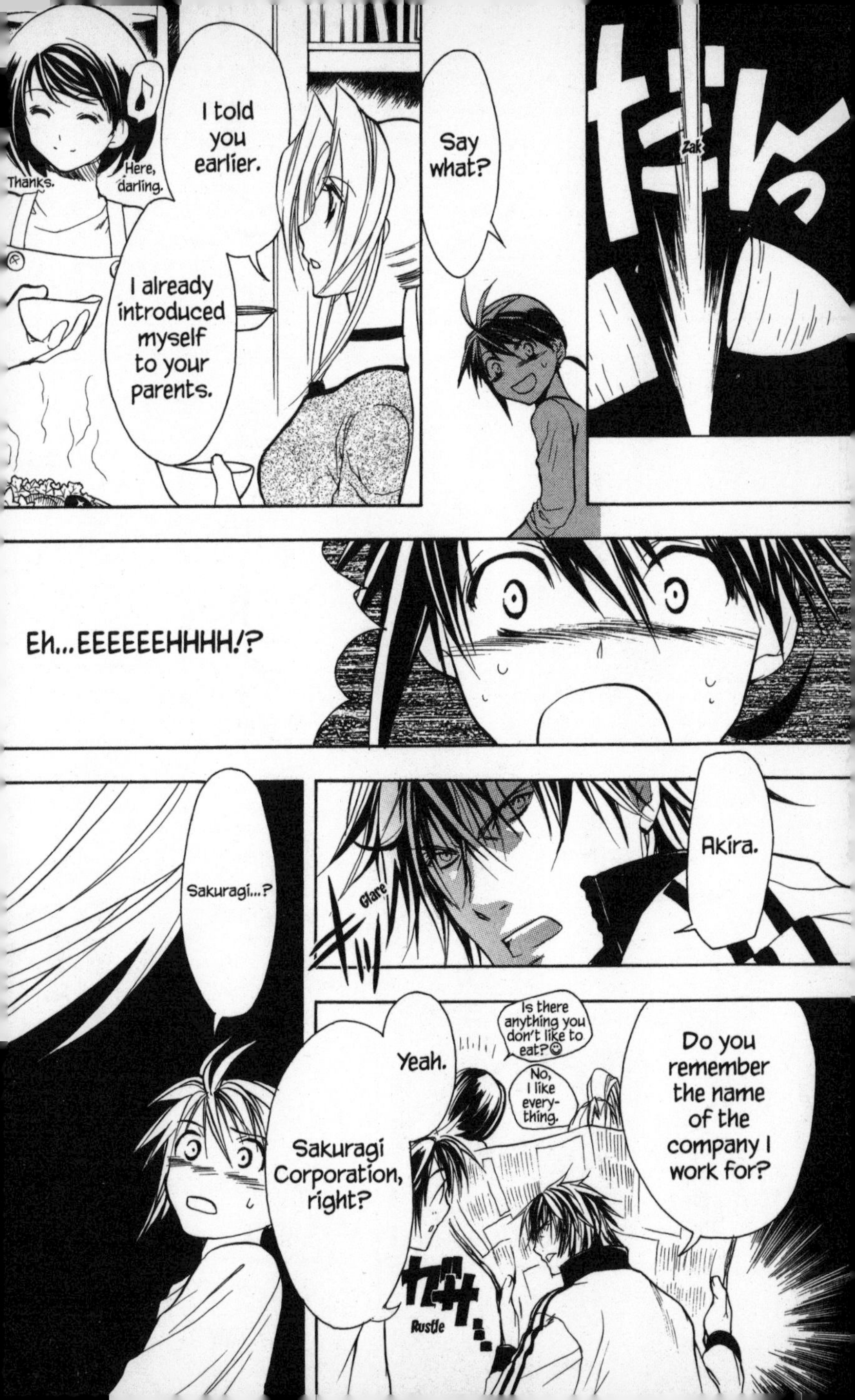
Zak
Say what?
I told you earlier.
Here, darling.
Thanks.
I already introduced myself to your parents.
Eh...EEEEEEHHHH!?
Akira.
Glare
Do you remember the name of the company I work for?
Is there anything you don't like to eat?
No, I like every-thing.
Yeah.
Sakuragi Corporation, right?
Rustle
Sakuragi...?

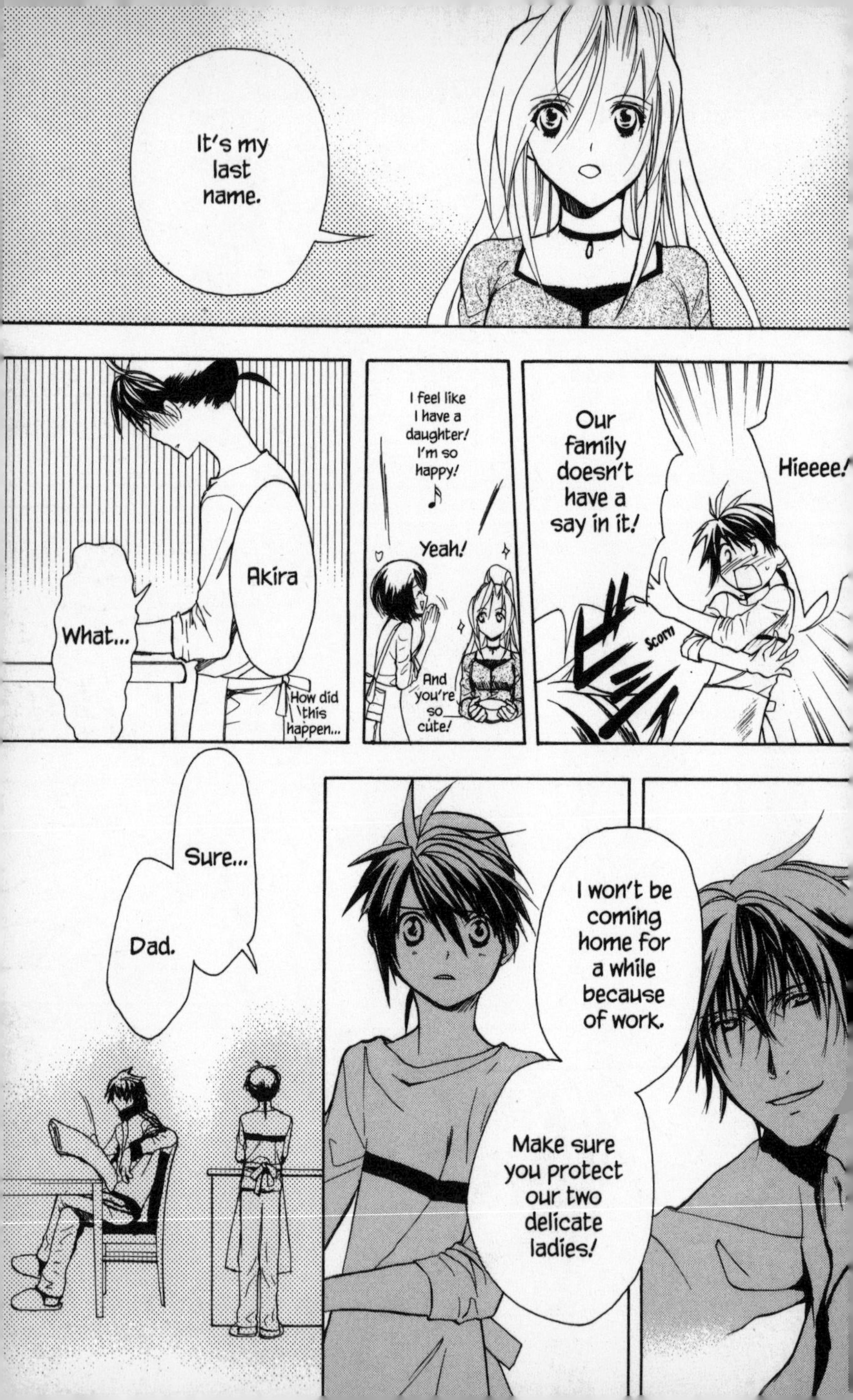
It's my last name.
Hieeee!
Our family doesn't have a say in it!
Scorn
I feel like I have a daughter! I'm so happy! ♪
Yeah!
And you're so cute!
Akira
What...
How did this happen...
I won't be coming home for a while because of work.
Make sure you protect our two delicate ladies!
Sure... Dad.

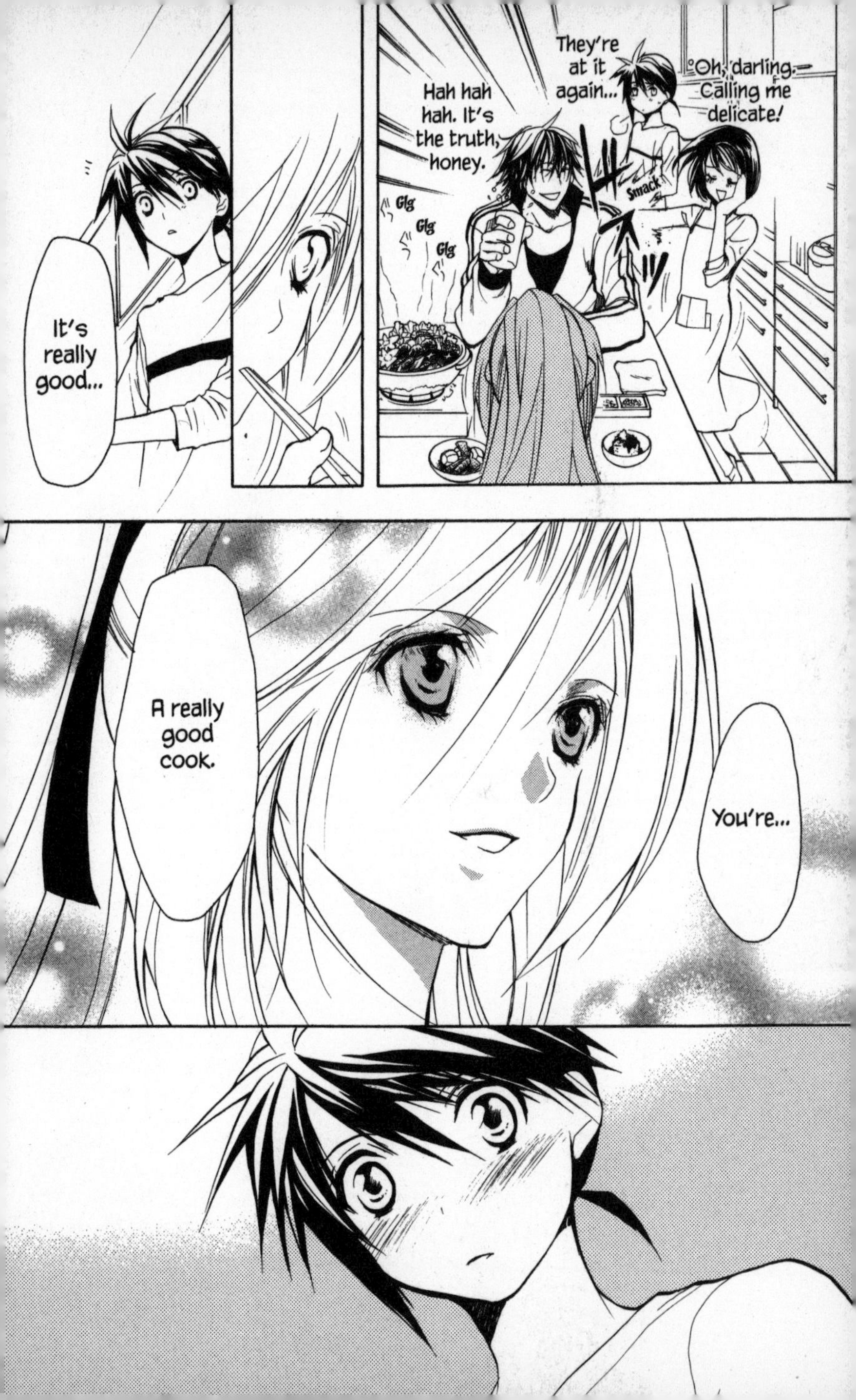
Oh, darling. Calling me delicate!
They're at it again...
Hah hah hah. It's the truth, honey.
Smack
Glg
Glg
Glg
It's really good...
You're...
A really good cook.

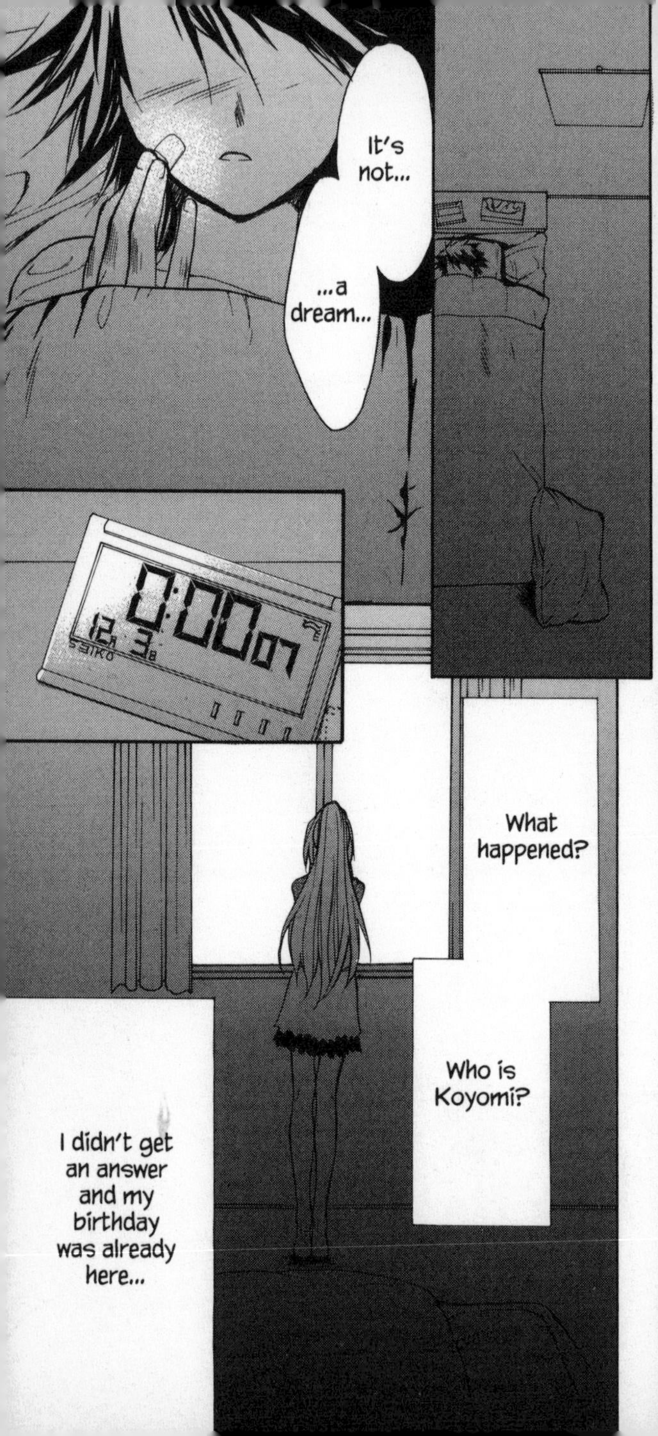
It's not...
...a dream...
0:00 07
What happened?
Who is Koyomi?
I didn't get an answer and my birthday was already here...

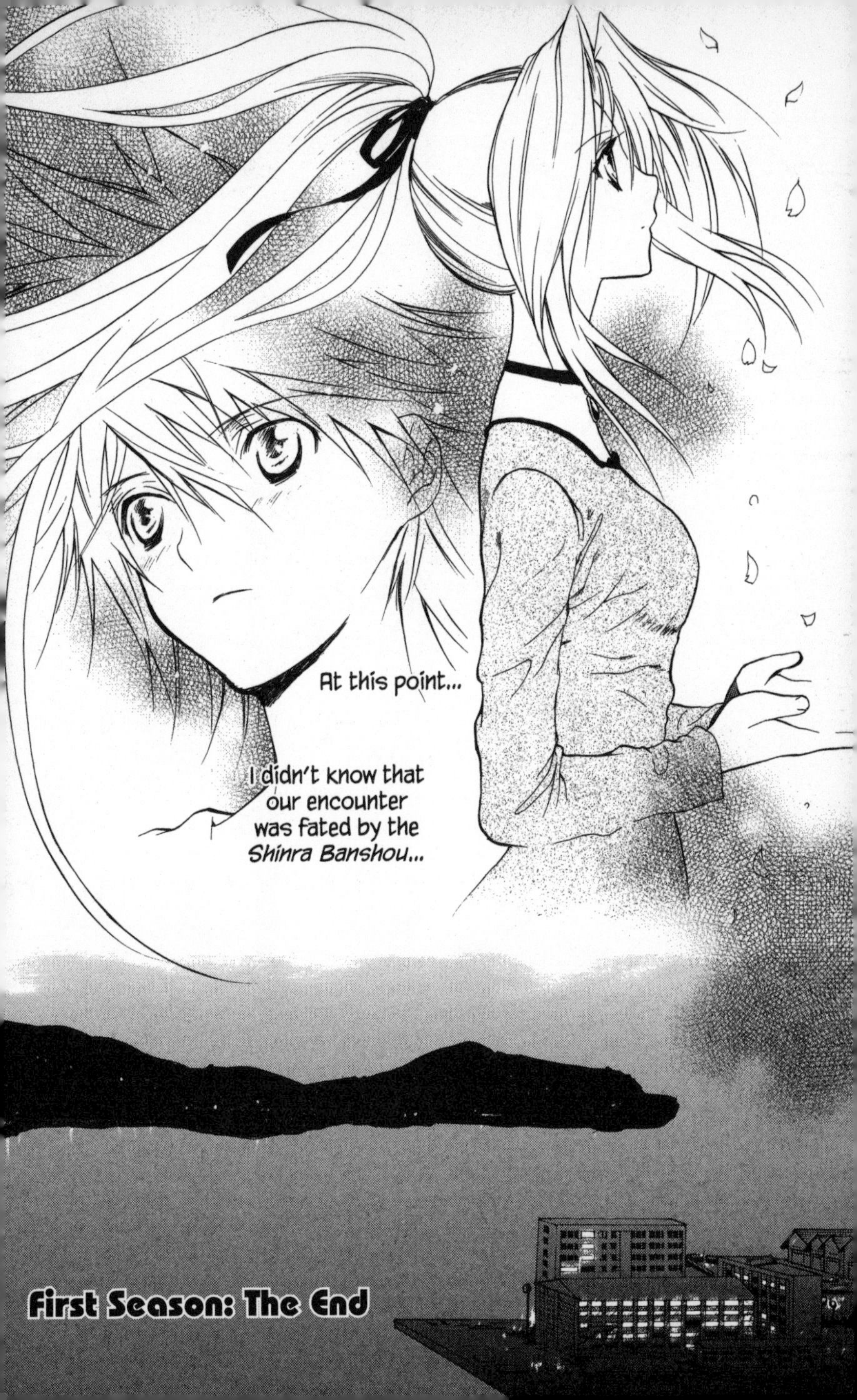
At this point...
I didn't know that our encounter was fated by the *Shinra Banshou*...
First Season: The End

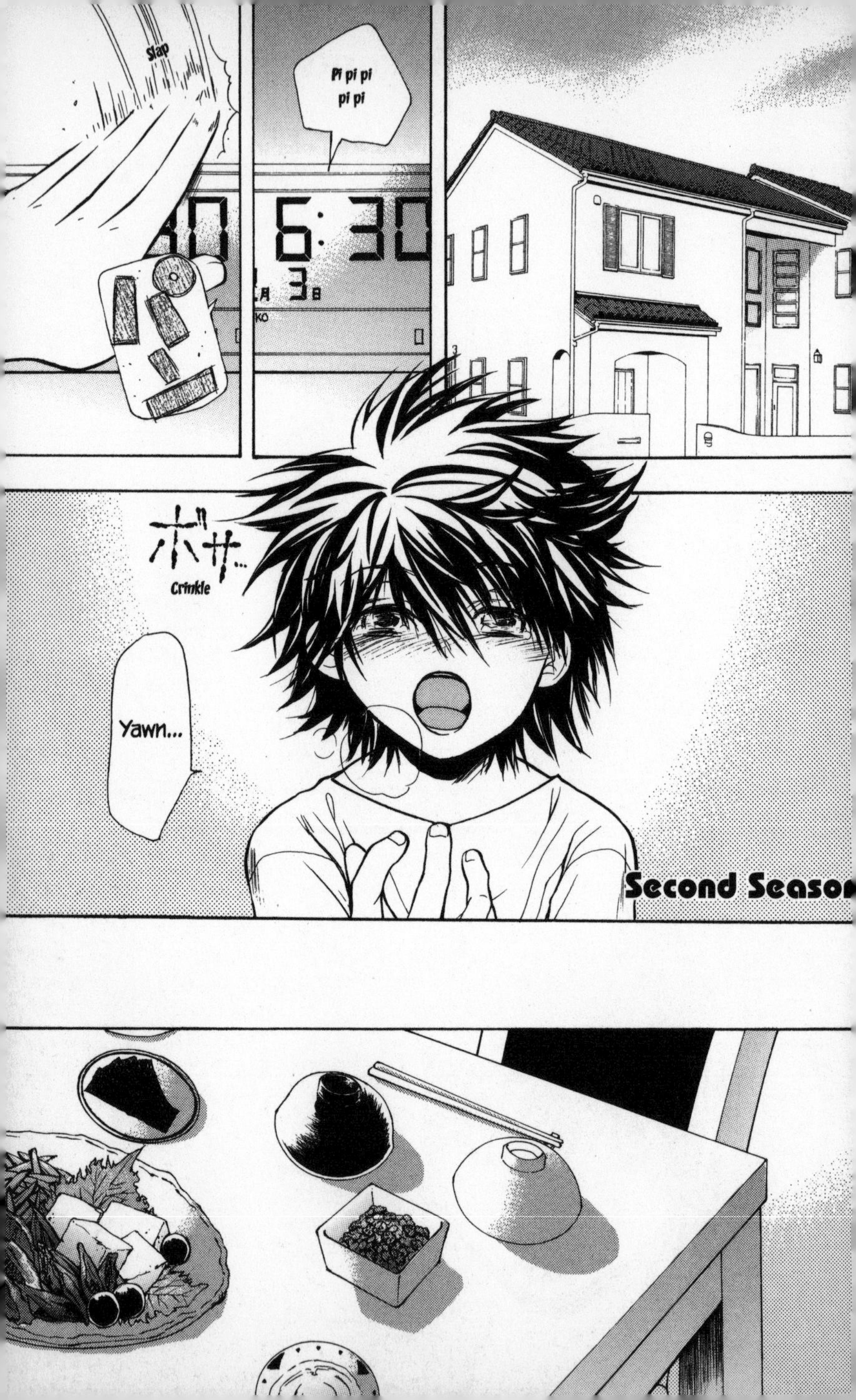

Pi pi pi
pi pi
Slap
ホサ...
Crinkle
Yawn...
Second Seaso

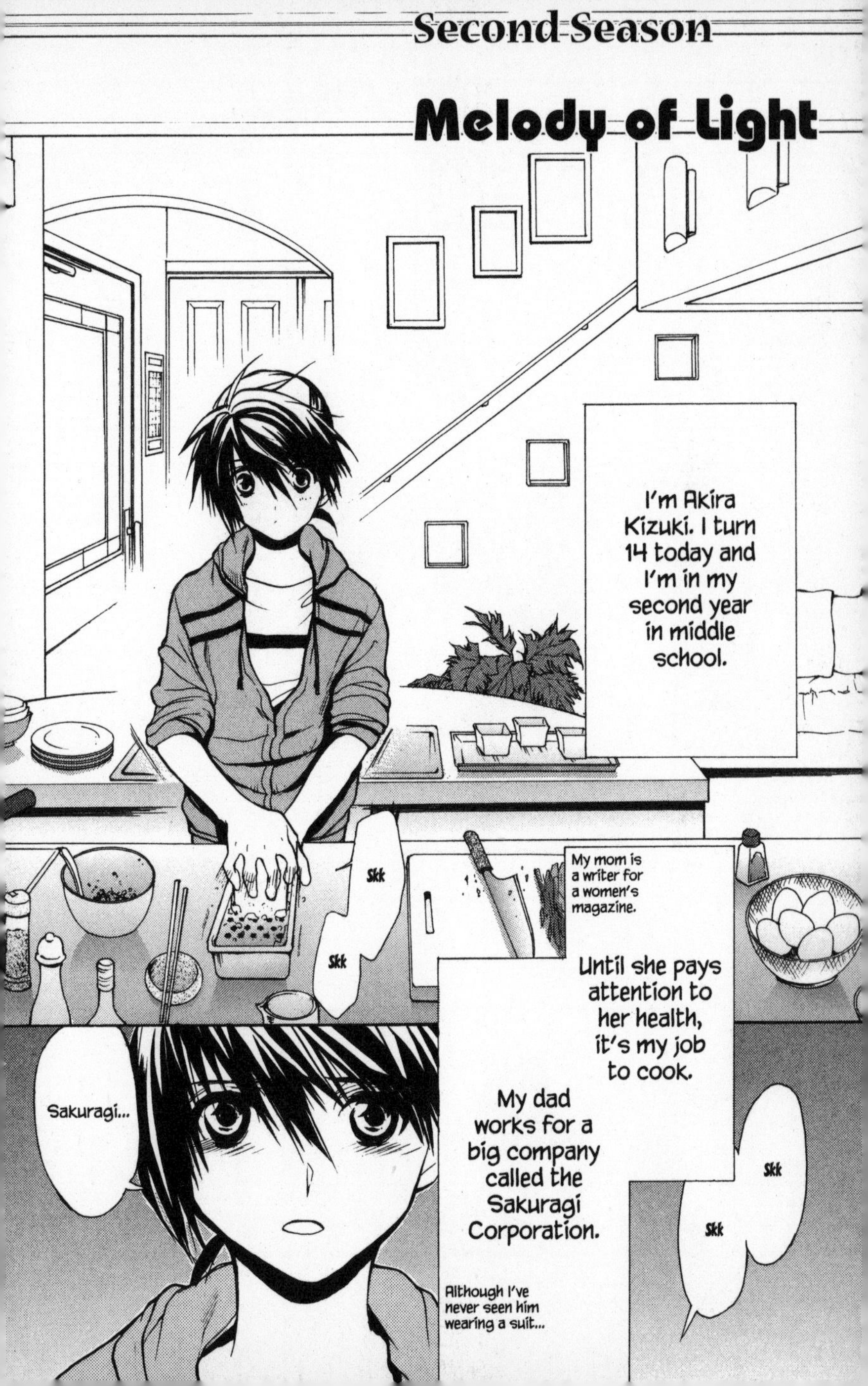
Second Season
Melody of Light
I'm Akira Kizuki. I turn 14 today and I'm in my second year in middle school.
My mom is a writer for a women's magazine.
Skk
Skk
Until she pays attention to her health, it's my job to cook.
My dad works for a big company called the Sakuragi Corporation.
Skk
Skk
Although I've never seen him wearing a suit...
Sakuragi...

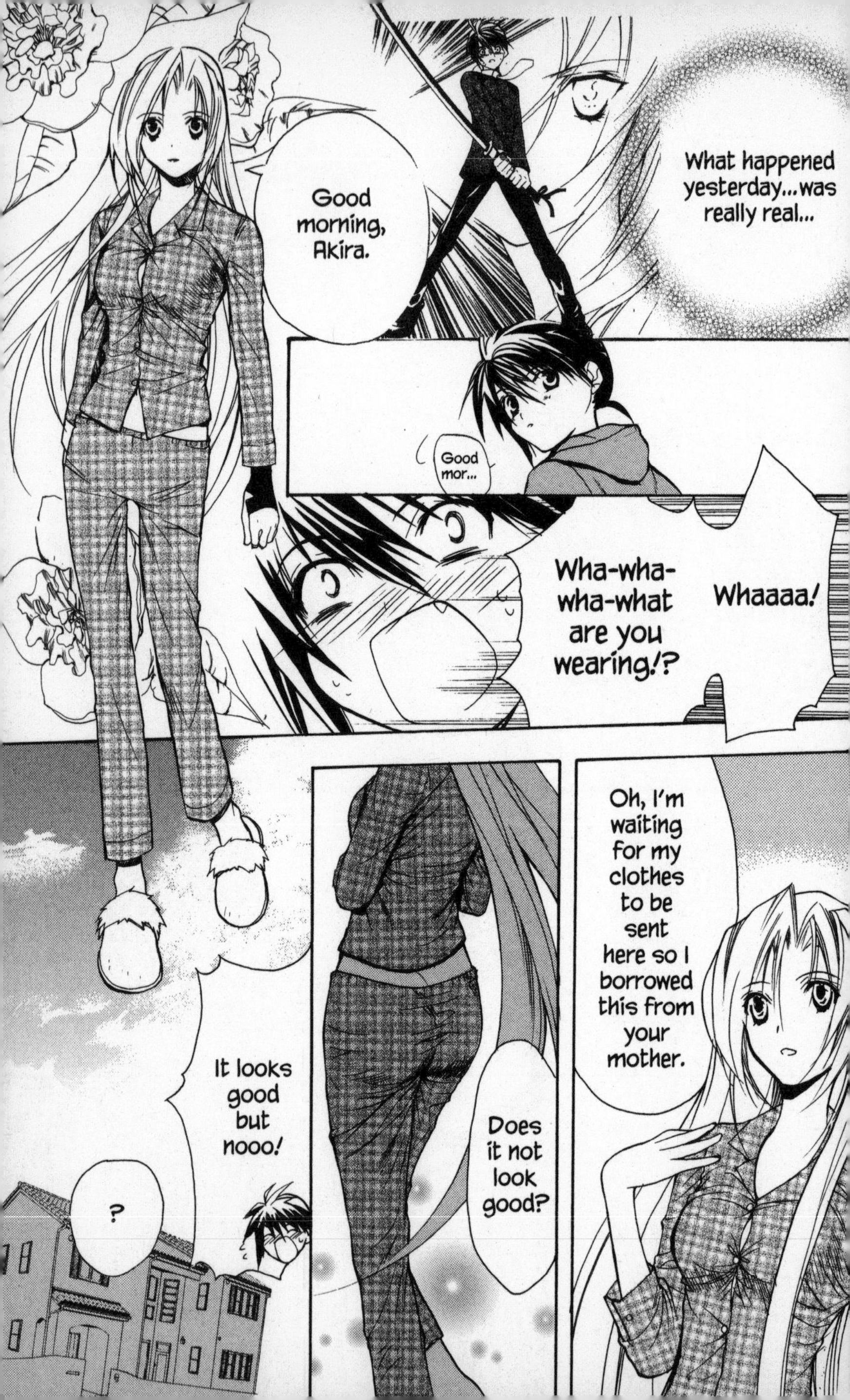
What happened yesterday...was really real...
Good morning, Akira.
Good mor...
Whaaaa!
Wha-wha-wha-what are you wearing!?
Oh, I'm waiting for my clothes to be sent here so I borrowed this from your mother.
Does it not look good?
It looks good but nooo!
?

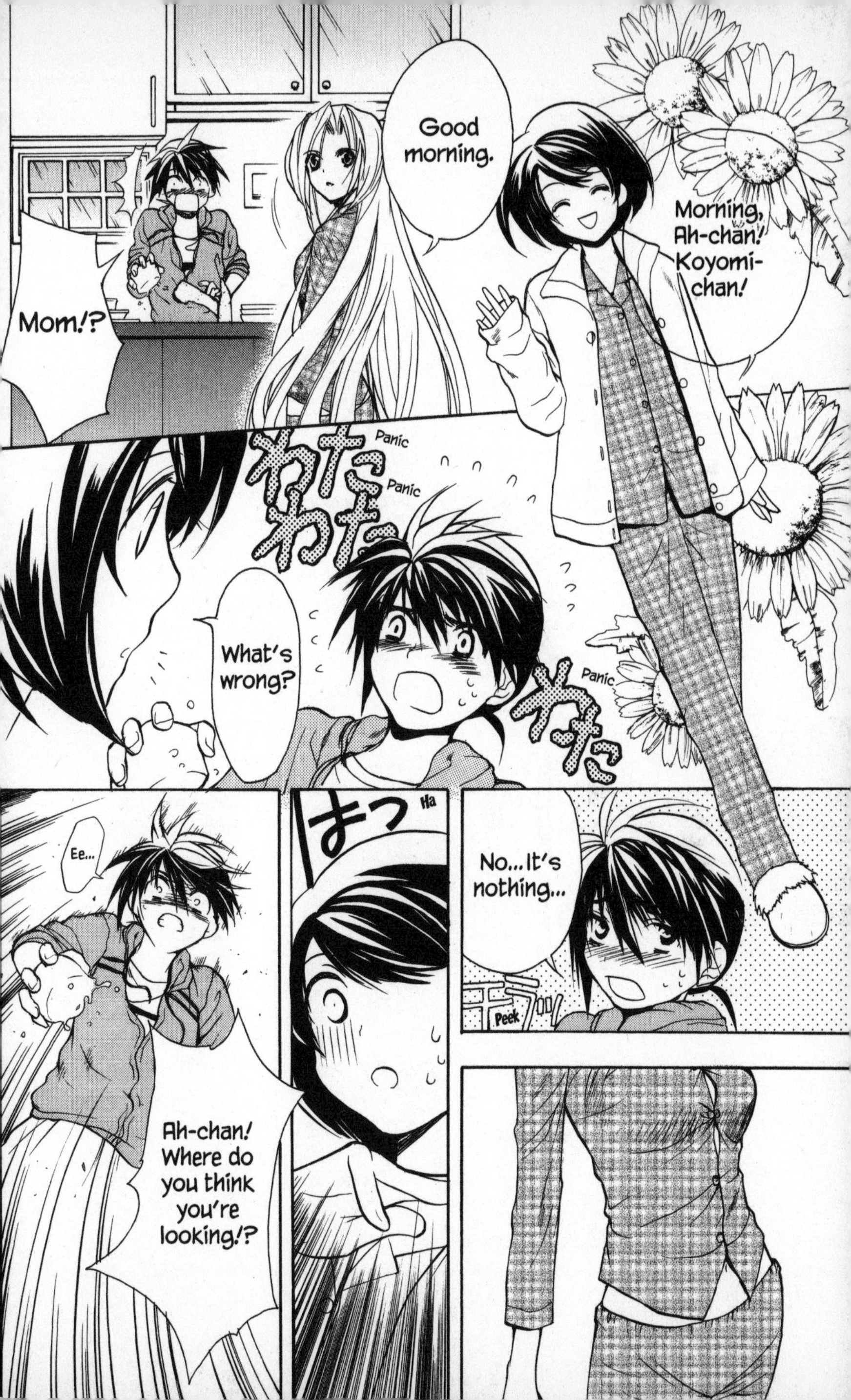
Morning, Ah-chan! Koyomi-chan!
Good morning.
Mom!?
Panic
Panic
Panic
What's wrong?
No... It's nothing...
Peek
Ha
Ee...
Ah-chan! Where do you think you're looking!?

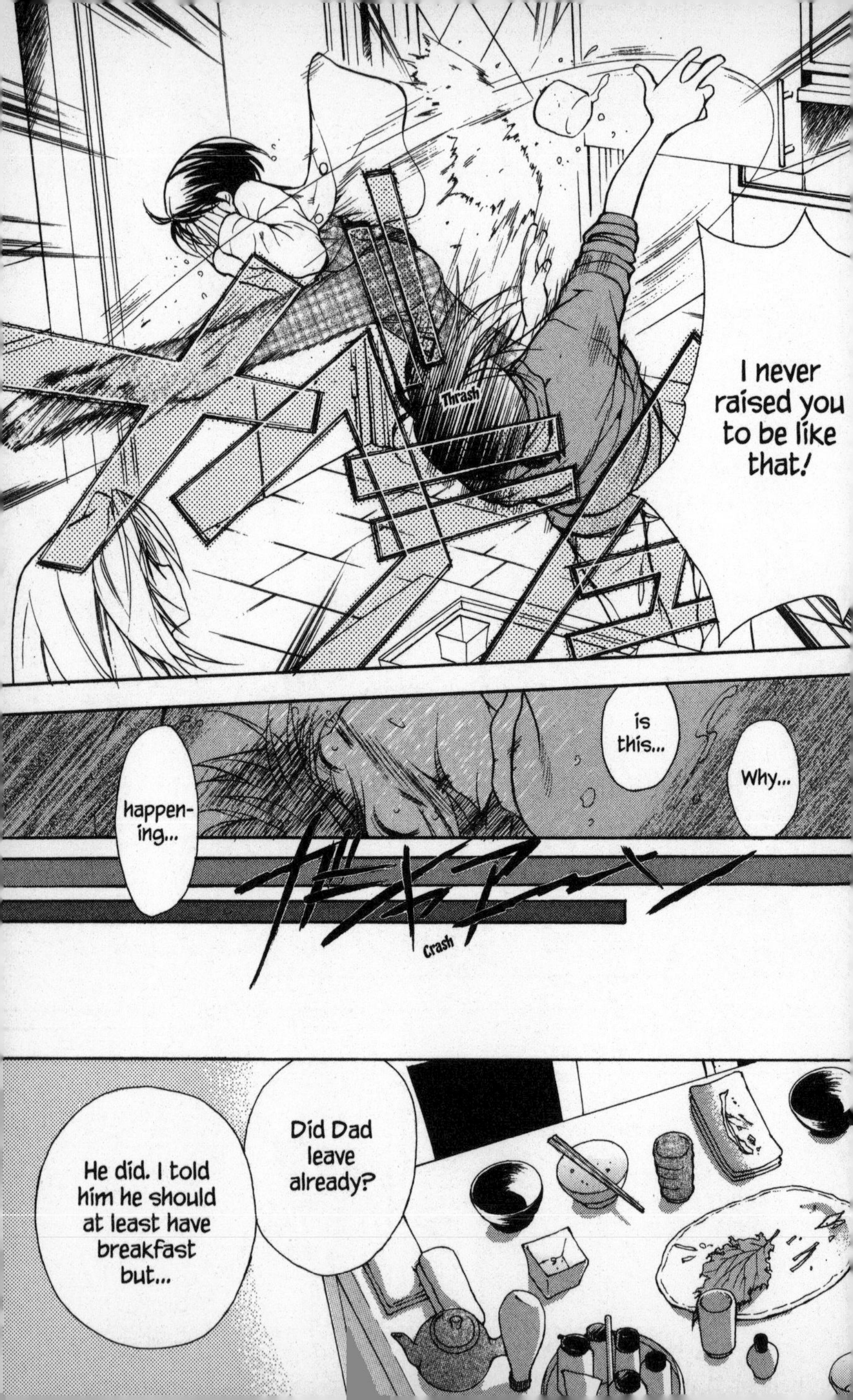
I never raised you to be like that!
Thrash
Why...
is this...
happen-ing...
Crash
Did Dad leave already?
He did. I told him he should at least have breakfast but...

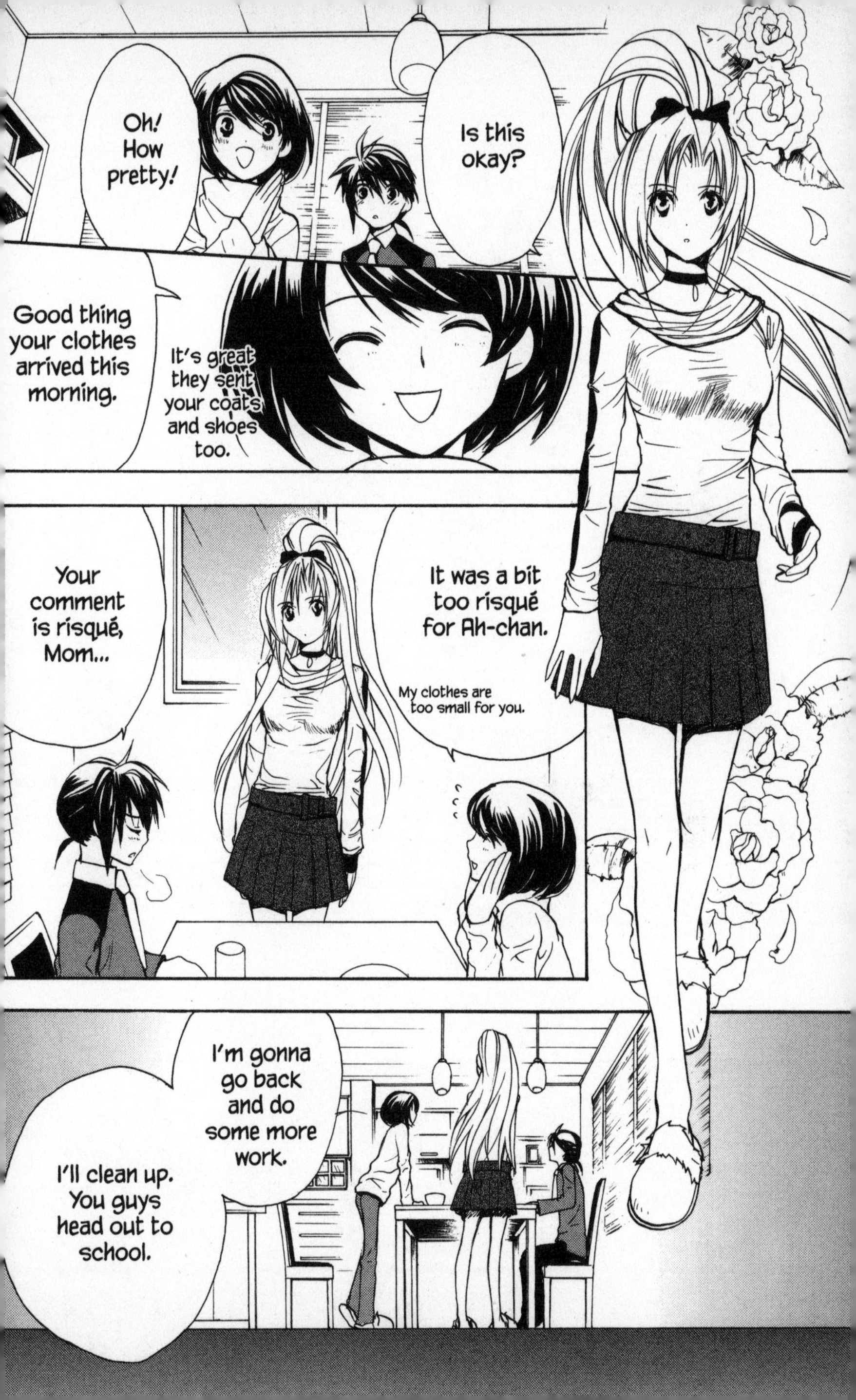
Is this okay?
Oh! How pretty!
Good thing your clothes arrived this morning.
It's great they sent your coats and shoes too.
It was a bit too risqué for Ah-chan.
My clothes are too small for you.
Your comment is risqué, Mom...
I'm gonna go back and do some more work.
I'll clean up. You guys head out to school.

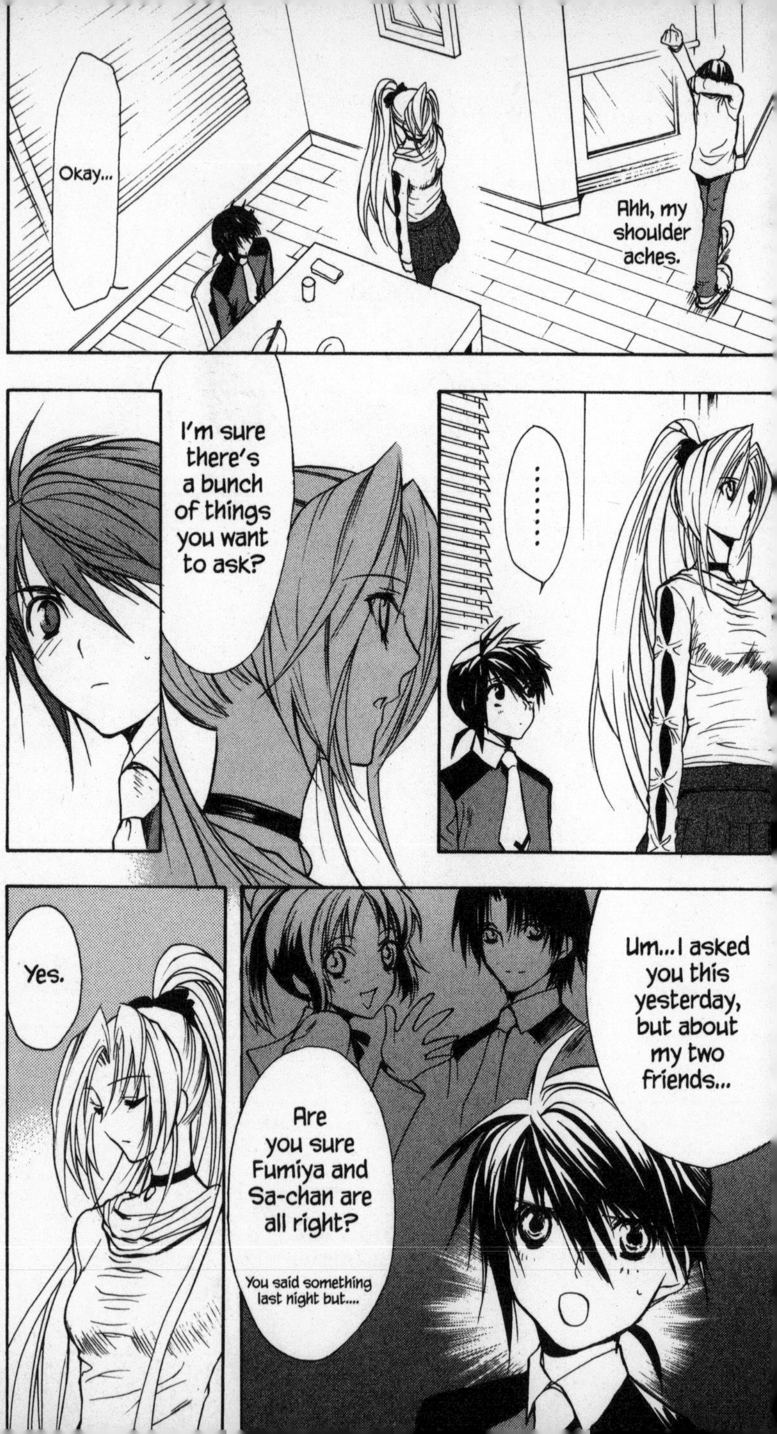
Ahh, my shoulder aches.
Okay...
....
I'm sure there's a bunch of things you want to ask?
Um...I asked you this yesterday, but about my two friends...
Are you sure Fumiya and Sa-chan are all right?
You said something last night but....
Yes.

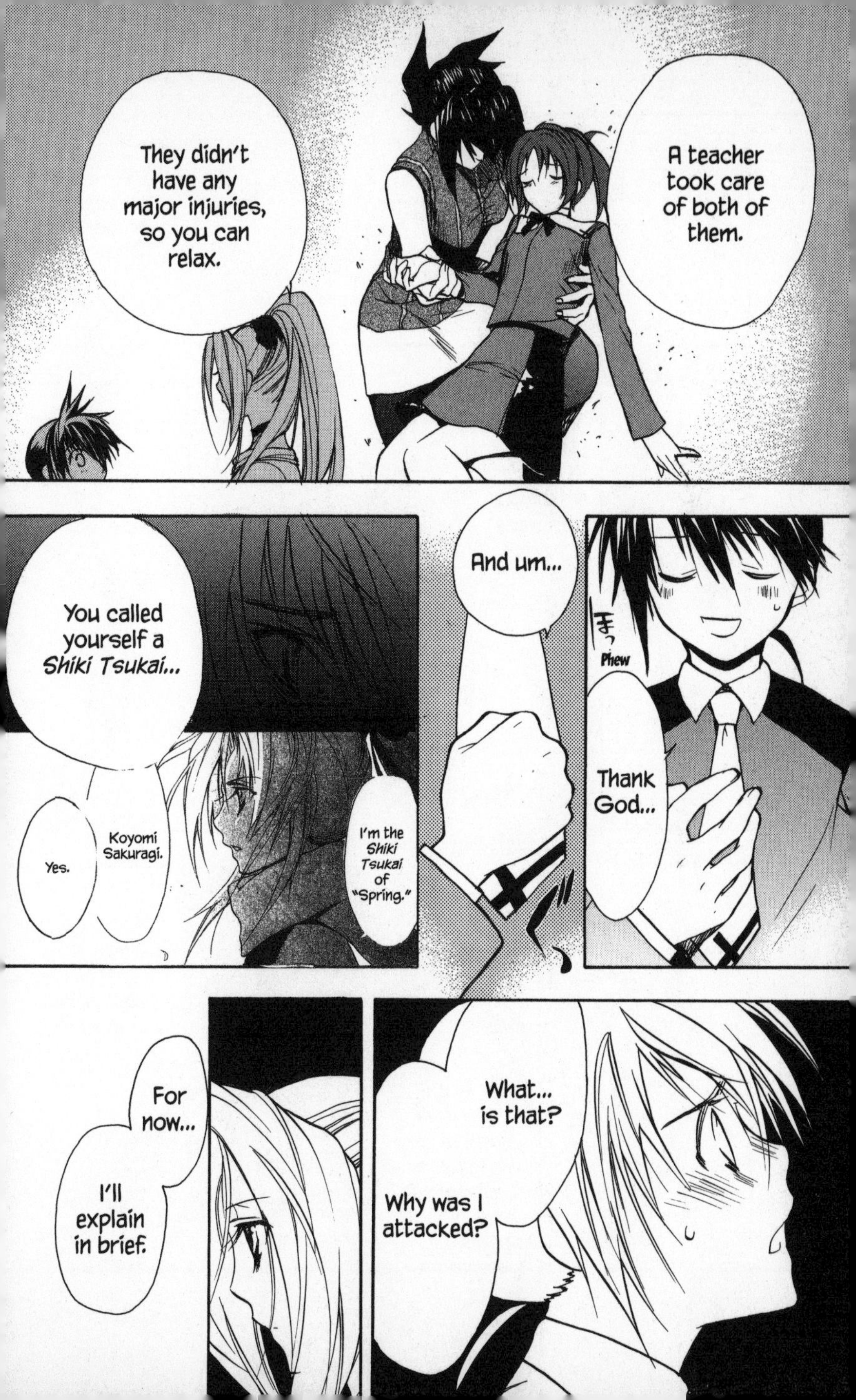
A teacher took care of both of them.
They didn't have any major injuries, so you can relax.
まっ
Phew
Thank God...
And um...
You called yourself a *Shiki Tsukai*...
I'm the *Shiki Tsukai* of "Spring."
Koyomi Sakuragi.
Yes.
What... is that?
Why was I attacked?
For now...
I'll explain in brief.

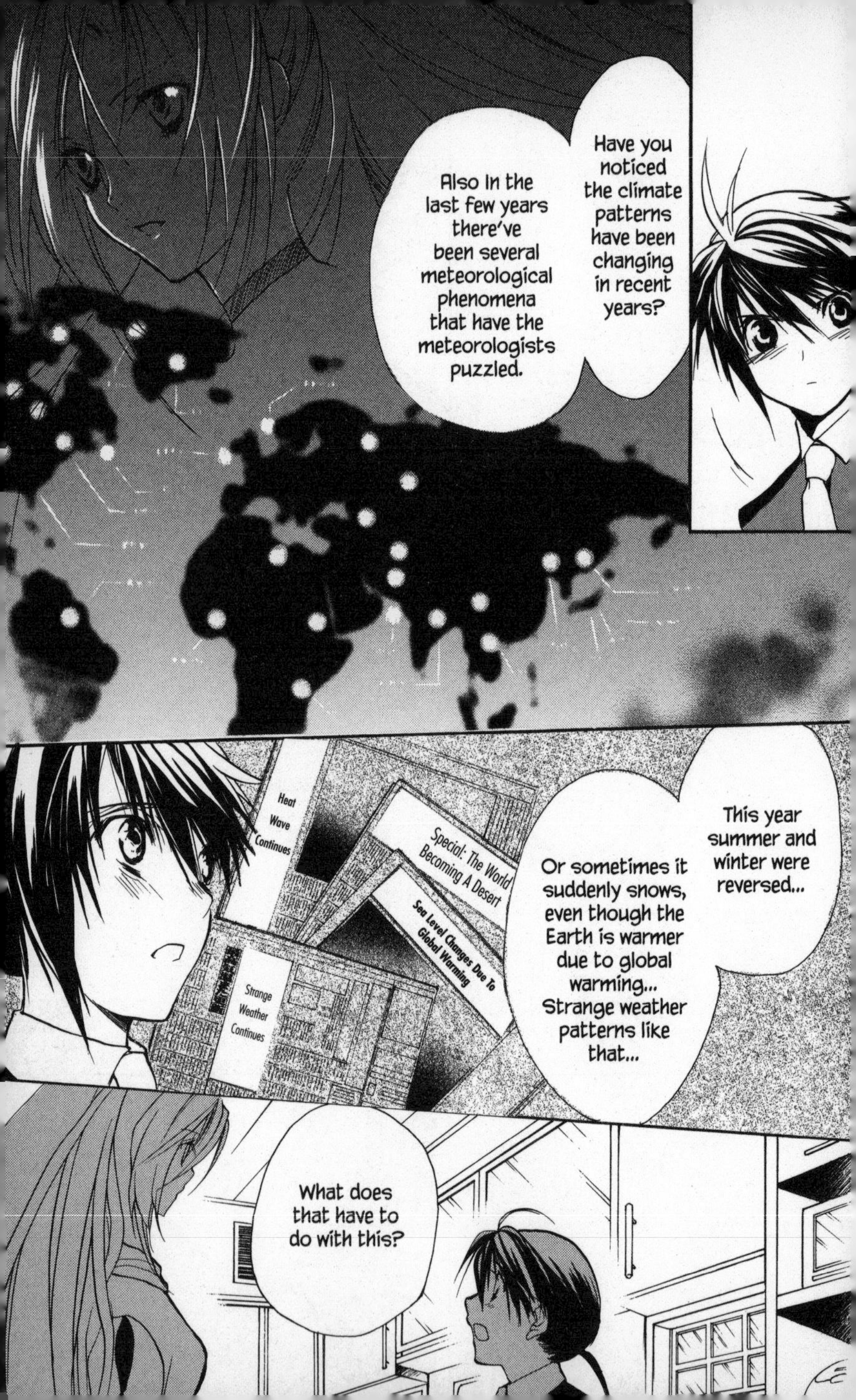
Have you noticed the climate patterns have been changing in recent years?
Also in the last few years there've been several meteorological phenomena that have the meteorologists puzzled.
This year summer and winter were reversed...
Or sometimes it suddenly snows, even though the Earth is warmer due to global warming... Strange weather patterns like that...
Sea Level Changes Due To Global Warming
Special: The World Becoming A Desert
Heat Wave Continues
Strange Weather Continues
What does that have to do with this?

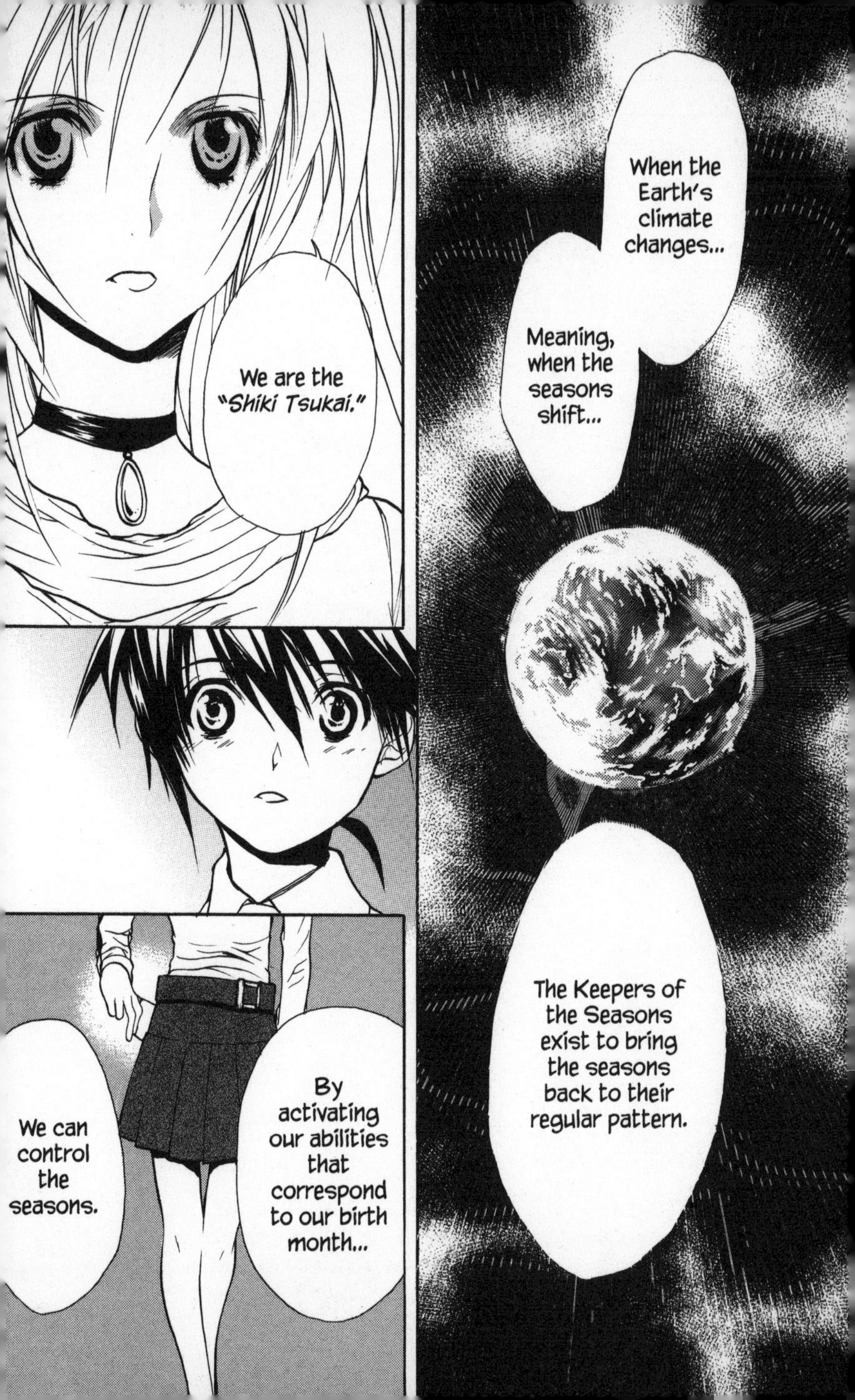
When the Earth's climate changes...
Meaning, when the seasons shift...
The Keepers of the Seasons exist to bring the seasons back to their regular pattern.
We are the "Shiki Tsukai."
By activating our abilities that correspond to our birth month...
We can control the seasons.

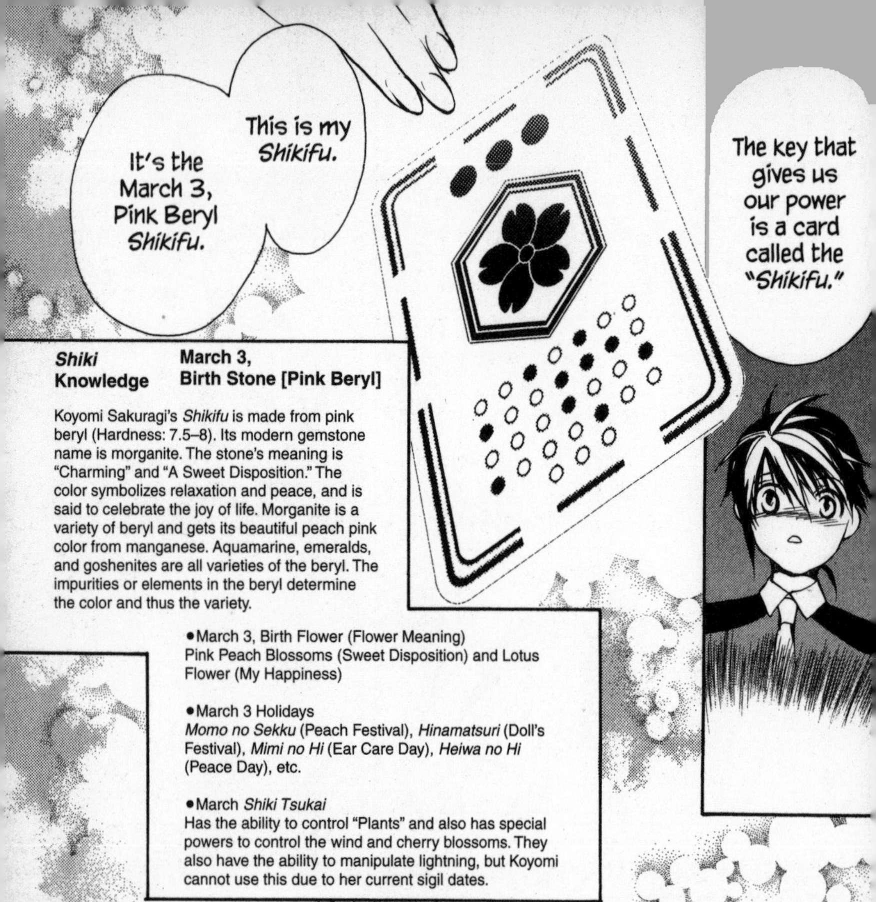
The key that gives us our power is a card called the "*Shikifu.*"
This is my *Shikifu.*
It's the March 3, Pink Beryl *Shikifu.*

***Shiki* Knowledge** **March 3, Birth Stone [Pink Beryl]**

Koyomi Sakuragi's *Shikifu* is made from pink beryl (Hardness: 7.5–8). Its modern gemstone name is morganite. The stone's meaning is "Charming" and "A Sweet Disposition." The color symbolizes relaxation and peace, and is said to celebrate the joy of life. Morganite is a variety of beryl and gets its beautiful peach pink color from manganese. Aquamarine, emeralds, and goshenites are all varieties of the beryl. The impurities or elements in the beryl determine the color and thus the variety.

- March 3, Birth Flower (Flower Meaning)
Pink Peach Blossoms (Sweet Disposition) and Lotus Flower (My Happiness)

- March 3 Holidays
Momo no Sekku (Peach Festival), *Hinamatsuri* (Doll's Festival), *Mimi no Hi* (Ear Care Day), *Heiwa no Hi* (Peace Day), etc.

- March *Shiki Tsukai*
Has the ability to control "Plants" and also has special powers to control the wind and cherry blossoms. They also have the ability to manipulate lightning, but Koyomi cannot use this due to her current sigil dates.

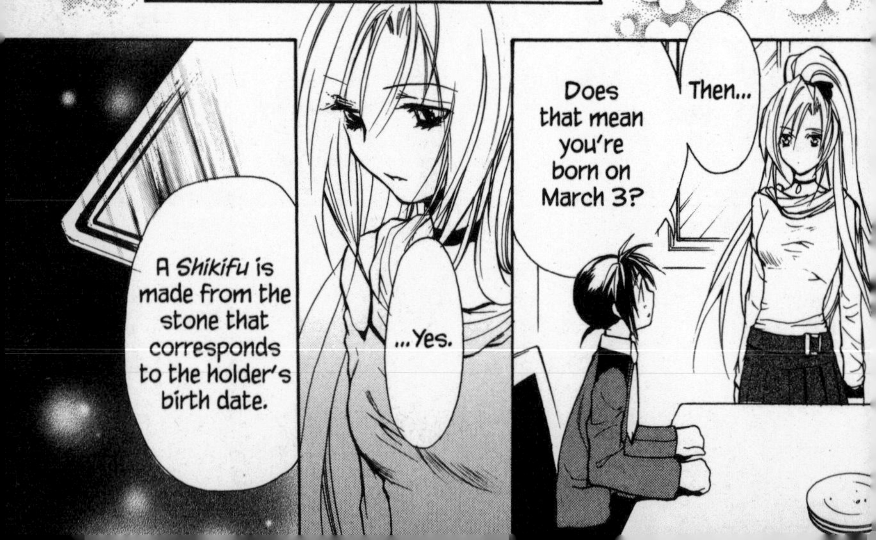
Then...
Does that mean you're born on March 3?
...Yes.
A *Shikifu* is made from the stone that corresponds to the holder's birth date.

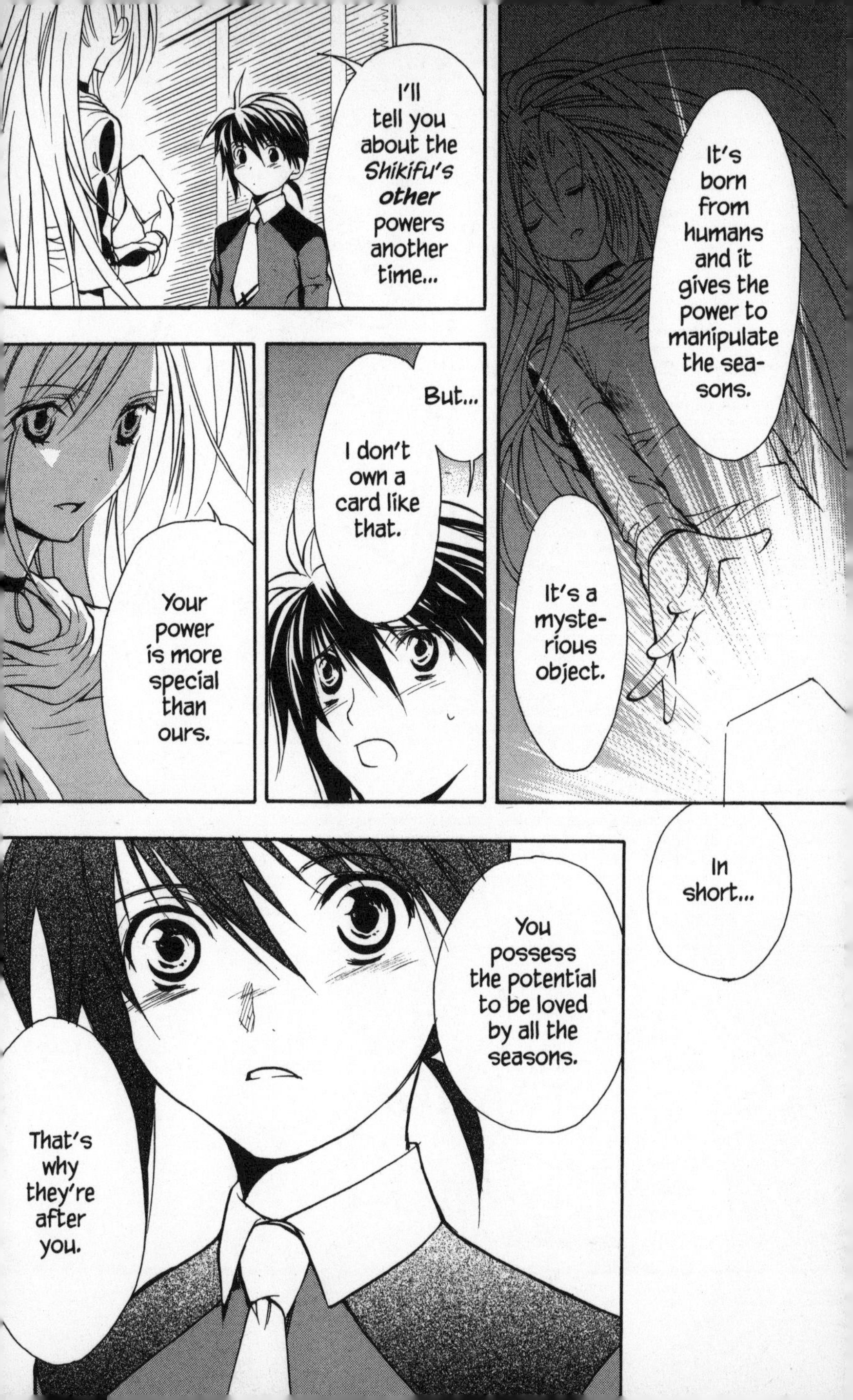
It's born from humans and it gives the power to manipulate the sea-sons.
It's a myste-rious object.
I'll tell you about the *Shikifu's* ***other*** powers another time...
But...
I don't own a card like that.
Your power is more special than ours.
In short...
You possess the potential to be loved by all the seasons.
That's why they're after you.

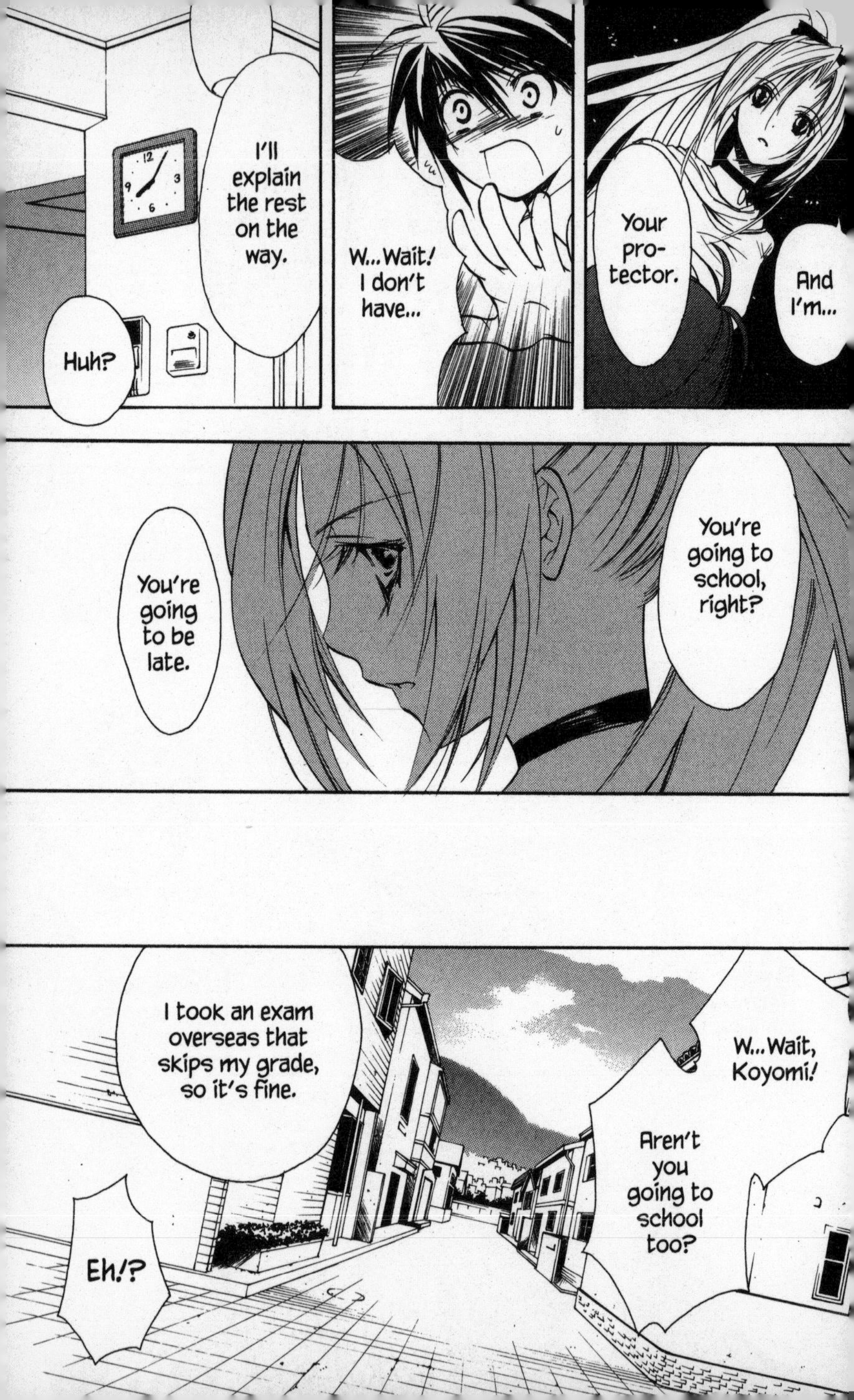
And I'm...
Your protector.
W...Wait! I don't have...
I'll explain the rest on the way.
Huh?
You're going to school, right?
You're going to be late.
W...Wait, Koyomi!
Aren't you going to school too?
I took an exam overseas that skips my grade, so it's fine.
Eh!?

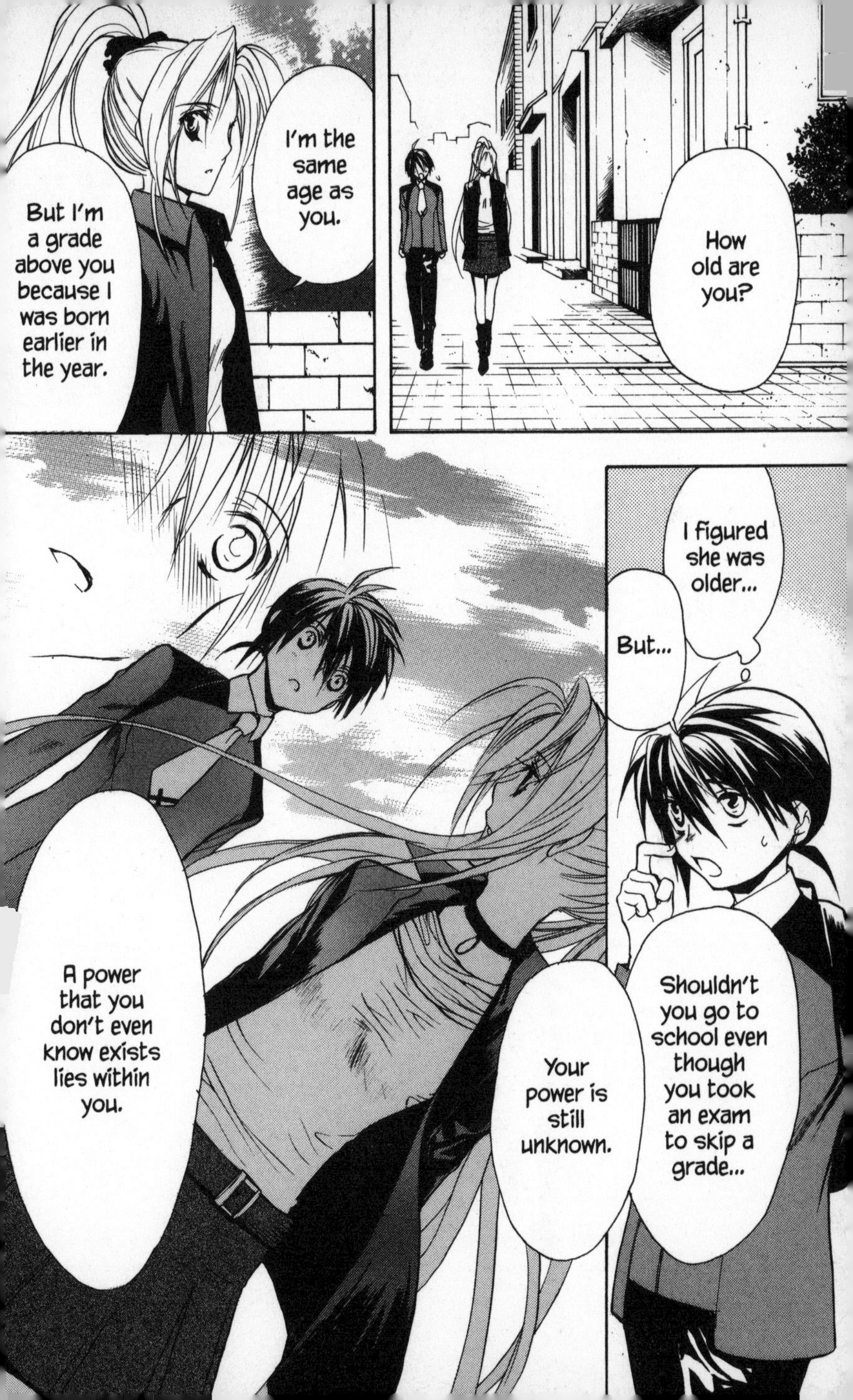
How old are you?
I'm the same age as you.
But I'm a grade above you because I was born earlier in the year.
I figured she was older...
But...
Shouldn't you go to school even though you took an exam to skip a grade...
Your power is still unknown.
A power that you don't even know exists lies within you.

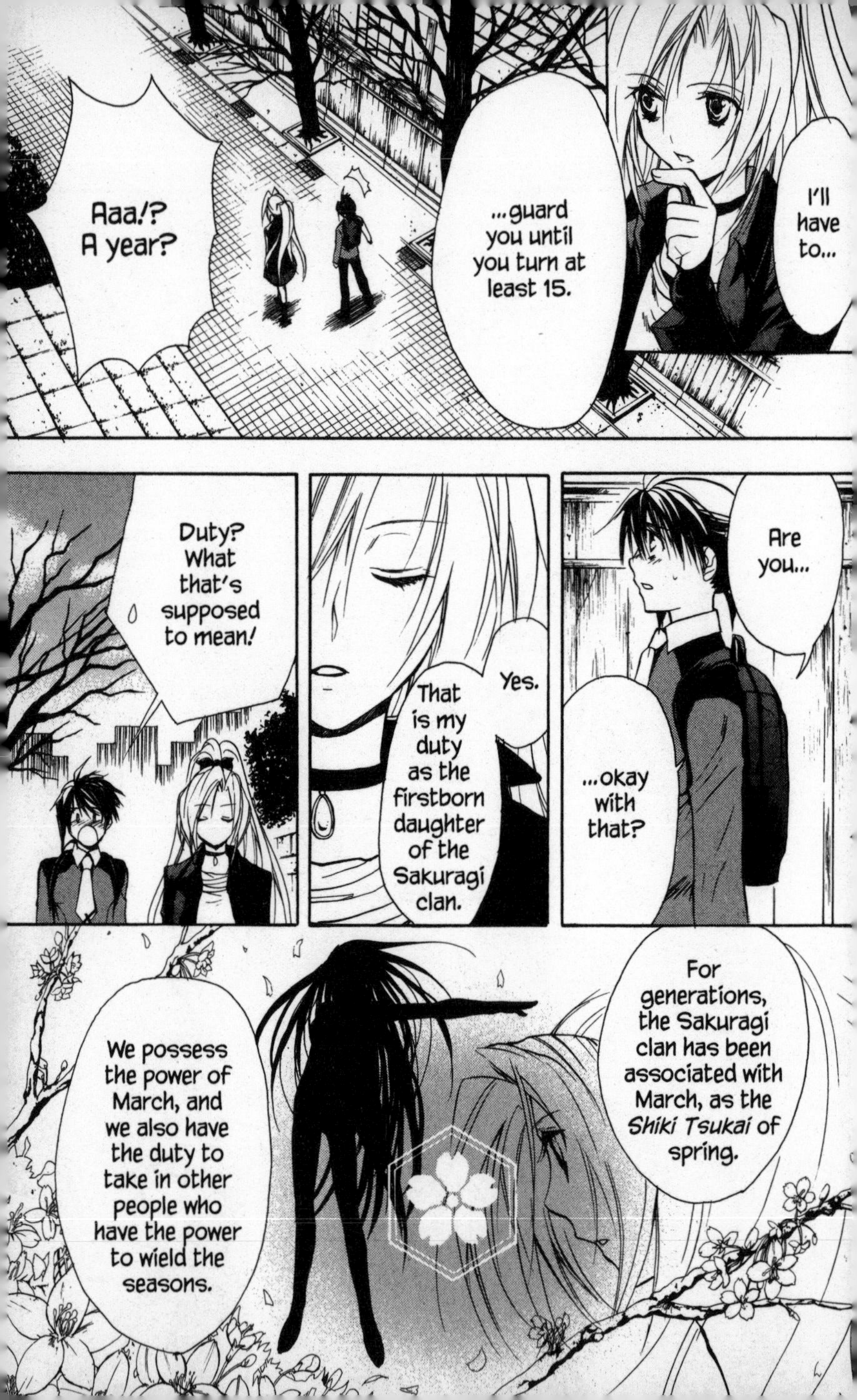
I'll have to...
...guard you until you turn at least 15.
Aaa!? A year?
Are you...
...okay with that?
Yes.
That is my duty as the firstborn daughter of the Sakuragi clan.
Duty? What that's supposed to mean!
For generations, the Sakuragi clan has been associated with March, as the *Shiki Tsukai* of spring.
We possess the power of March, and we also have the duty to take in other people who have the power to wield the seasons.

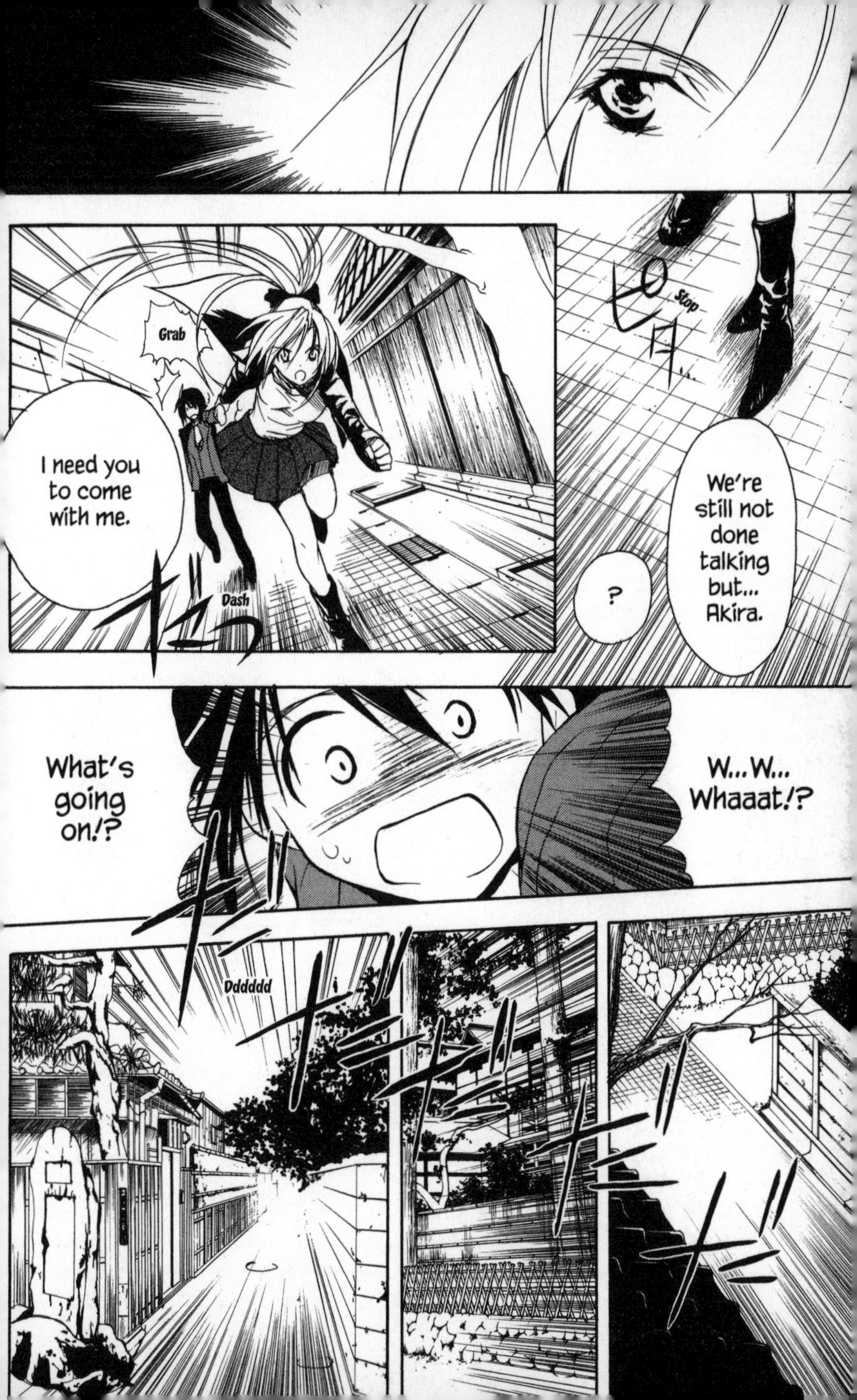
Stop
We're still not done talking but... Akira.
?
Grab
I need you to come with me.
Dash
W...W... Whaaat!?
What's going on!?
Dddddd

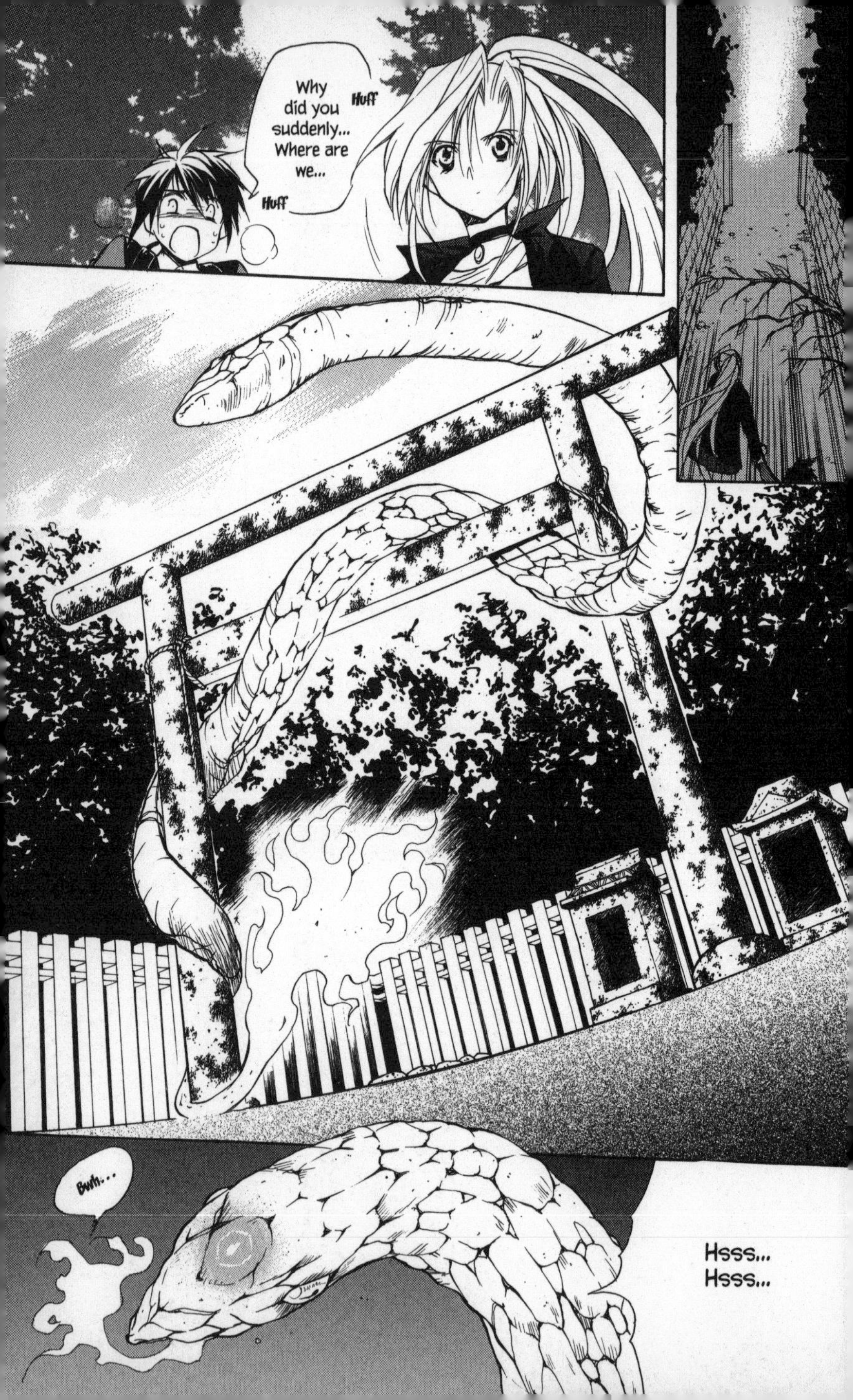
Why did you suddenly... Where are we...
Huff
Huff
Hsss... Hsss...
Buh...

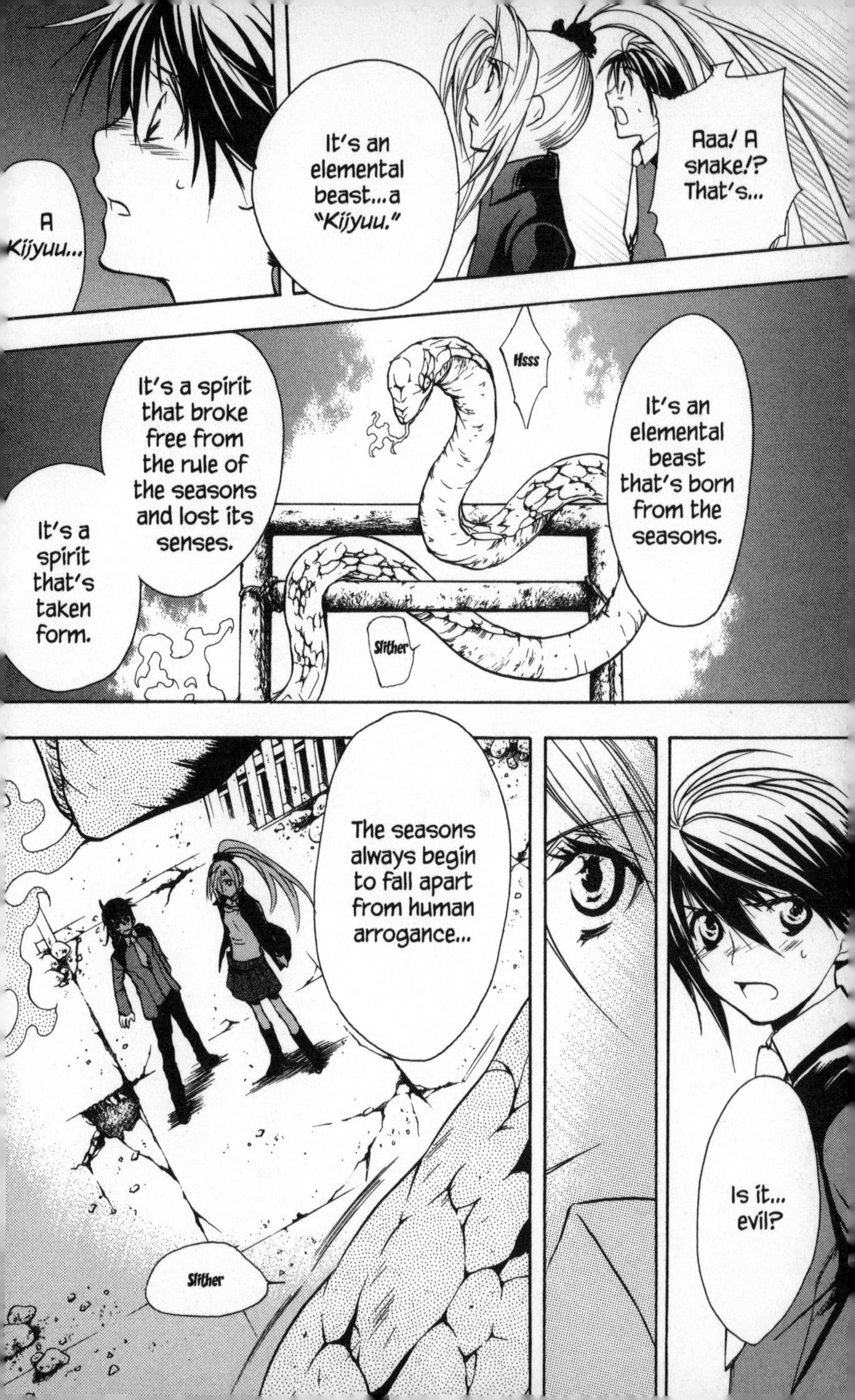
Aaa! A snake!? That's...
It's an elemental beast...a "Kijyuu."
A Kijyuu...
It's an elemental beast that's born from the seasons.
Hsss
It's a spirit that broke free from the rule of the seasons and lost its senses.
It's a spirit that's taken form.
Slither
Is it... evil?
The seasons always begin to fall apart from human arrogance...
Slither

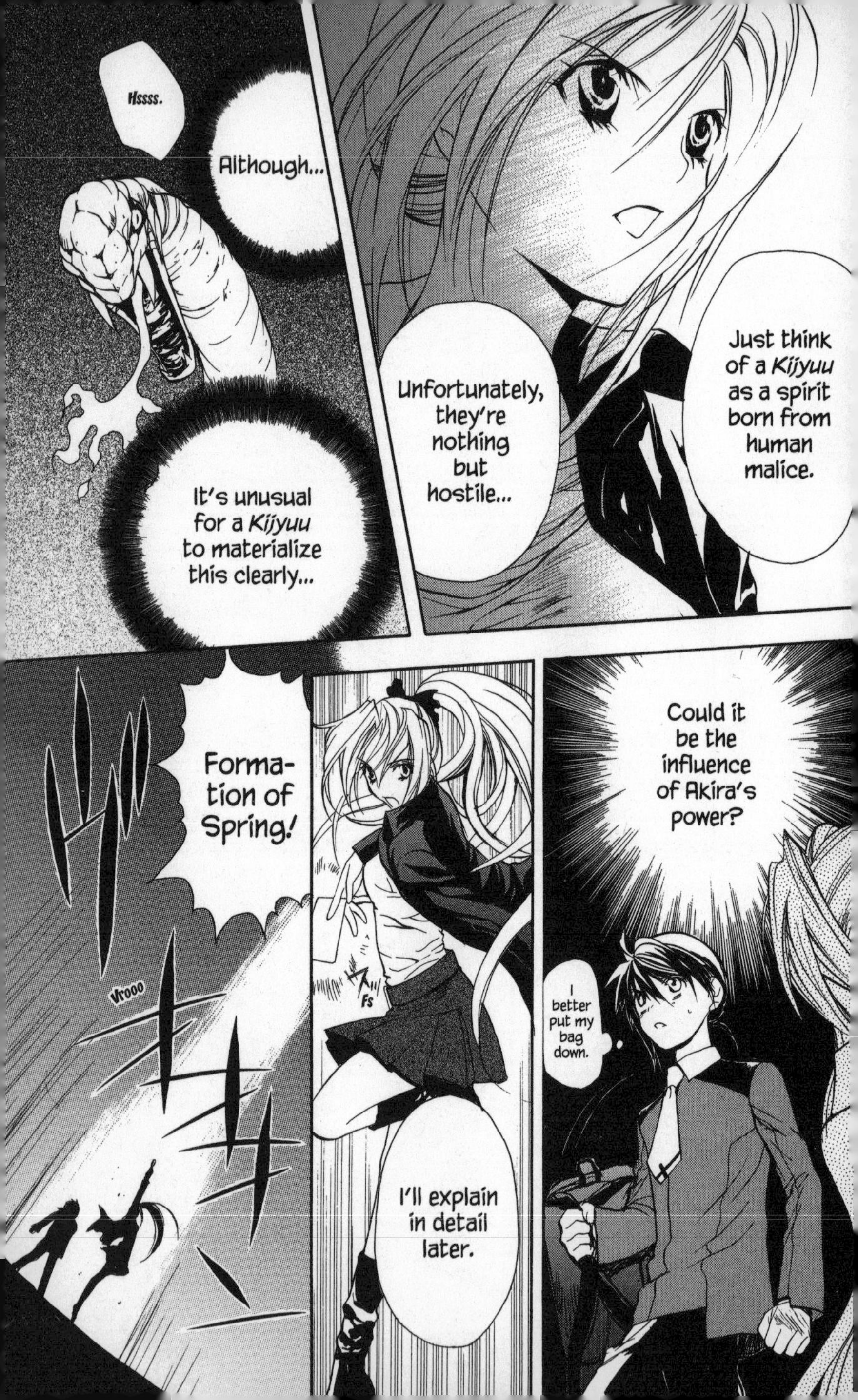
Just think of a *Kijyuu* as a spirit born from human malice.
Unfortunately, they're nothing but hostile...
Hssss.
Although...
It's unusual for a *Kijyuu* to materialize this clearly...
Could it be the influence of Akira's power?
I better put my bag down.
Fs
I'll explain in detail later.
Formation of Spring!
Vrooo

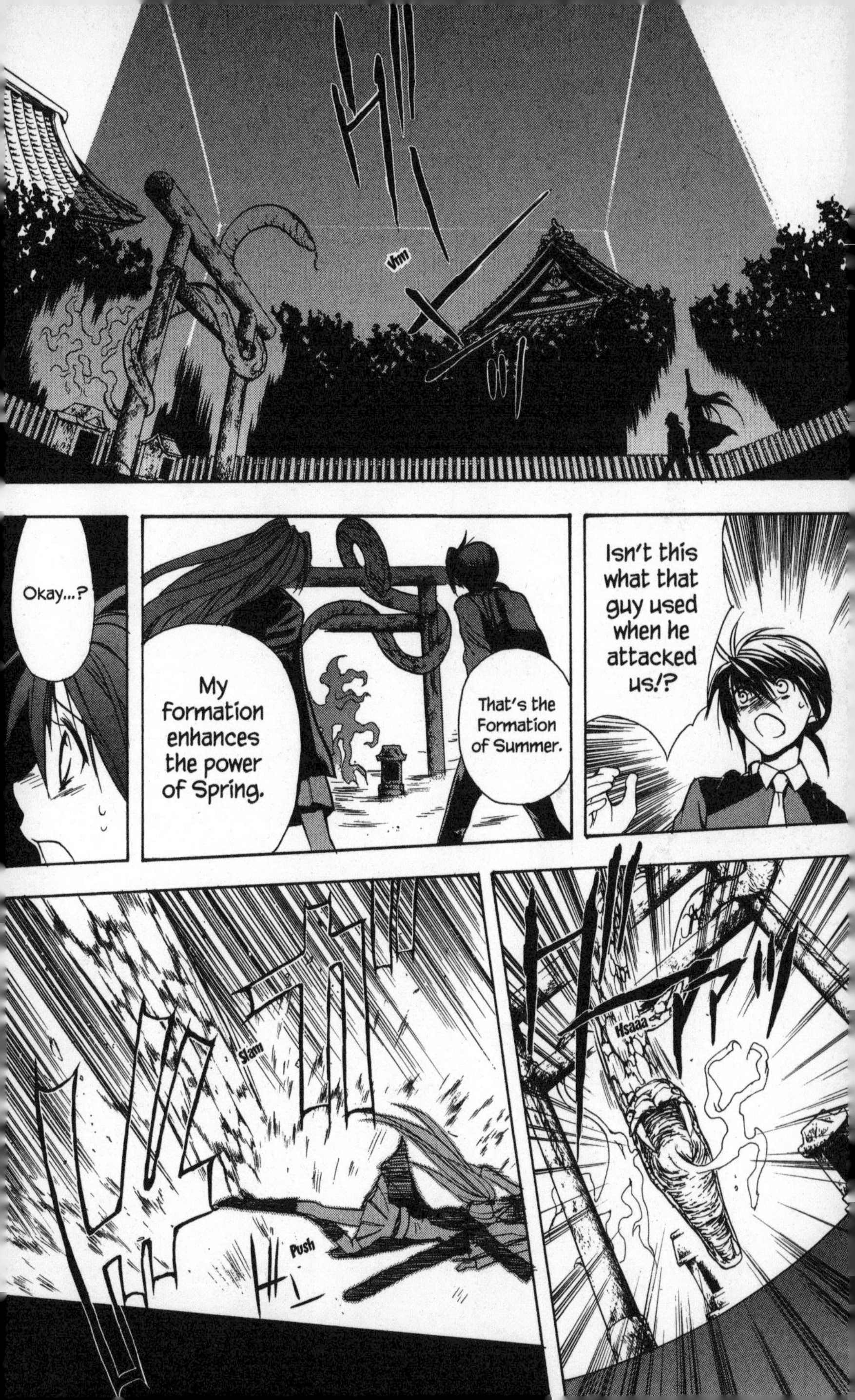
Vm
Isn't this what that guy used when he attacked us!?
That's the Formation of Summer.
My formation enhances the power of Spring.
Okay...?
Hsaaa
Slam
Push

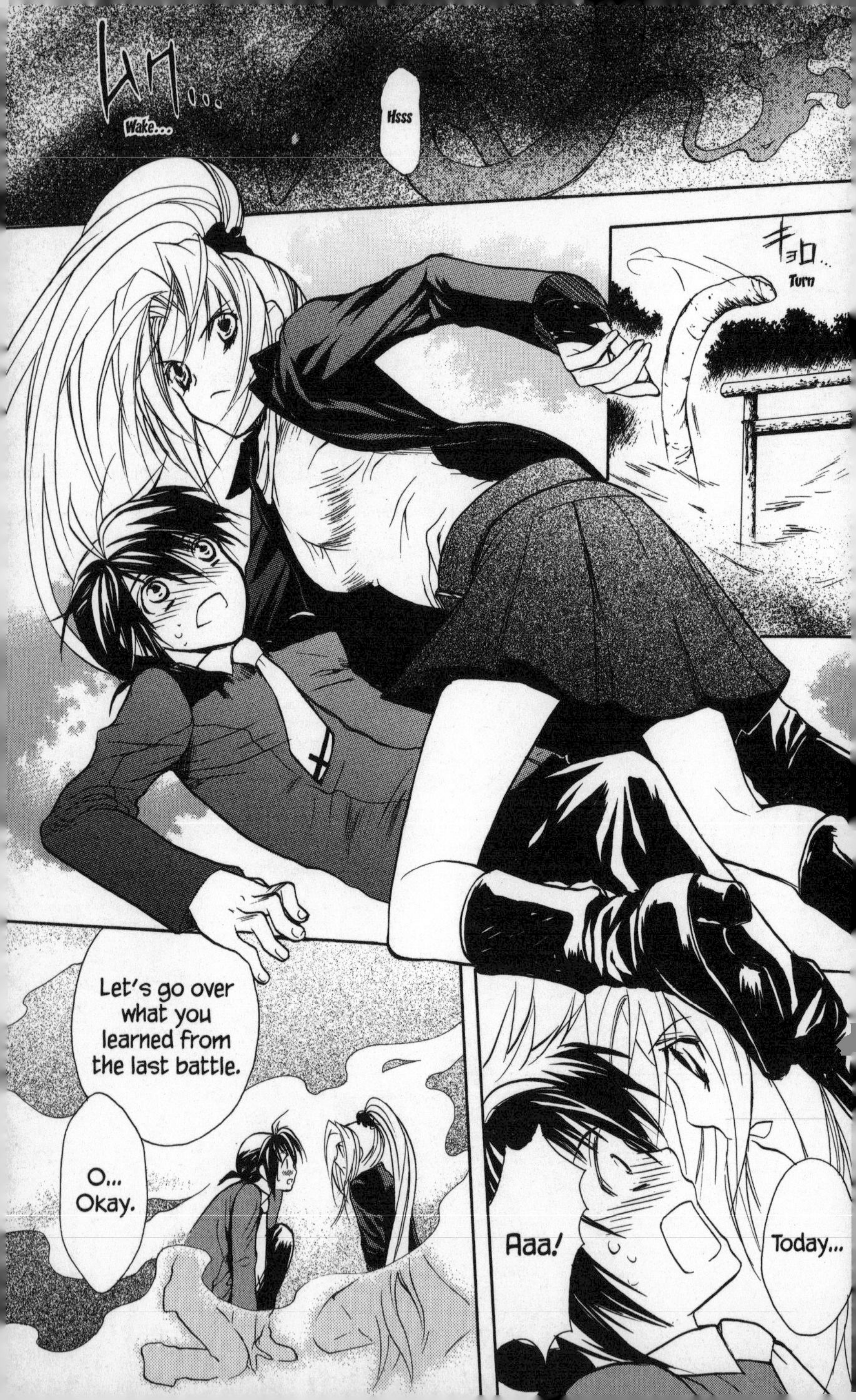
Hsss
Wake...
キョロ...
Turn
Today...
Aaa!
Let's go over what you learned from the last battle.
O... Okay.

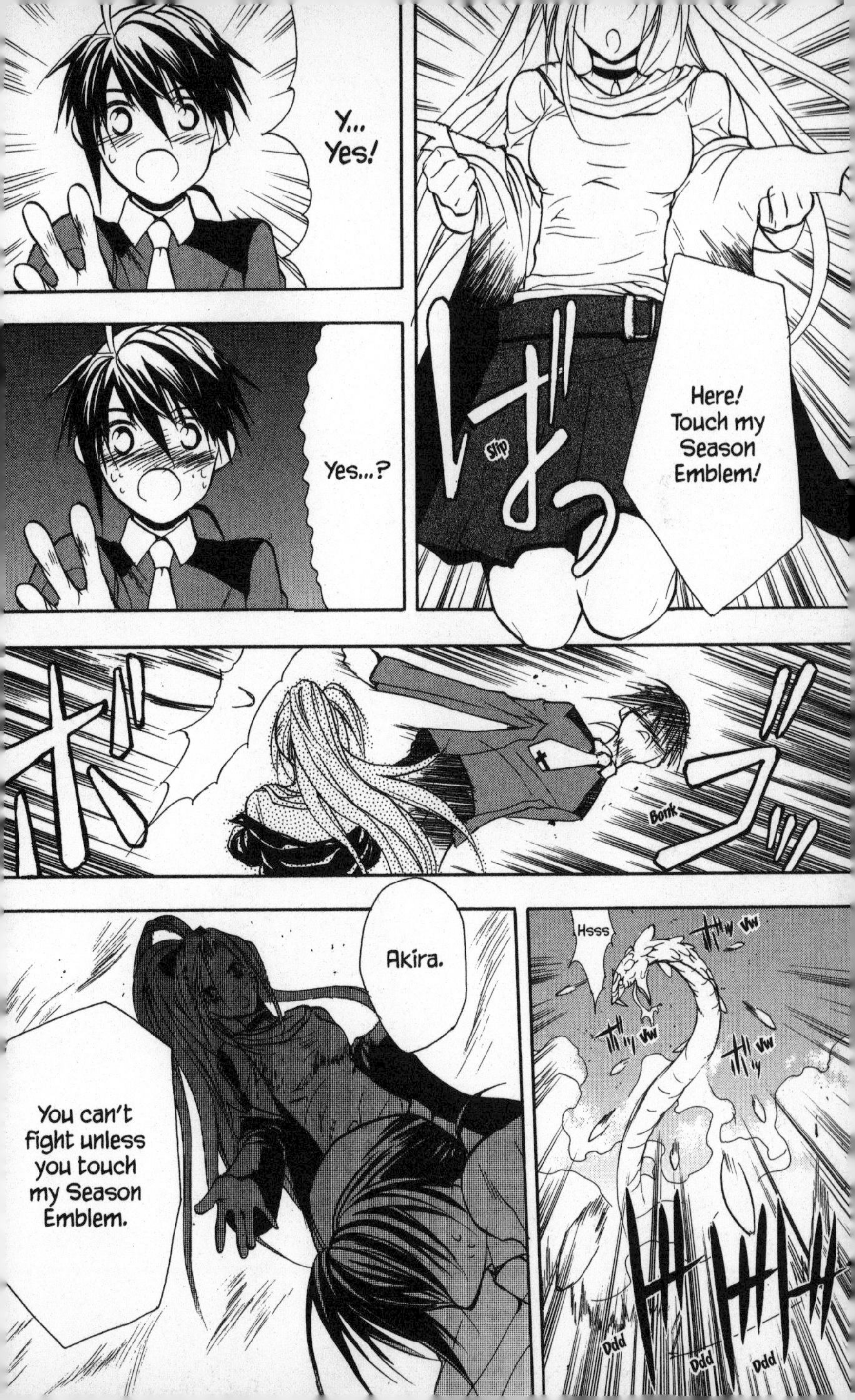
Here! Touch my Season Emblem!
Slip
Y... Yes!
Yes...?
Bonk
Hsss
vw
vw
vw
Ddd
Ddd
Ddd
Akira.
You can't fight unless you touch my Season Emblem.

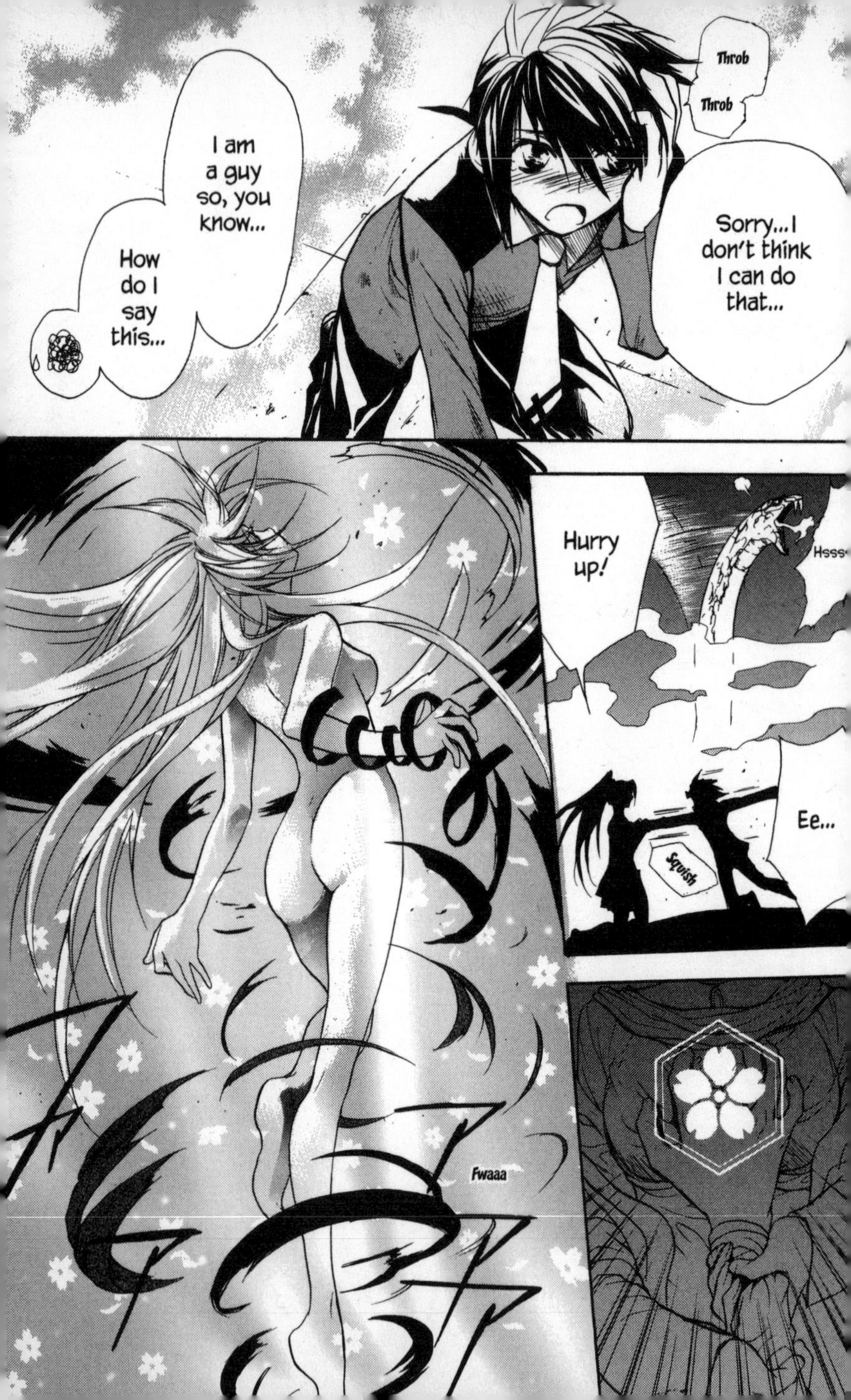
Throb
Throb
Sorry...I don't think I can do that...
I am a guy so, you know...
How do I say this...
Hsss
Hurry up!
Ee...
Squish
Fwaaa

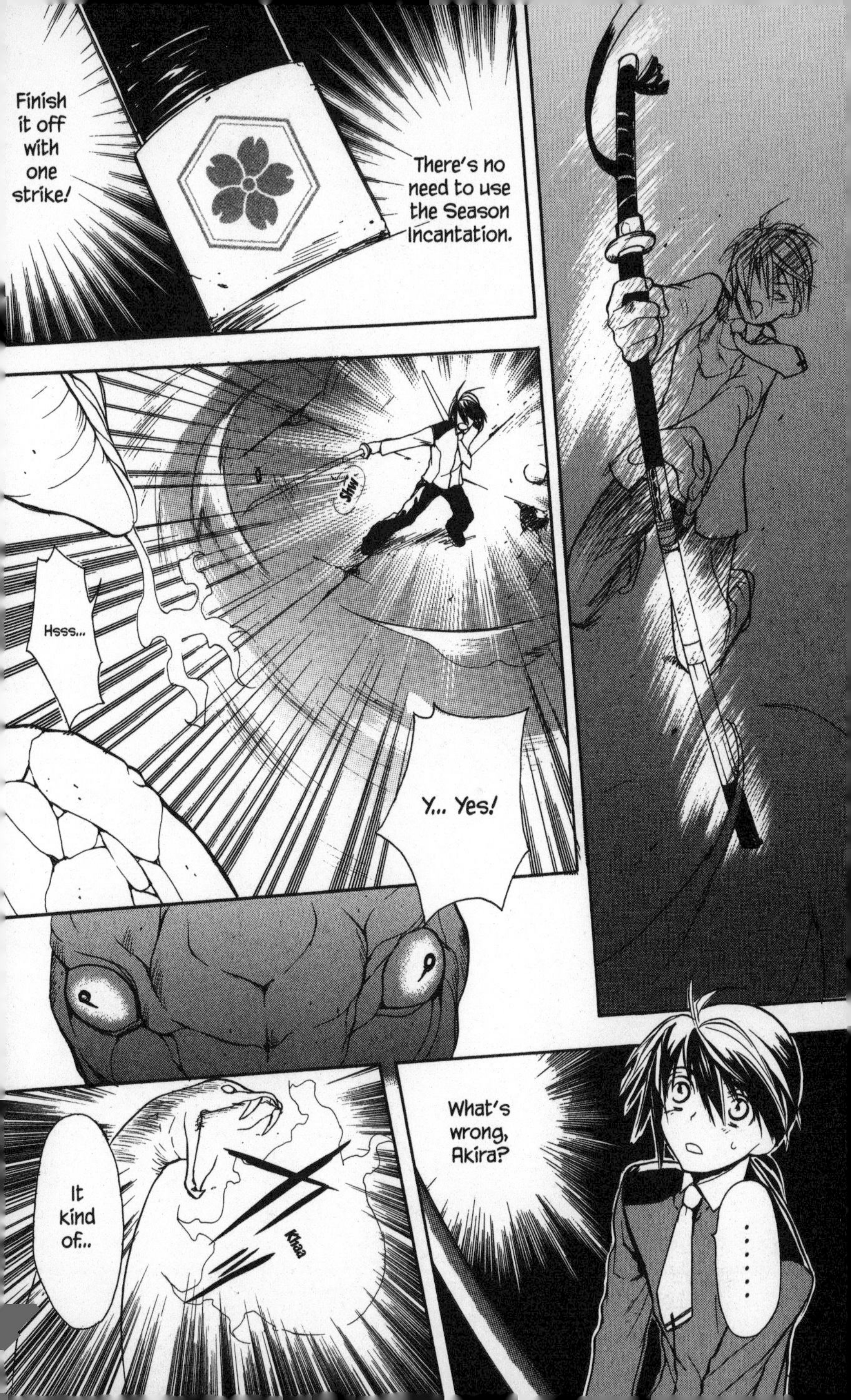
There's no need to use the Season Incantation.
Finish it off with one strike!
Shw
Y... Yes!
Hsss...
What's wrong, Akira?
......
It kind of...
Khaa

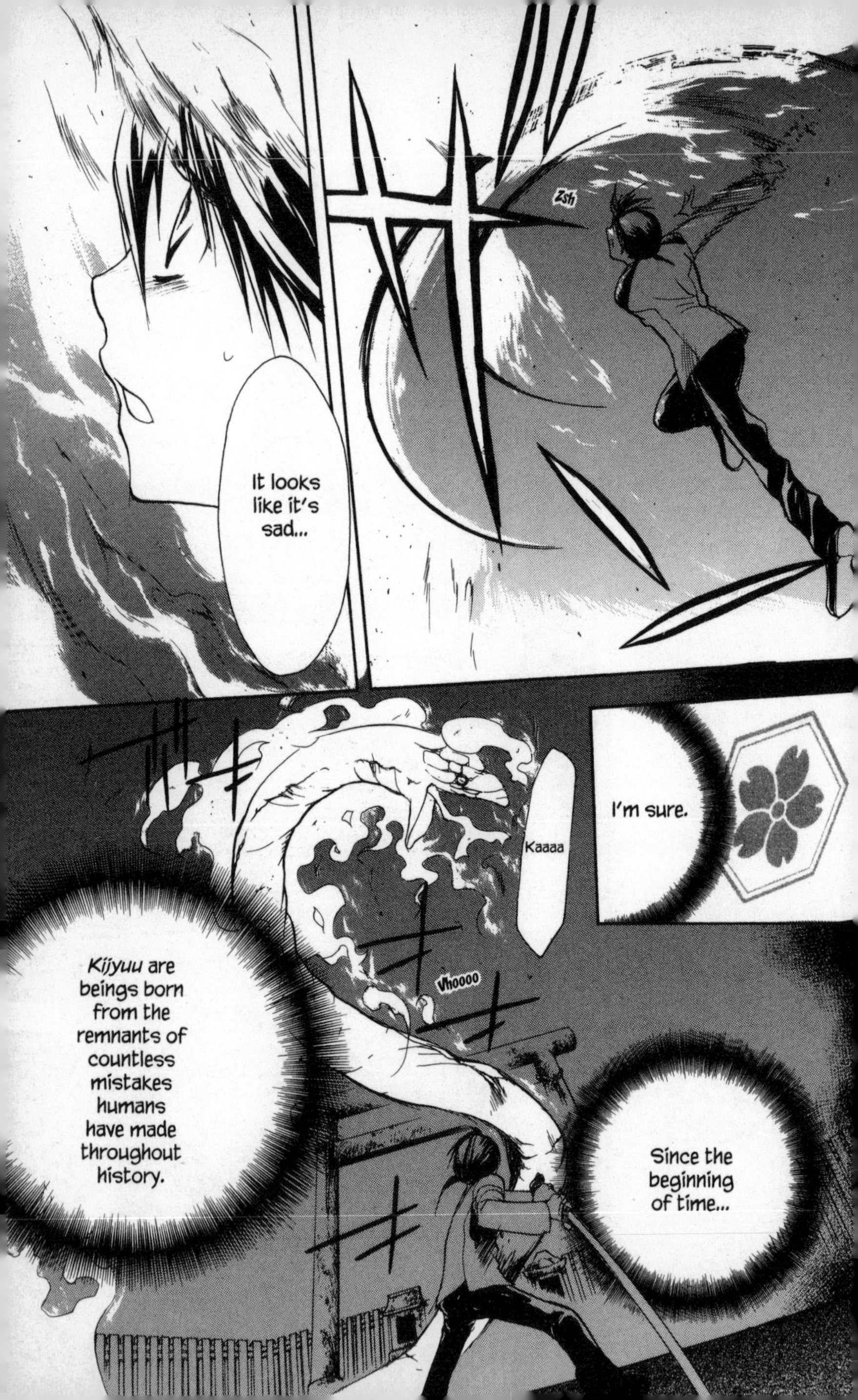
Zsh
It looks like it's sad...
I'm sure.
Kaaaa
Vhoooo
Kijyuu are beings born from the remnants of countless mistakes humans have made throughout history.
Since the beginning of time...

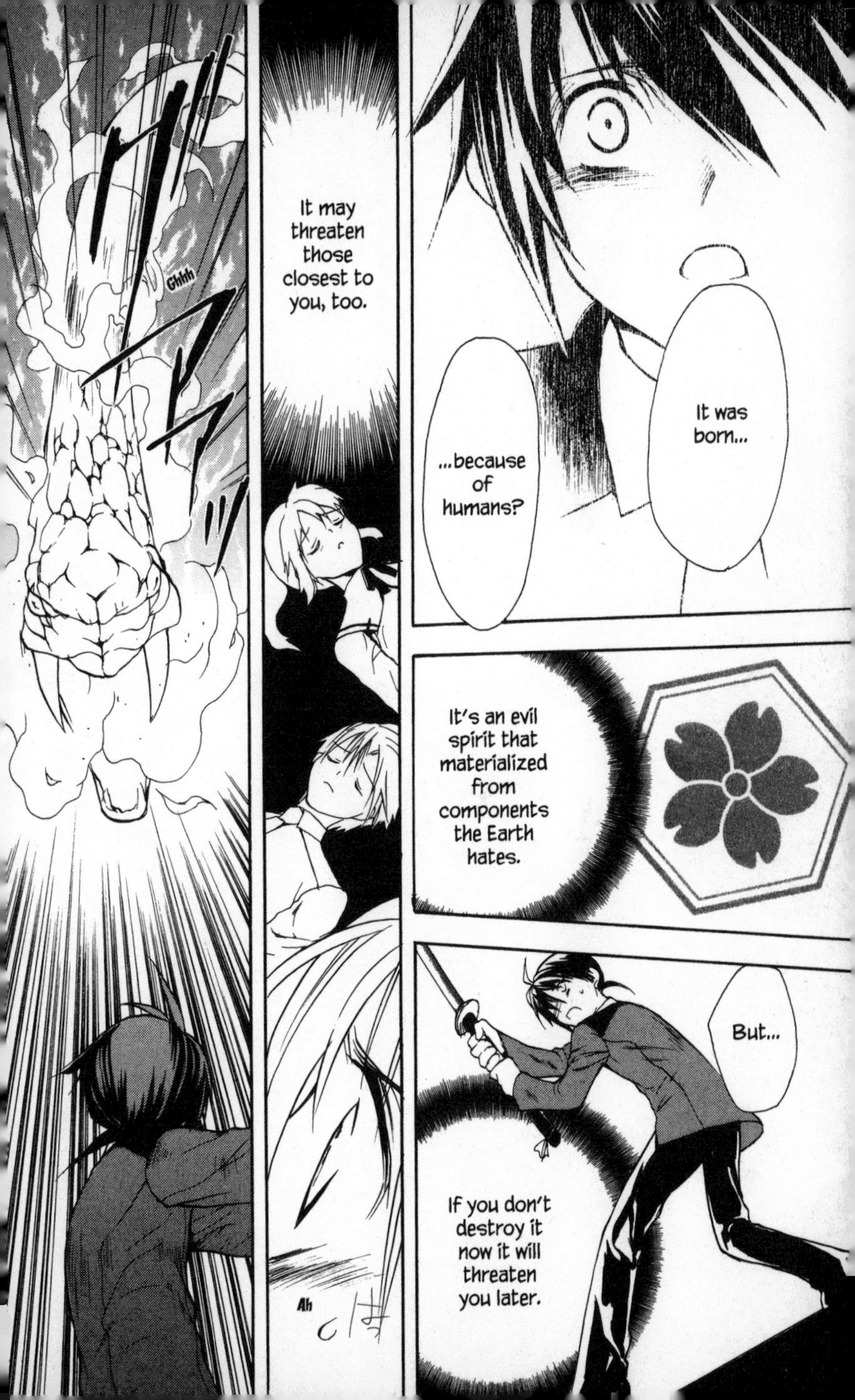
It was born...
...because of humans?
It's an evil spirit that materialized from components the Earth hates.
But...
If you don't destroy it now it will threaten you later.
It may threaten those closest to you, too.
Ah
Ghhh

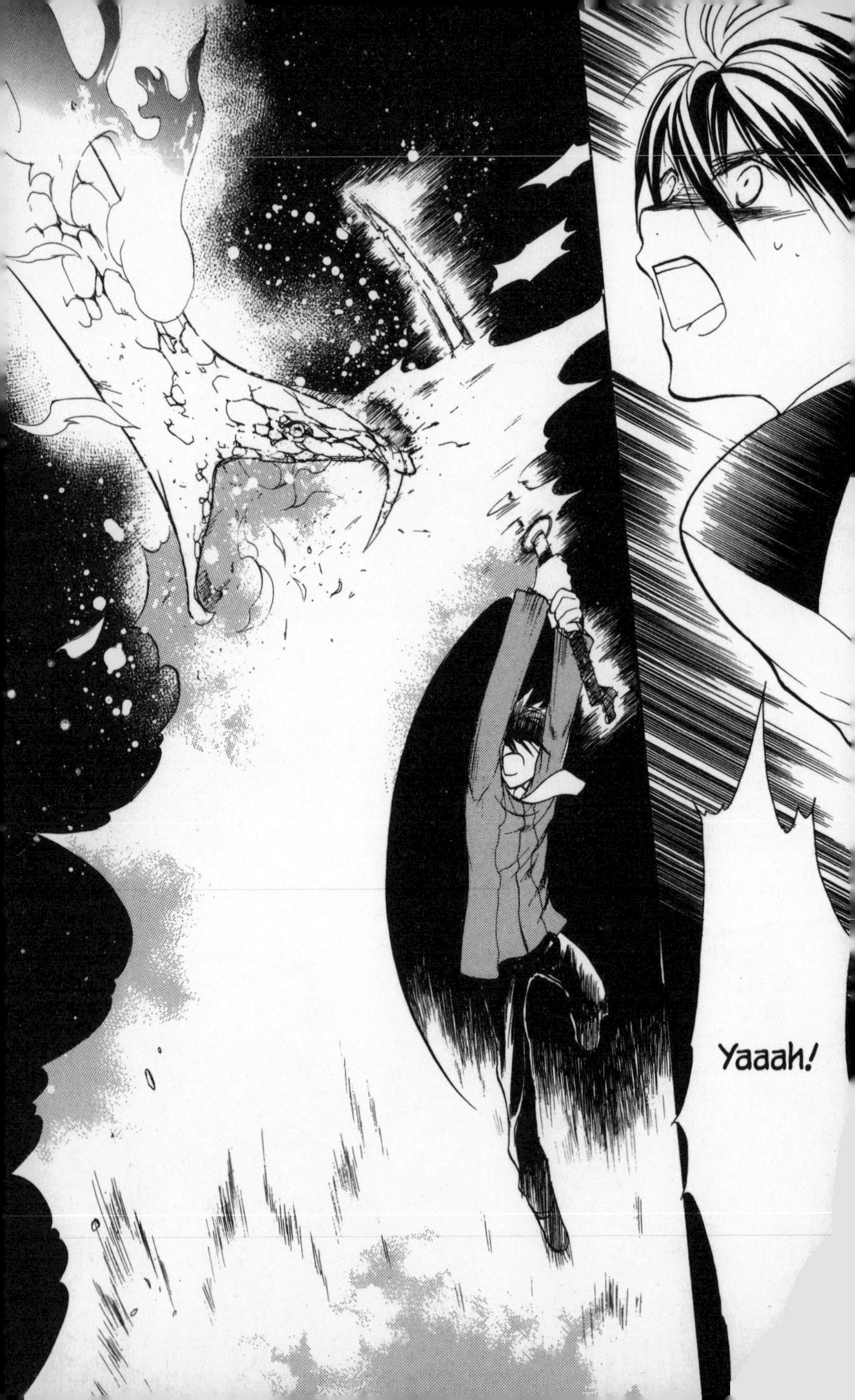
Yaaah!

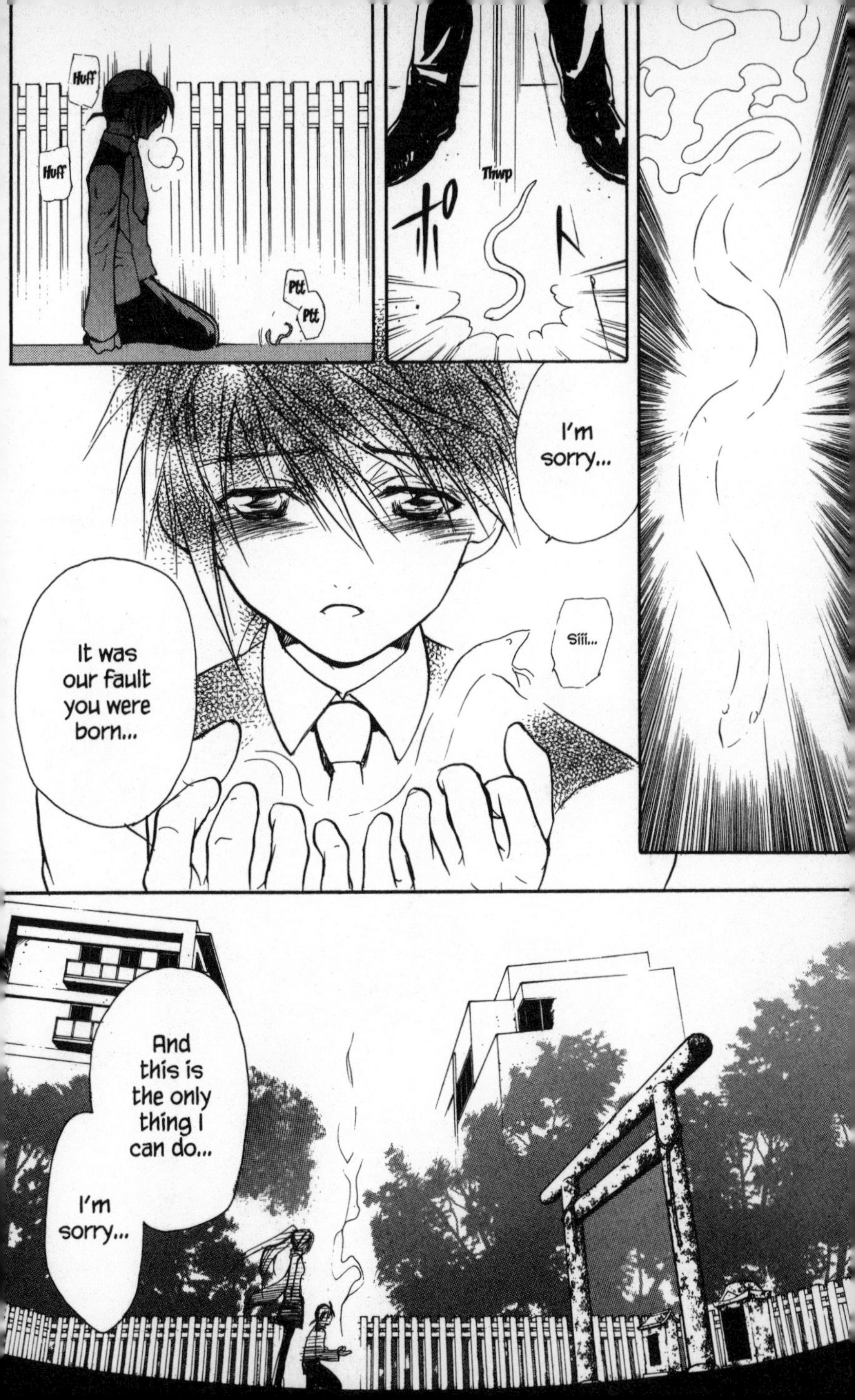
Thwp
Huff
Huff
Ptt
Ptt
I'm sorry...
Siii...
It was our fault you were born...
And this is the only thing I can do...
I'm sorry...

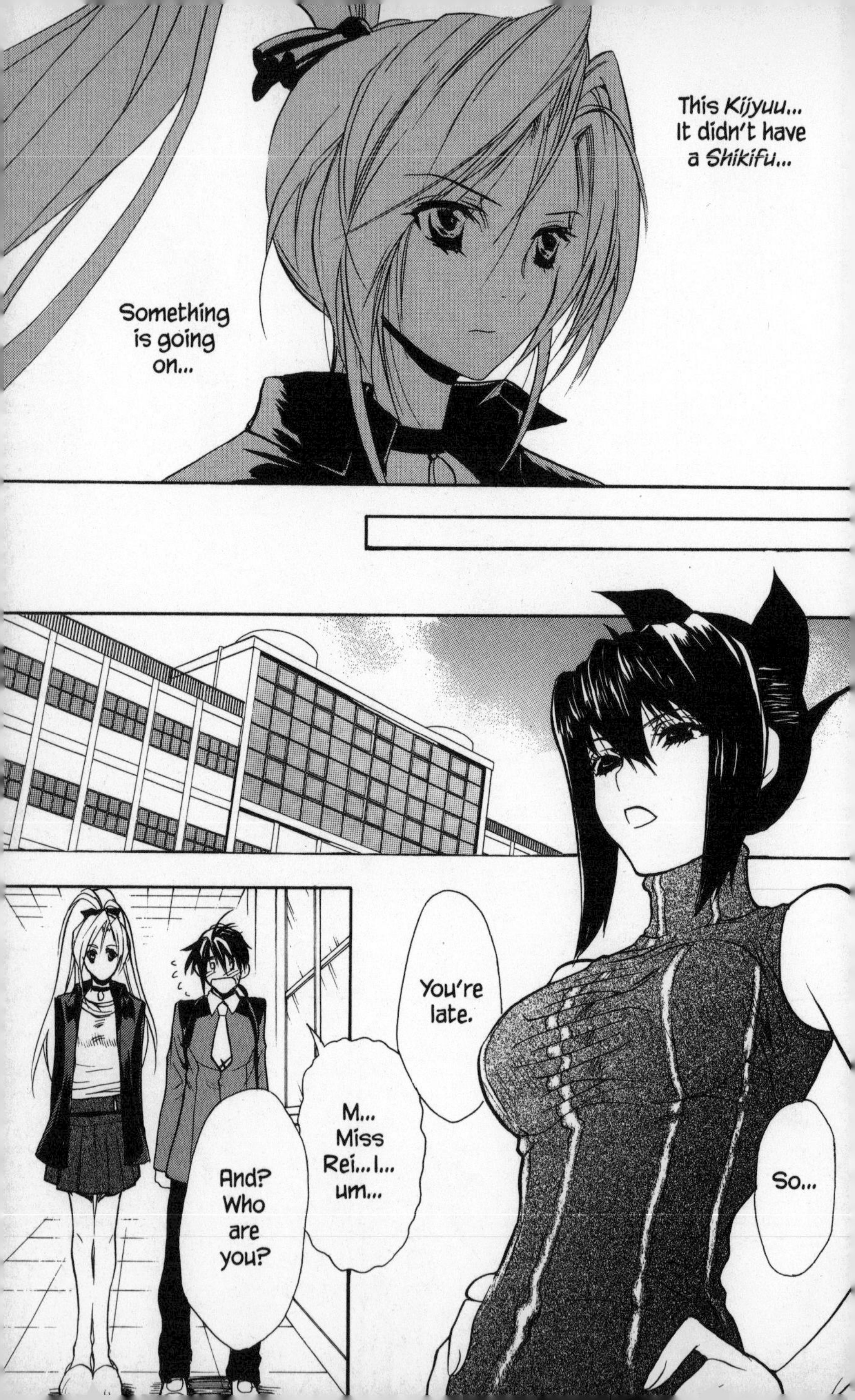
This *Kijyuu*... It didn't have a *Shikifu*...
Something is going on...
You're late.
M... Miss Rei...I... um...
So...
And? Who are you?

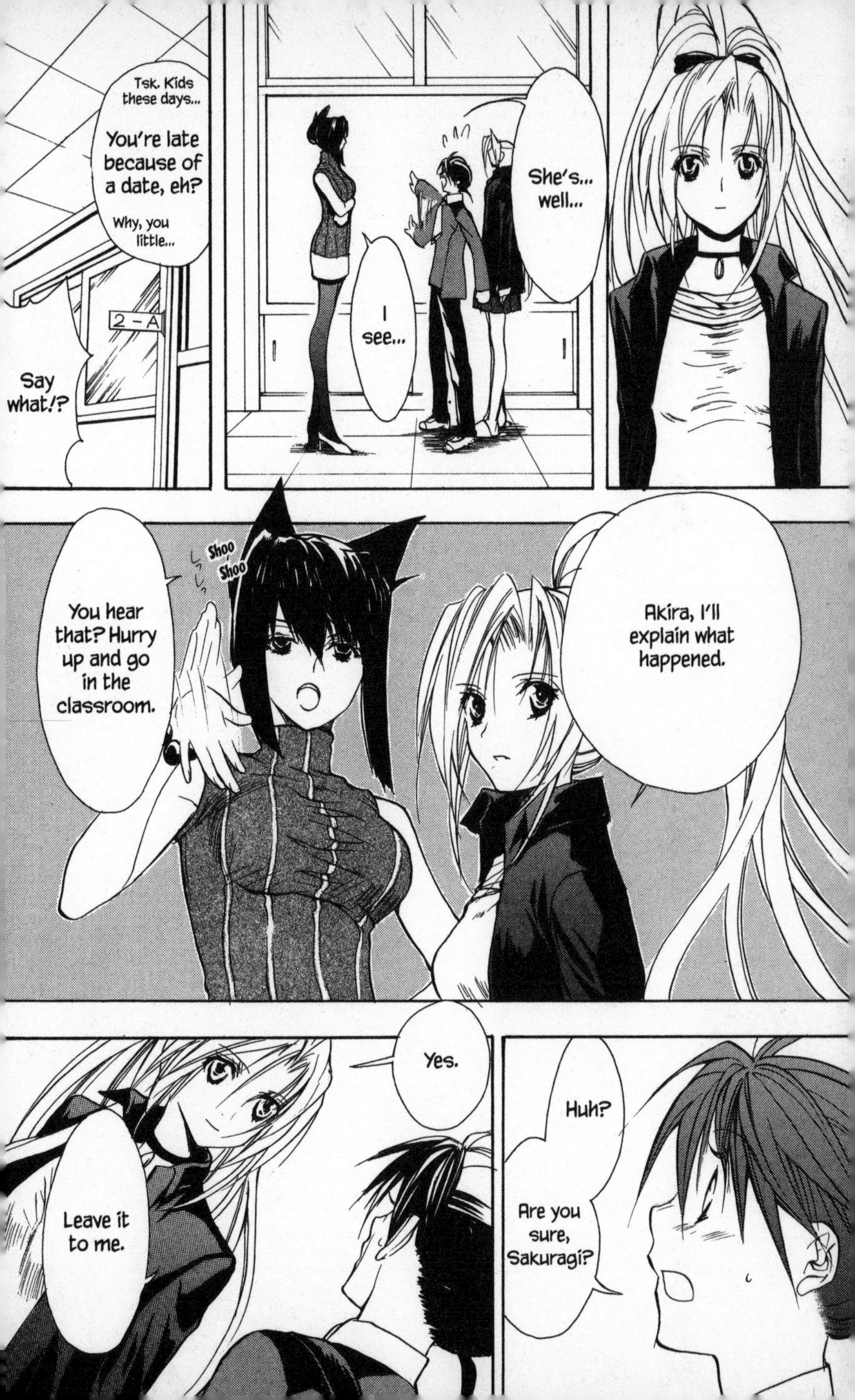
She's... well...
I see...
Tsk. Kids these days...
You're late because of a date, eh?
Why, you little...
2-A
Say what!?
Akira, I'll explain what happened.
Shoo Shoo
You hear that? Hurry up and go in the classroom.
Huh?
Are you sure, Sakuragi?
Yes.
Leave it to me.

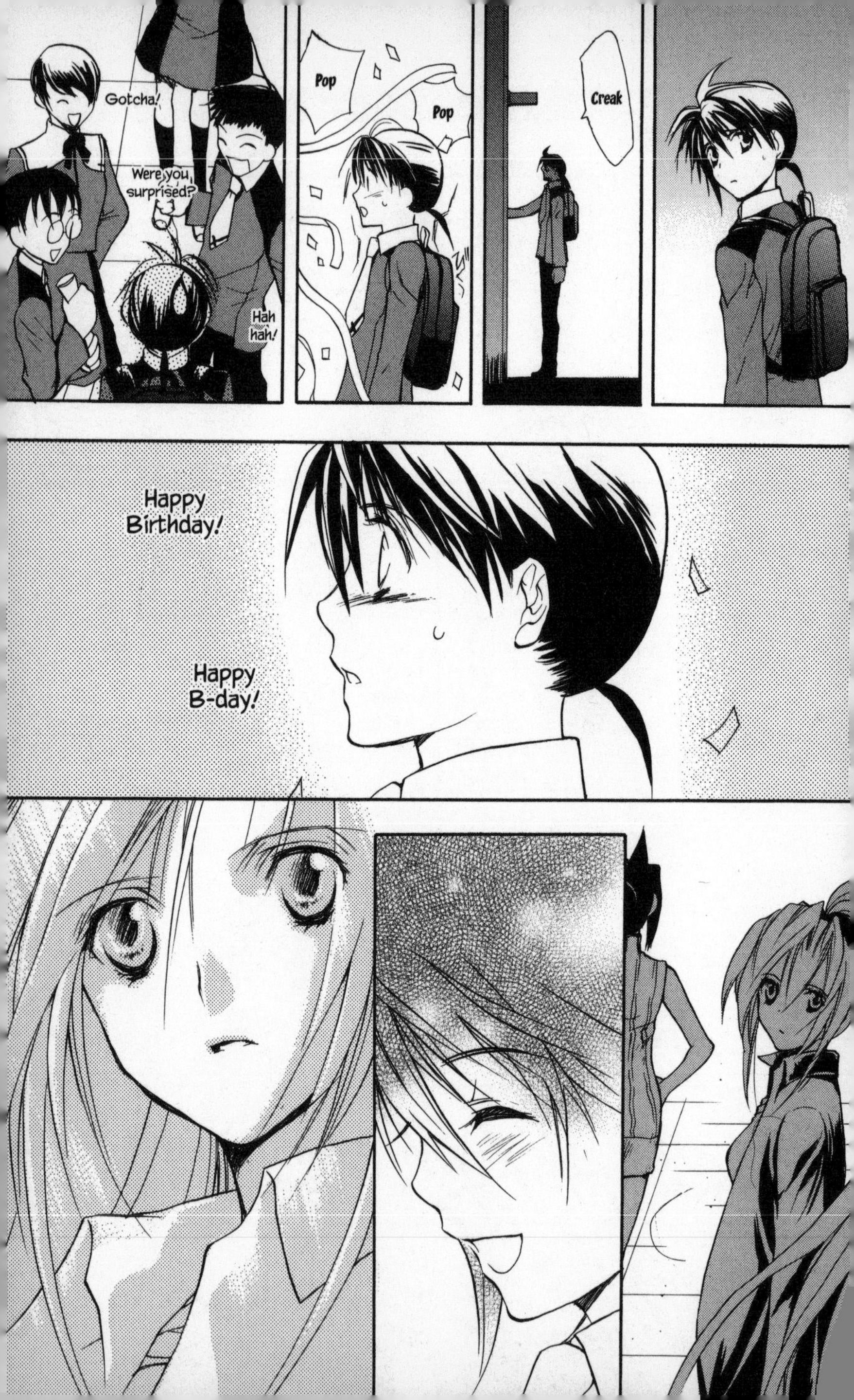
Creak
Pop
Pop
Gotcha!
Were you surprised?
Hah hah!
Happy Birthday!
Happy B-day!

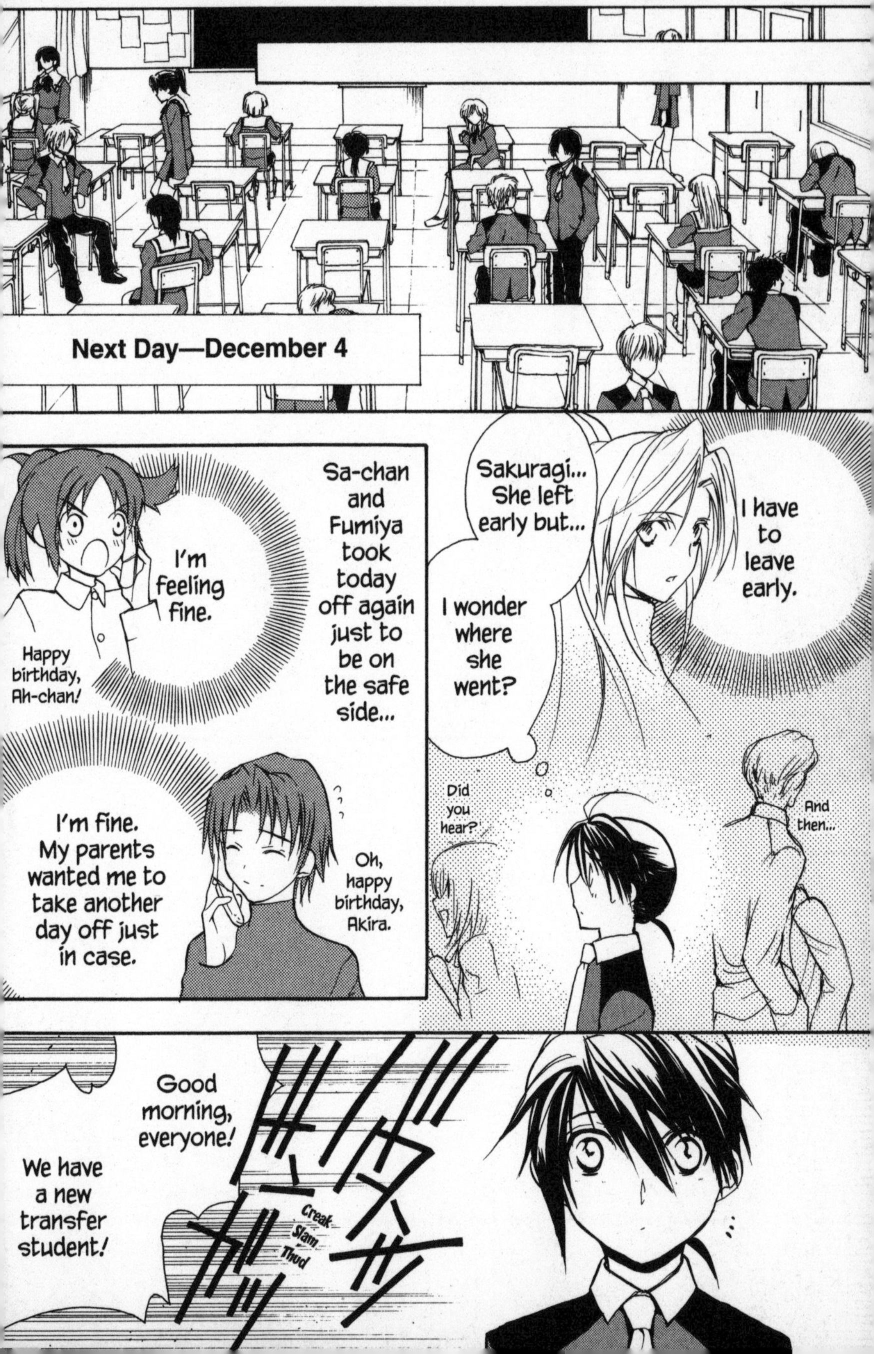
Next Day—December 4
I have to leave early.
Sakuragi... She left early but...
I wonder where she went?
And then...
Did you hear?
Sa-chan and Fumiya took today off again just to be on the safe side...
I'm feeling fine.
Happy birthday, Ah-chan!
Oh, happy birthday, Akira.
I'm fine. My parents wanted me to take another day off just in case.
Good morning, everyone!
Creak
Slam
Thud
We have a new transfer student!

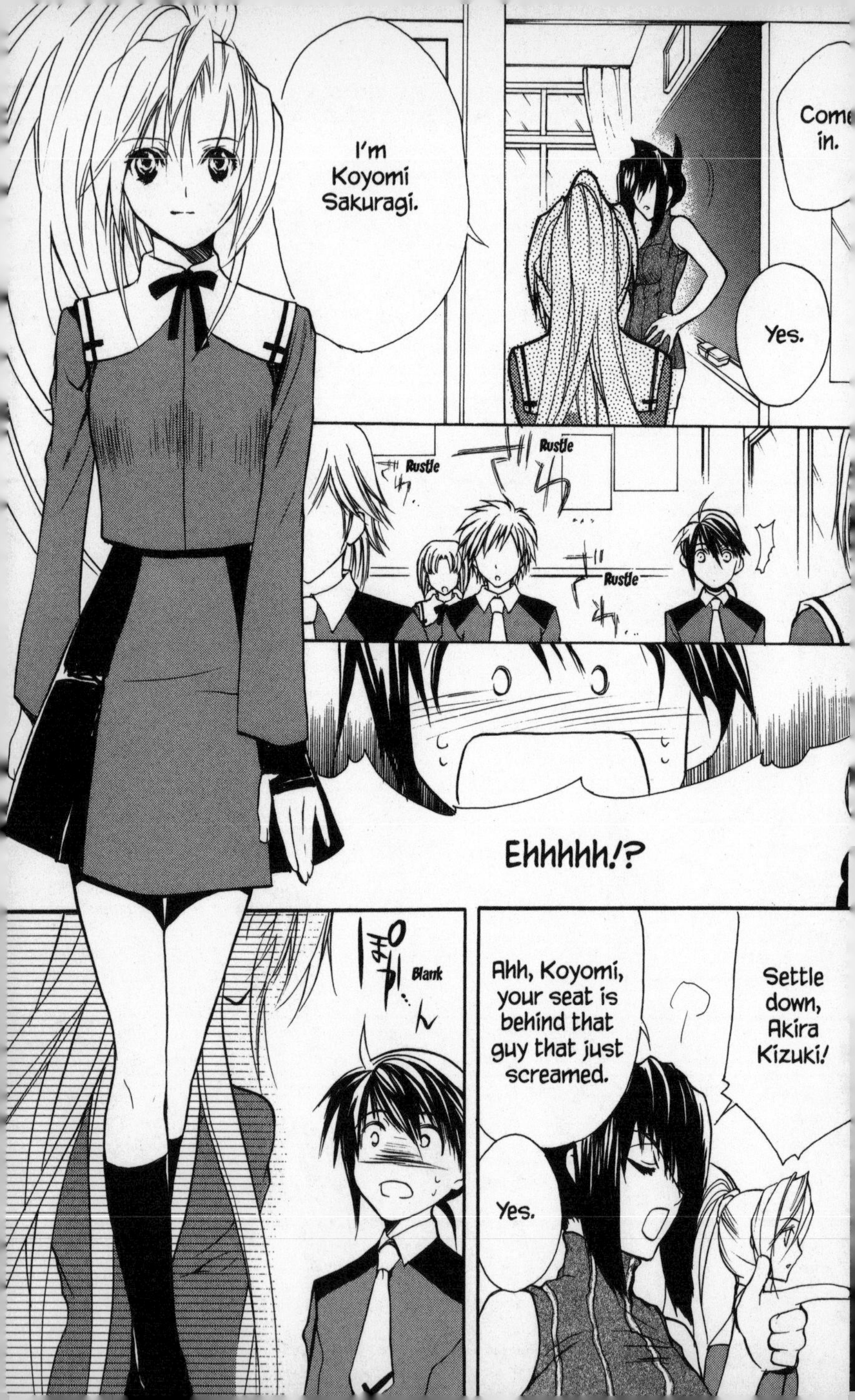

Come in.
Yes.
I'm Koyomi Sakuragi.
Rustle
Rustle
Rustle
Ehhhhh!?
Settle down, Akira Kizuki!
Ahh, Koyomi, your seat is behind that guy that just screamed.
Yes.
Blank

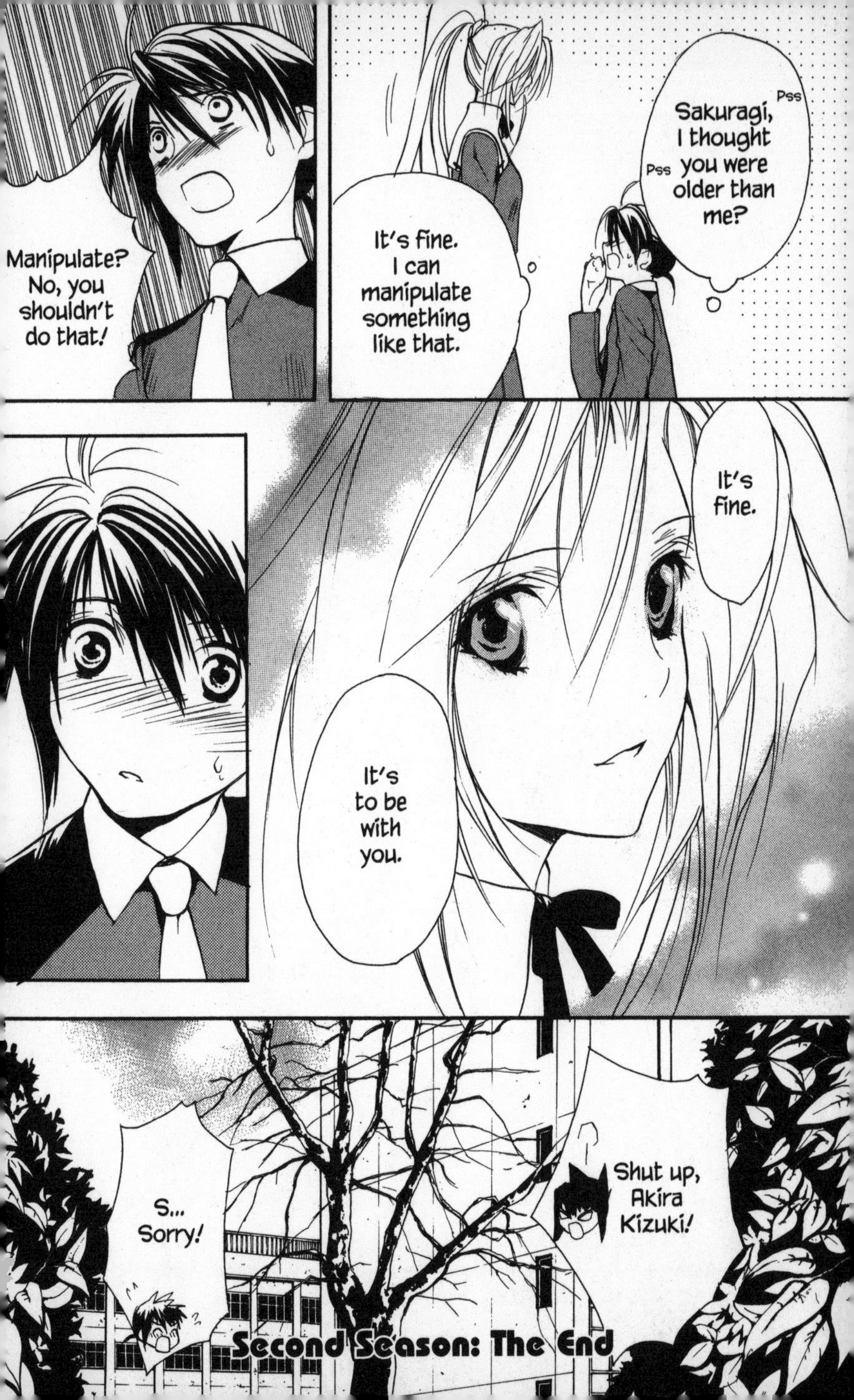
Pss
Pss
Sakuragi, I thought you were older than me?
It's fine. I can manipulate something like that.
Manipulate? No, you shouldn't do that!
It's fine.
It's to be with you.
Shut up, Akira Kizuki!
S... Sorry!
Second Season: The End

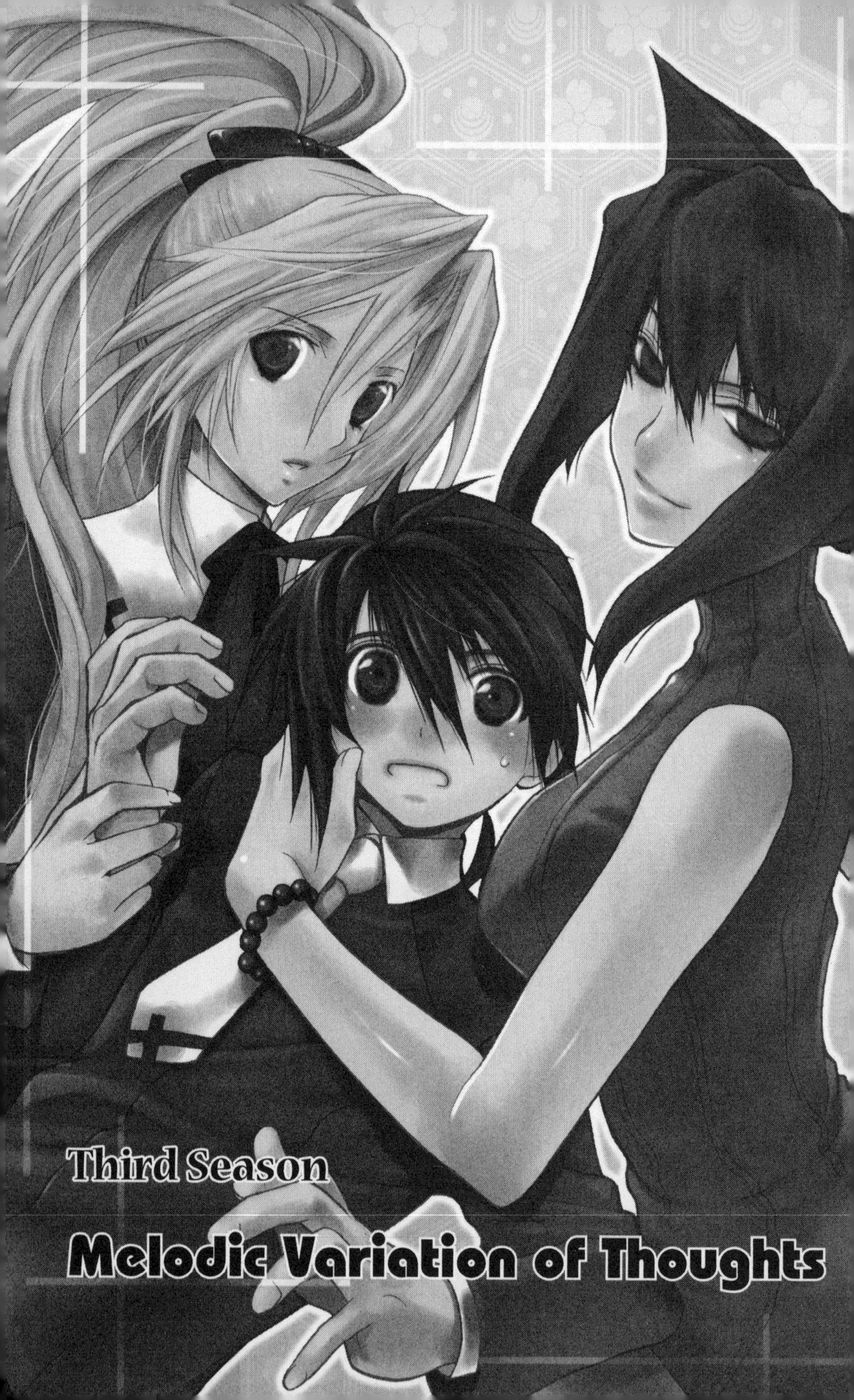
Third Season
Melodic Variation of Thoughts

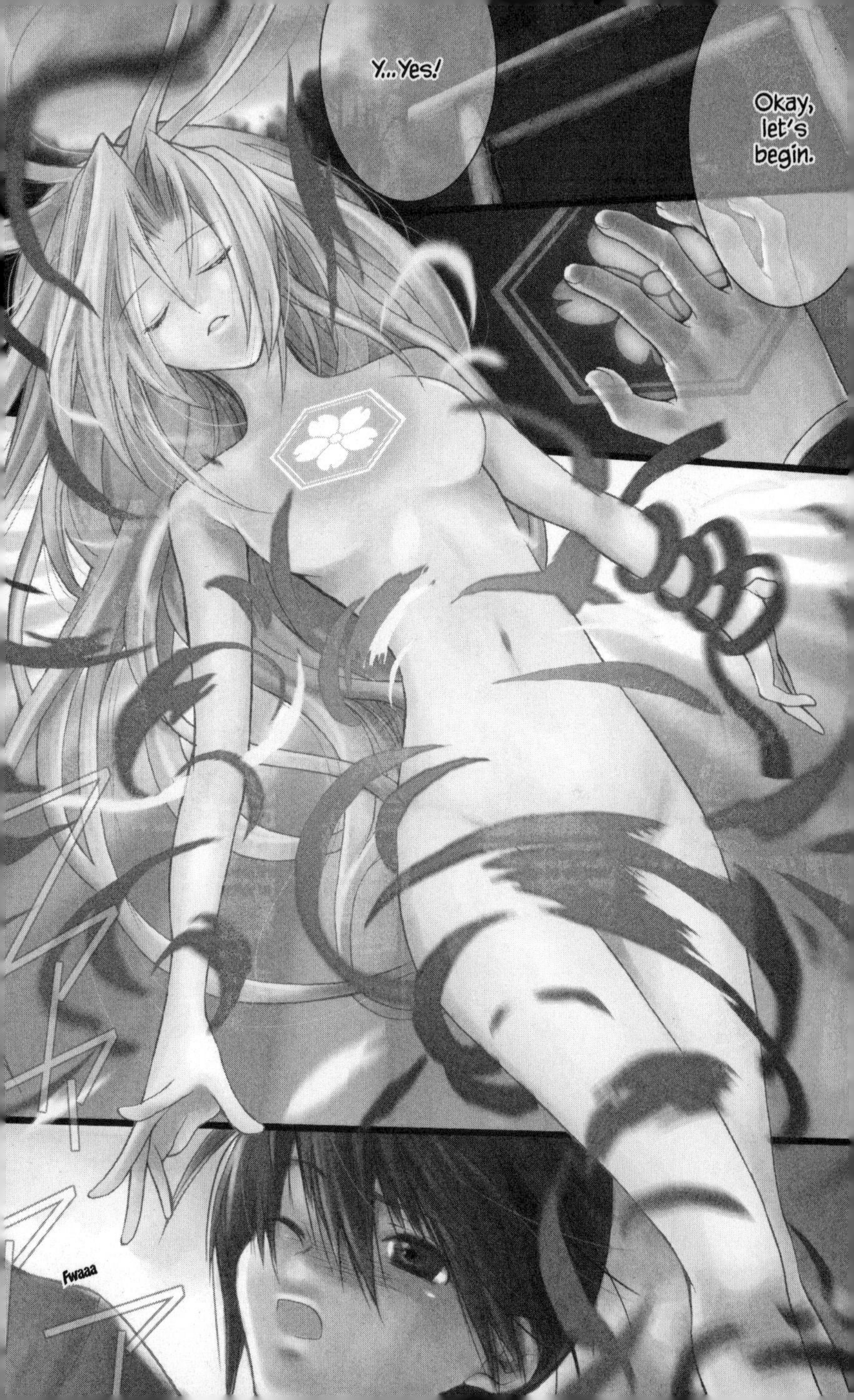
Okay, let's begin.
Y...Yes!
Fwaaa

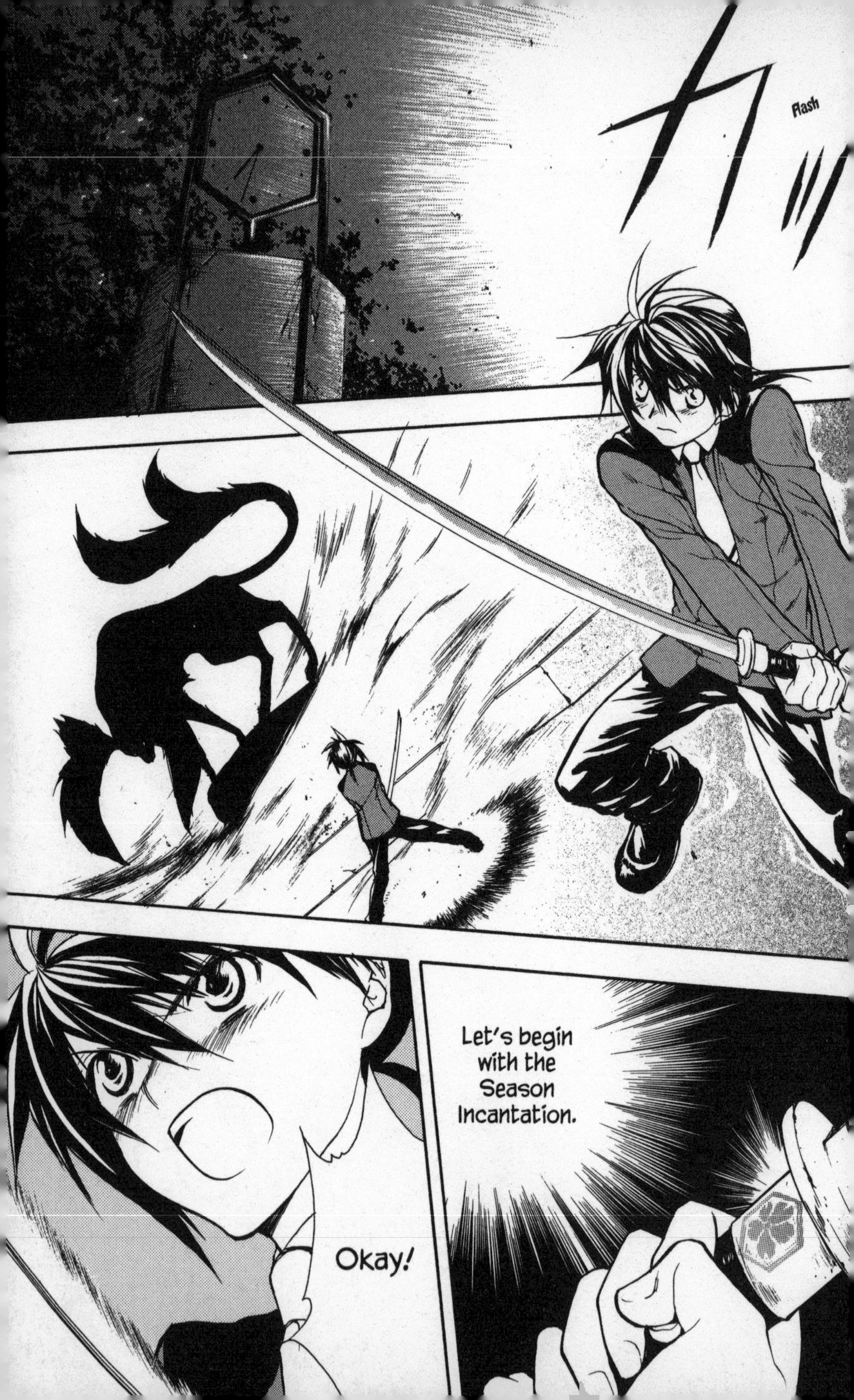
Flash
Let's begin with the Season Incantation.
Okay!

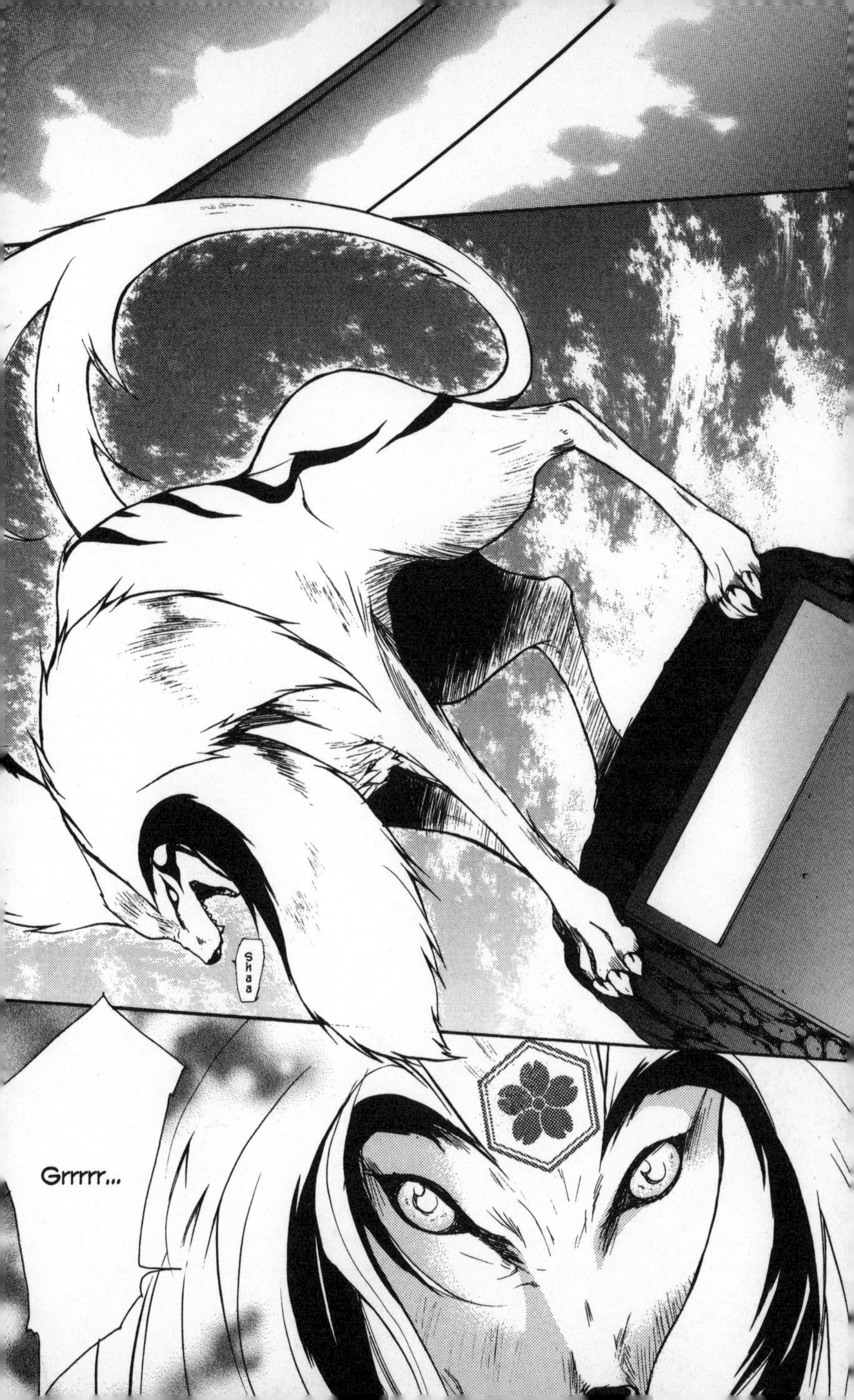
Shaa
Grrrrr...

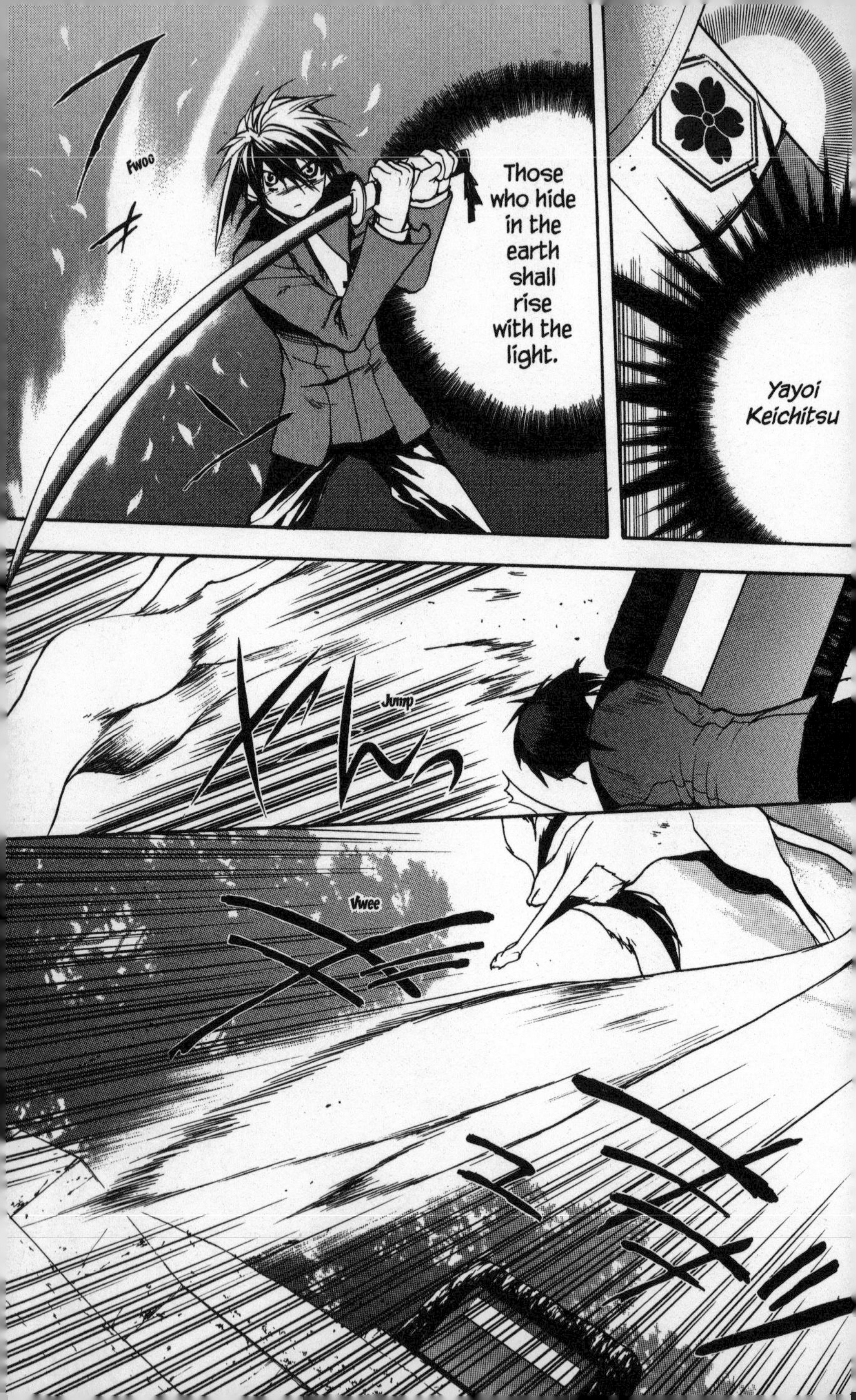
Yayoi Keichitsu
Those who hide in the earth shall rise with the light.
Fwoo
Jump
Vwee

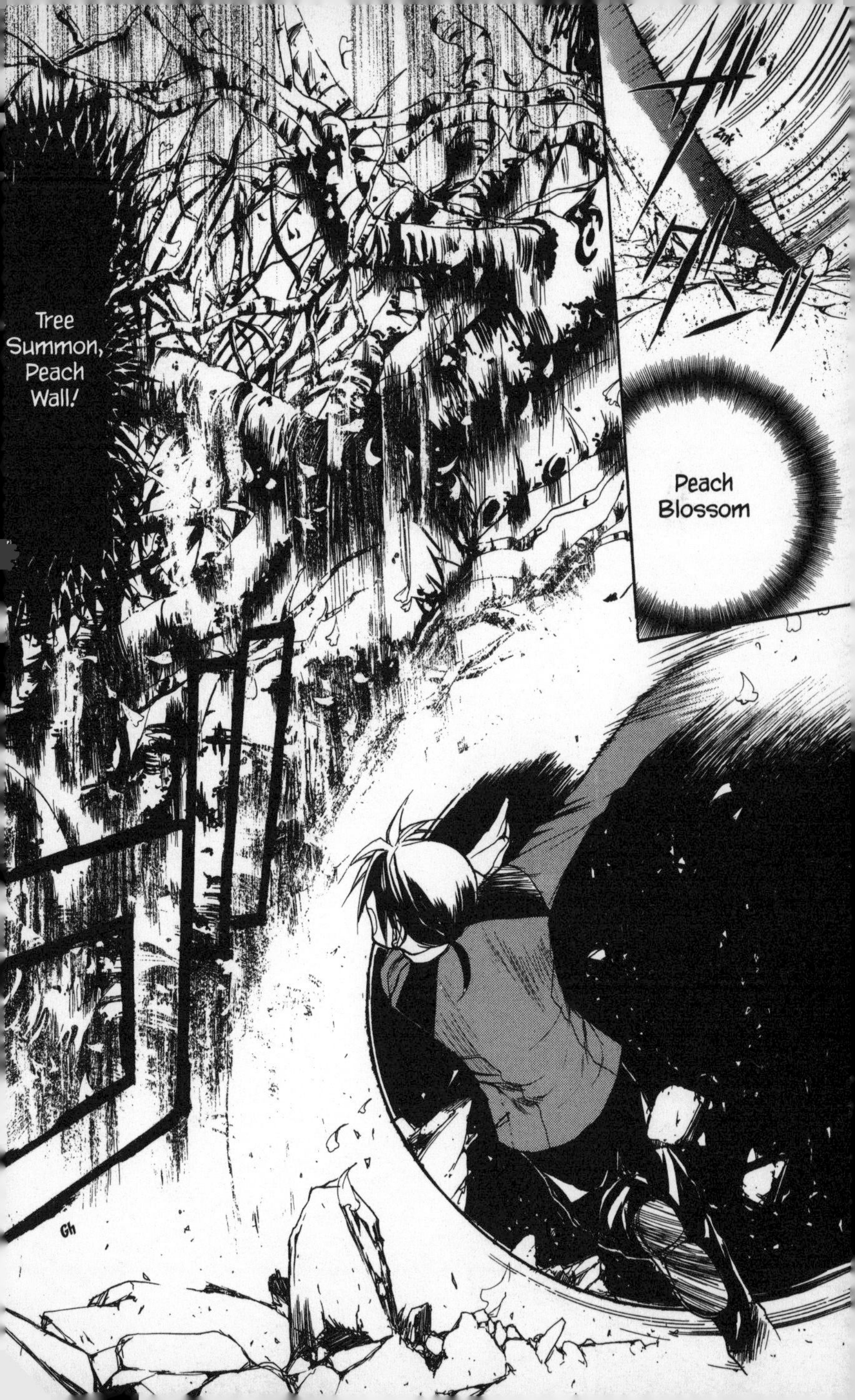
Znk
Peach Blossom
Tree Summon, Peach Wall!
Gh

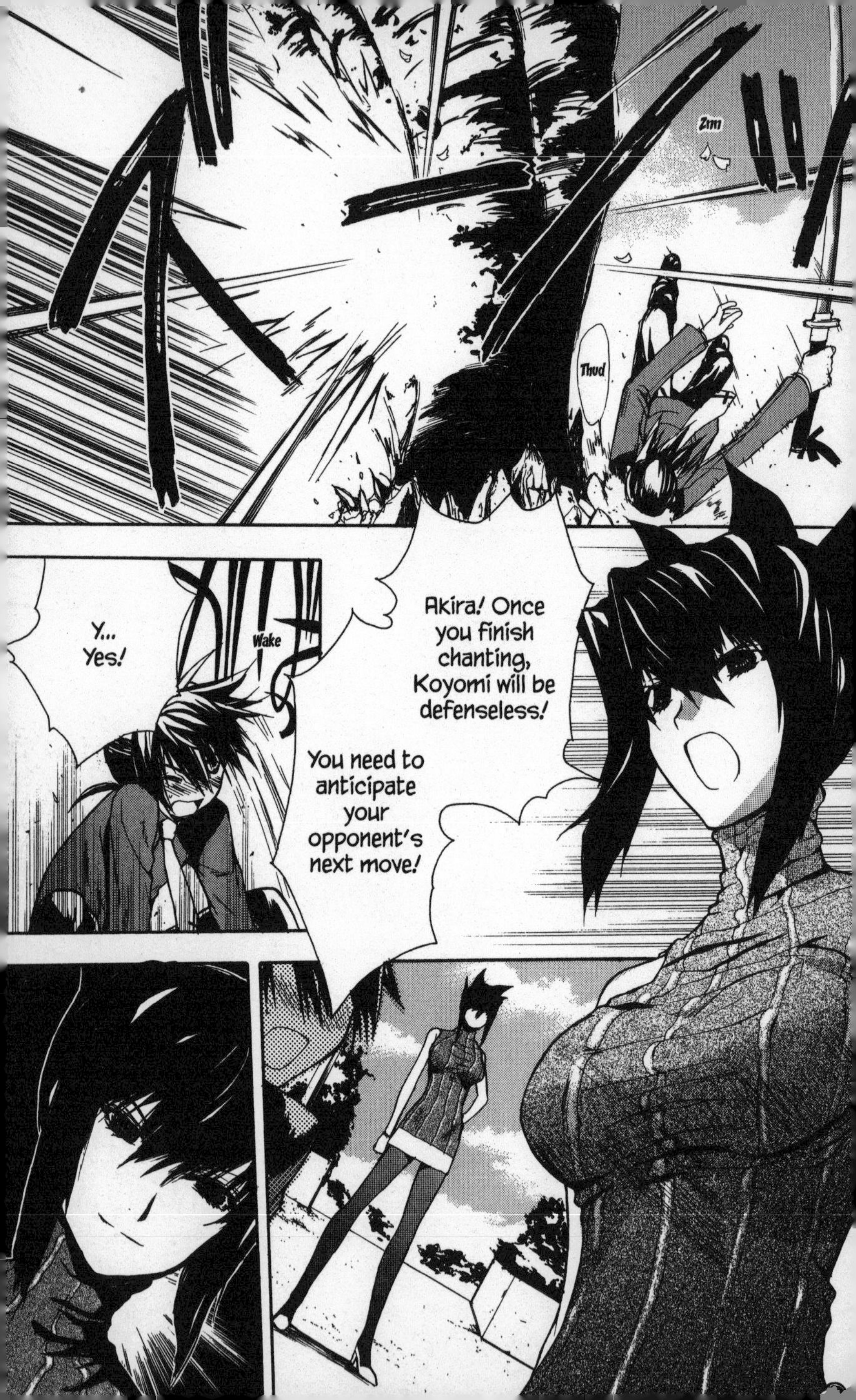
Zm
Thud
Akira! Once you finish chanting, Koyomi will be defenseless!
You need to anticipate your opponent's next move!
Wake
Y... Yes!

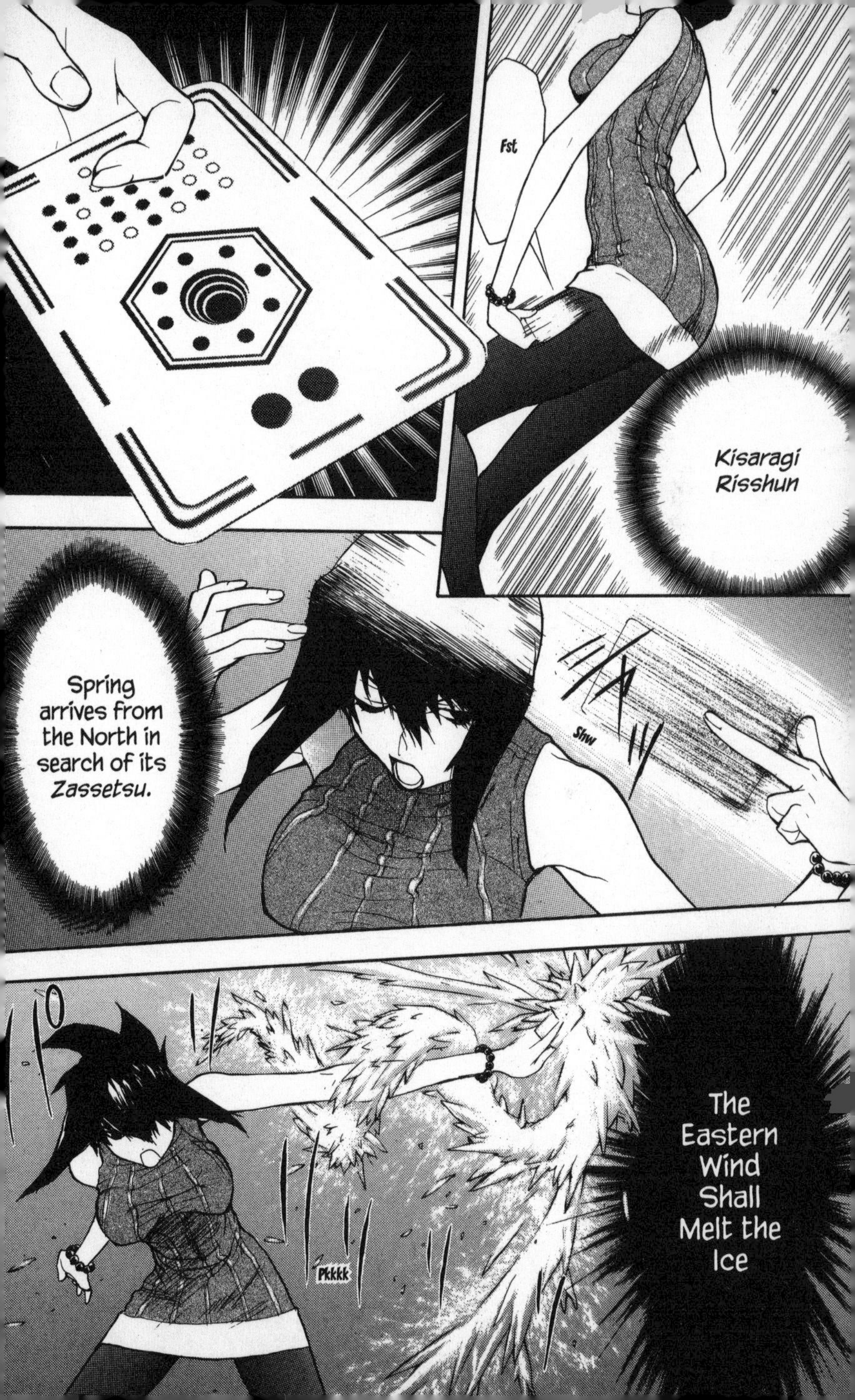
Fst
Kisaragi Risshun
Shw
Spring arrives from the North in search of its Zassetsu.
The Eastern Wind Shall Melt the Ice
Pkkkk

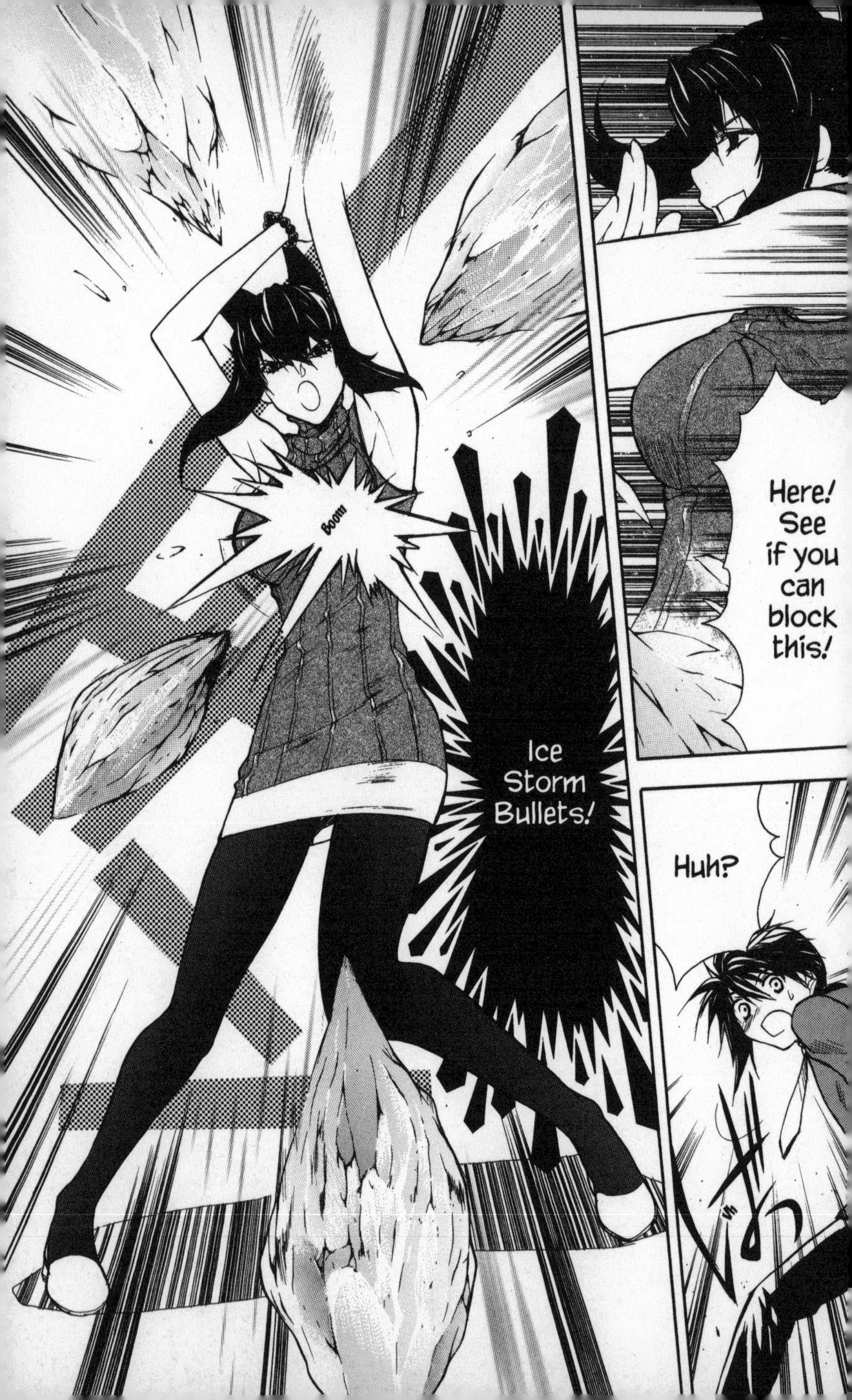
Here! See if you can block this!
Huh?
Ice Storm Bullets!
Boom

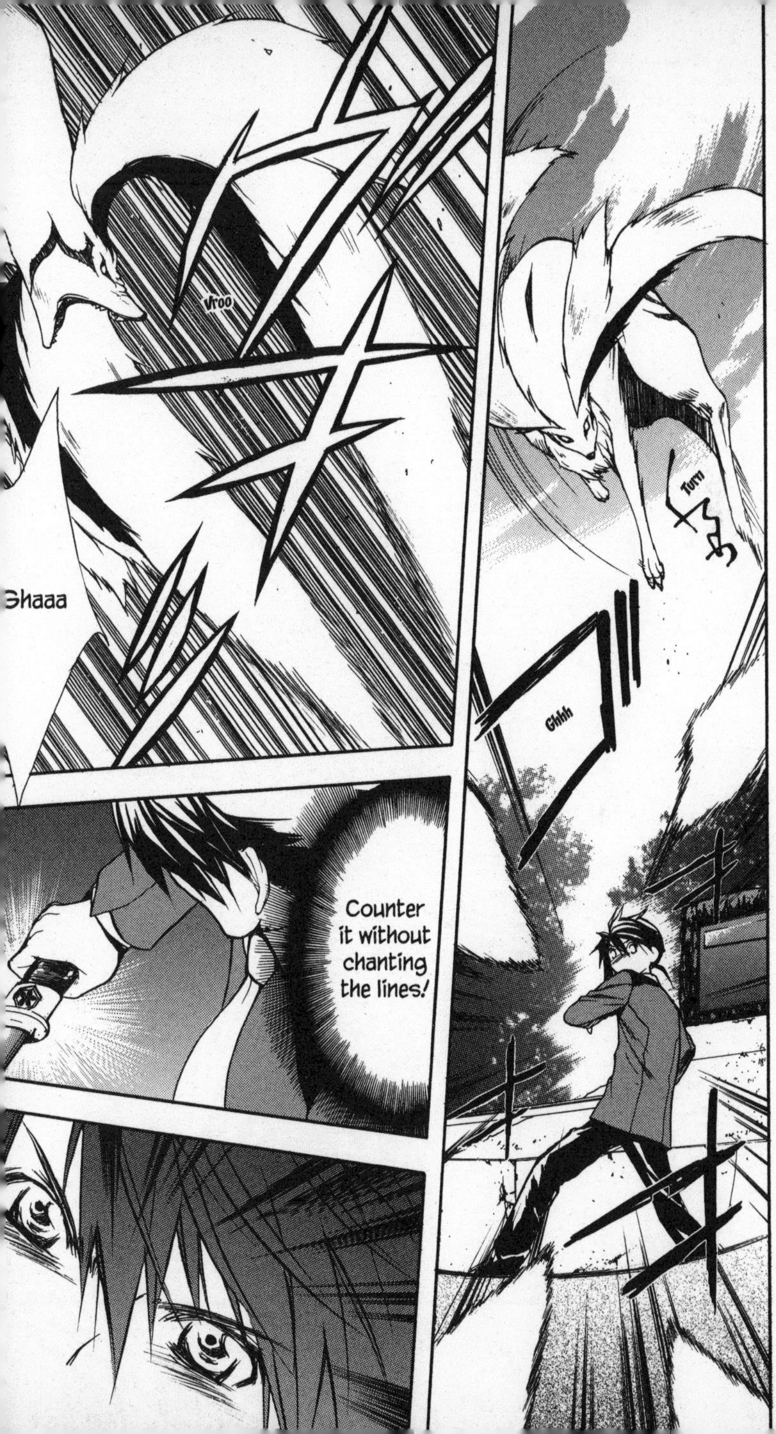
Turn
Ghhh
Vroo
Ghaaa
Counter it without chanting the lines!

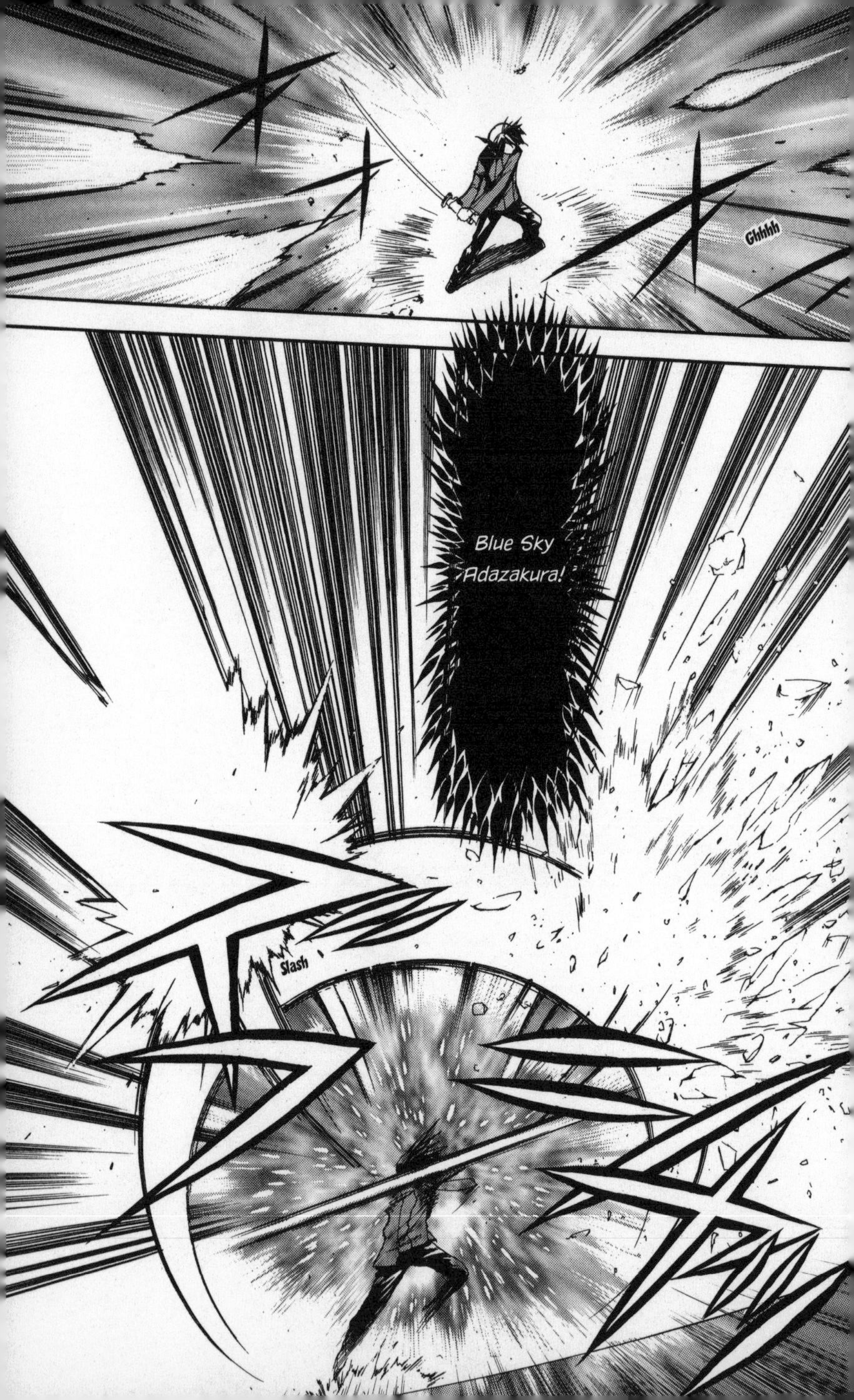
Ghhhh
Blue Sky Adazakura!
Slash

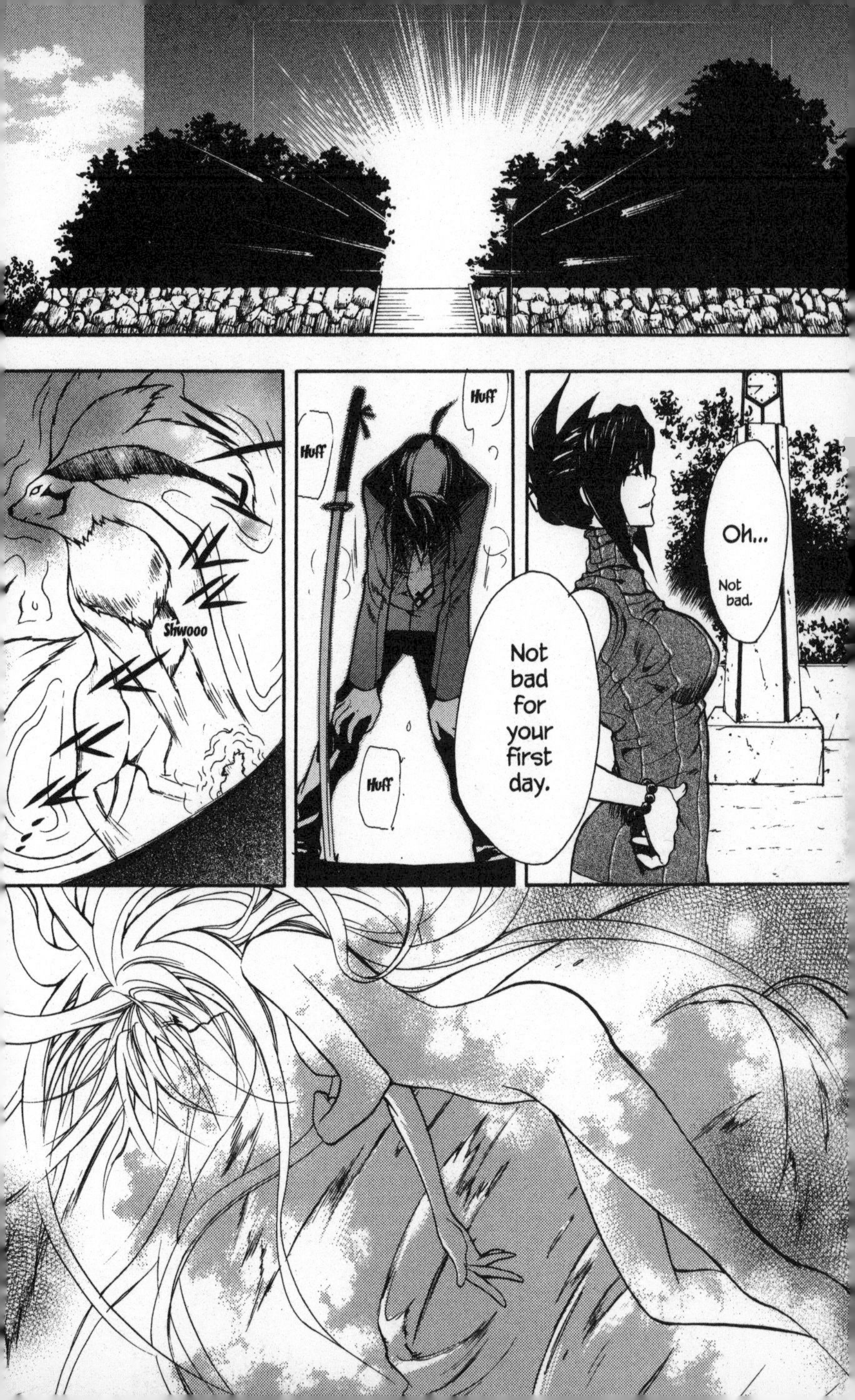
Oh...
Not bad.
Not bad for your first day.
Huff
Huff
Huff
Shwooo

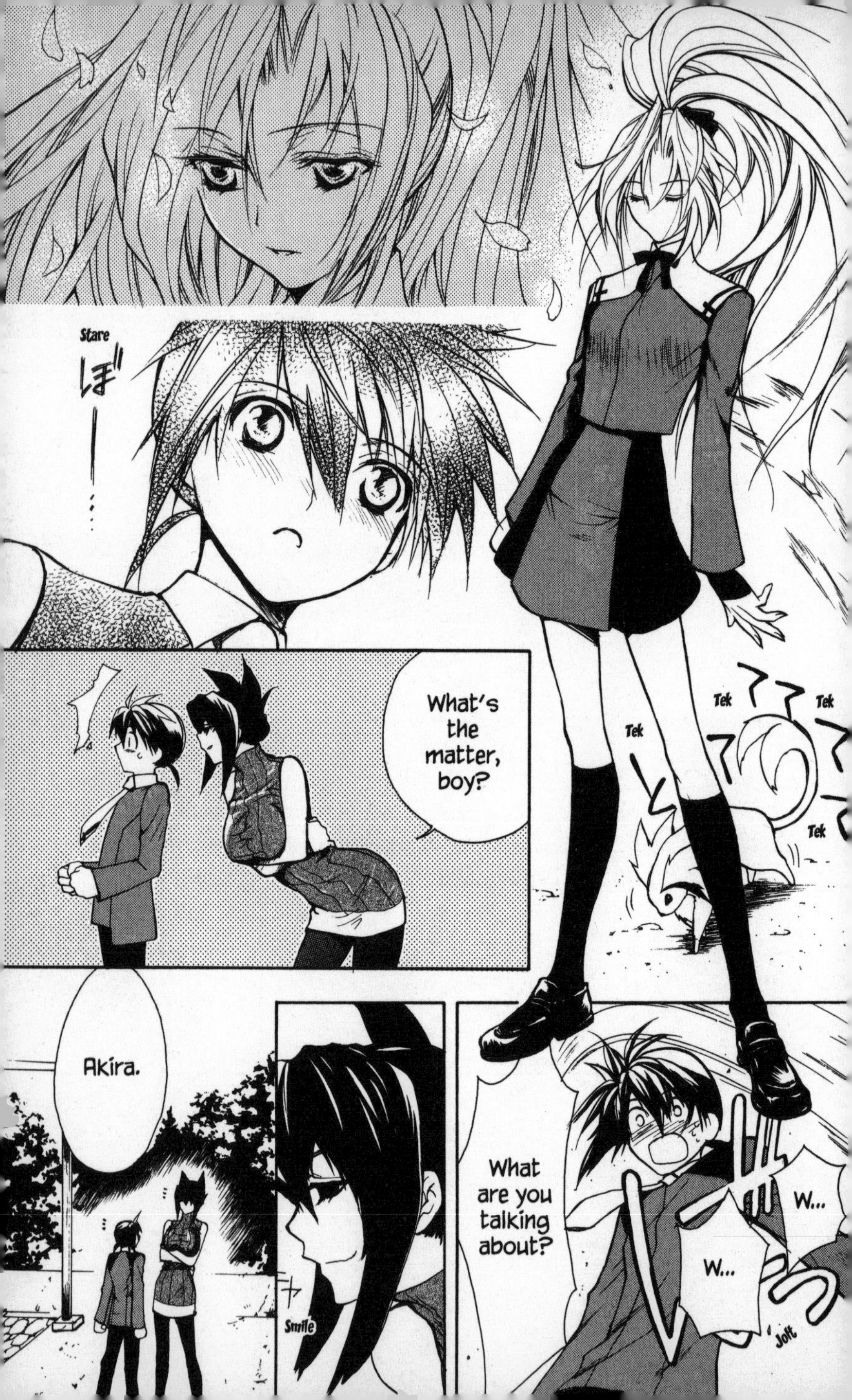
Tek
Tek
Tek
Tek
Stare
What's the matter, boy?
W...
W...
What are you talking about?
Jolt
Smile
Akira.

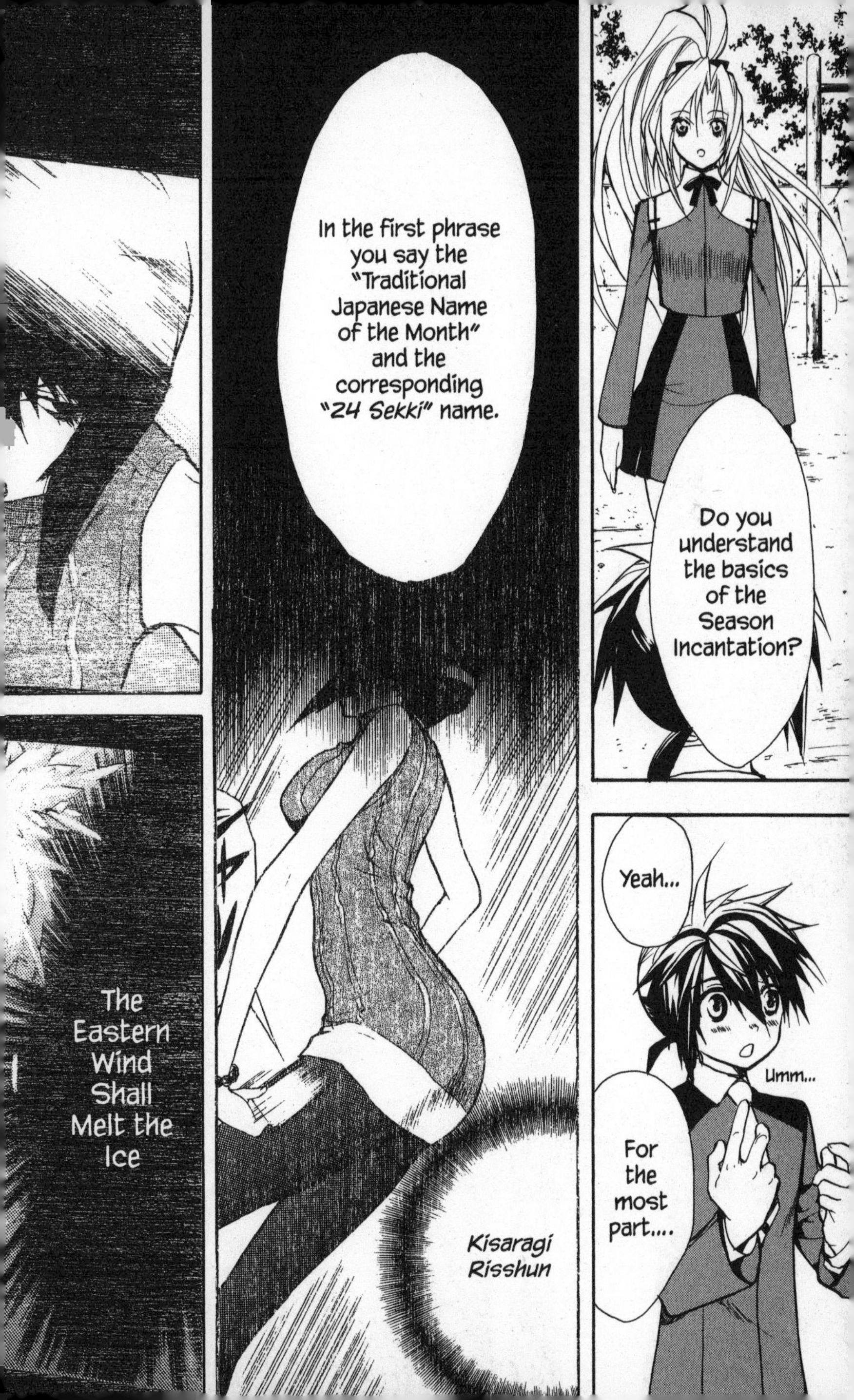
Do you understand the basics of the Season Incantation?
Yeah...
Umm...
For the most part....
In the first phrase you say the "Traditional Japanese Name of the Month" and the corresponding "24 Sekki" name.
Kisaragi Risshun
The Eastern Wind Shall Melt the Ice

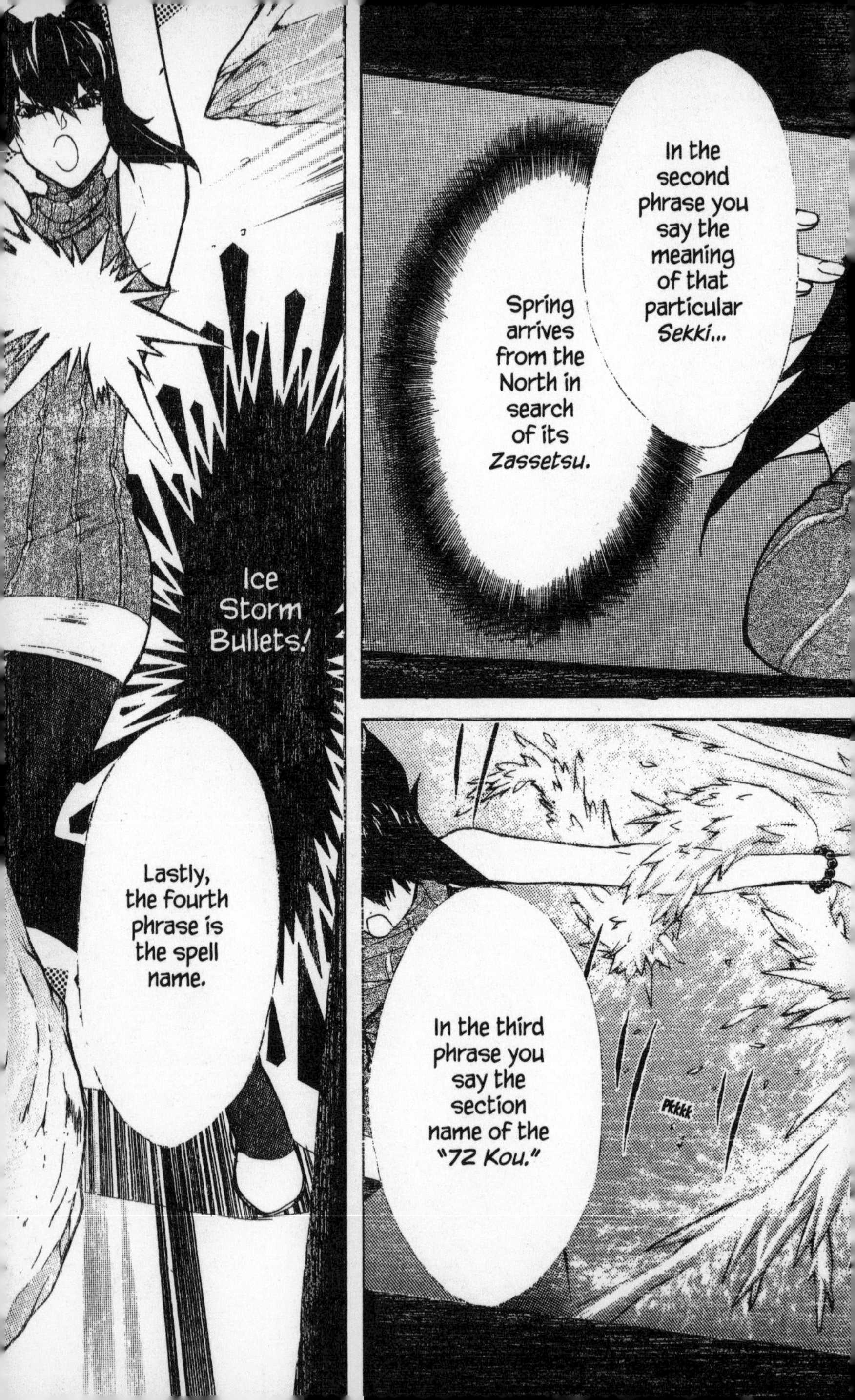

In the second phrase you say the meaning of that particular *Sekki*...
Spring arrives from the North in search of its *Zassetsu*.
In the third phrase you say the section name of the "*72 Kou*."
Pkkkk
Lastly, the fourth phrase is the spell name.
Ice Storm Bullets!

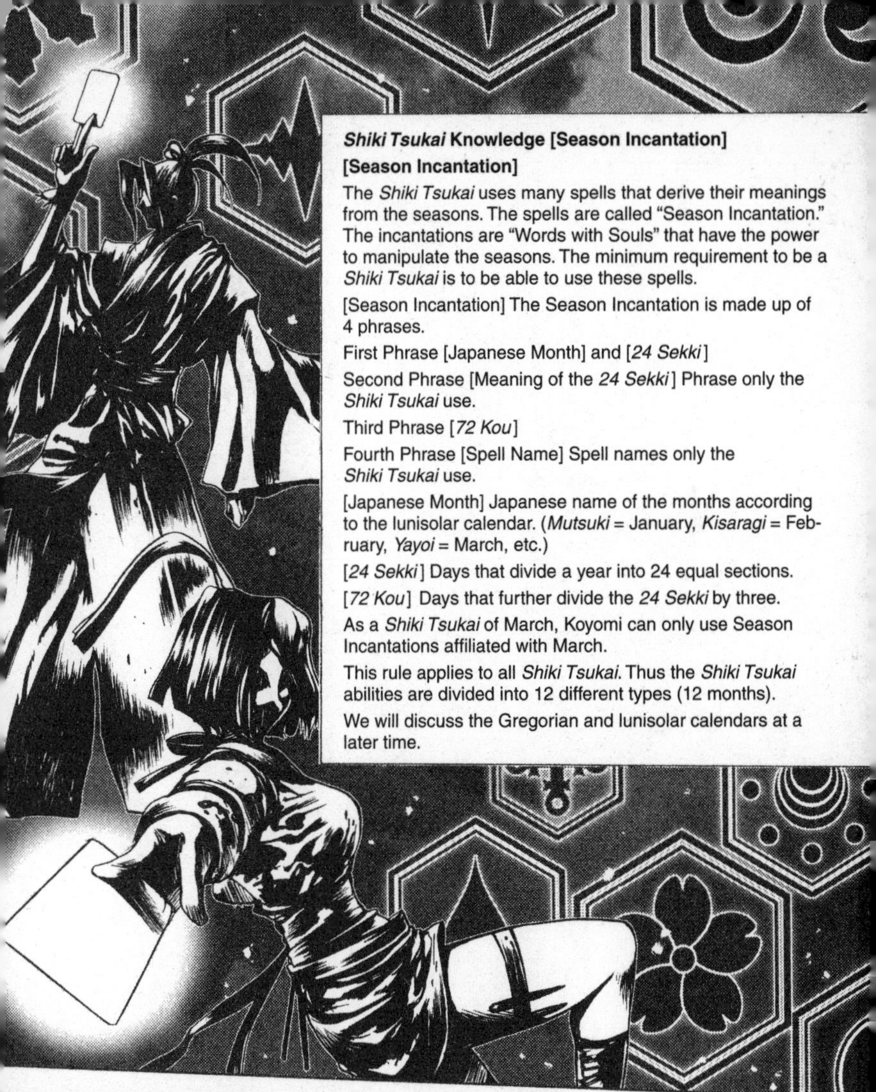

Shiki Tsukai Knowledge [Season Incantation]

[Season Incantation]

The *Shiki Tsukai* uses many spells that derive their meanings from the seasons. The spells are called "Season Incantation." The incantations are "Words with Souls" that have the power to manipulate the seasons. The minimum requirement to be a *Shiki Tsukai* is to be able to use these spells.

[Season Incantation] The Season Incantation is made up of 4 phrases.

First Phrase [Japanese Month] and [*24 Sekki*]

Second Phrase [Meaning of the *24 Sekki*] Phrase only the *Shiki Tsukai* use.

Third Phrase [*72 Kou*]

Fourth Phrase [Spell Name] Spell names only the *Shiki Tsukai* use.

[Japanese Month] Japanese name of the months according to the lunisolar calendar. (*Mutsuki* = January, *Kisaragi* = February, *Yayoi* = March, etc.)

[*24 Sekki*] Days that divide a year into 24 equal sections.

[*72 Kou*] Days that further divide the *24 Sekki* by three.

As a *Shiki Tsukai* of March, Koyomi can only use Season Incantations affiliated with March.

This rule applies to all *Shiki Tsukai*. Thus the *Shiki Tsukai* abilities are divided into 12 different types (12 months).

We will discuss the Gregorian and lunisolar calendars at a later time.

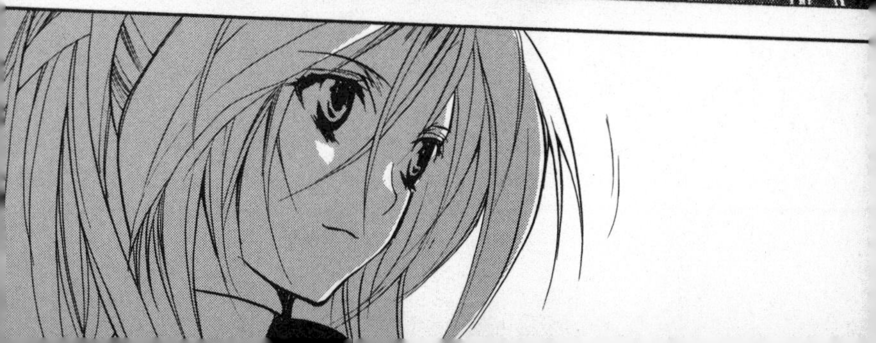

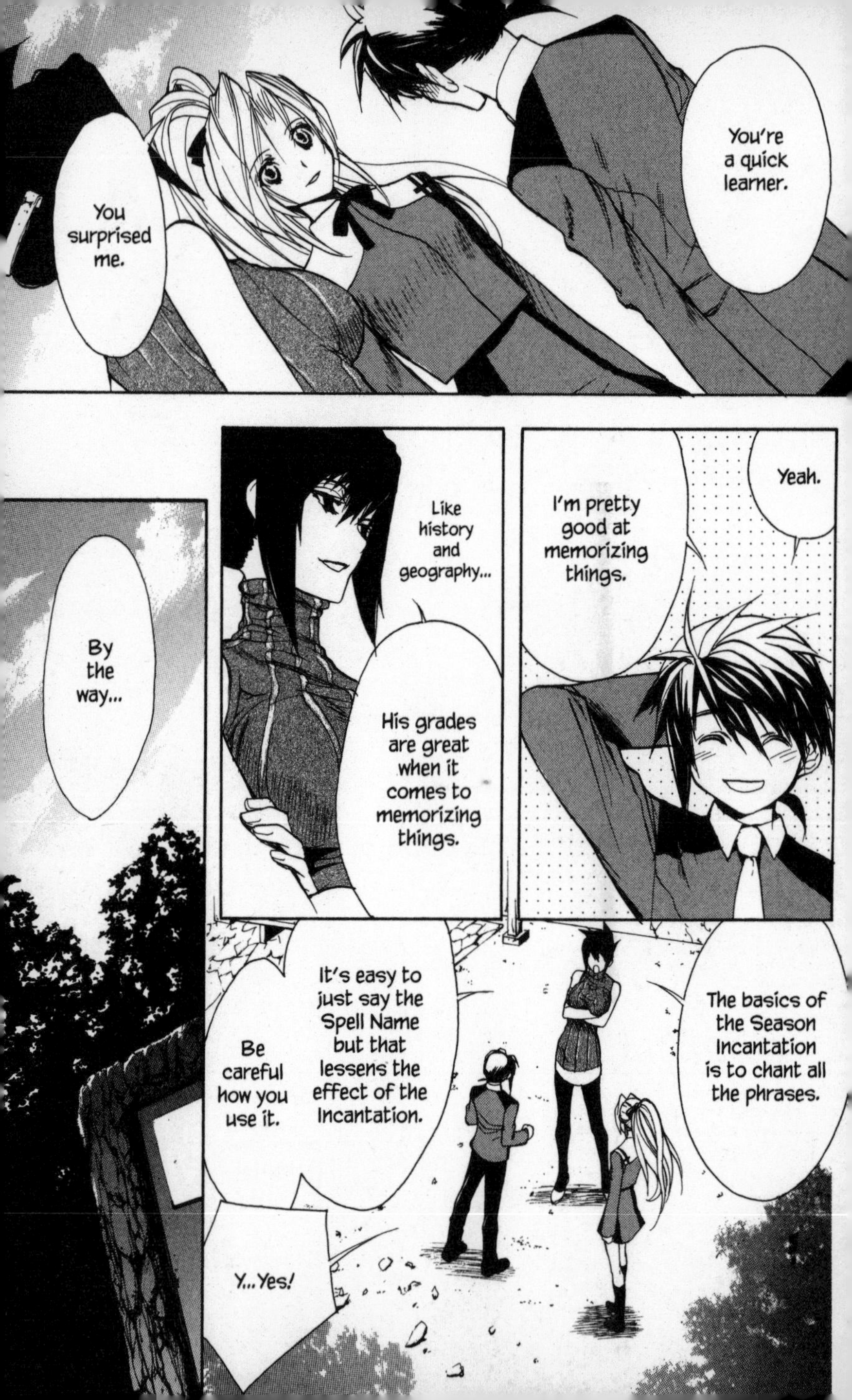
You're a quick learner.
You surprised me.
Yeah.
I'm pretty good at memorizing things.
Like history and geography...
His grades are great when it comes to memorizing things.
The basics of the Season Incantation is to chant all the phrases.
It's easy to just say the Spell Name but that lessens the effect of the Incantation.
Be careful how you use it.
Y...Yes!
By the way...

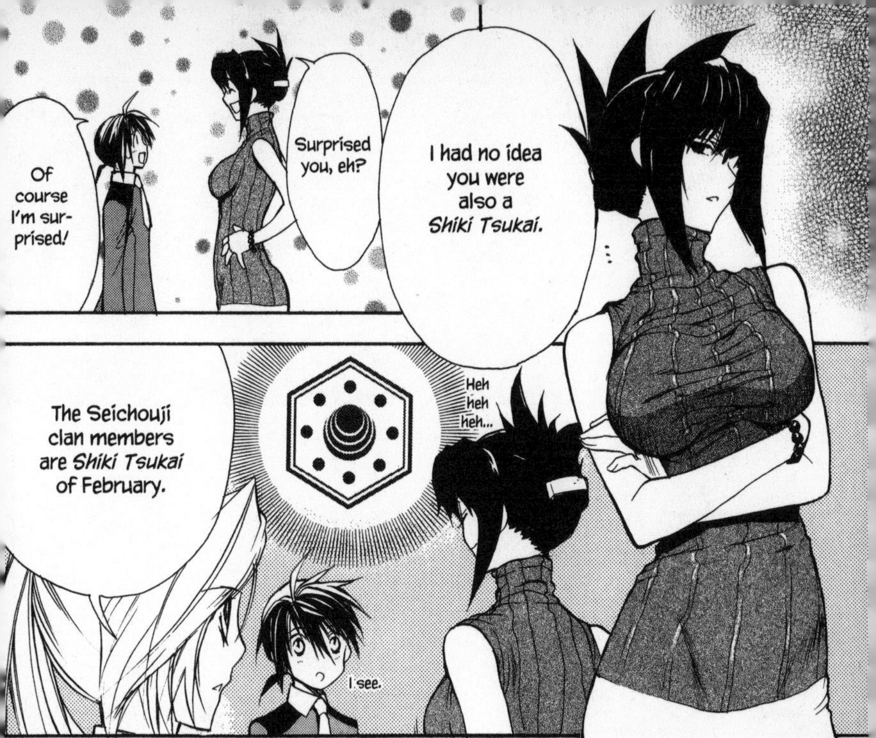
I had no idea you were also a *Shiki Tsukai.*
...
Surprised you, eh?
Of course I'm sur-prised!
Heh heh heh...
The Seichouji clan members are *Shiki Tsukai* of February.
I see.

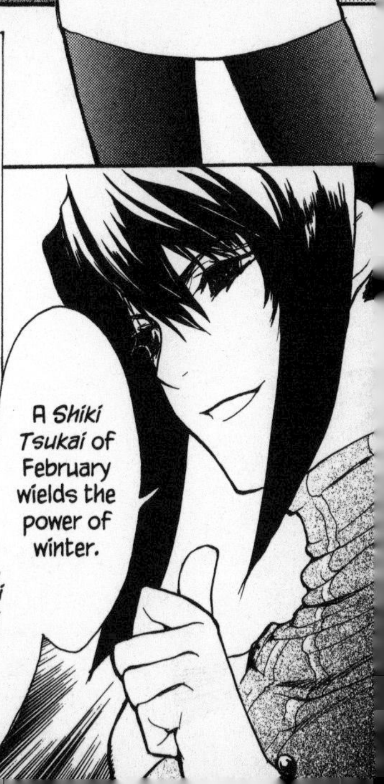
A *Shiki Tsukai* of February wields the power of winter.
I, Rei Seichouji, am a *Shiki Tsukai* of "Winter."

***Shiki* Knowledge** **February 2, Birth Stone [Conch Pearl]**

Rei Seichiouji's *Shikifu* is made of from a Conch Pearl (Hardness: 2.5–4.5). The stone means, "My Dearest." It's a type of pearl that typically has a teardrop shape unlike a perfectly circular pearl. This pearl comes from the conch shell. Its characteristic is its pink color, similar to a coral pink, and it is very rare.

• February 2, Birth Flower (Flower Meaning)
White Freesia (Innocence, Virginity), Quince (Ordinary, Fairy's Sparkle), etc.

• February 2 Holidays
[Candlemas], [Married Couples Day], [Moxibustion Day], [Police Booth Installation Day], etc.

• February *Shiki Tsukai*
Has the ability to amplify, manipulate, and shoot their "Chi." Also has healing abilities. They also use illusion incantations.

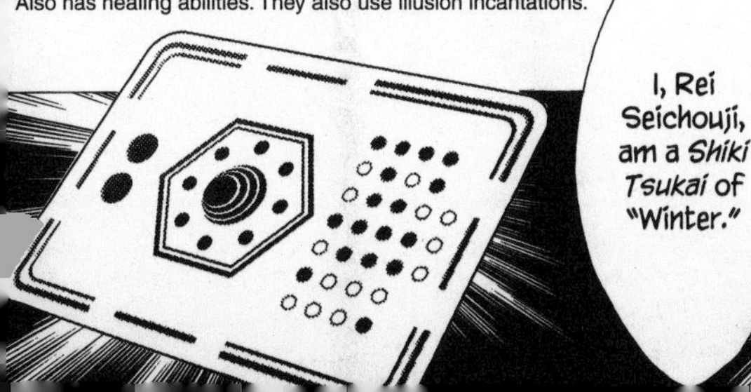

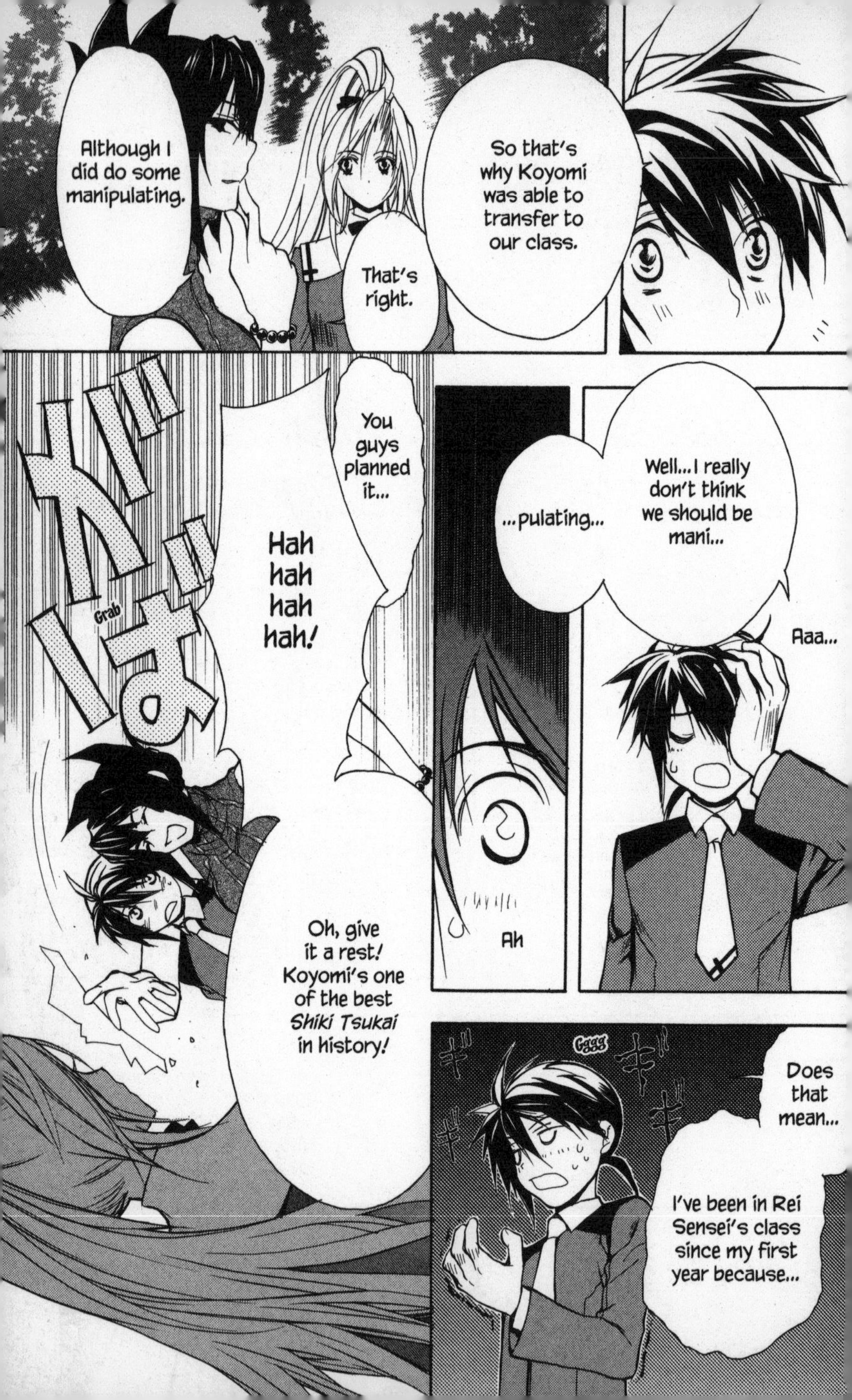
So that's why Koyomi was able to transfer to our class.
That's right.
Although I did do some manipulating.
Well...I really don't think we should be mani...
...pulating...
Aaa...
Ah
Does that mean...
Gggg
I've been in Rei Sensei's class since my first year because...
You guys planned it...
Hah hah hah hah!
Grab
Oh, give it a rest! Koyomi's one of the best *Shiki Tsukai* in history!

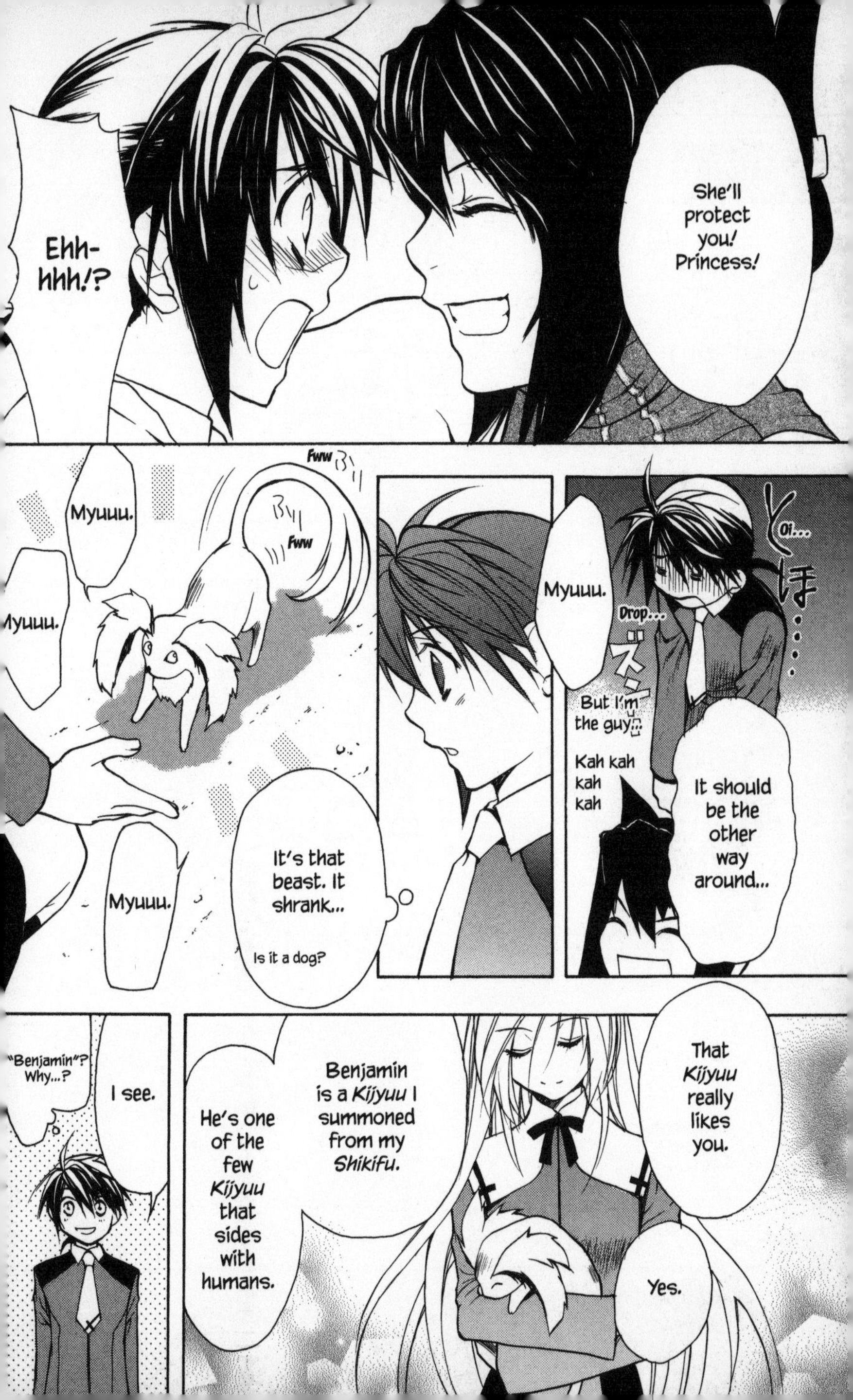
She'll protect you! Princess!
Ehh-hhh!?
Oi...
Drop...
But I'm the guy...
Kah kah kah kah
It should be the other way around...
Myuuu.
Fww
Fww
Myuuu.
Myuuu.
Myuuu.
It's that beast. It shrank...
Is it a dog?
That *Kijyuu* really likes you.
Yes.
Benjamin is a *Kijyuu* I summoned from my *Shikifu*.
He's one of the few *Kijyuu* that sides with humans.
I see.
"Benjamin"? Why...?

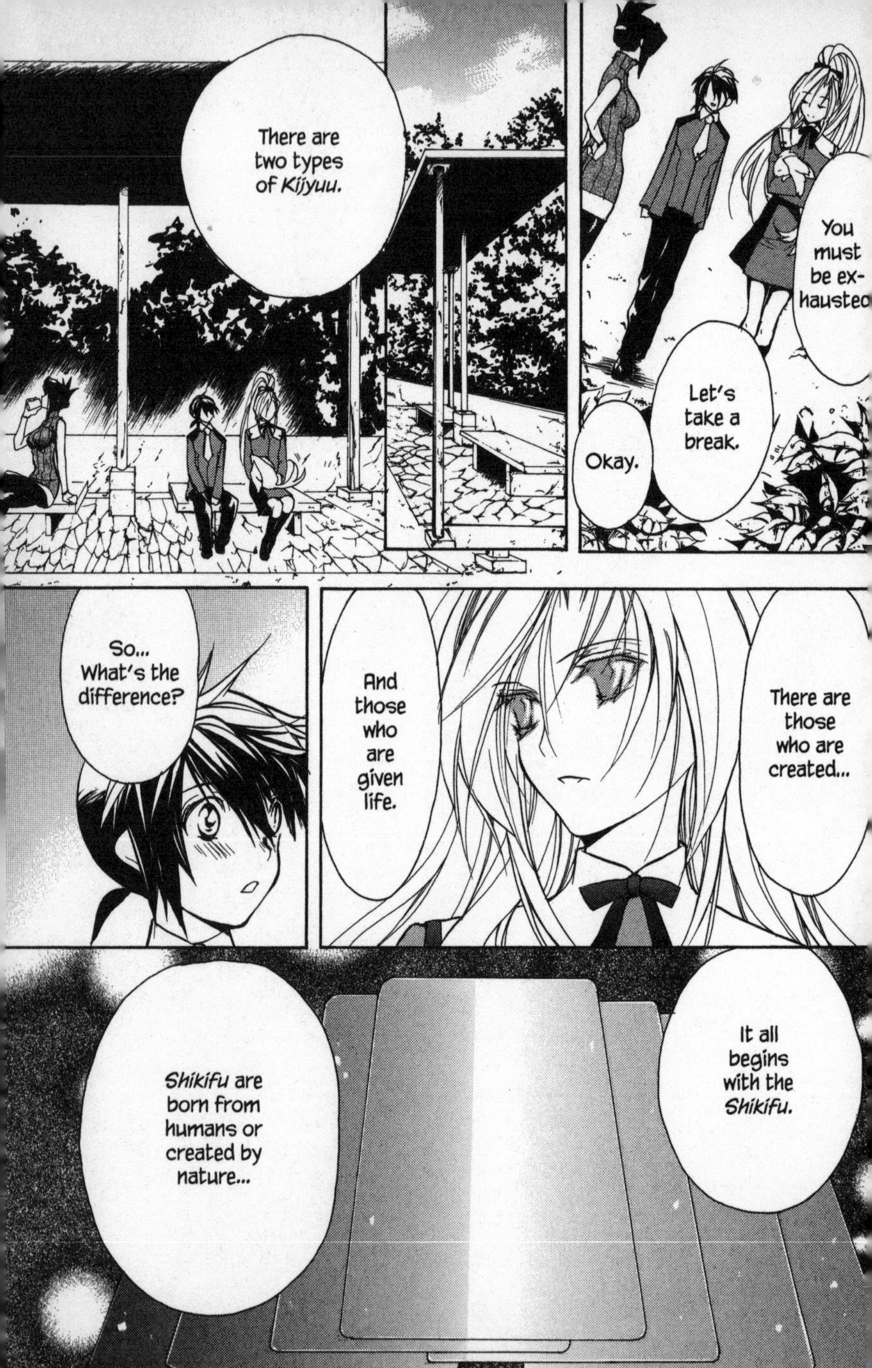
You must be exhausted
Let's take a break.
Okay.
There are two types of Kijyuu.
There are those who are created...
And those who are given life.
So... What's the difference?
It all begins with the Shikifu.
Shikifu are born from humans or created by nature...

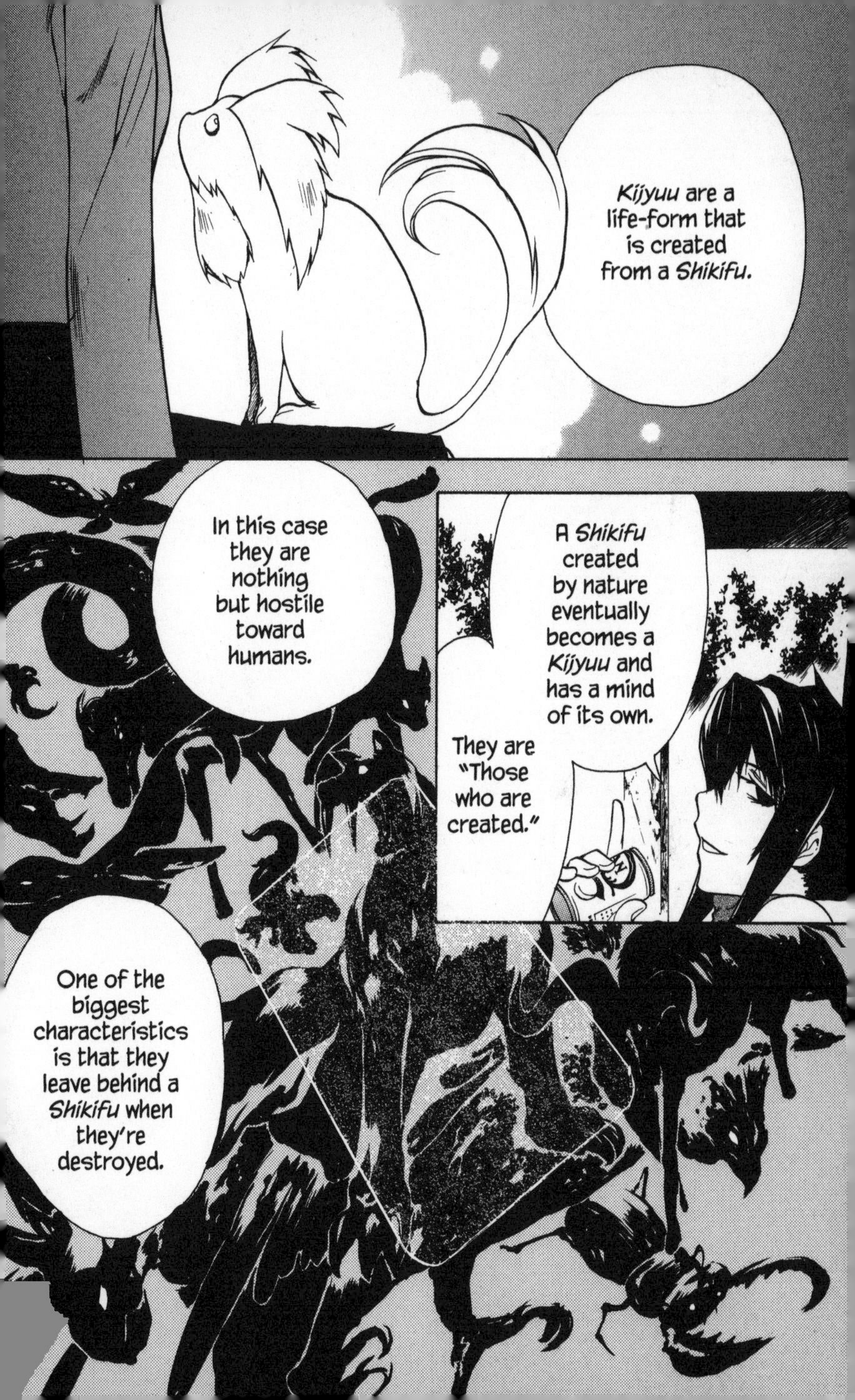
Kijyuu are a life-form that is created from a Shikifu.
A Shikifu created by nature eventually becomes a Kijyuu and has a mind of its own.
They are "Those who are created."
In this case they are nothing but hostile toward humans.
One of the biggest characteristics is that they leave behind a Shikifu when they're destroyed.

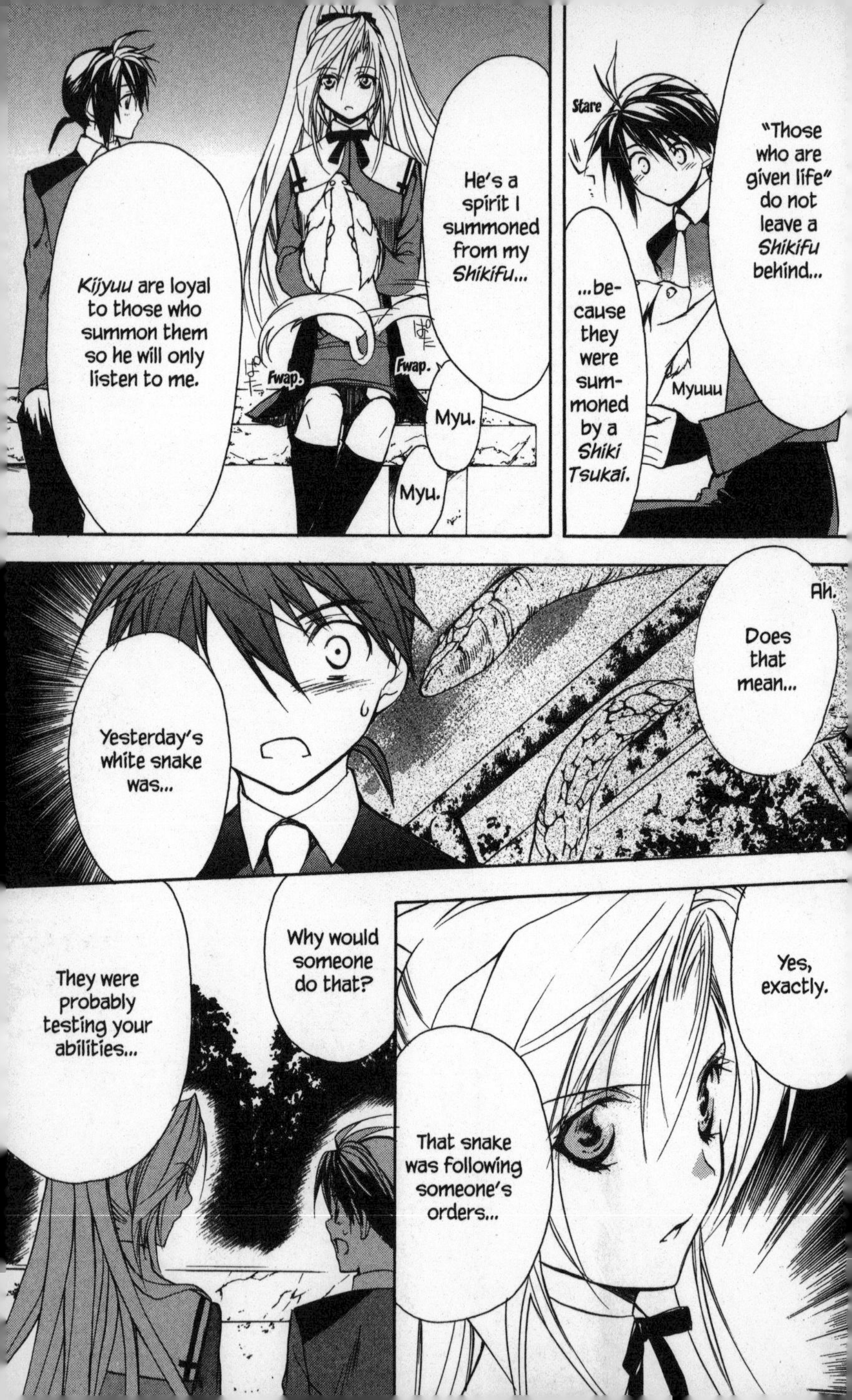
"Those who are given life" do not leave a Shikifu behind...
Stare
...be-cause they were sum-moned by a Shiki Tsukai.
Myuuu
He's a spirit I summoned from my Shikifu...
Kijyuu are loyal to those who summon them so he will only listen to me.
Fwap.
Fwap.
Myu.
Myu.
Ah.
Does that mean...
Yesterday's white snake was...
Yes, exactly.
That snake was following someone's orders...
Why would someone do that?
They were probably testing your abilities...

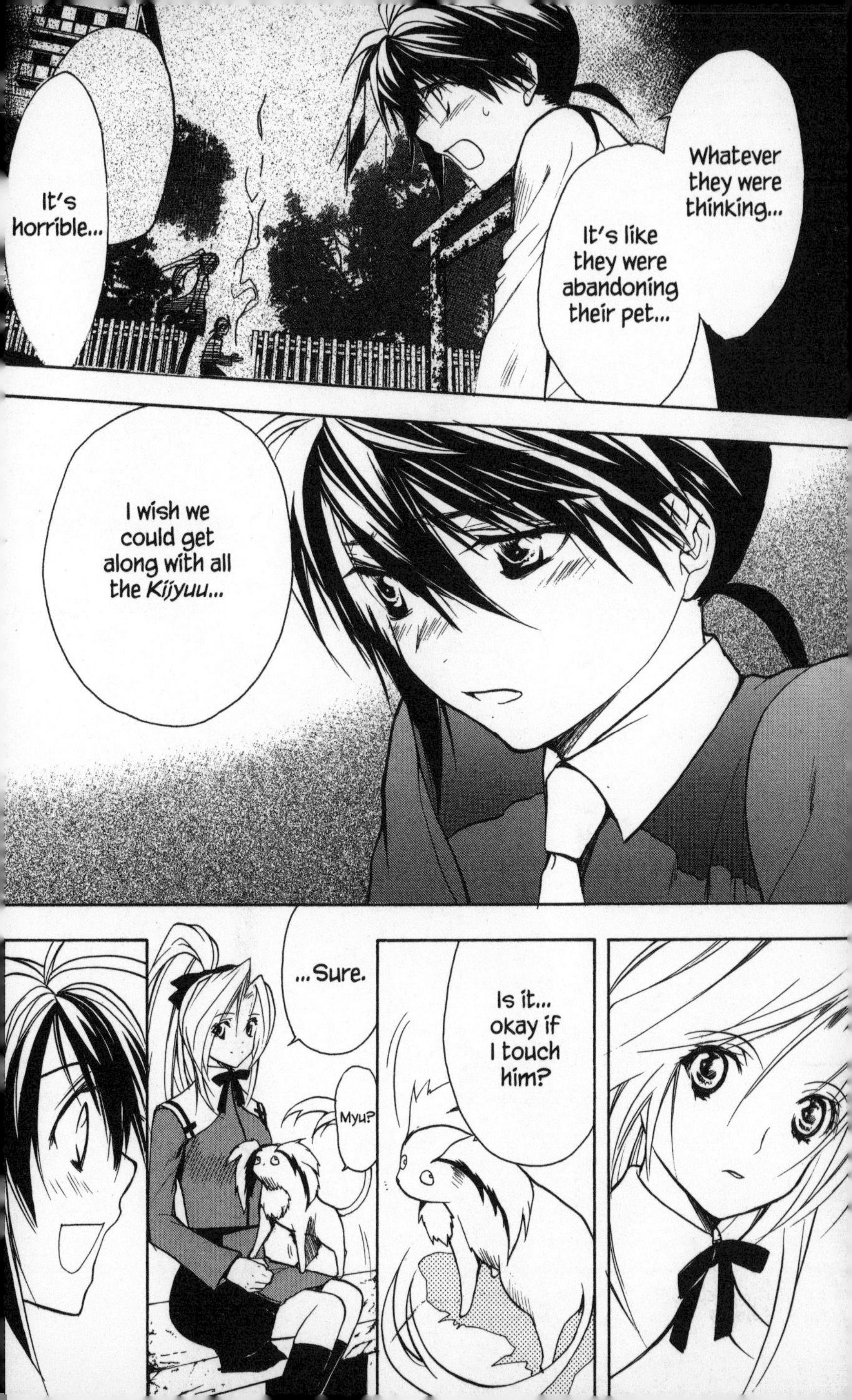
Whatever they were thinking...
It's like they were abandoning their pet...
It's horrible...
I wish we could get along with all the *Kijyuu*...
Is it... okay if I touch him?
...Sure.
Myu?

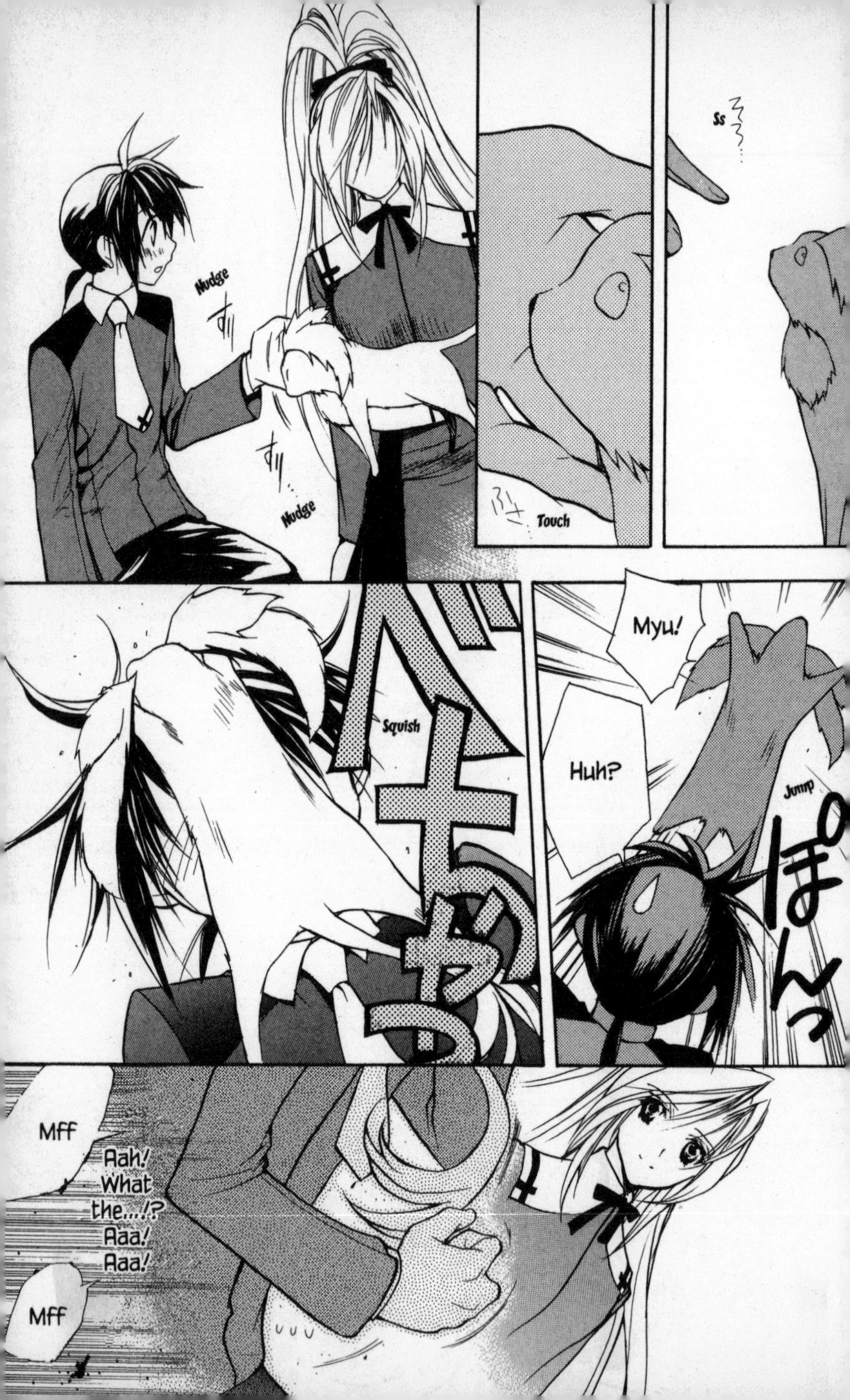

Ss
Touch
Nudge
Nudge
Myu!
Huh?
Jump
ぽんっ
Squish
Mff
Aah! What the...!? Aaa! Aaa!
Mff

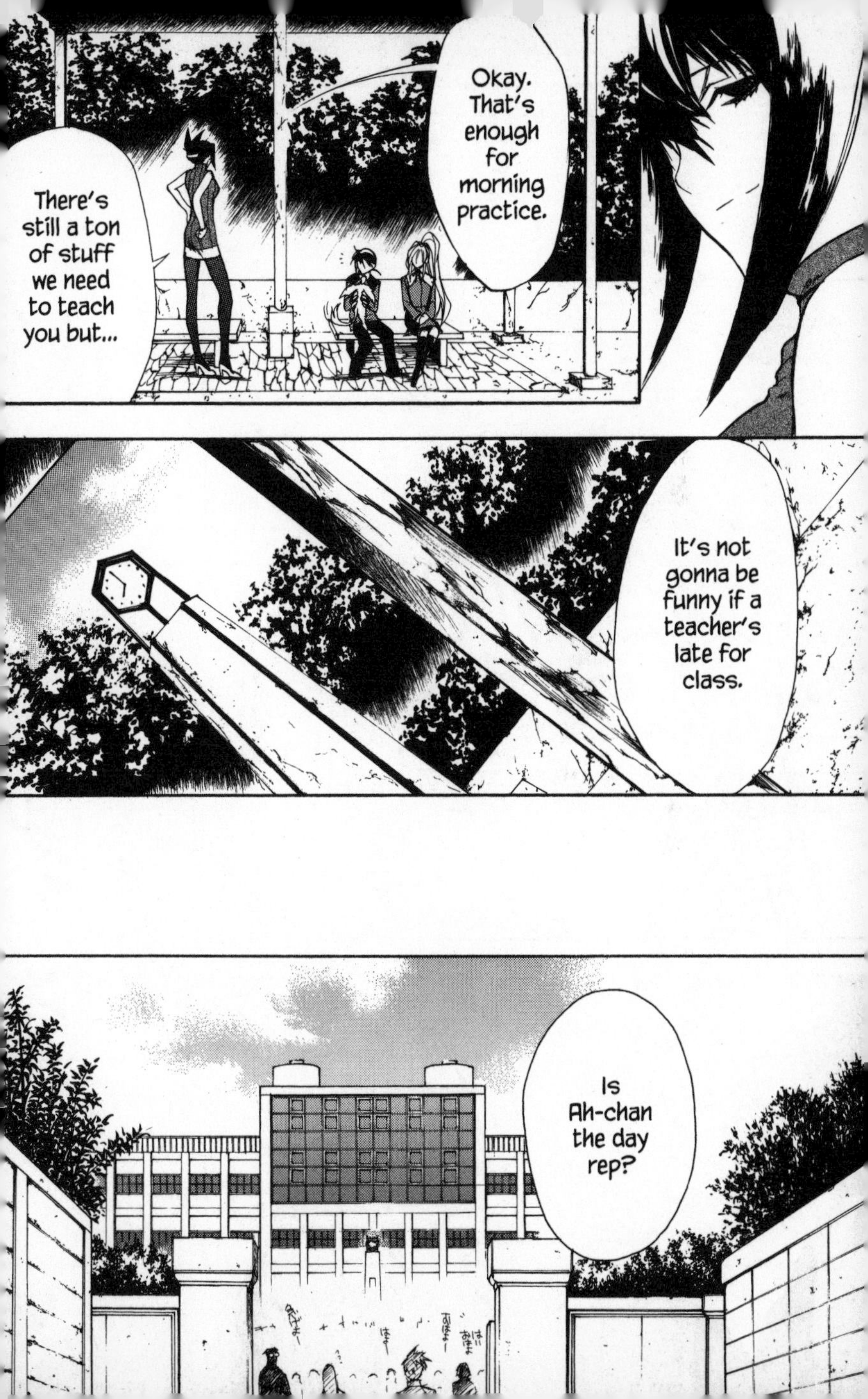
Okay. That's enough for morning practice.
There's still a ton of stuff we need to teach you but...
It's not gonna be funny if a teacher's late for class.
Is Ah-chan the day rep?

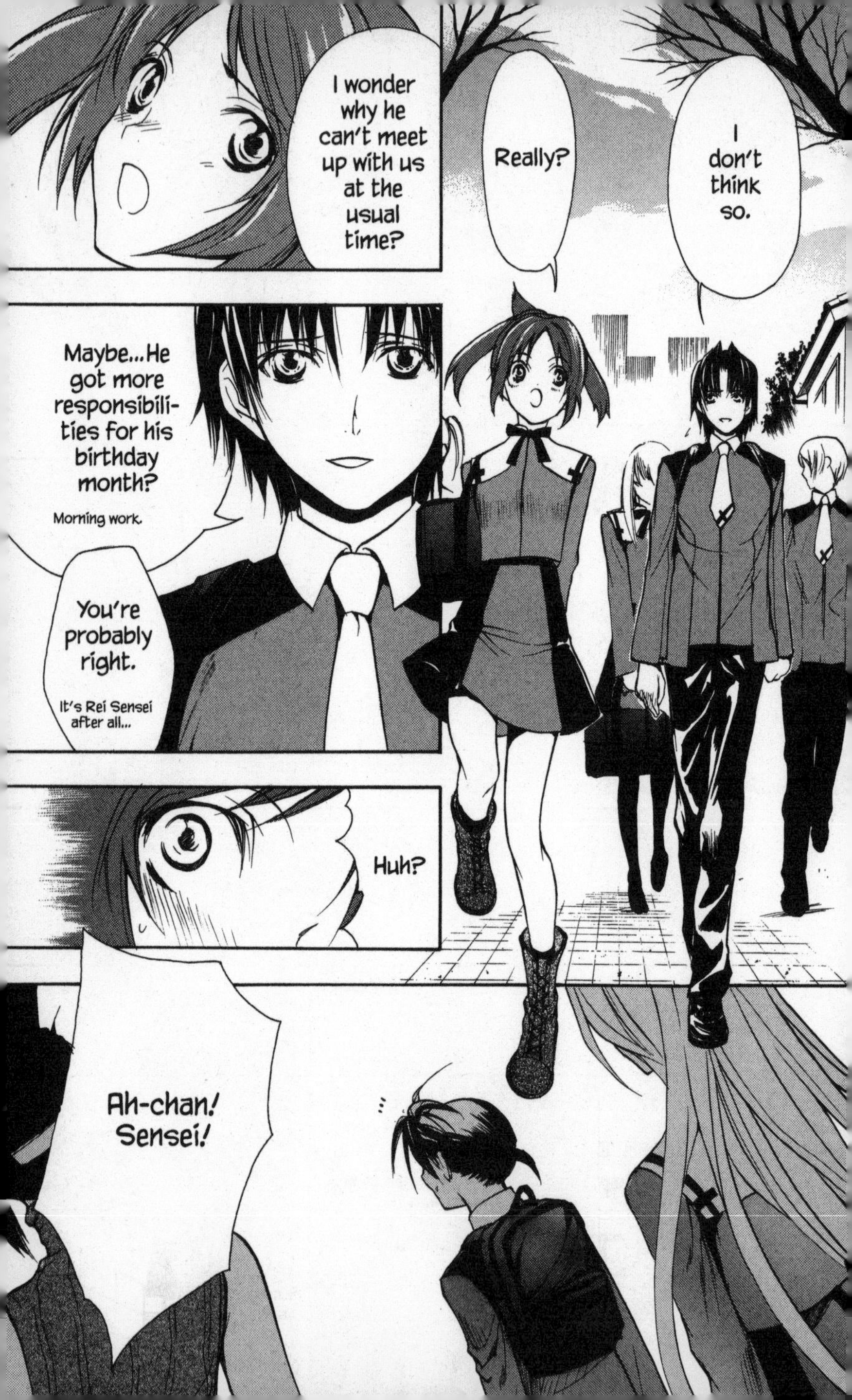
I don't think so.
Really?
I wonder why he can't meet up with us at the usual time?
Maybe...He got more responsibilities for his birthday month?
Morning work.
You're probably right.
It's Rei Sensei after all...
Huh?
Ah-chan! Sensei!

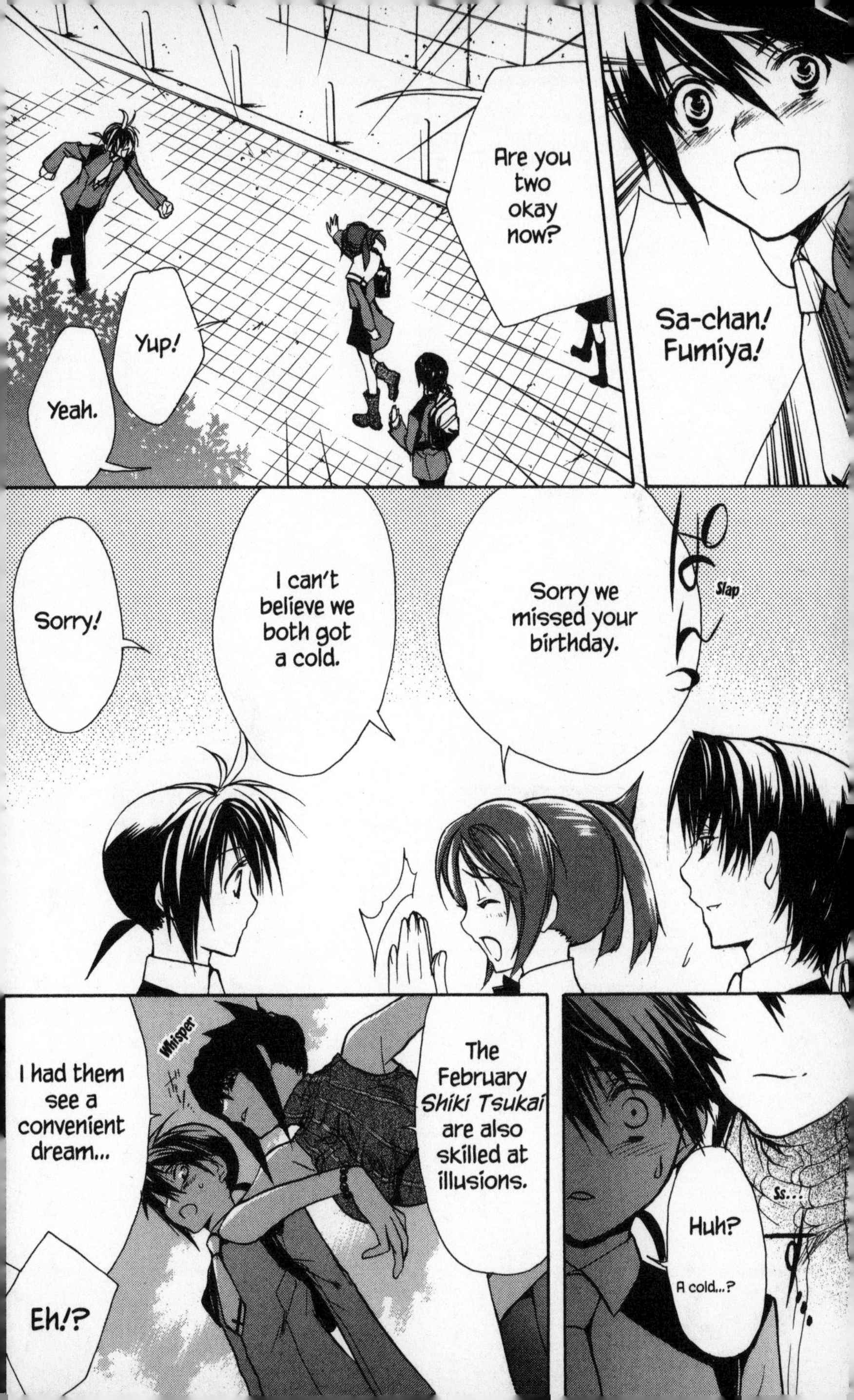
Sa-chan! Fumiya!
Are you two okay now?
Yup!
Yeah.
Slap
Sorry we missed your birthday.
I can't believe we both got a cold.
Sorry!
Ss...
Huh?
A cold...?
The February *Shiki Tsukai* are also skilled at illusions.
Whisper
I had them see a convenient dream...
Eh!?

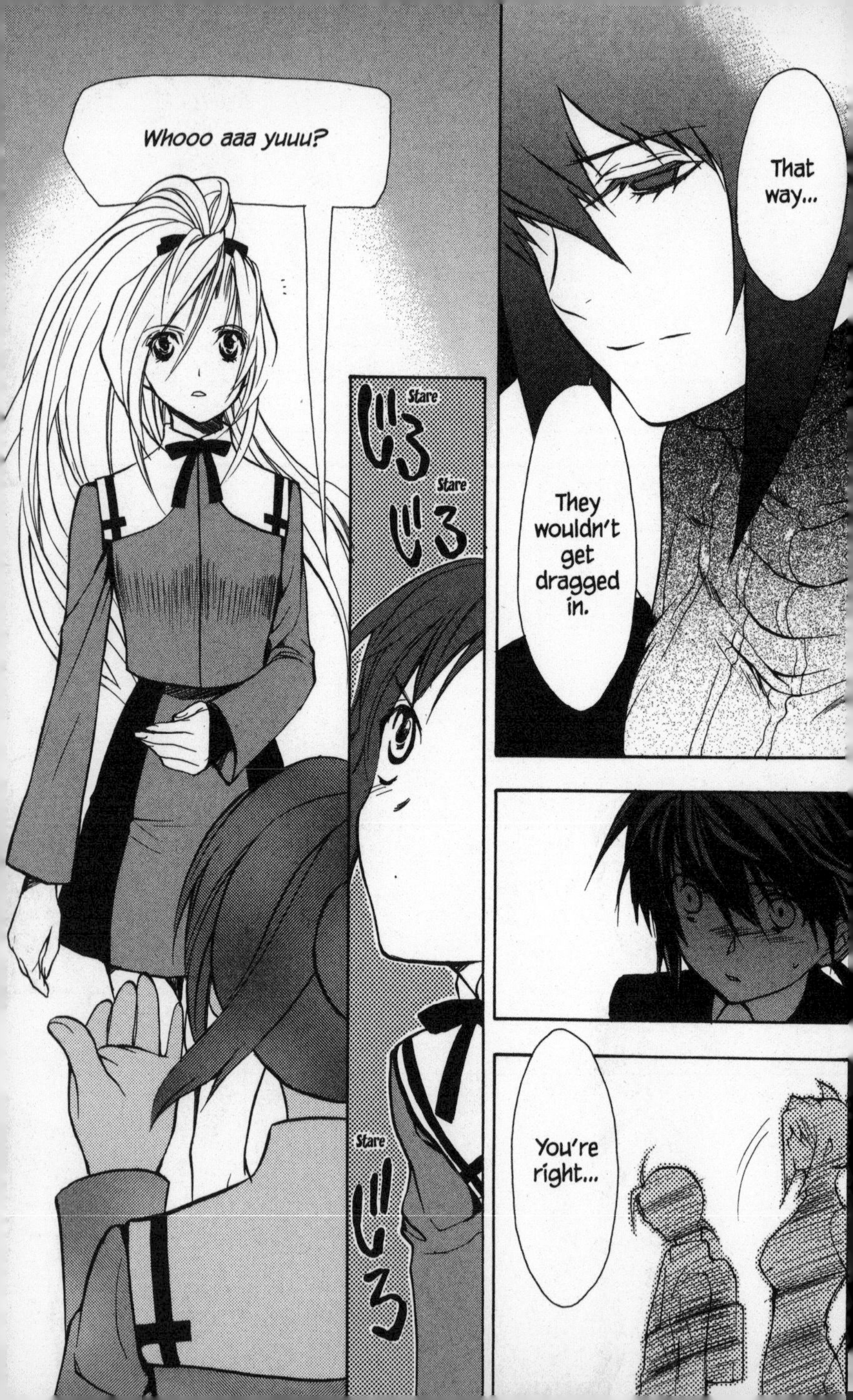

That way...
They wouldn't get dragged in.
You're right...
Whooo aaa yuuu?
じろ
Stare
じろ
Stare
じろ
Stare

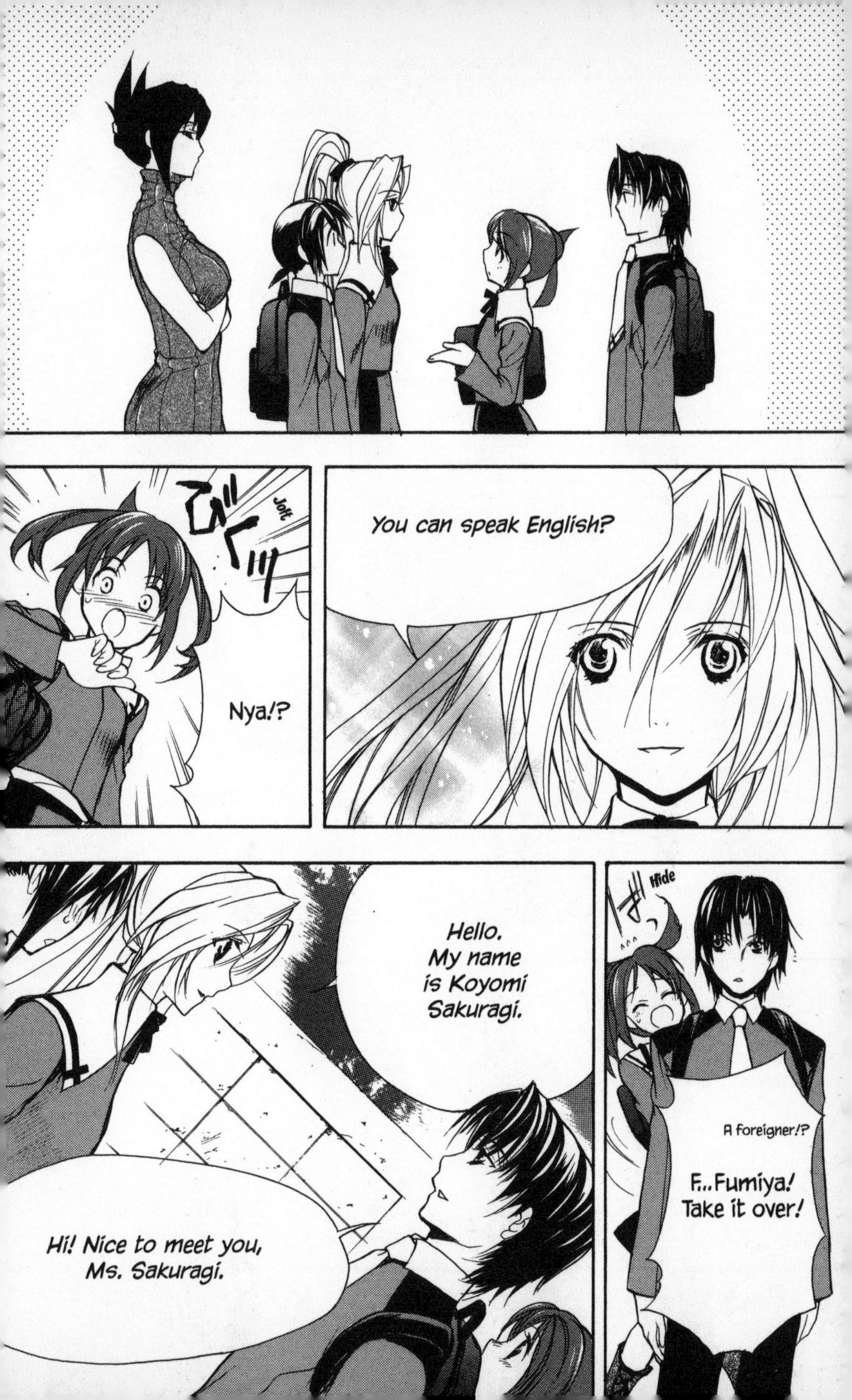
You can speak English?
Jolt
Nya!?
Hide
A foreigner!?
F...Fumiya! Take it over!
Hello. My name is Koyomi Sakuragi.
Hi! Nice to meet you, Ms. Sakuragi.

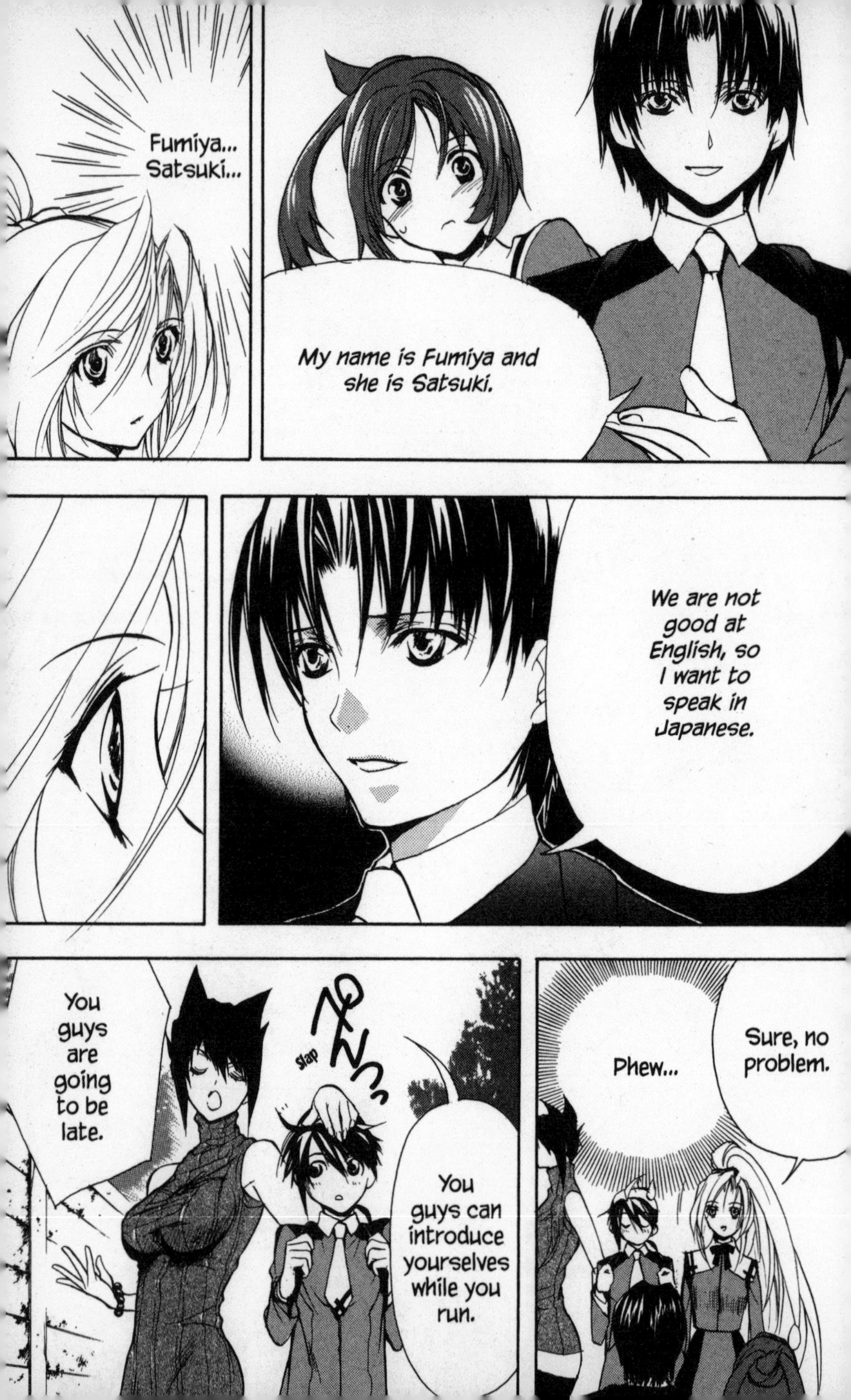
My name is Fumiya and she is Satsuki.
Fumiya... Satsuki...
We are not good at English, so I want to speak in Japanese.
Sure, no problem.
Phew...
You guys are going to be late.
Slap
You guys can introduce yourselves while you run.

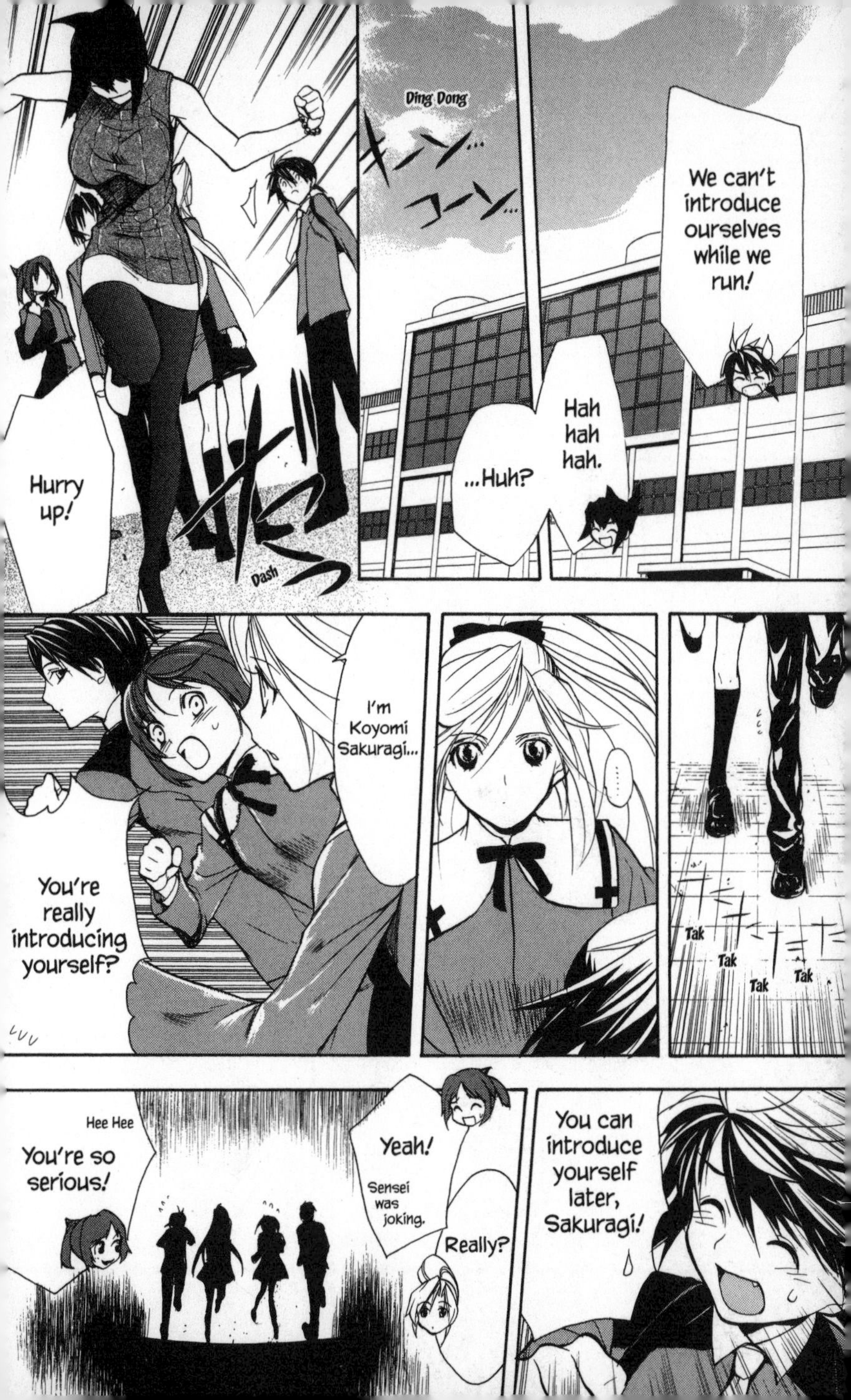
We can't introduce ourselves while we run!
Ding Dong
Hah hah hah.
...Huh?
Hurry up!
Dash
Tak
Tak
Tak
Tak
I'm Koyomi Sakuragi...
......
You're really introducing yourself?
You can introduce yourself later, Sakuragi!
Yeah!
Sensei was joking.
Really?
Hee Hee
You're so serious!

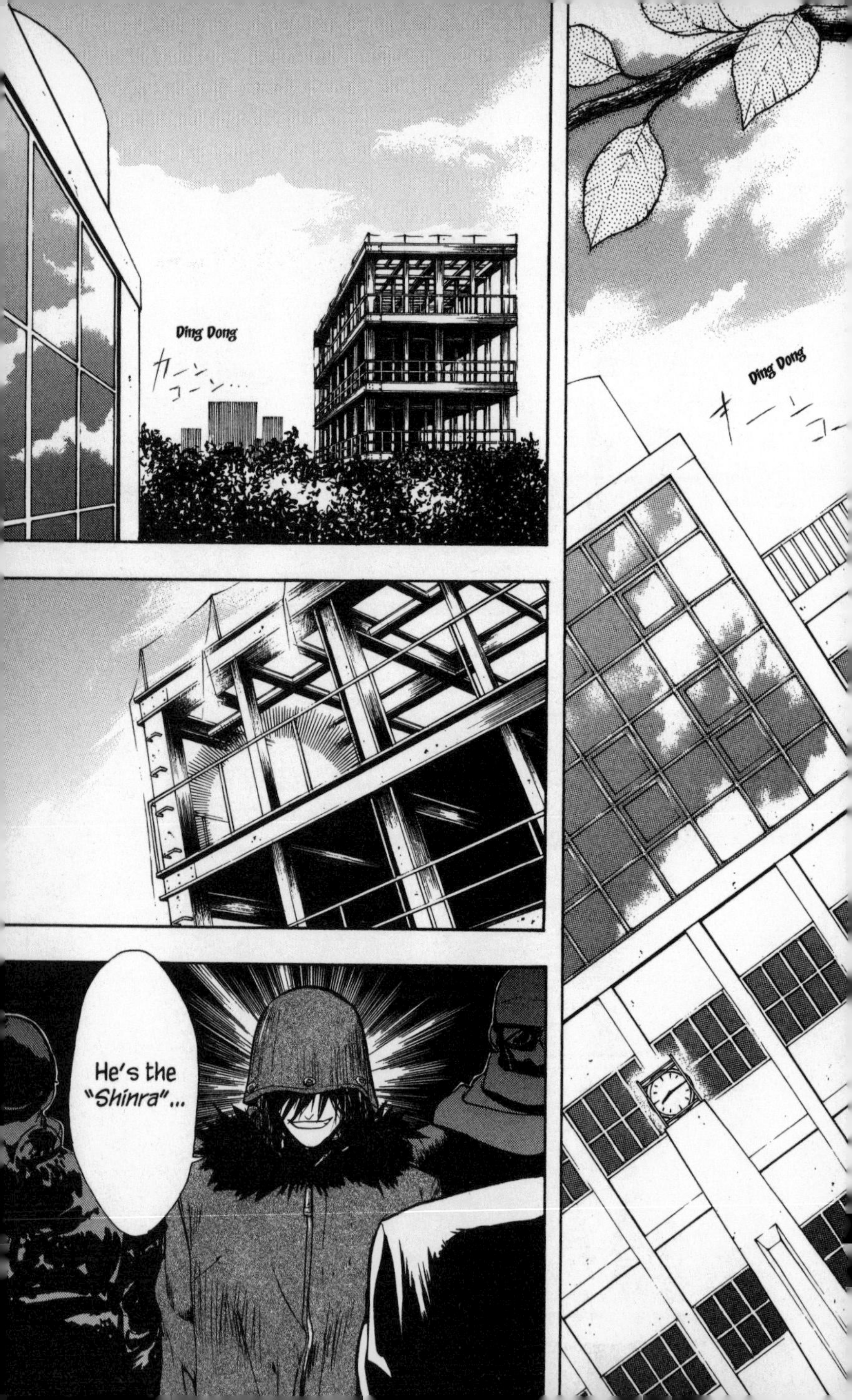
Ding Dong
Ding Dong
カーンコーン…
He's the "Shinra"...

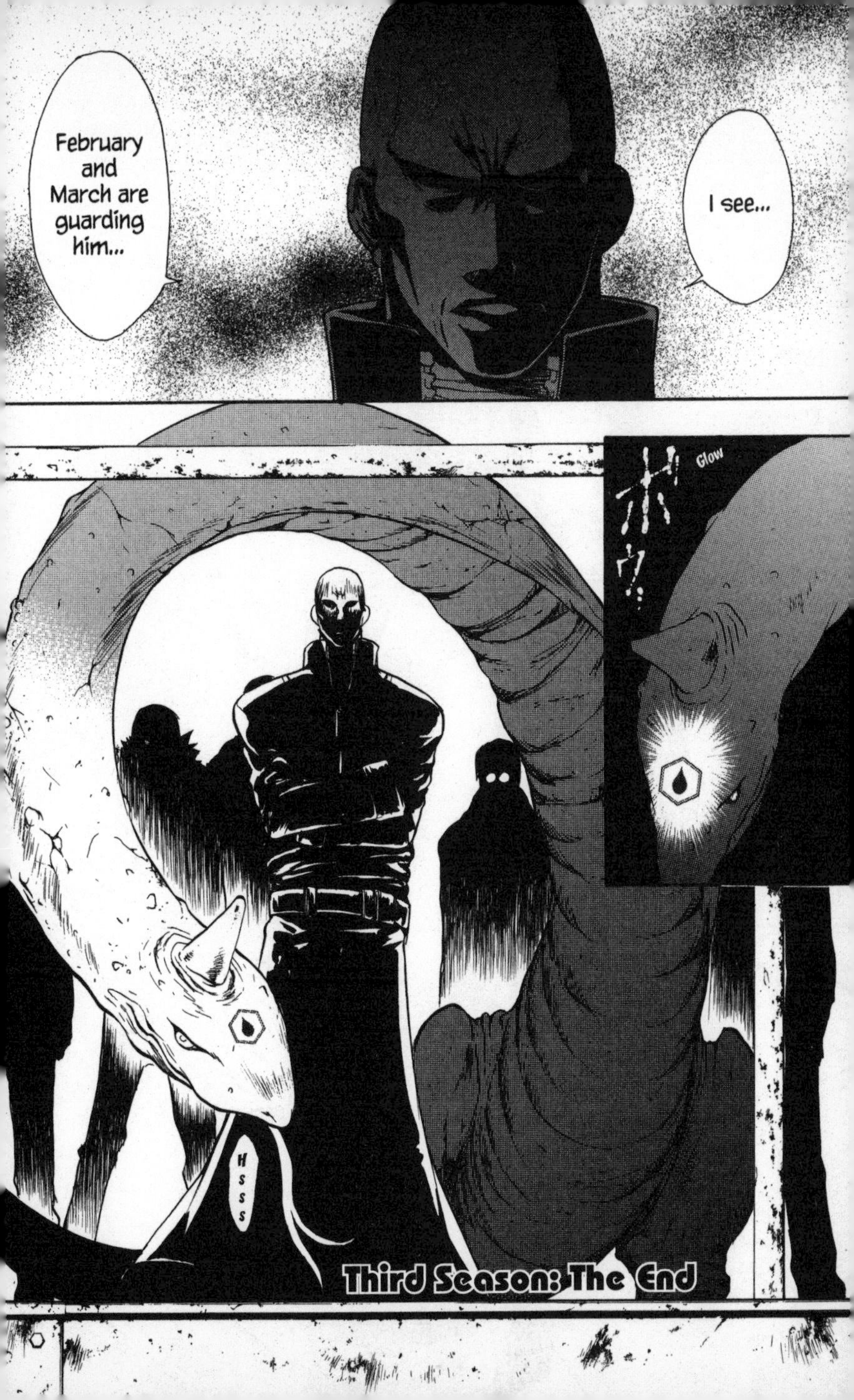
February and March are guarding him...
I see...
Glow
Hsss
Third Season: The End

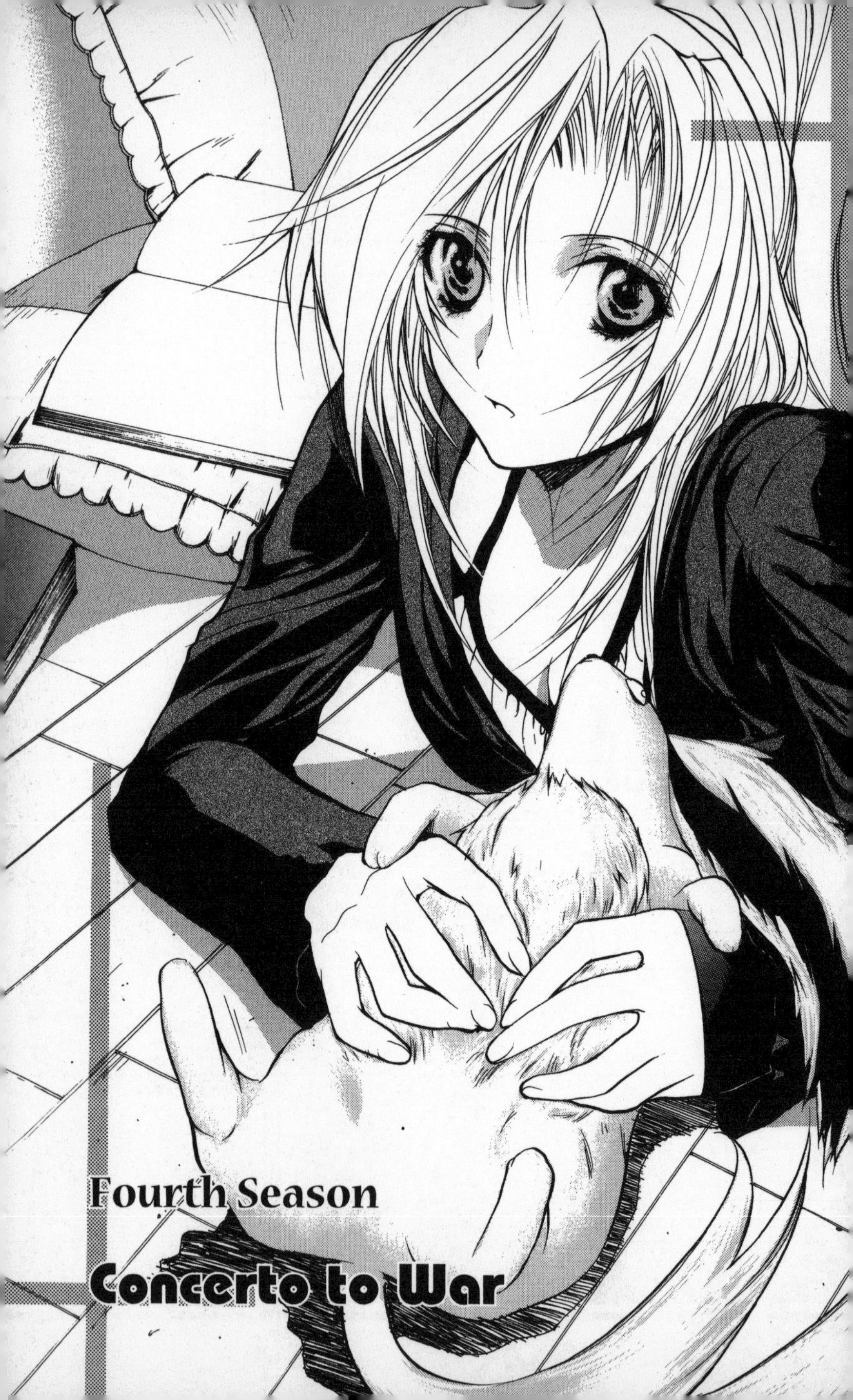
Fourth Season
Concerto to War

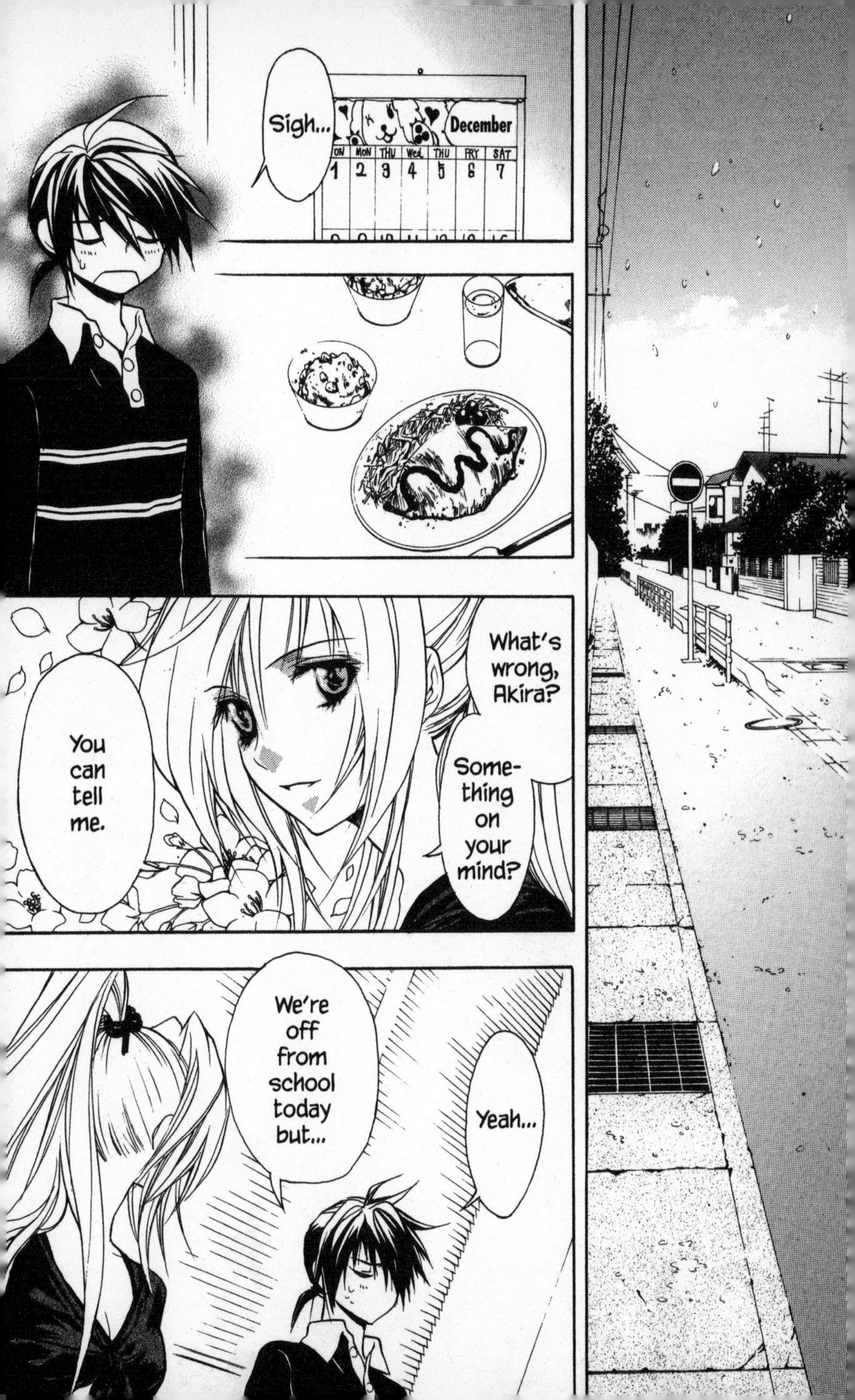
Sigh...
December
What's wrong, Akira?
Some-thing on your mind?
You can tell me.
We're off from school today but...
Yeah...

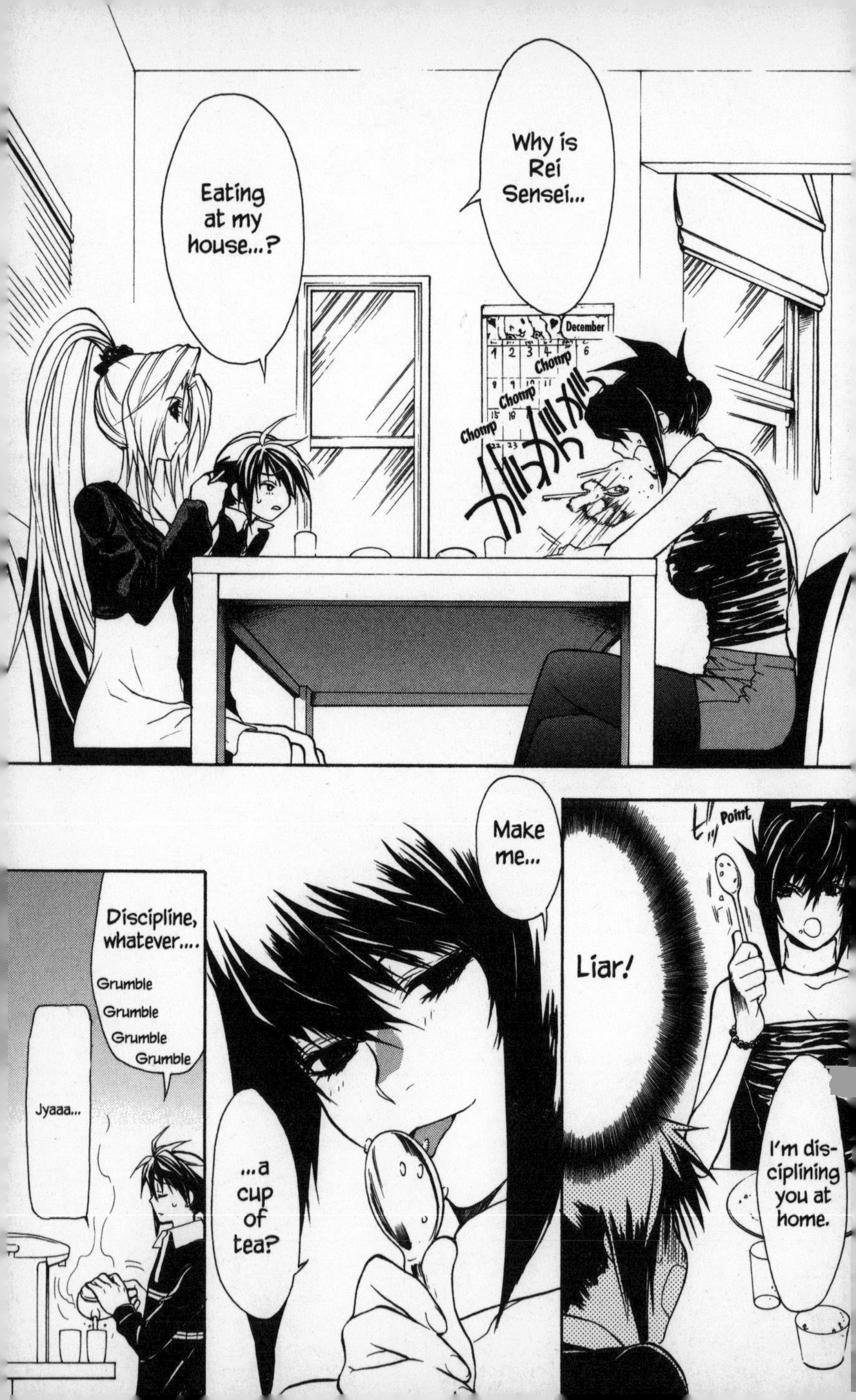
Why is Rei Sensei...
December
Chomp
Chomp
Chomp
Eating at my house...?
Point
Liar!
I'm disciplining you at home.
Make me...
...a cup of tea?
Discipline, whatever....
Grumble
Grumble
Grumble
Grumble
Jyaaa...

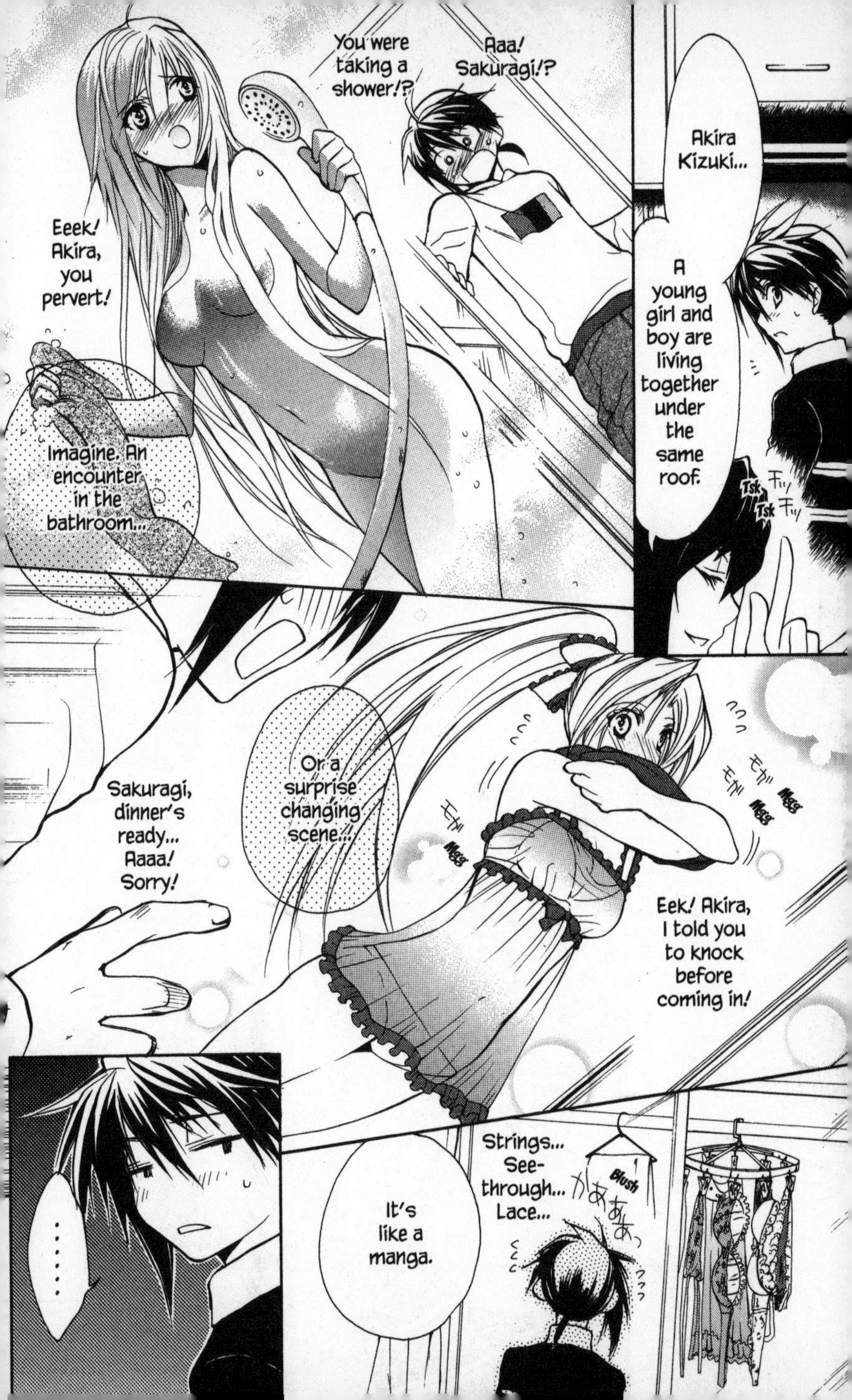

Akira Kizuki...
A young girl and boy are living together under the same roof.
Tsk
Tsk
Aaa! Sakuragi!?
You were taking a shower!?
Eeek! Akira, you pervert!
Imagine. An encounter in the bathroom...
Or a surprise changing scene...
Sakuragi, dinner's ready... Aaaa! Sorry!
Mgg
Mgg
Mgg
Eek! Akira, I told you to knock before coming in!
Strings... See-through... Lace...
Blush
It's like a manga.
......

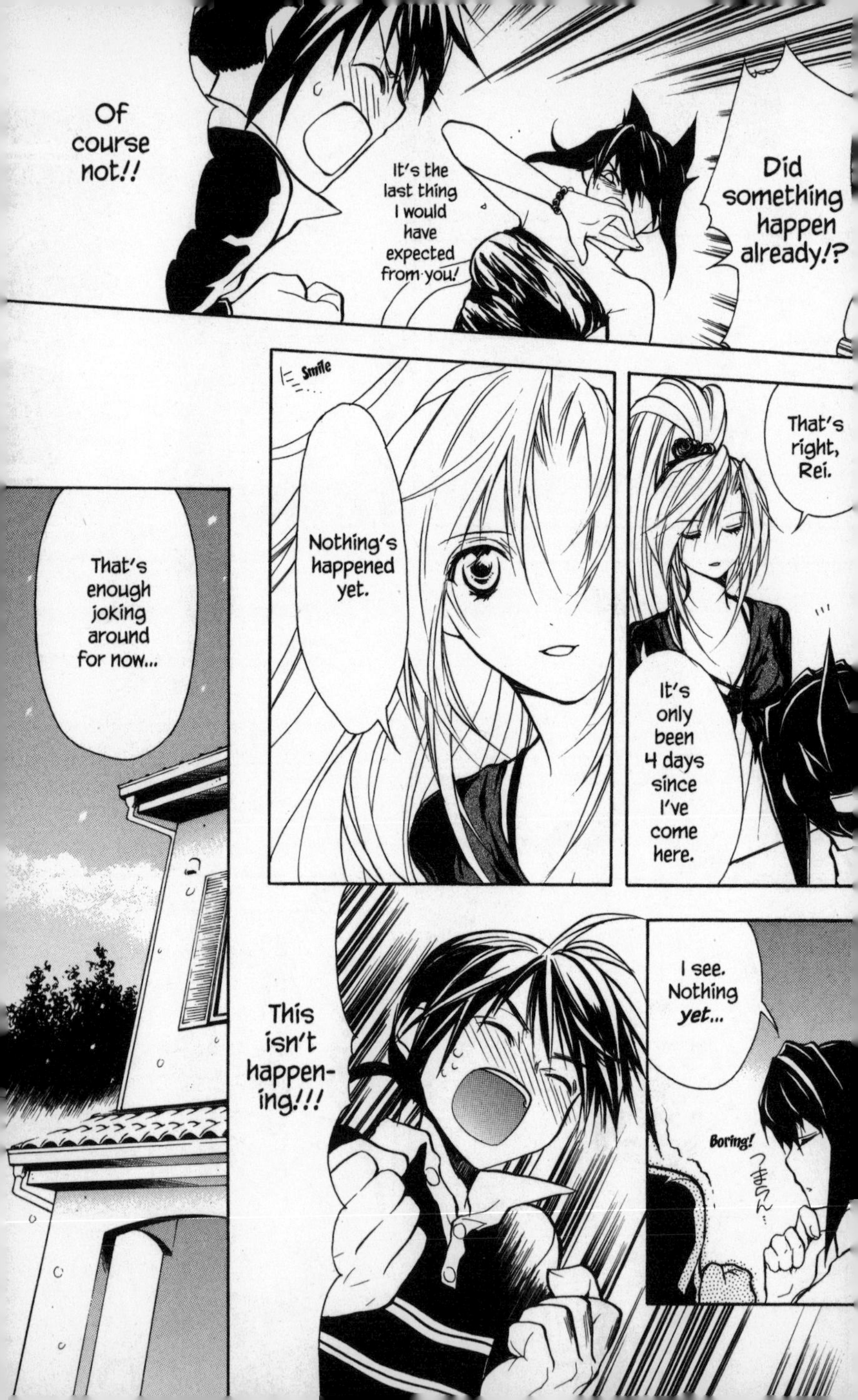
Did something happen already!?
It's the last thing I would have expected from you!
Of course not!!
That's right, Rei.
It's only been 4 days since I've come here.
Smile
Nothing's happened yet.
I see. Nothing *yet*...
Boring!
つまらん…
This isn't happening!!!
That's enough joking around for now...

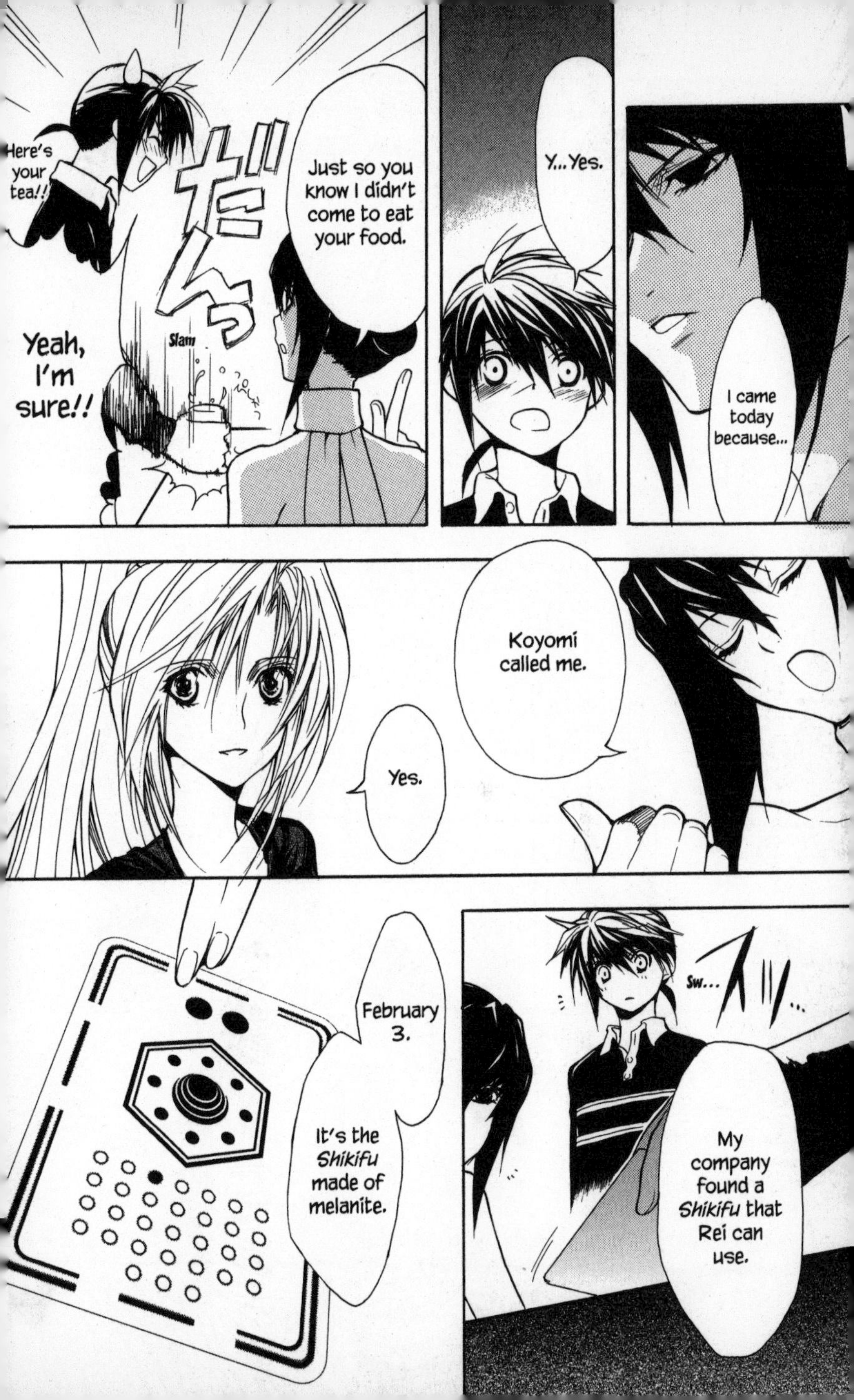
I came today because...
Y...Yes.
Just so you know I didn't come to eat your food.
Here's your tea!!
Slam
Yeah, I'm sure!!
Koyomi called me.
Yes.
Sw...
My company found a *Shikifu* that Rei can use.
February 3.
It's the *Shikifu* made of melanite.

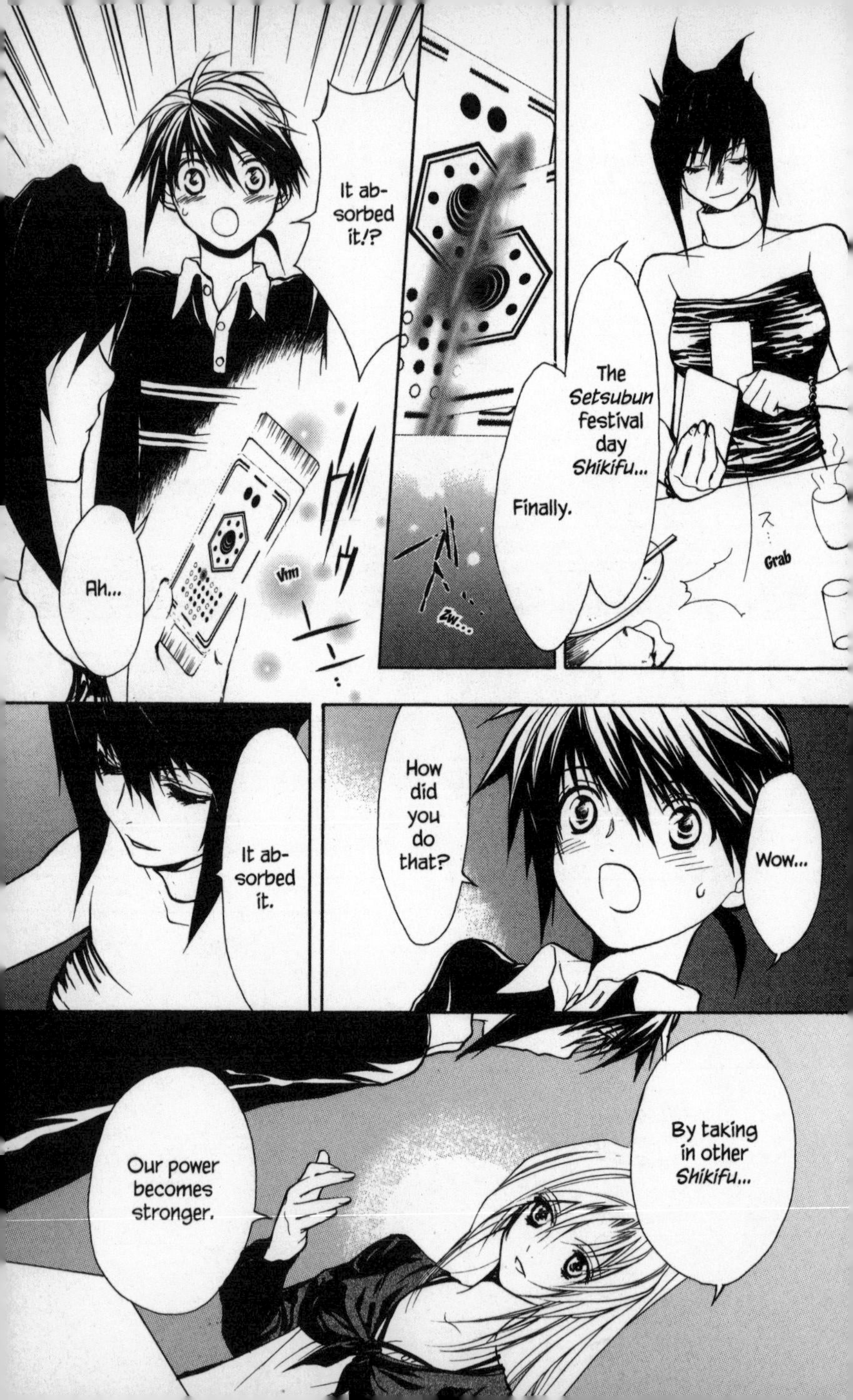
The Setsubun festival day Shikifu...
Finally.
Grab
Zw...
It absorbed it!?
Vm
Ah...
Wow...
How did you do that?
It absorbed it.
By taking in other Shikifu...
Our power becomes stronger.

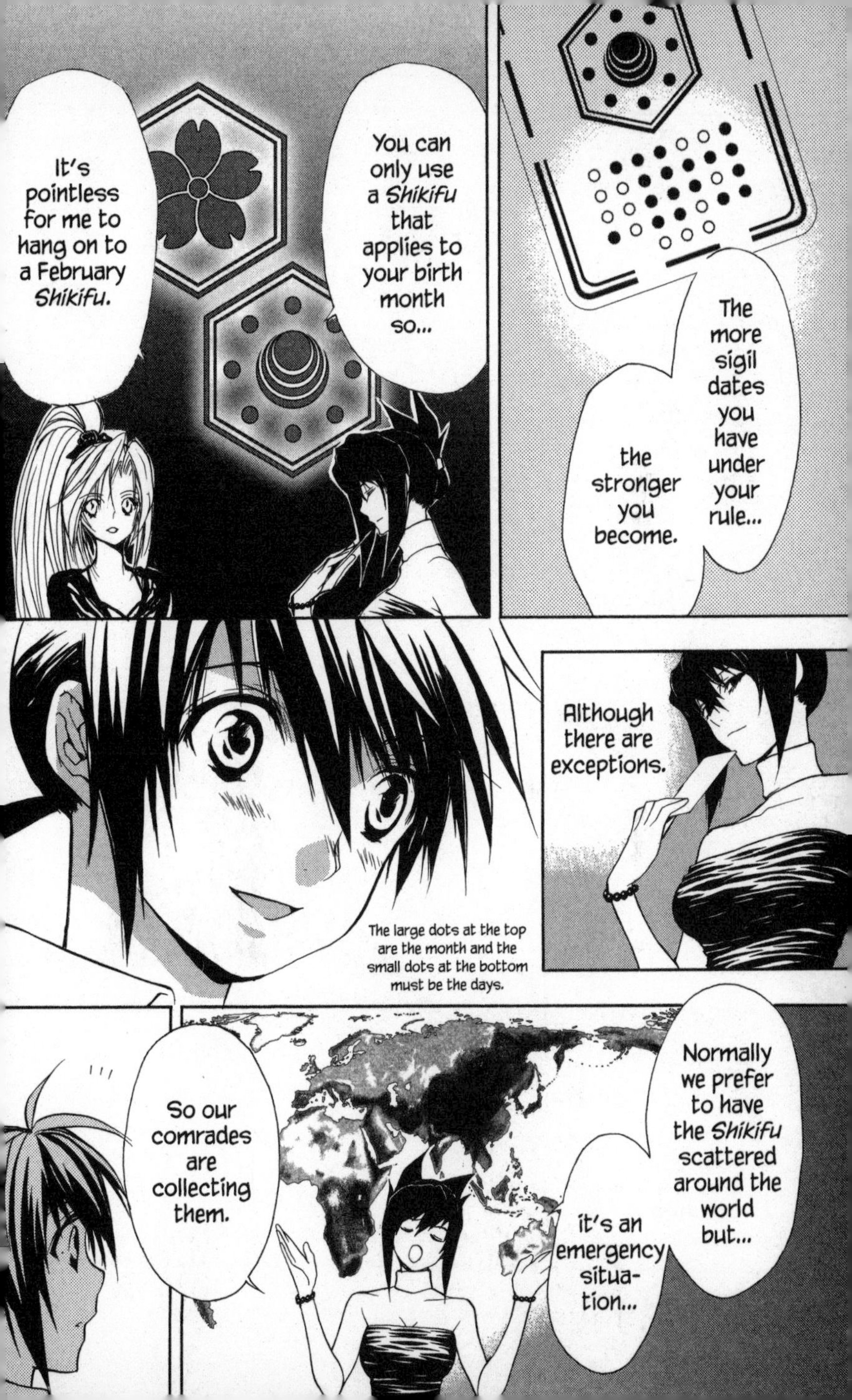
The more sigil dates you have under your rule...
the stronger you become.
You can only use a *Shikifu* that applies to your birth month so...
It's pointless for me to hang on to a February *Shikifu*.
Although there are exceptions.
The large dots at the top are the month and the small dots at the bottom must be the days.
Normally we prefer to have the *Shikifu* scattered around the world but...
it's an emergency situation...
So our comrades are collecting them.

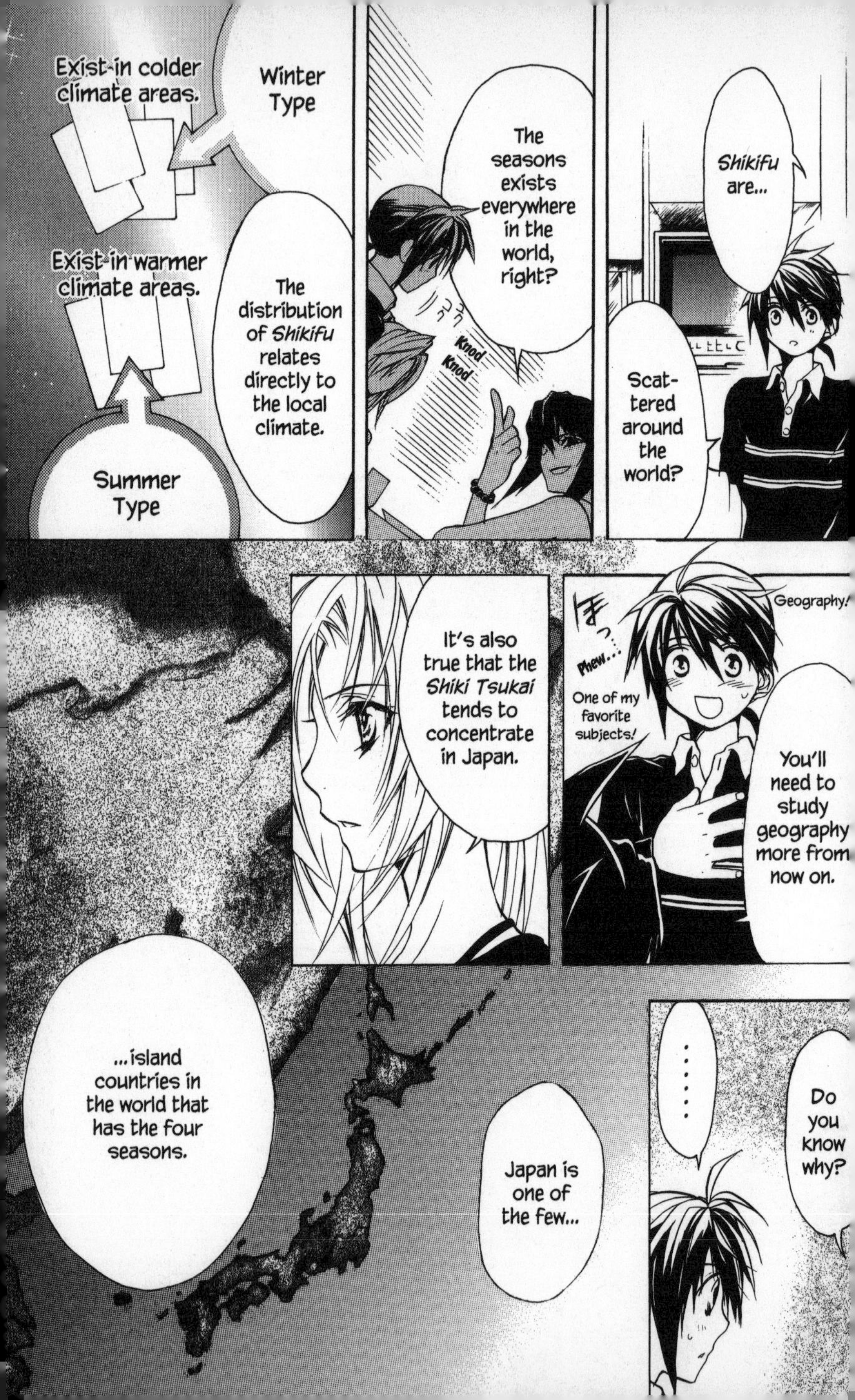
Shikifu are...
Scat-tered around the world?
The seasons exists everywhere in the world, right?
Knod
Knod
Winter Type
Exist in colder climate areas.
The distribution of Shikifu relates directly to the local climate.
Exist in warmer climate areas.
Summer Type
Geography!
Phew...
One of my favorite subjects!
You'll need to study geography more from now on.
It's also true that the Shiki Tsukai tends to concentrate in Japan.
Do you know why?
......
Japan is one of the few...
...island countries in the world that has the four seasons.

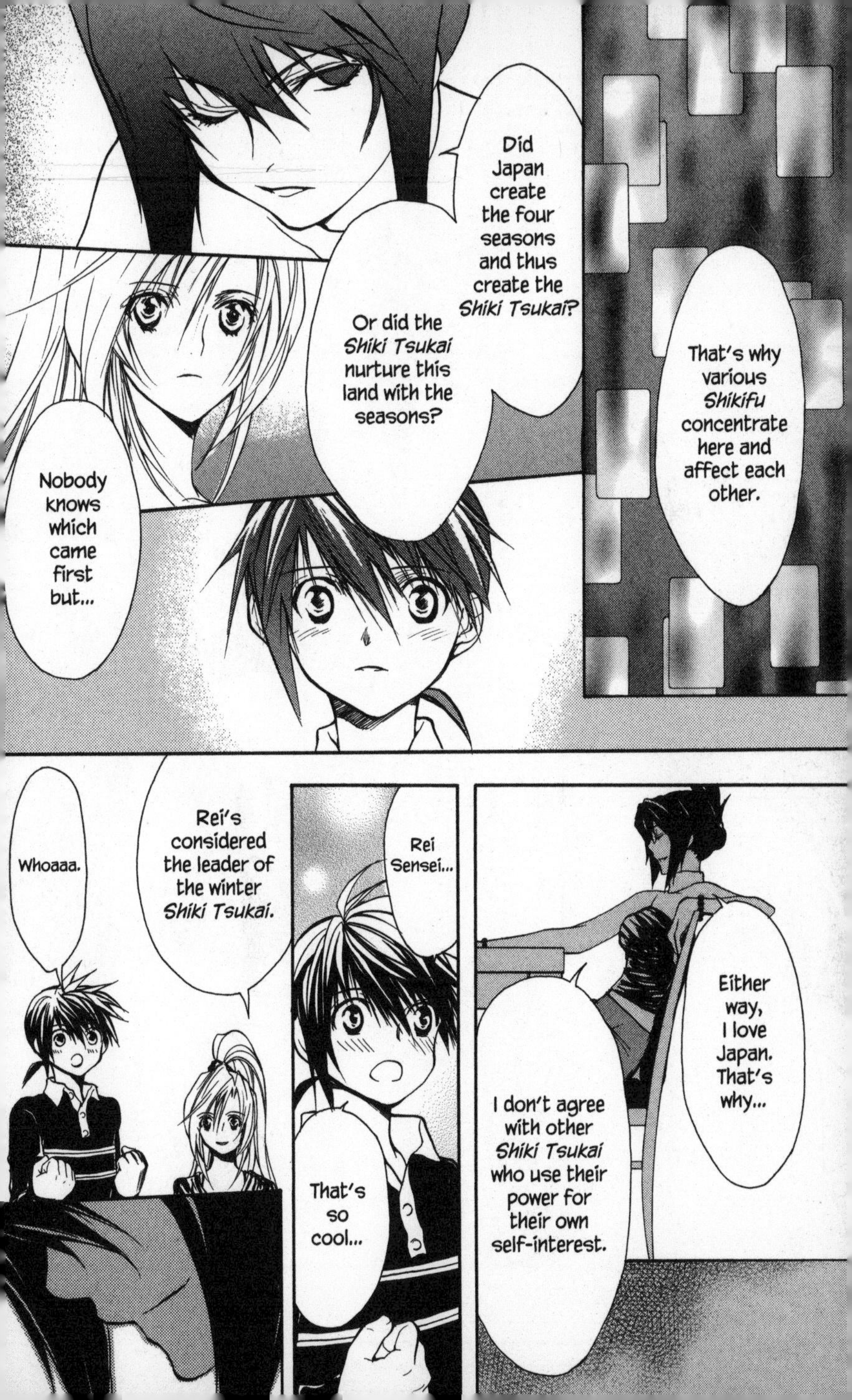

Did Japan create the four seasons and thus create the *Shiki Tsukai*?
Or did the *Shiki Tsukai* nurture this land with the seasons?
Nobody knows which came first but...
That's why various *Shikifu* concentrate here and affect each other.
Either way, I love Japan. That's why...
I don't agree with other *Shiki Tsukai* who use their power for their own self-interest.
Rei Sensei...
That's so cool...
Rei's considered the leader of the winter *Shiki Tsukai*.
Whoaaa.

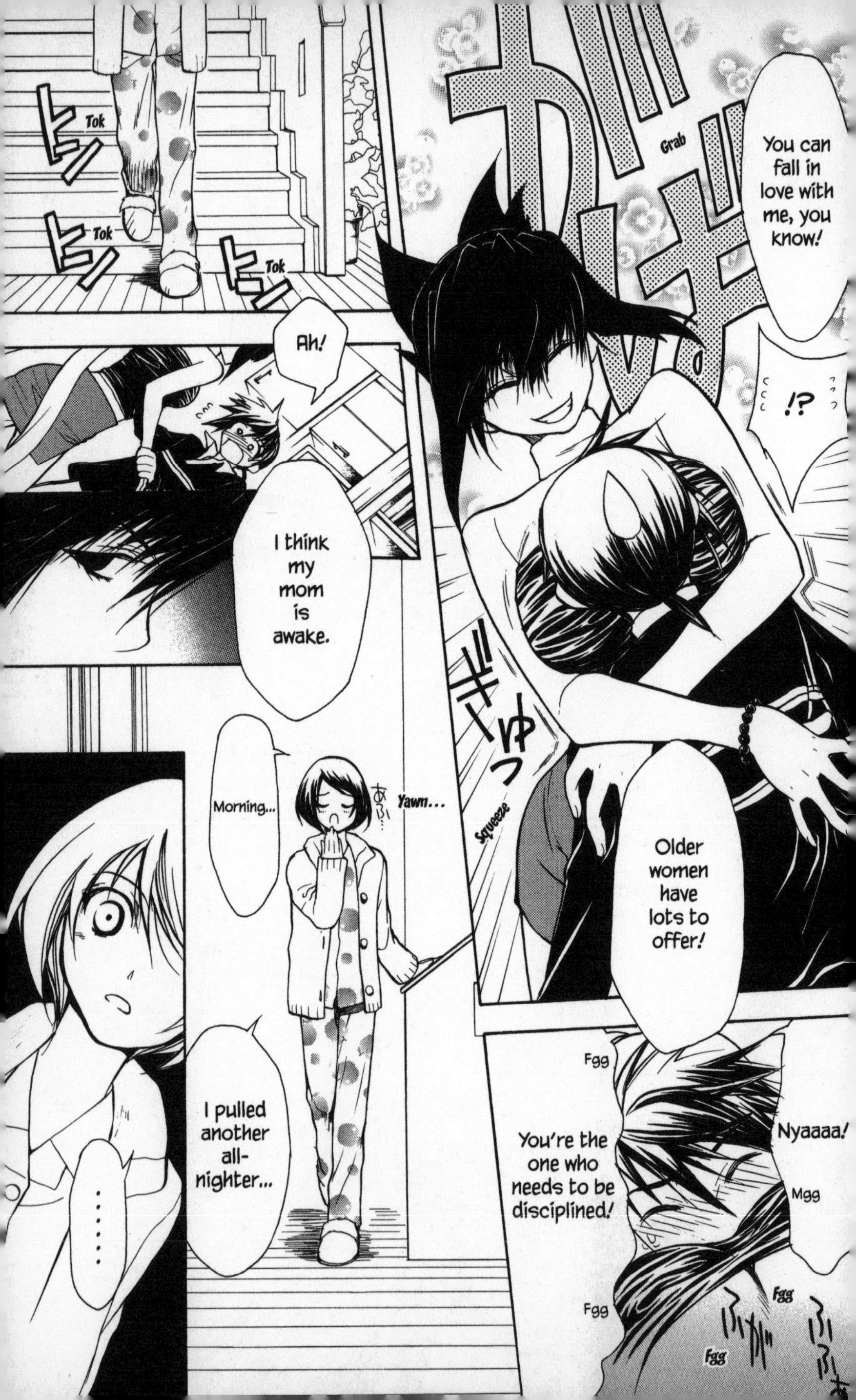

Grab
You can fall in love with me, you know!
!?
Older women have lots to offer!
Squeeze
Tok
Tok
Tok
Ah!
I think my mom is awake.
Nyaaaa!
Fgg
Mgg
You're the one who needs to be disciplined!
Fgg
Fgg
Fgg
Yawn...
Morning...
I pulled another all-nighter...
......

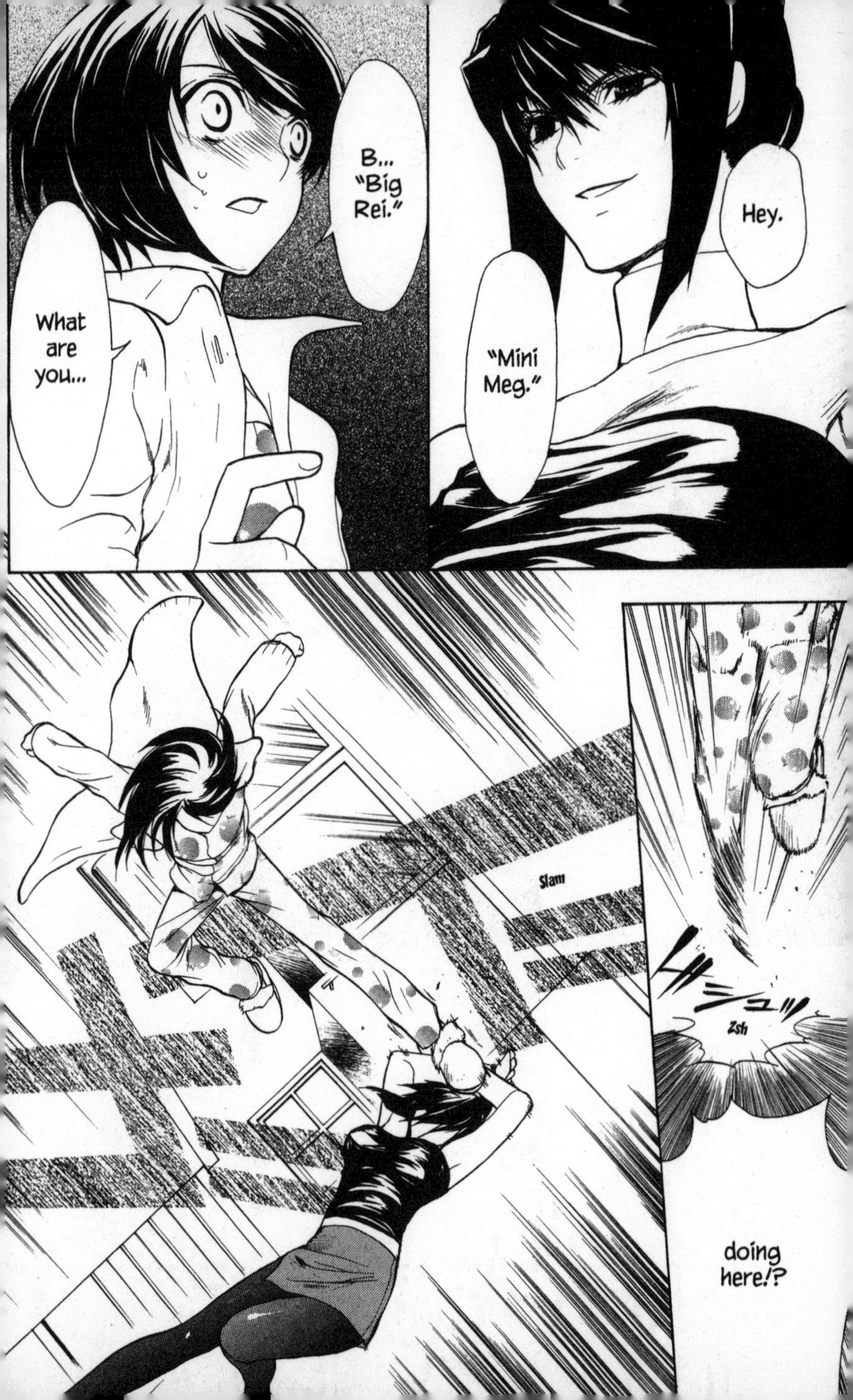
Hey.
"Mini Meg."
B... "Big Rei."
What are you...
Zsh
doing here!?
Slam

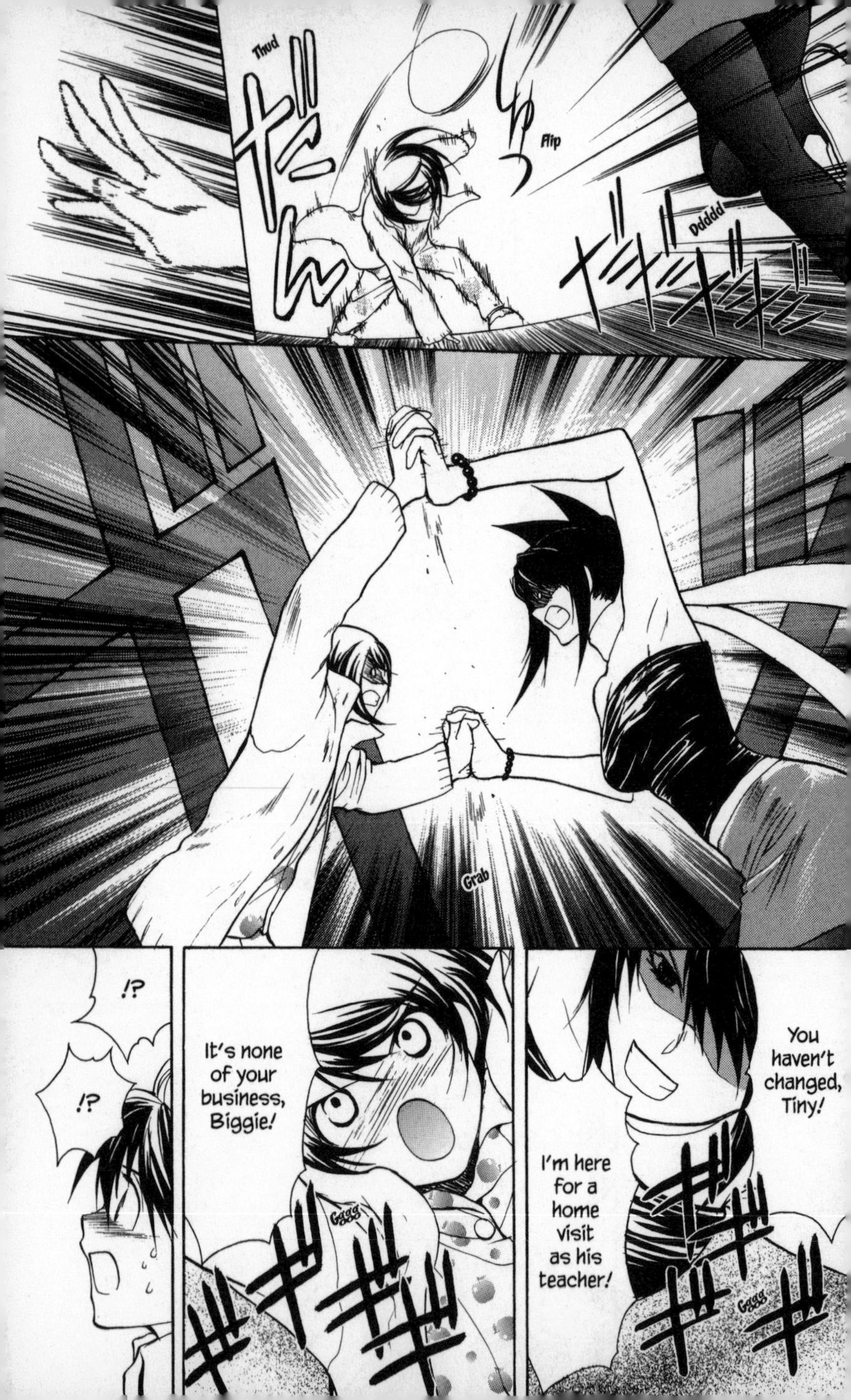

Flip
Ddddd
Thud
Grab
You haven't changed, Tiny!
I'm here for a home visit as his teacher!
Gagg
It's none of your business, Biggie!
Gagg
!?
!?

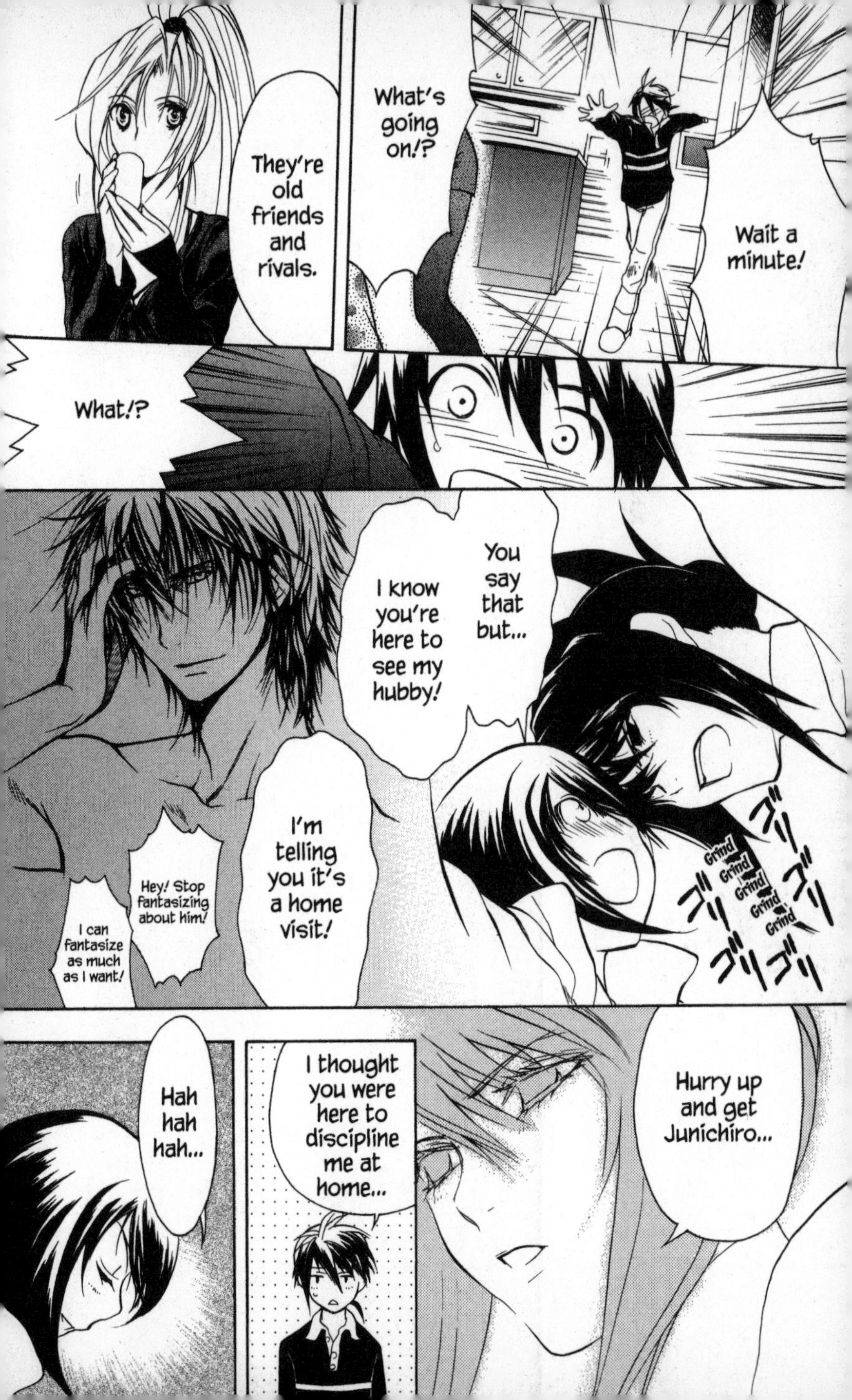
Wait a minute!
What's going on!?
They're old friends and rivals.
What!?
You say that but...
I know you're here to see my hubby!
ゴリゴリ
Grind Grind Grind Grind Grind
ゴリゴリ
I'm telling you it's a home visit!
Hey! Stop fantasizing about him!
I can fantasize as much as I want!
Hurry up and get Junichiro...
I thought you were here to discipline me at home...
Hah hah hah...

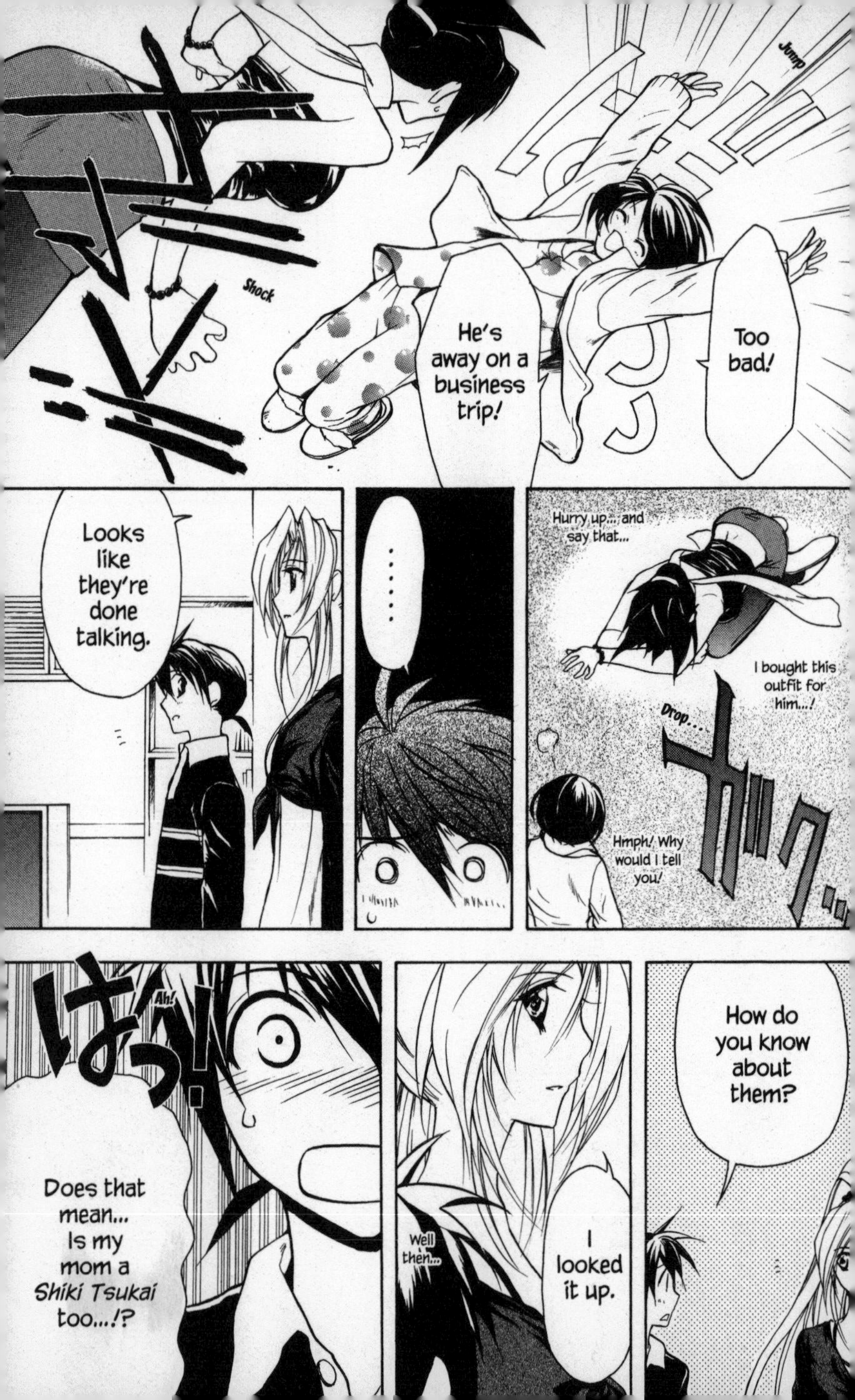
Jump
Too bad!
He's away on a business trip!
Shock
Hurry up... and say that...
I bought this outfit for him...!
Drop...
Hmph! Why would I tell you!
......
Looks like they're done talking.
How do you know about them?
I looked it up.
Well then...
Ah!
Does that mean... Is my mom a Shiki Tsukai too...!?

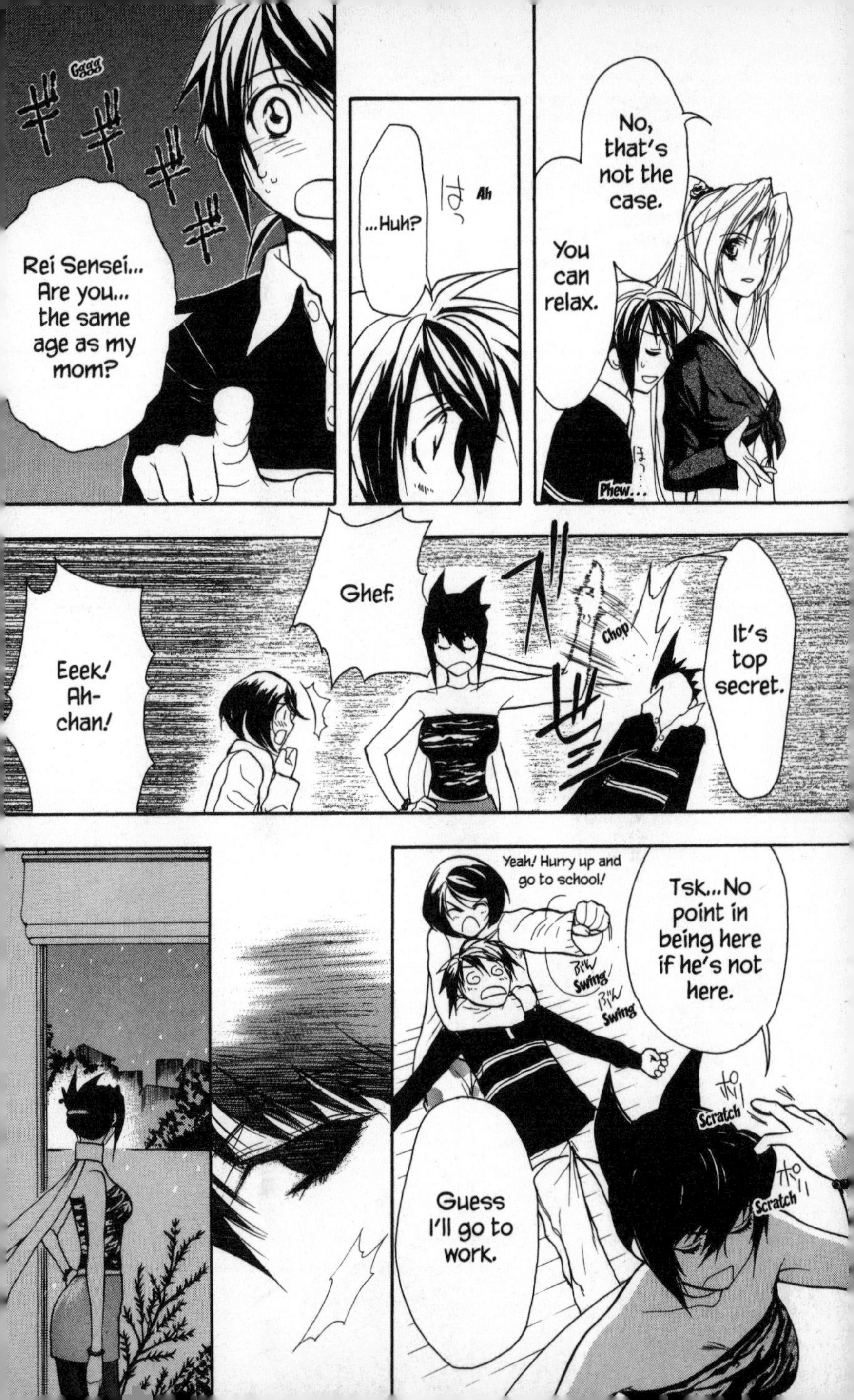
No, that's not the case.
You can relax.
Phew...
...Huh?
Ah
Rei Sensei... Are you... the same age as my mom?
It's top secret.
Chop
Ghef.
Eeek! Ah-chan!
Tsk...No point in being here if he's not here.
Yeah! Hurry up and go to school!
Swing
Swing
Scratch
Scratch
Guess I'll go to work.

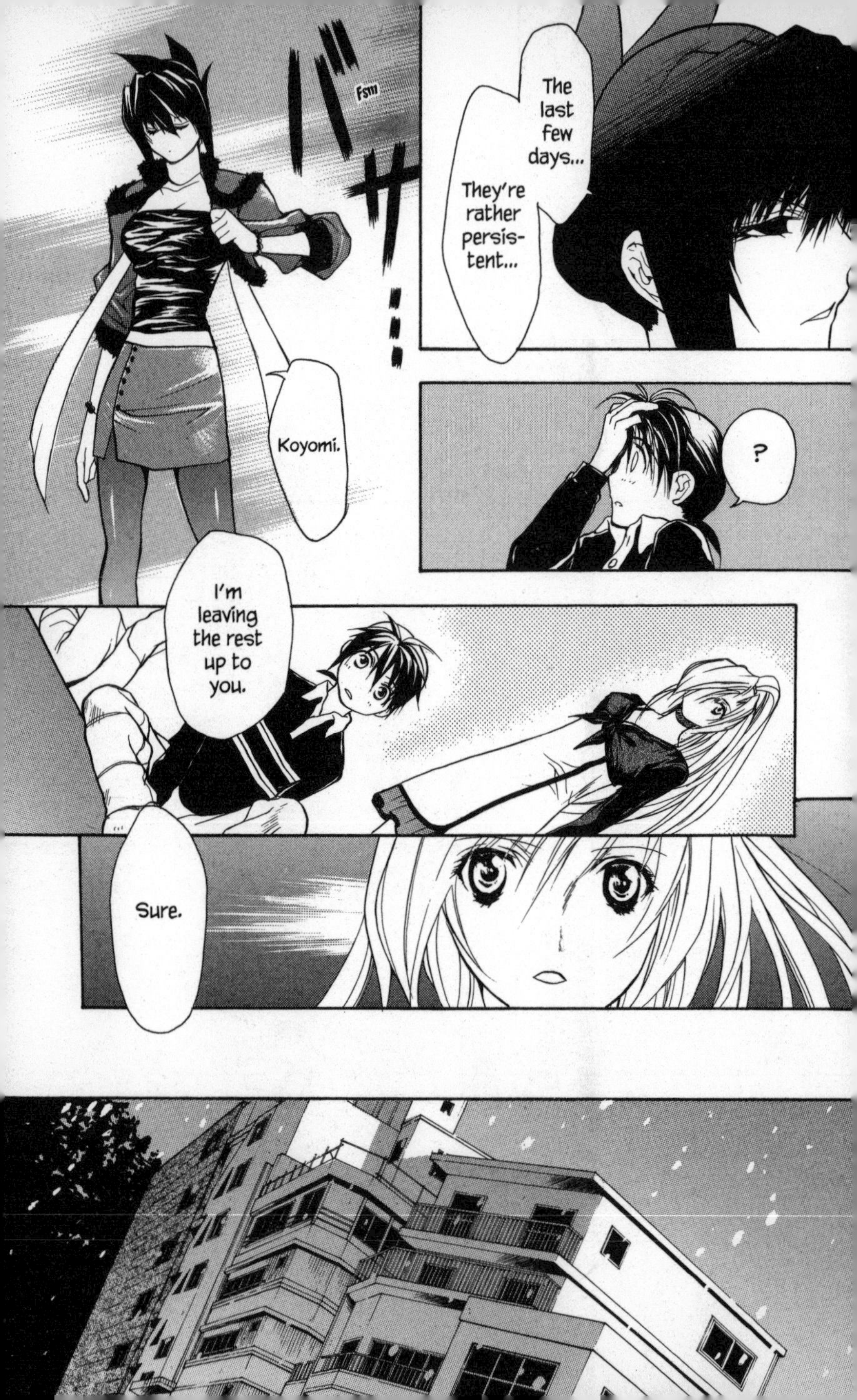
The last few days...
They're rather persistent...
?
バサ
Fsm
Koyomi.
I'm leaving the rest up to you.
Sure.

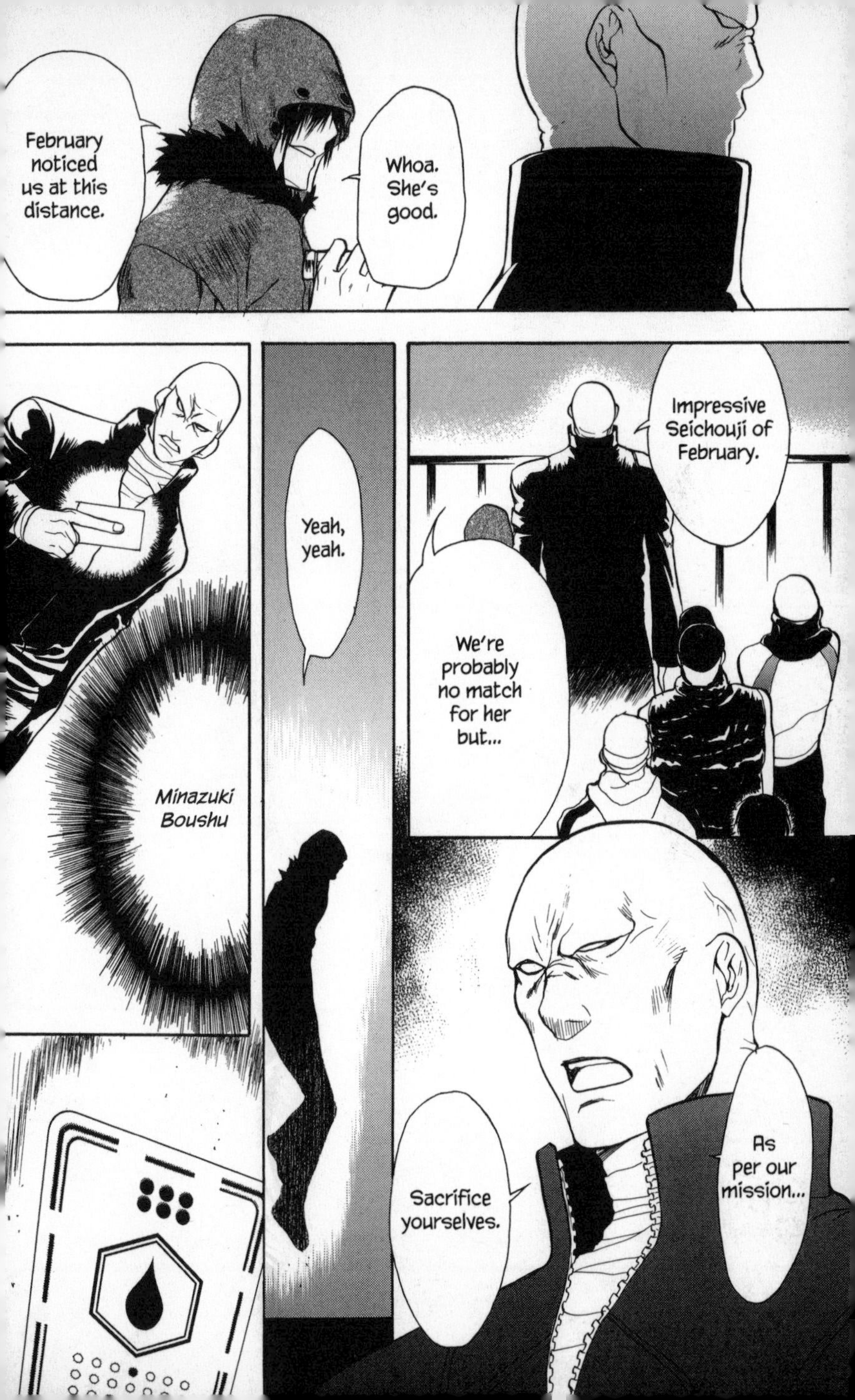
Whoa. She's good.
February noticed us at this distance.
Impressive Seichouji of February.
We're probably no match for her but...
As per our mission...
Sacrifice yourselves.
Yeah, yeah.
Minazuki Boushu

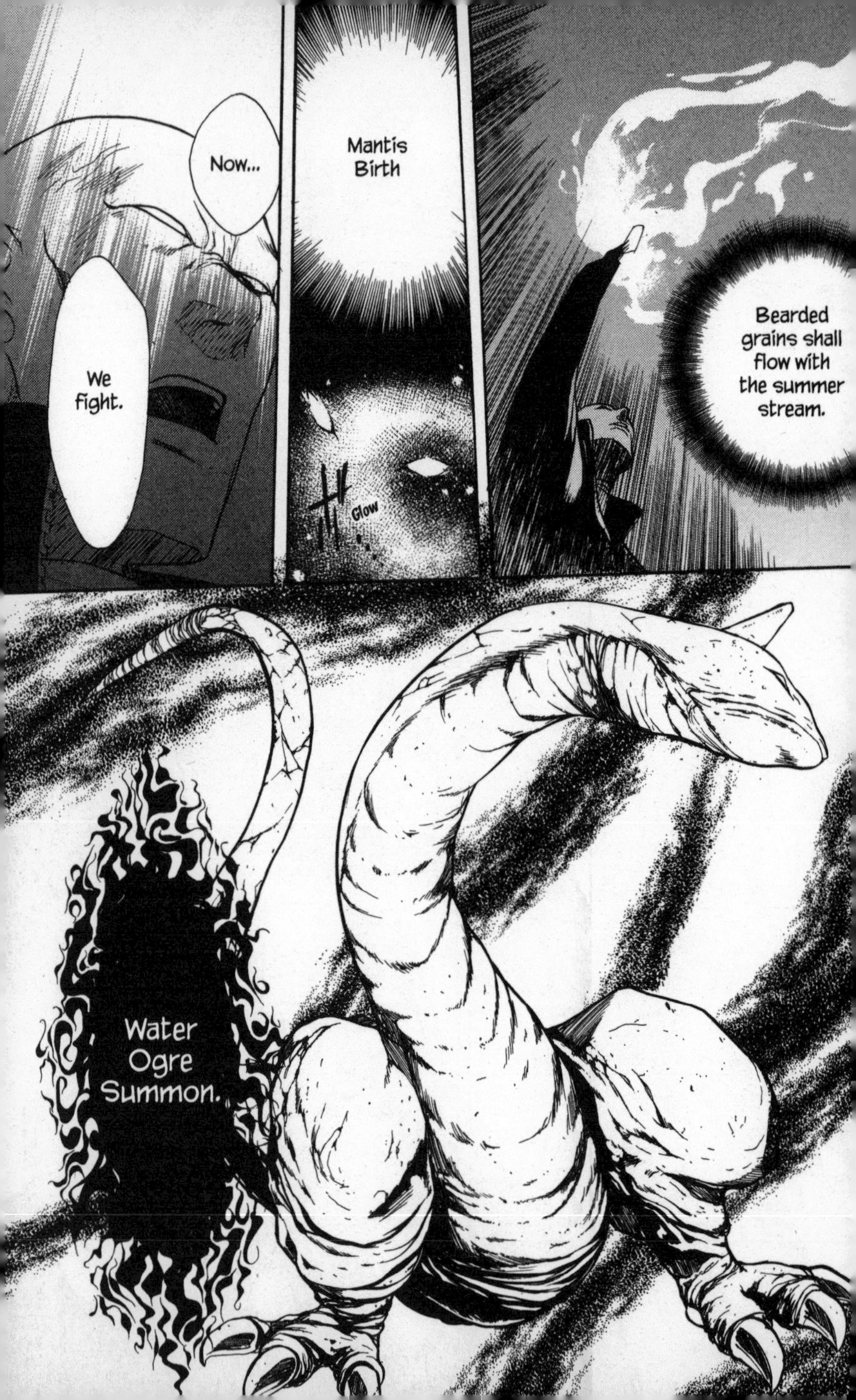
Bearded grains shall flow with the summer stream.
Mantis Birth
Glow
Now...
We fight.
Water Ogre Summon.

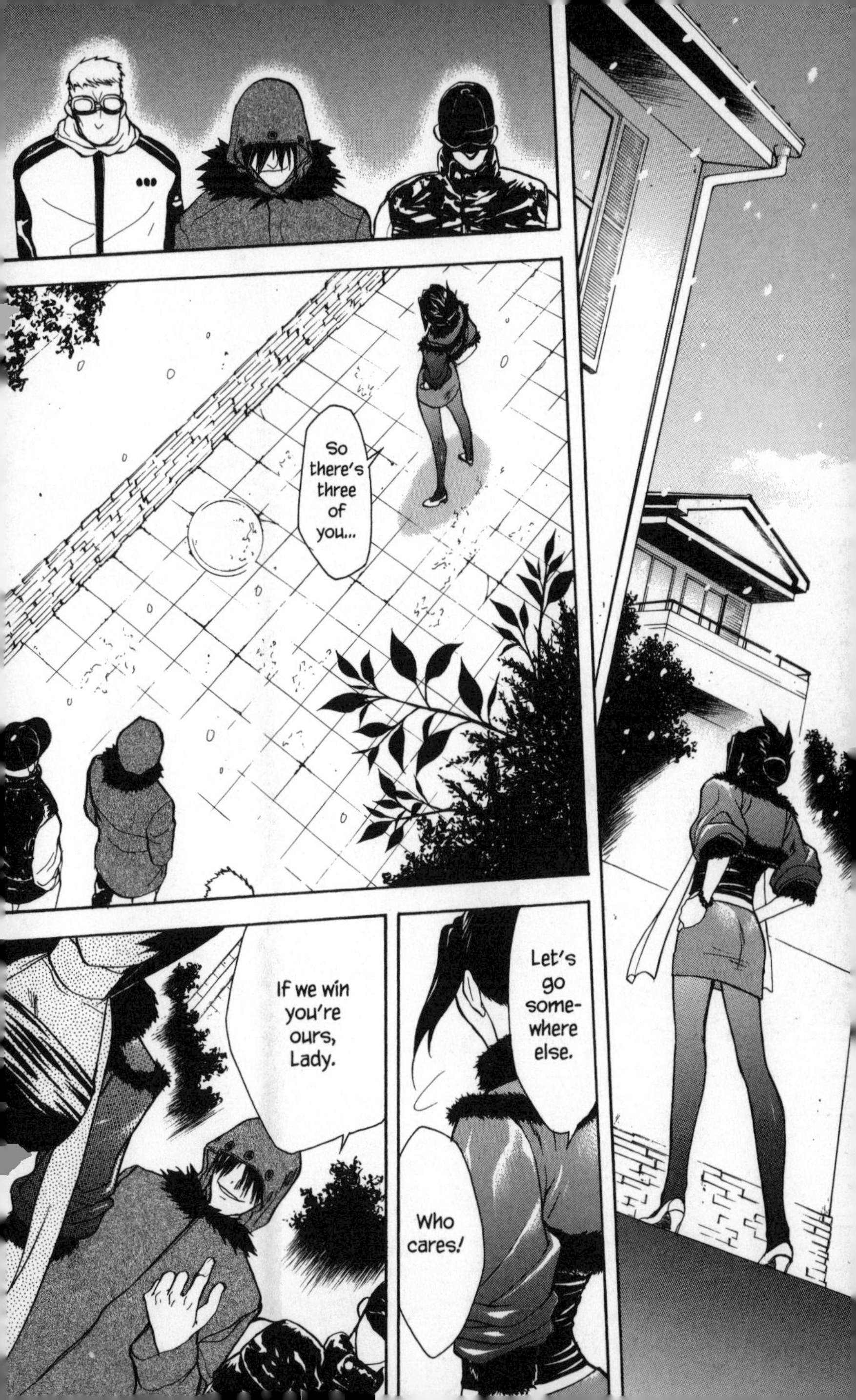
So there's three of you...
Let's go somewhere else.
Who cares!
If we win you're ours, Lady.

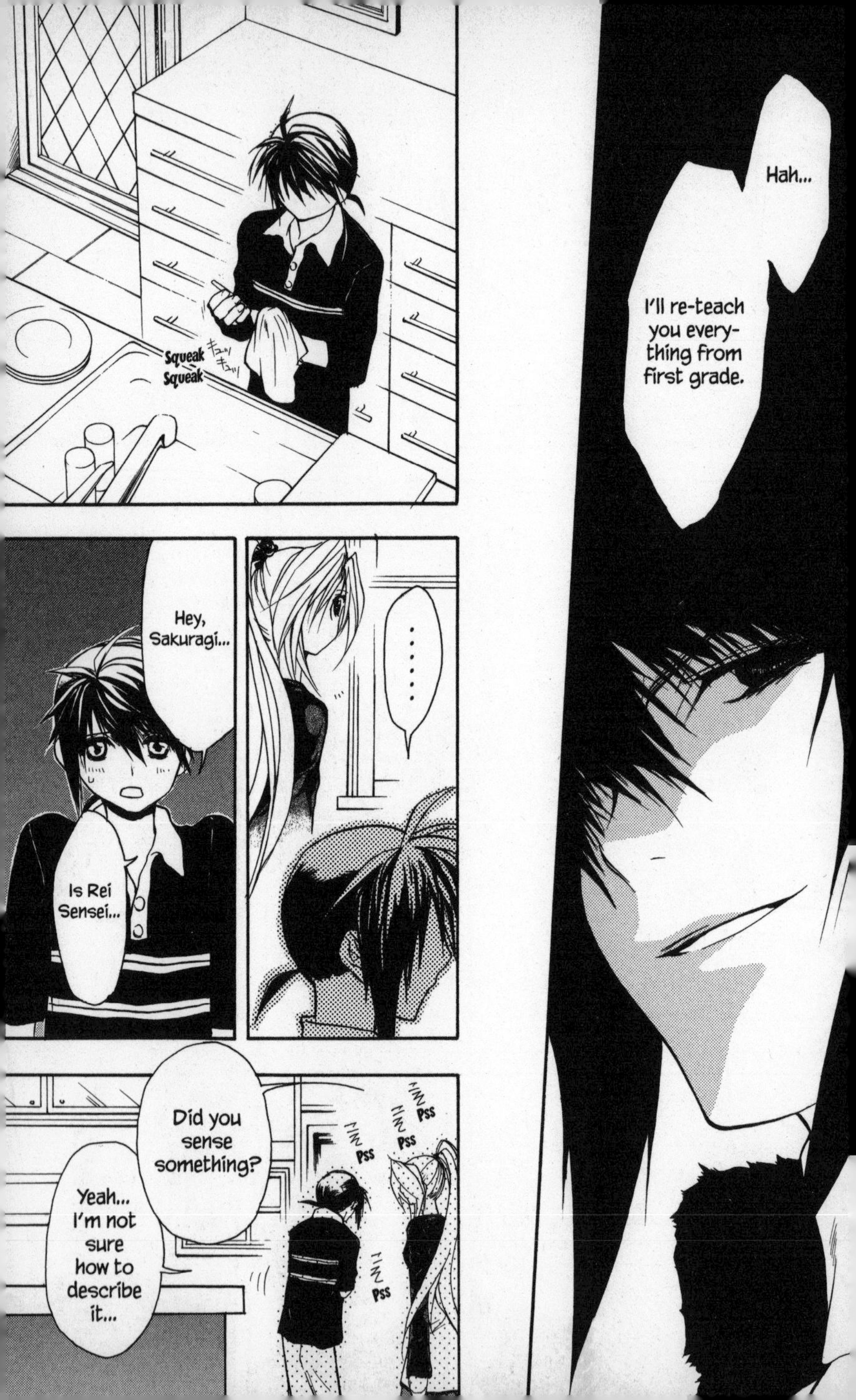
Hah...
I'll re-teach you every-thing from first grade.
Squeak Squeak
キュッ キュッ
......
Hey, Sakuragi...
Is Rei Sensei...
Pss Pss Pss Pss
Did you sense something?
Yeah... I'm not sure how to describe it...

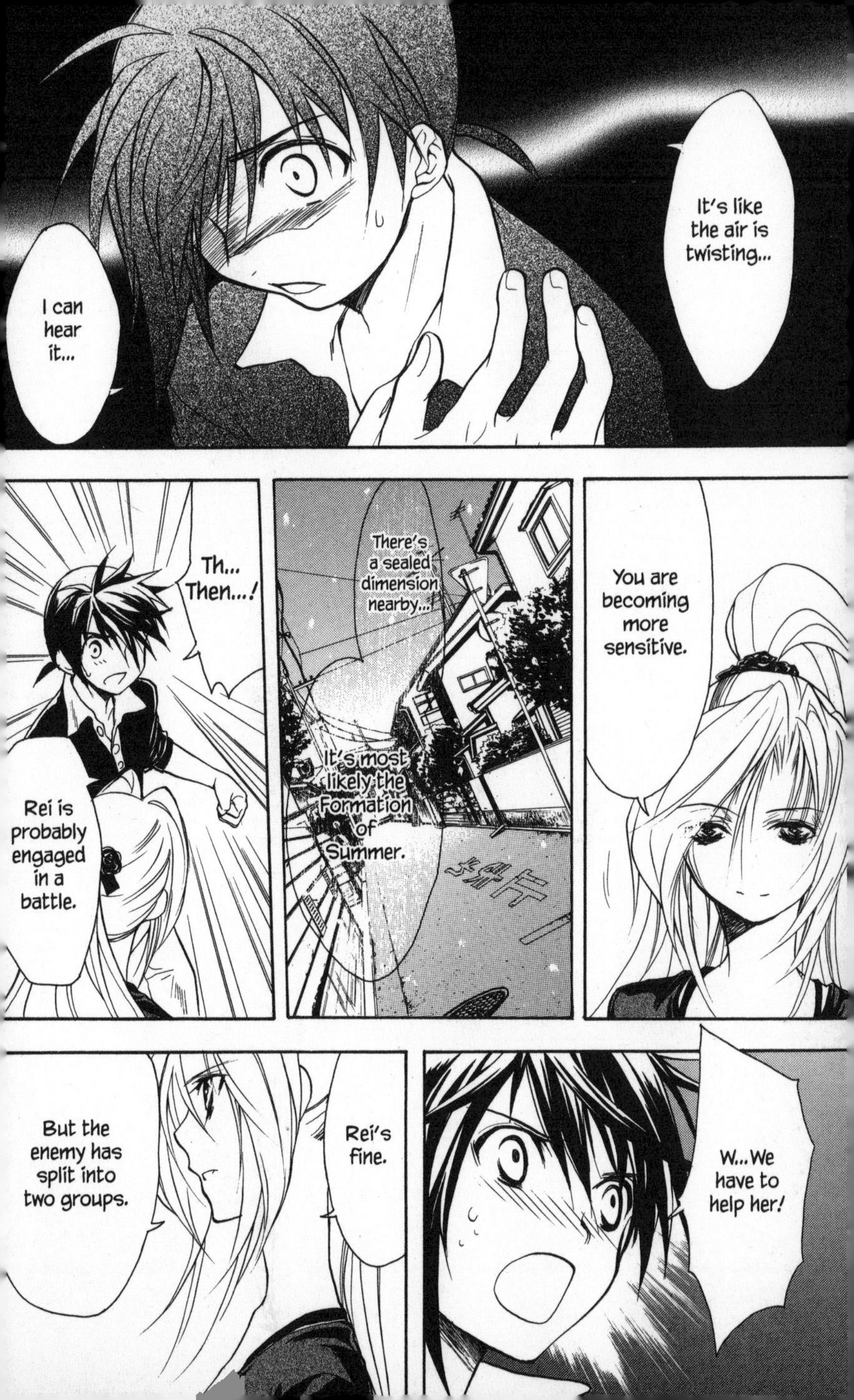
It's like the air is twisting...
I can hear it...
You are becoming more sensitive.
There's a sealed dimension nearby...
It's most likely the Formation of Summer.
Th... Then...!
Rei is probably engaged in a battle.
W...We have to help her!
Rei's fine.
But the enemy has split into two groups.

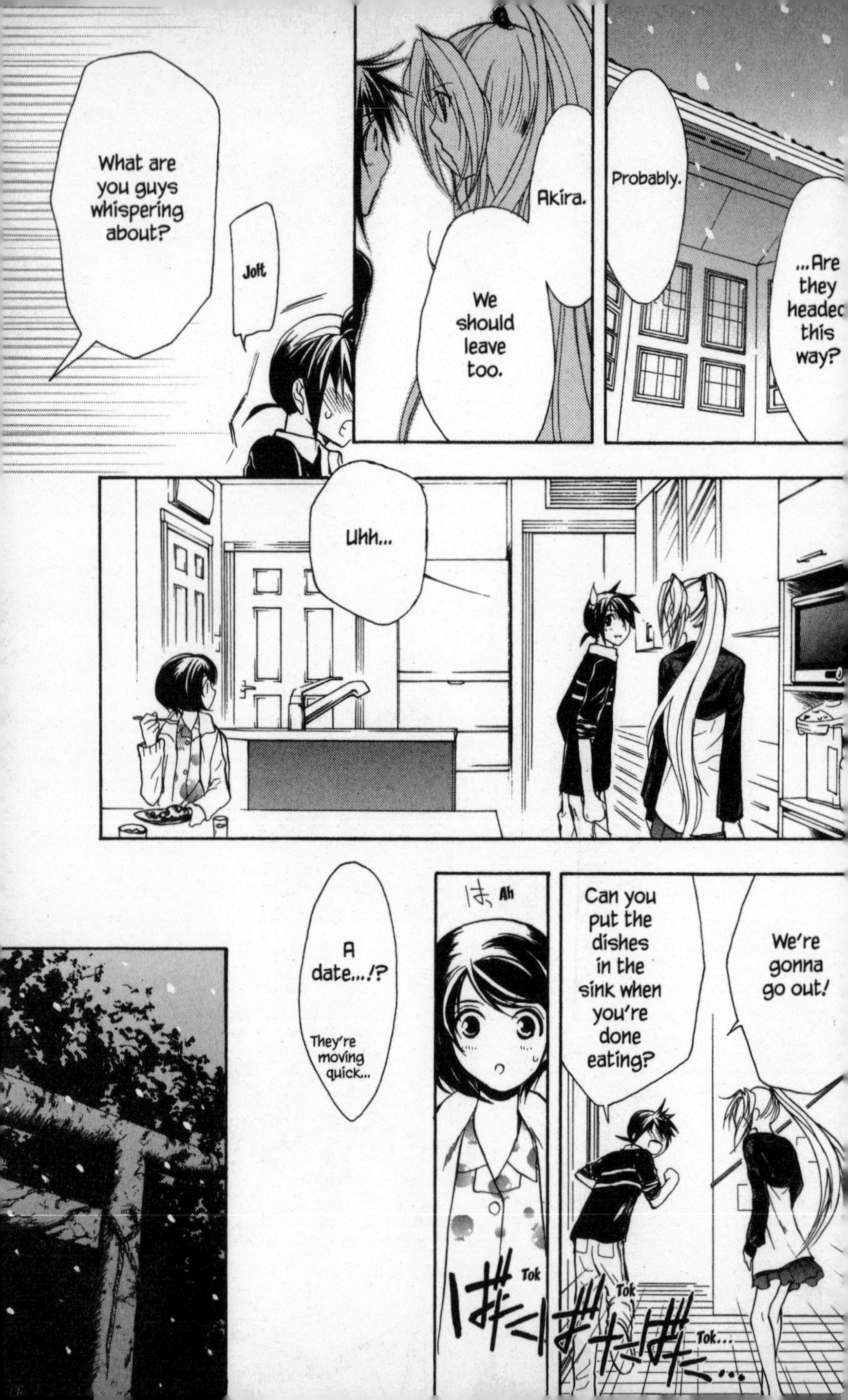
...Are they headec this way?
Probably.
Akira.
We should leave too.
Jolt
What are you guys whispering about?
Uhh...
We're gonna go out!
Can you put the dishes in the sink when you're done eating?
Tok
Tok
Tok...
は Ah
A date...!?
They're moving quick...

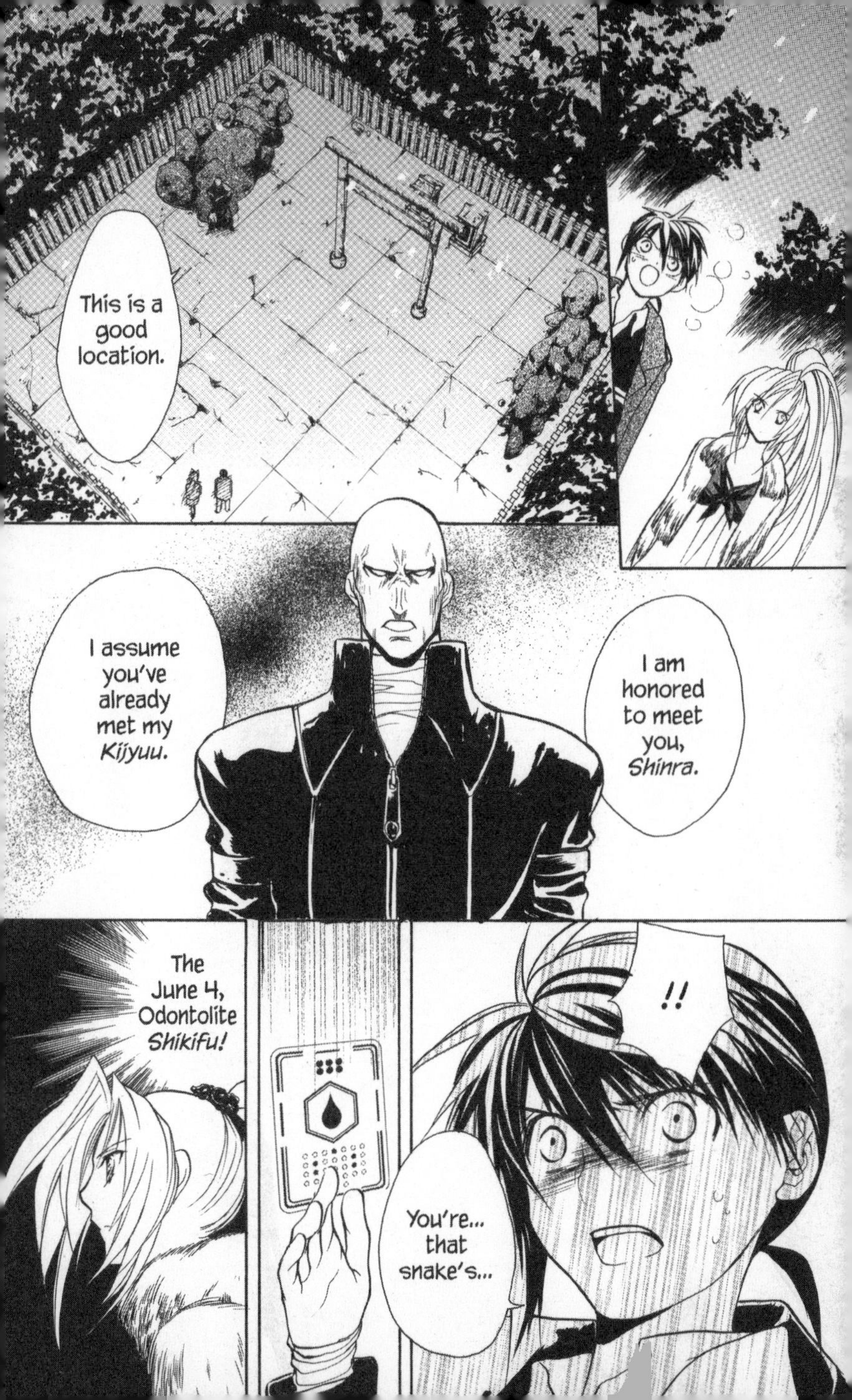
This is a good location.
I am honored to meet you, *Shinra.*
I assume you've already met my *Kijyuu.*
!!
You're... that snake's...
The June 4, Odontolite *Shikifu!*

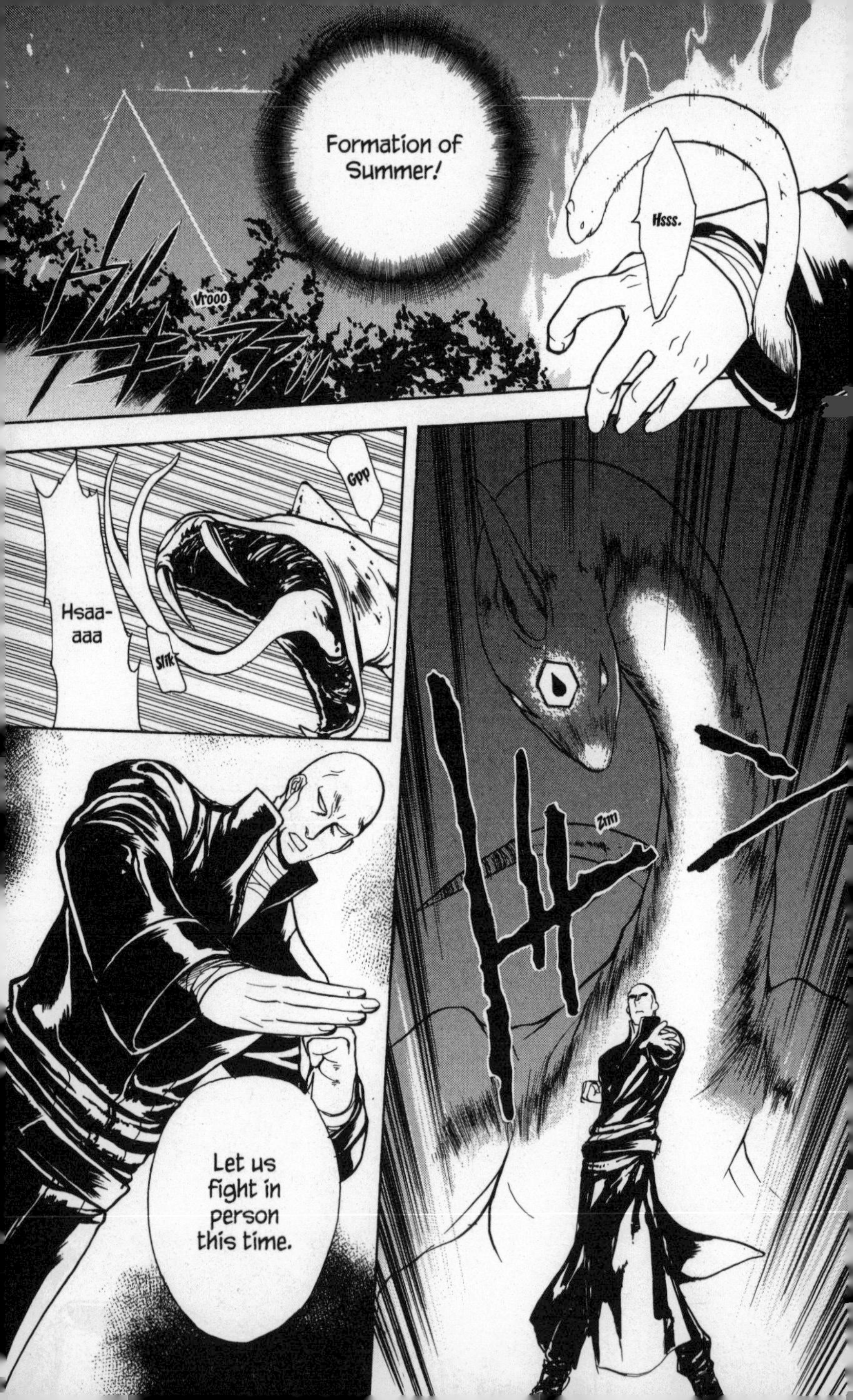
Formation of Summer!
Hsss.
Vrooo
Zim
Gpp
Hsaa-aaa
Slik
Let us fight in person this time.

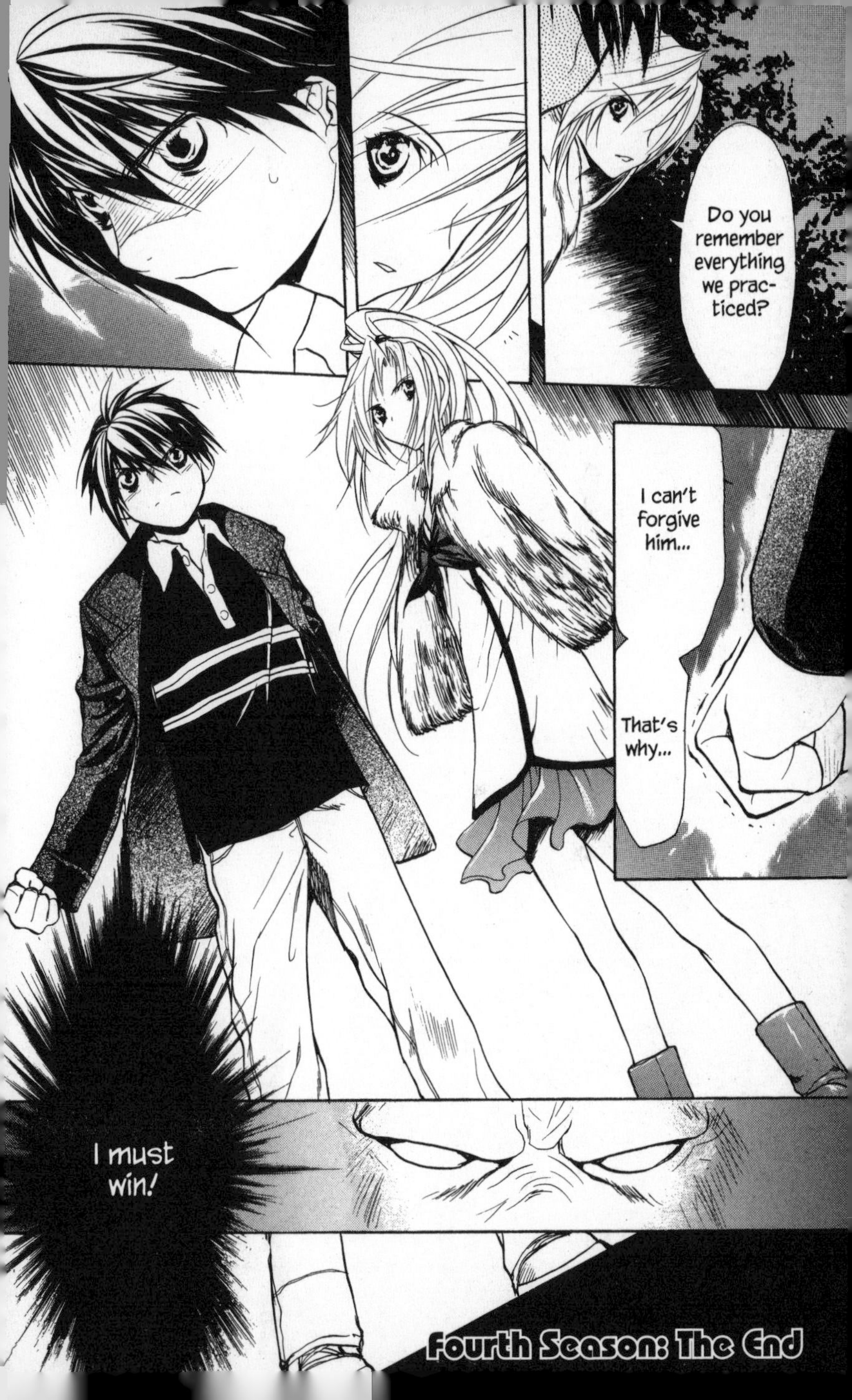
Do you remember everything we practiced?
I can't forgive him...
That's why...
I must win!
Fourth Season: The End

Fifth Season

Doubting the Melody of the Music Box

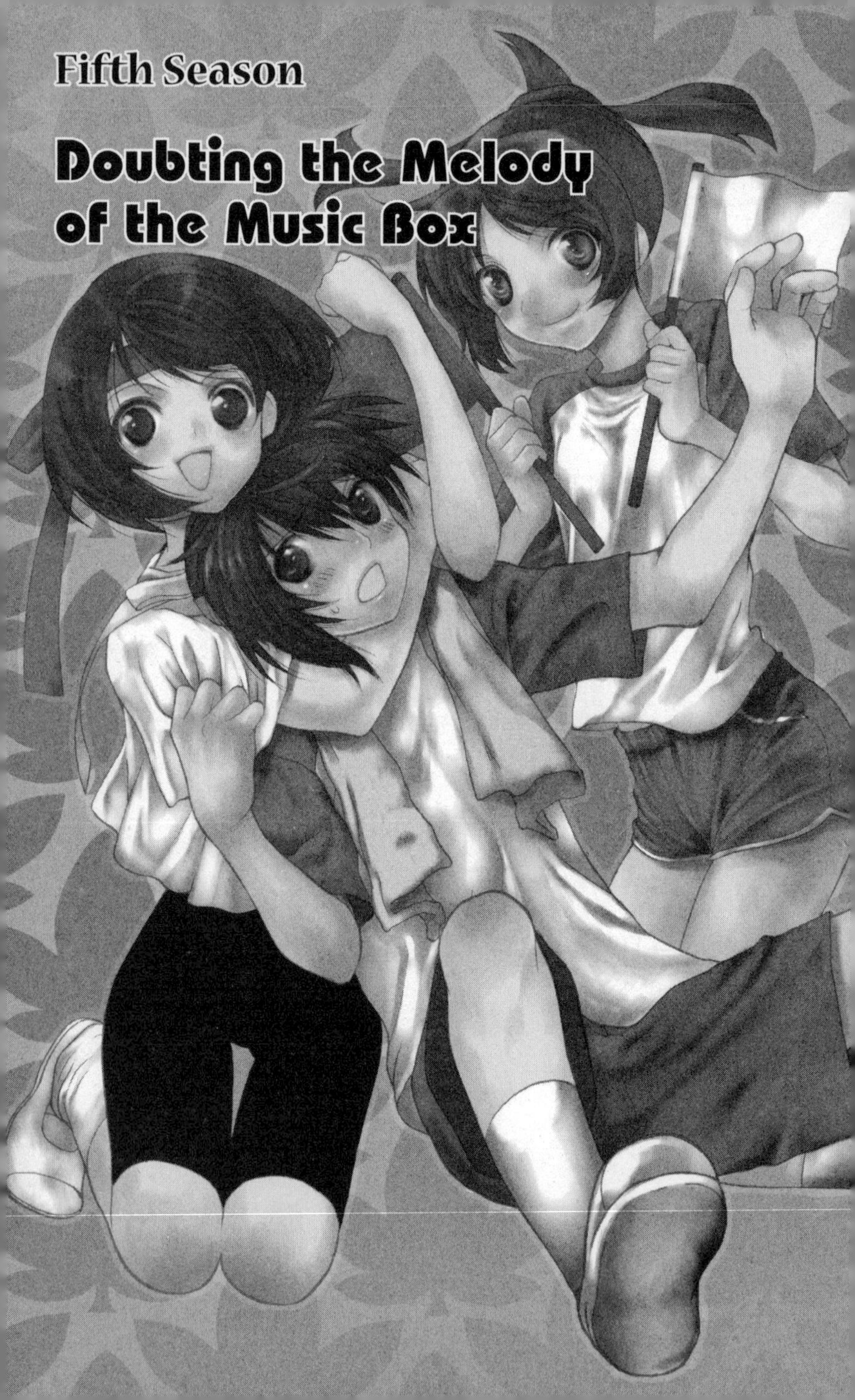

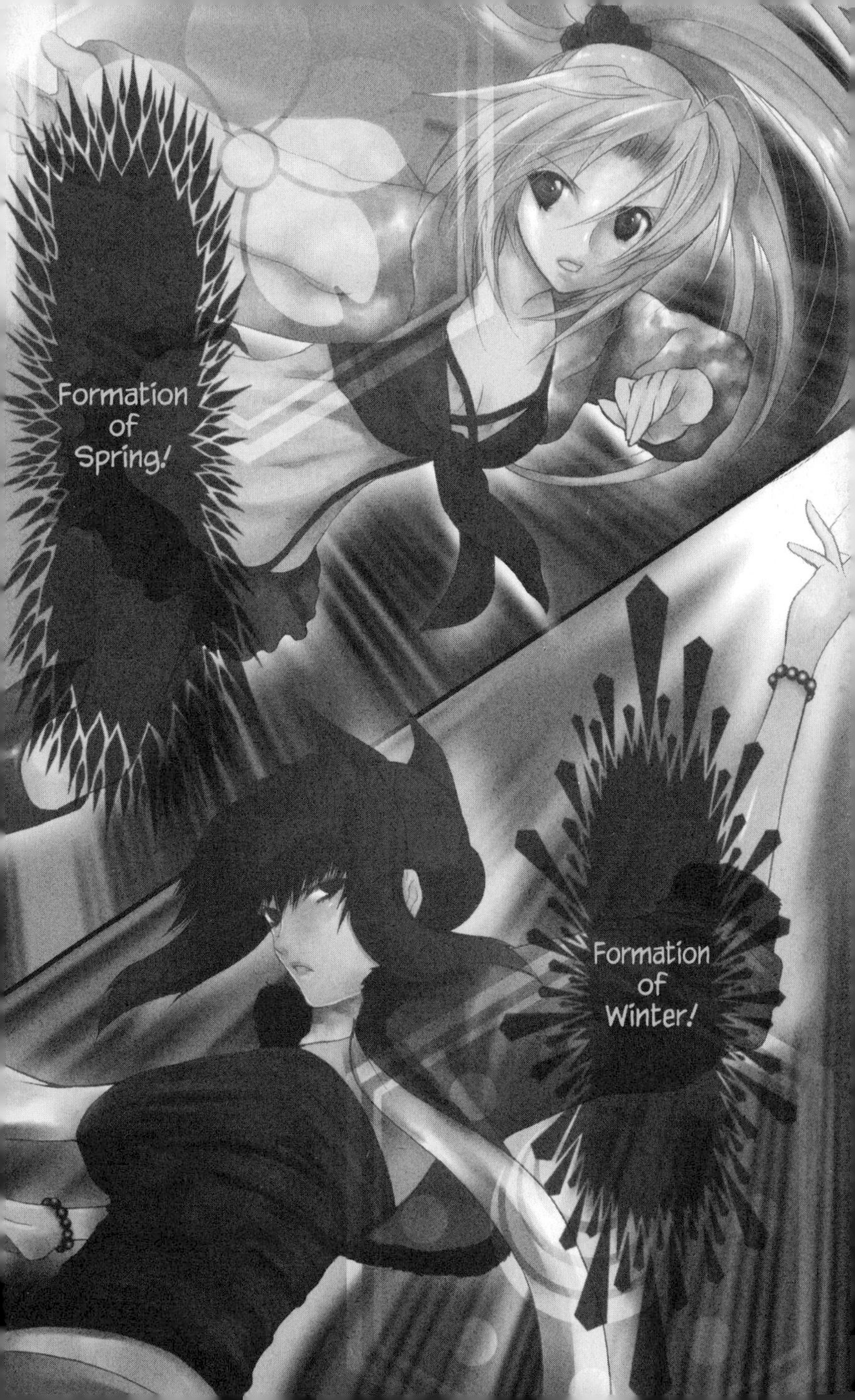
Formation of Spring!
Formation of Winter!

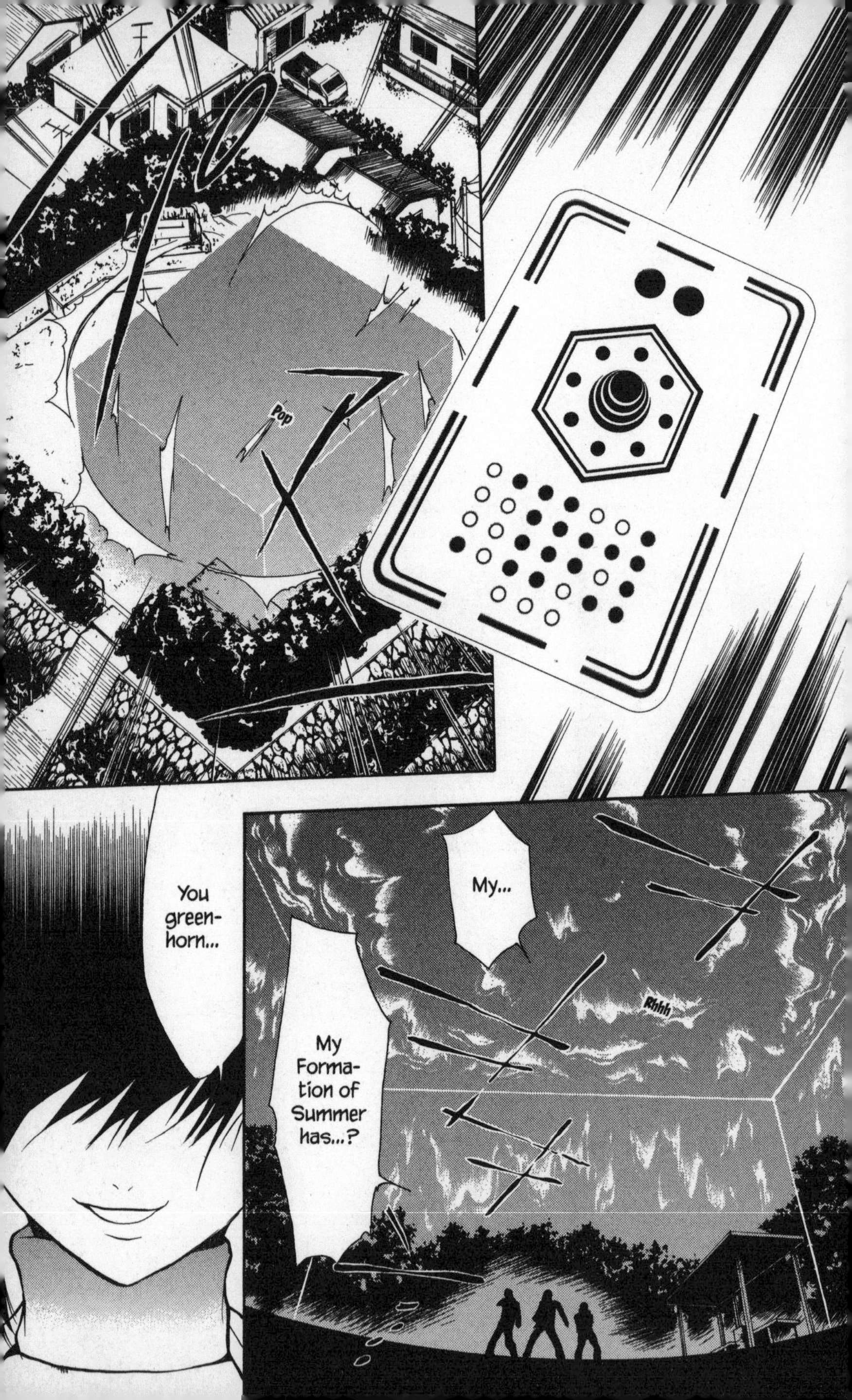
Pop
My...
Rhhh
My Formation of Summer has...?
You greenhorn...

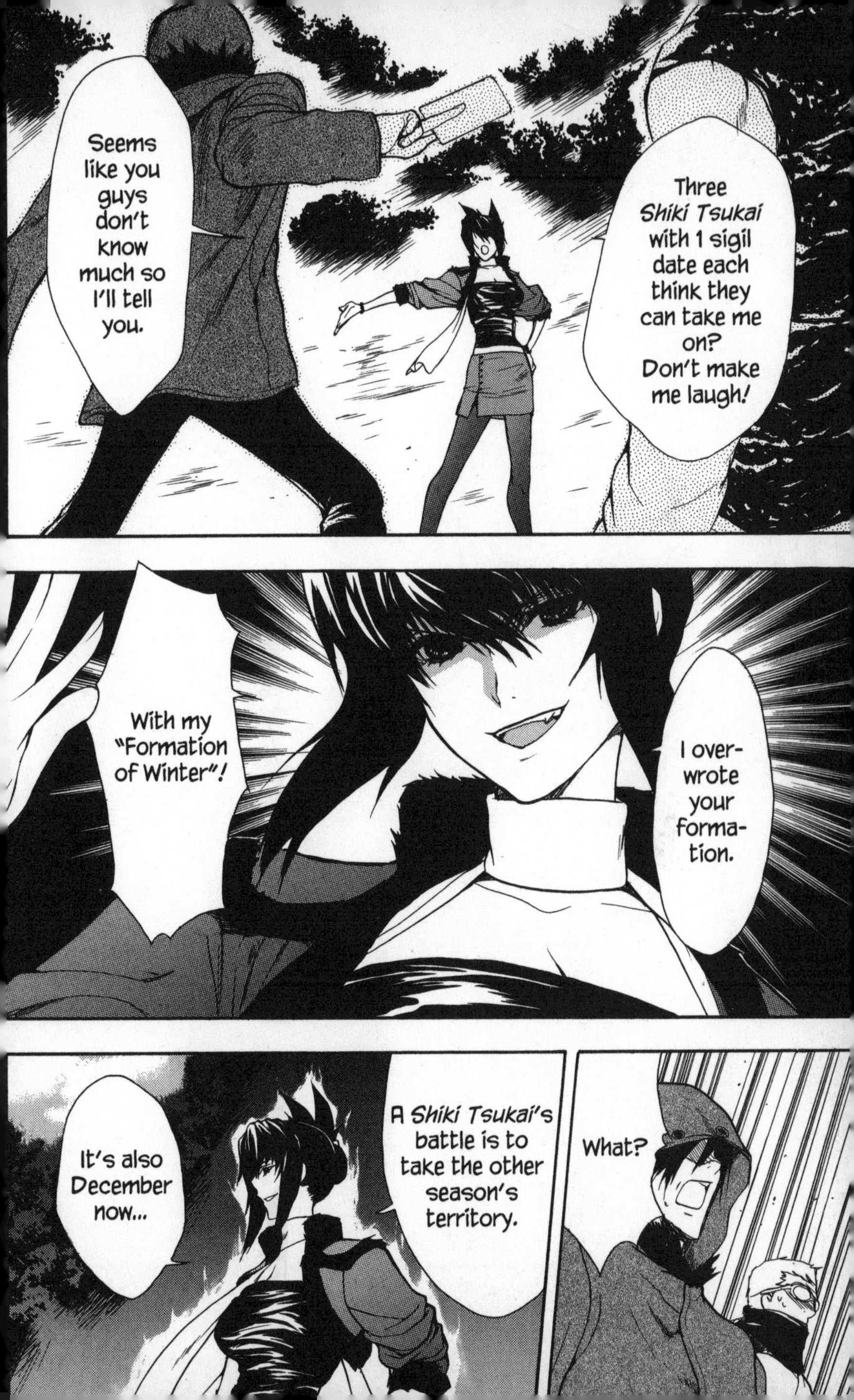
Three *Shiki Tsukai* with 1 sigil date each think they can take me on? Don't make me laugh!
Seems like you guys don't know much so I'll tell you.
I over-wrote your formation.
With my "Formation of Winter"!
What?
A *Shiki Tsukai*'s battle is to take the other season's territory.
It's also December now...

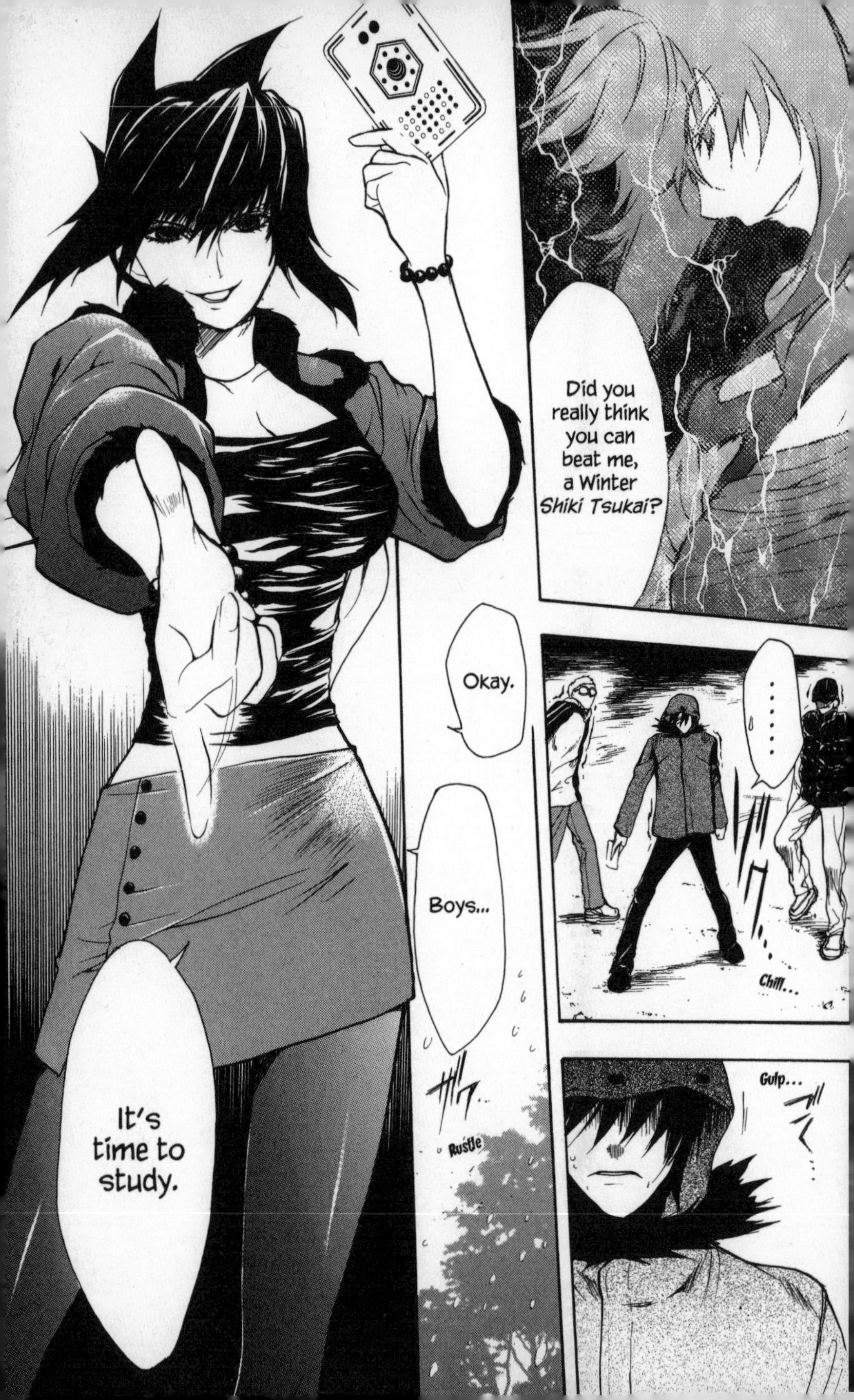
Did you really think you can beat me, a Winter Shiki Tsukai?
......
Chill...
Gulp...
Okay.
Boys...
Rustle
It's time to study.

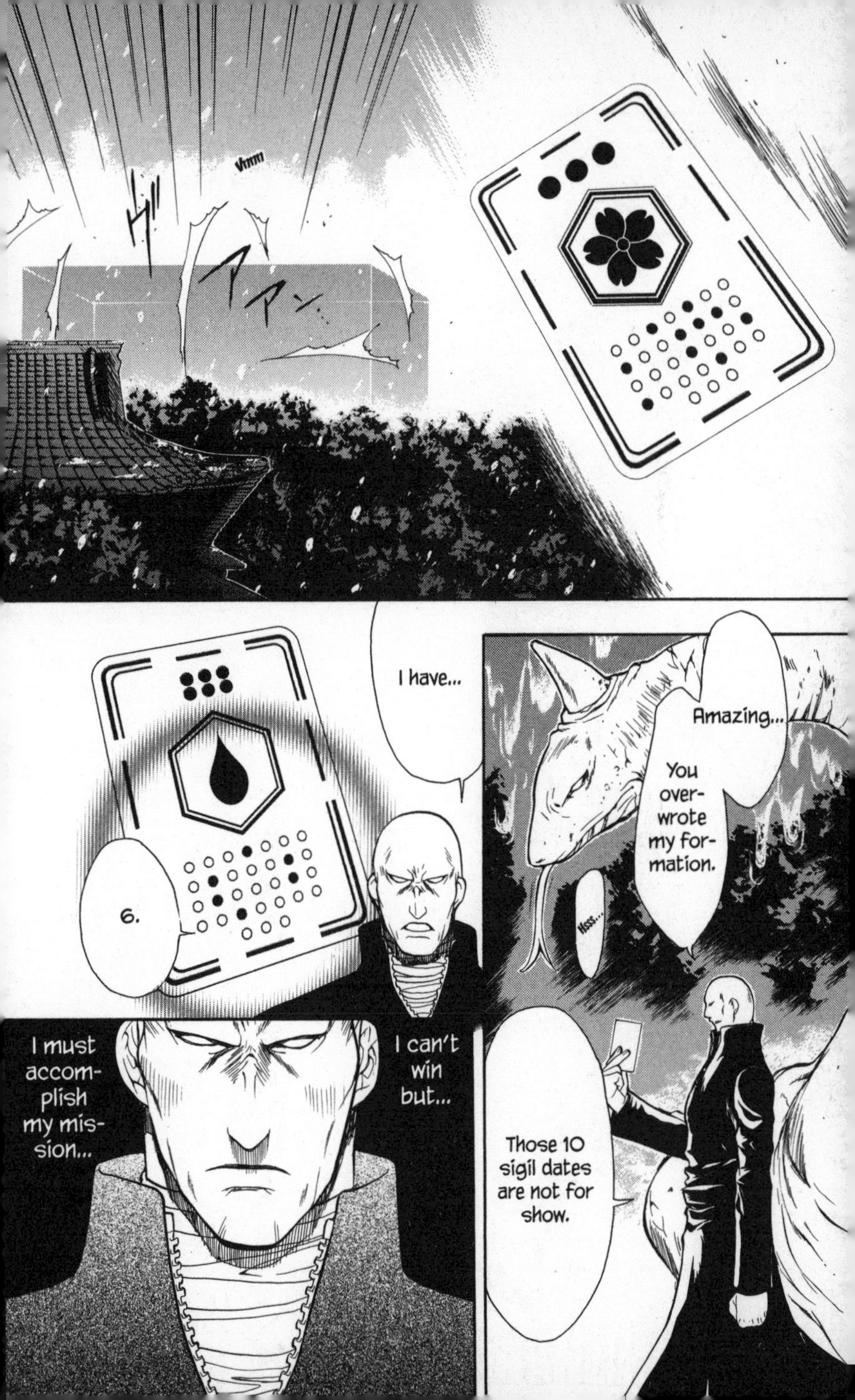
Vmm
Amazing...
You over-wrote my for-mation.
Hsss...
I have...
6.
Those 10 sigil dates are not for show.
I can't win but...
I must accom-plish my mis-sion...

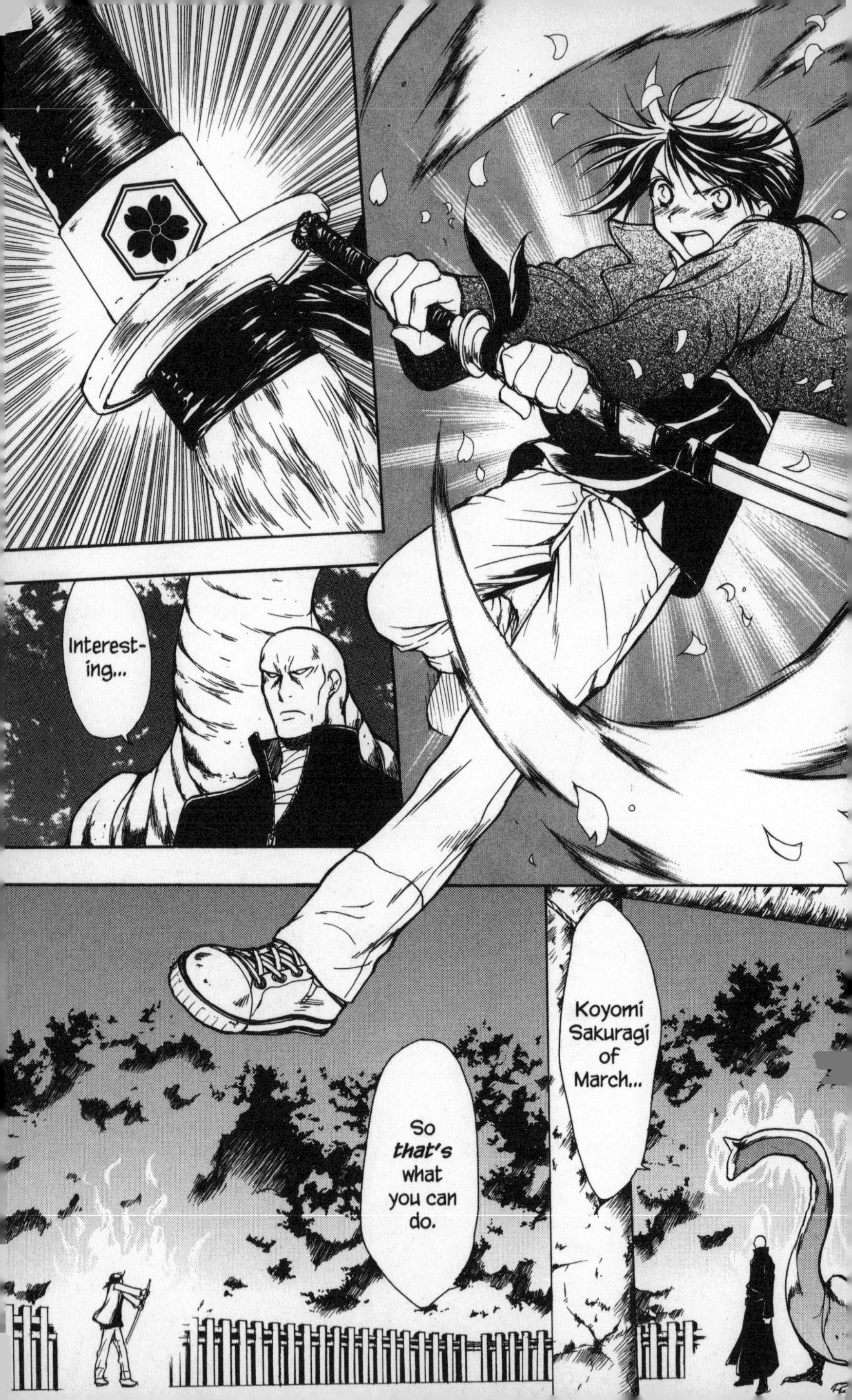
Interesting...
Koyomi Sakuragi of March...
So *that's* what you can do.

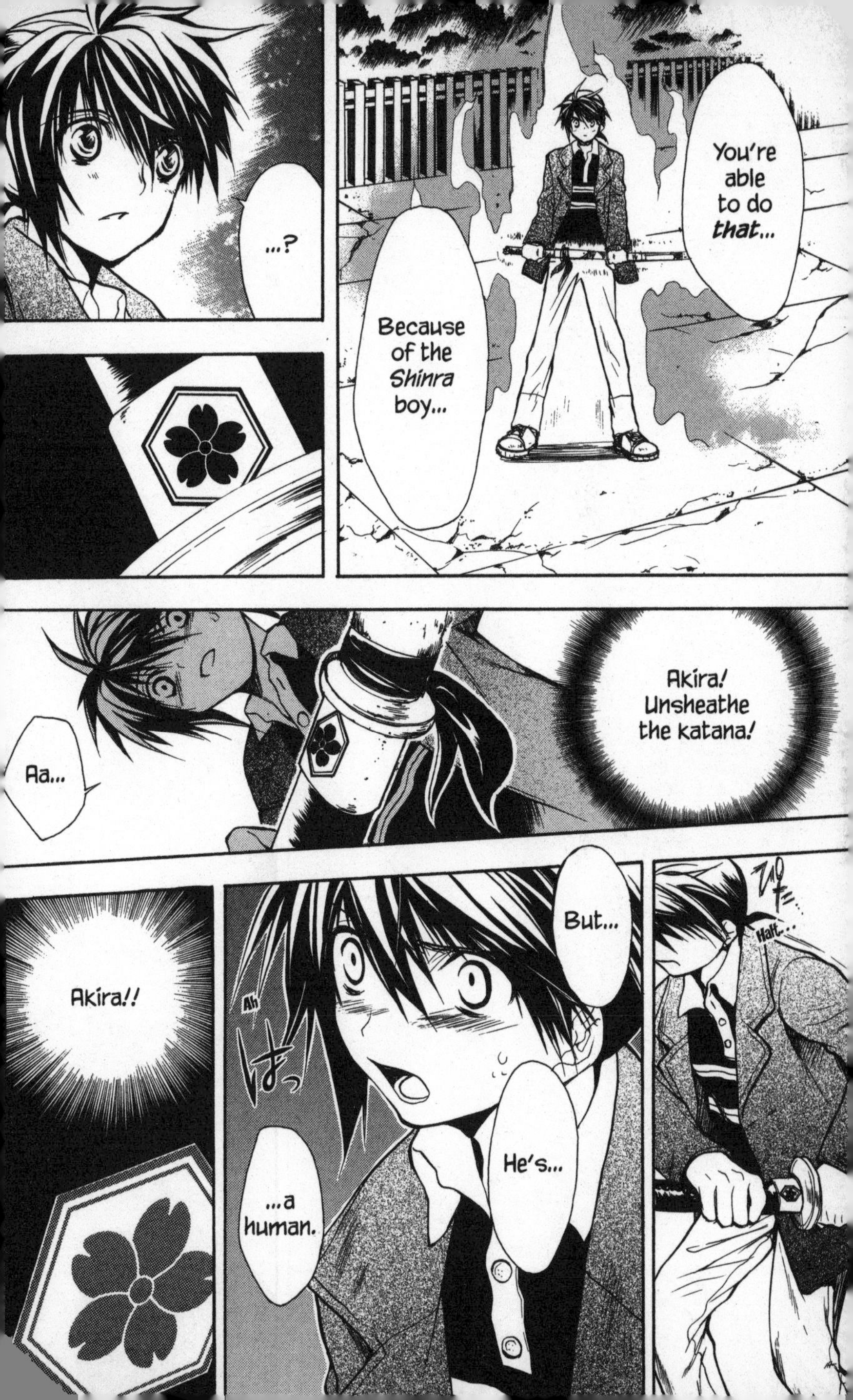

You're able to do *that*...
Because of the *Shinra* boy...
...?
Akira! Unsheathe the katana!
Aa...
Halt...
But...
Ah
He's...
...a human.
Akira!!

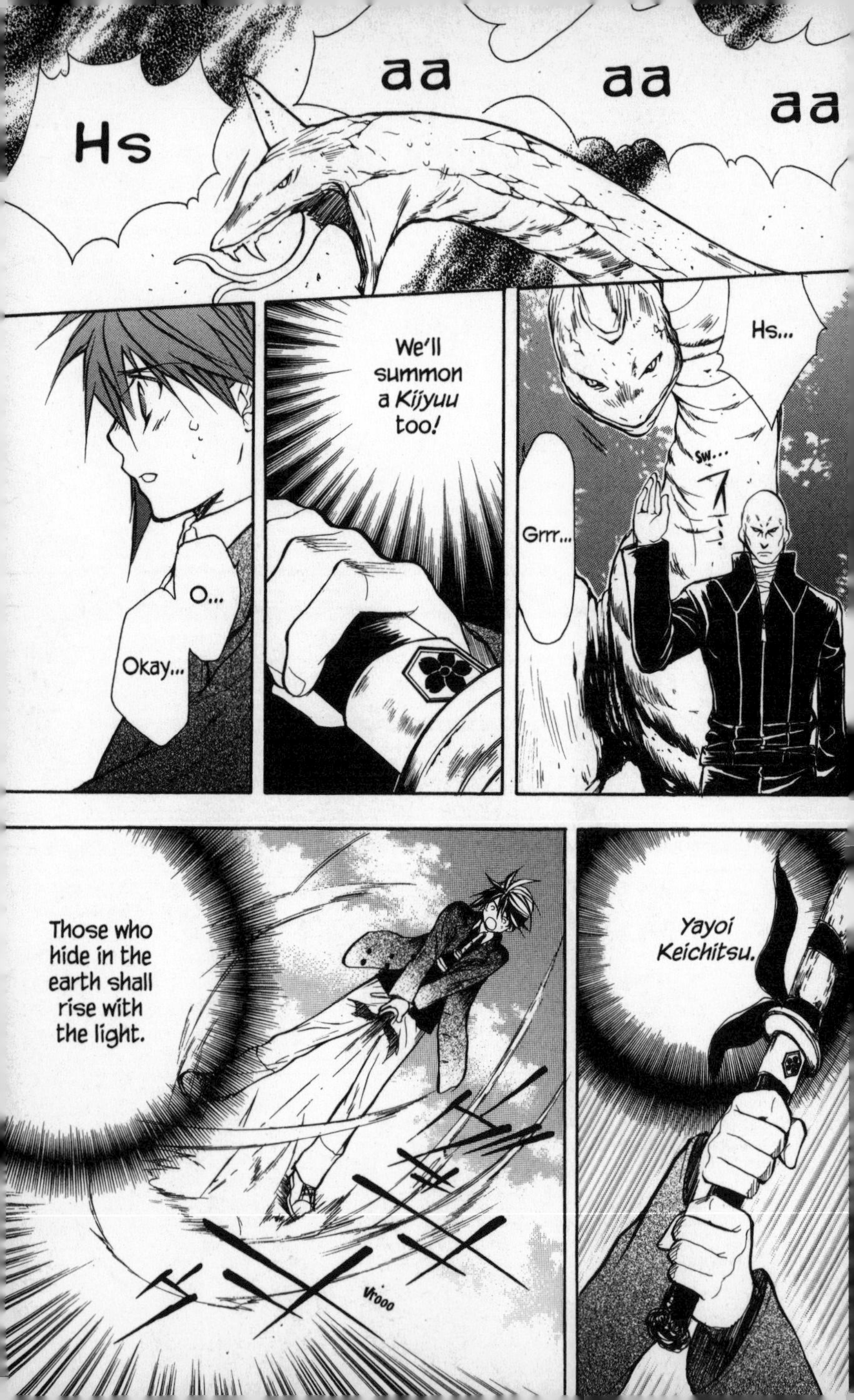
Hs
aa
aa
aa
Hs...
sw...
Grrr...
We'll summon a *Kijyuu* too!
O...
Okay...
Yayoi Keichitsu.
Those who hide in the earth shall rise with the light.
Vrooo

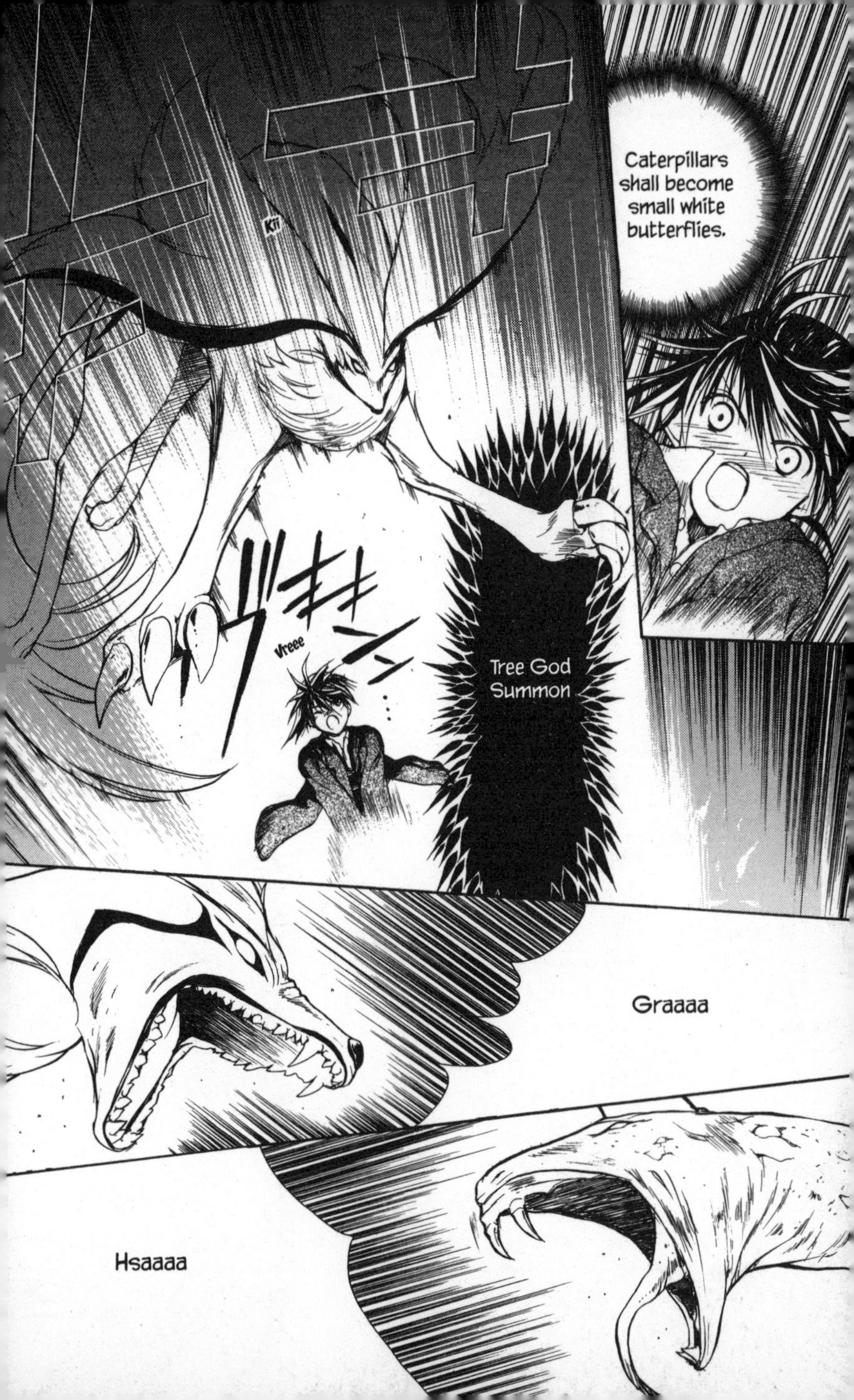
Caterpillars shall become small white butterflies.
Kii
Vreee
Tree God Summon
Graaaa
Hsaaaa

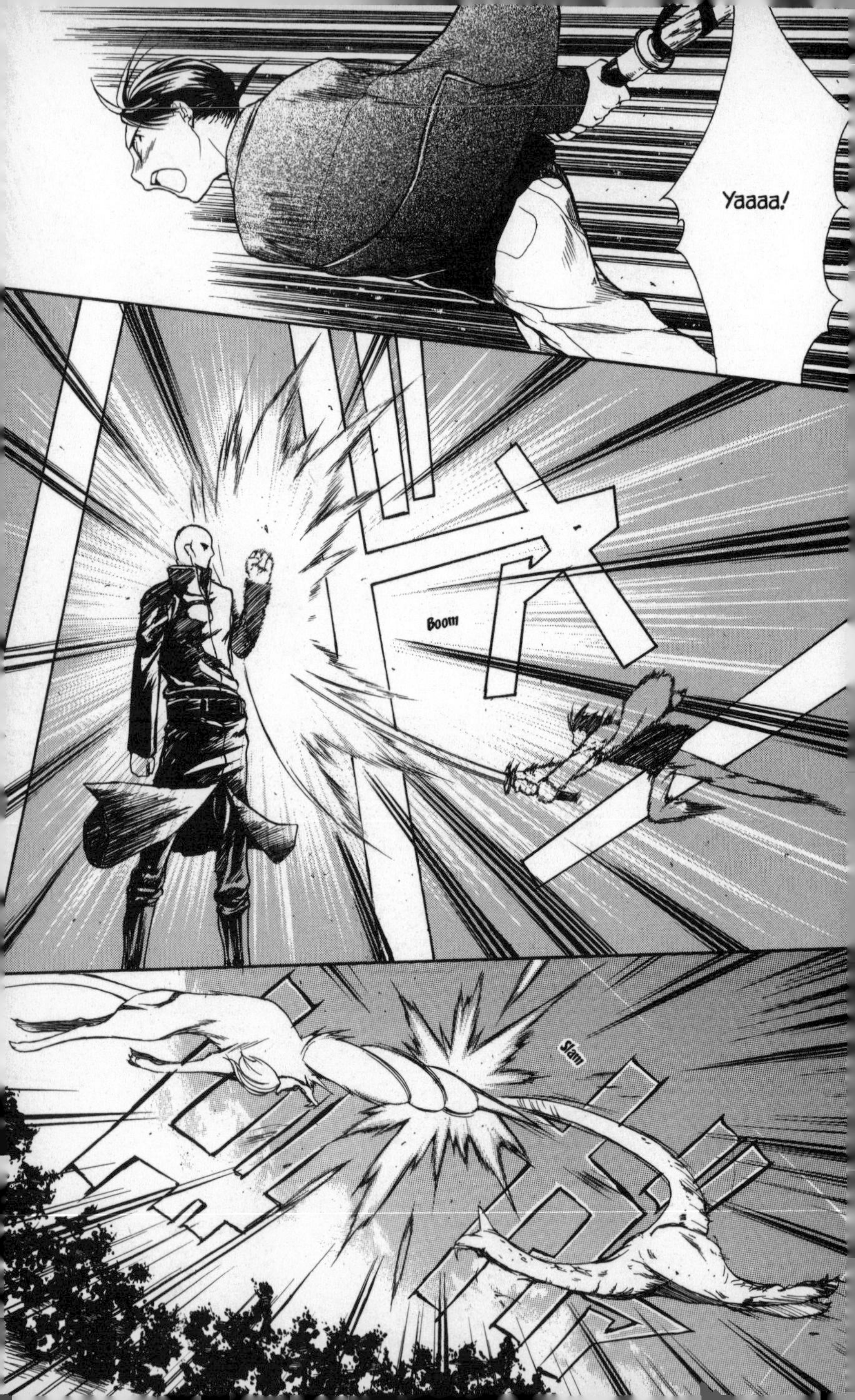
Yaaaa!
Boom
Slam

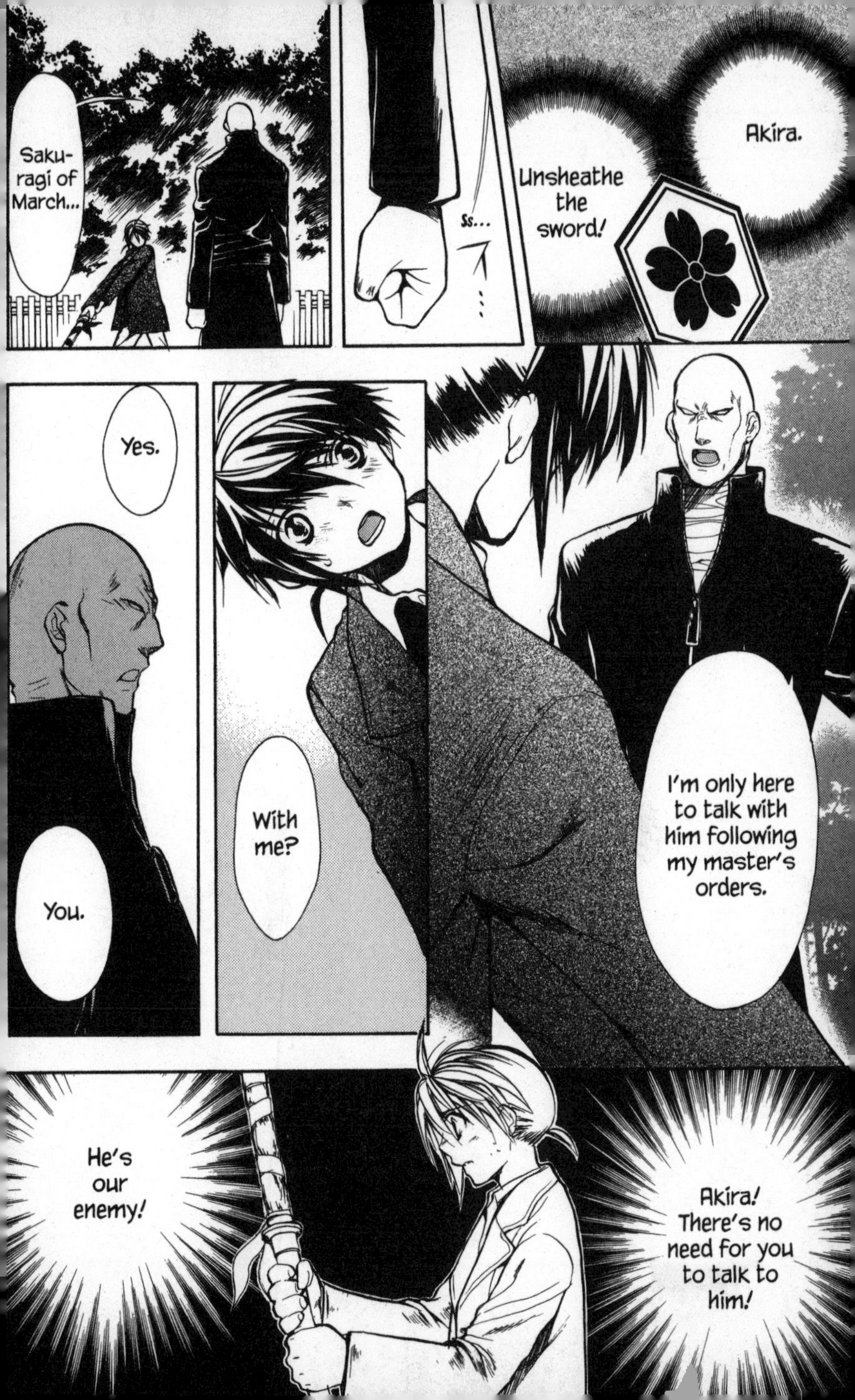
Akira.
Unsheathe the sword!
Ss...
Saku-ragi of March...
I'm only here to talk with him following my master's orders.
With me?
Yes.
You.
Akira! There's no need for you to talk to him!
He's our enemy!

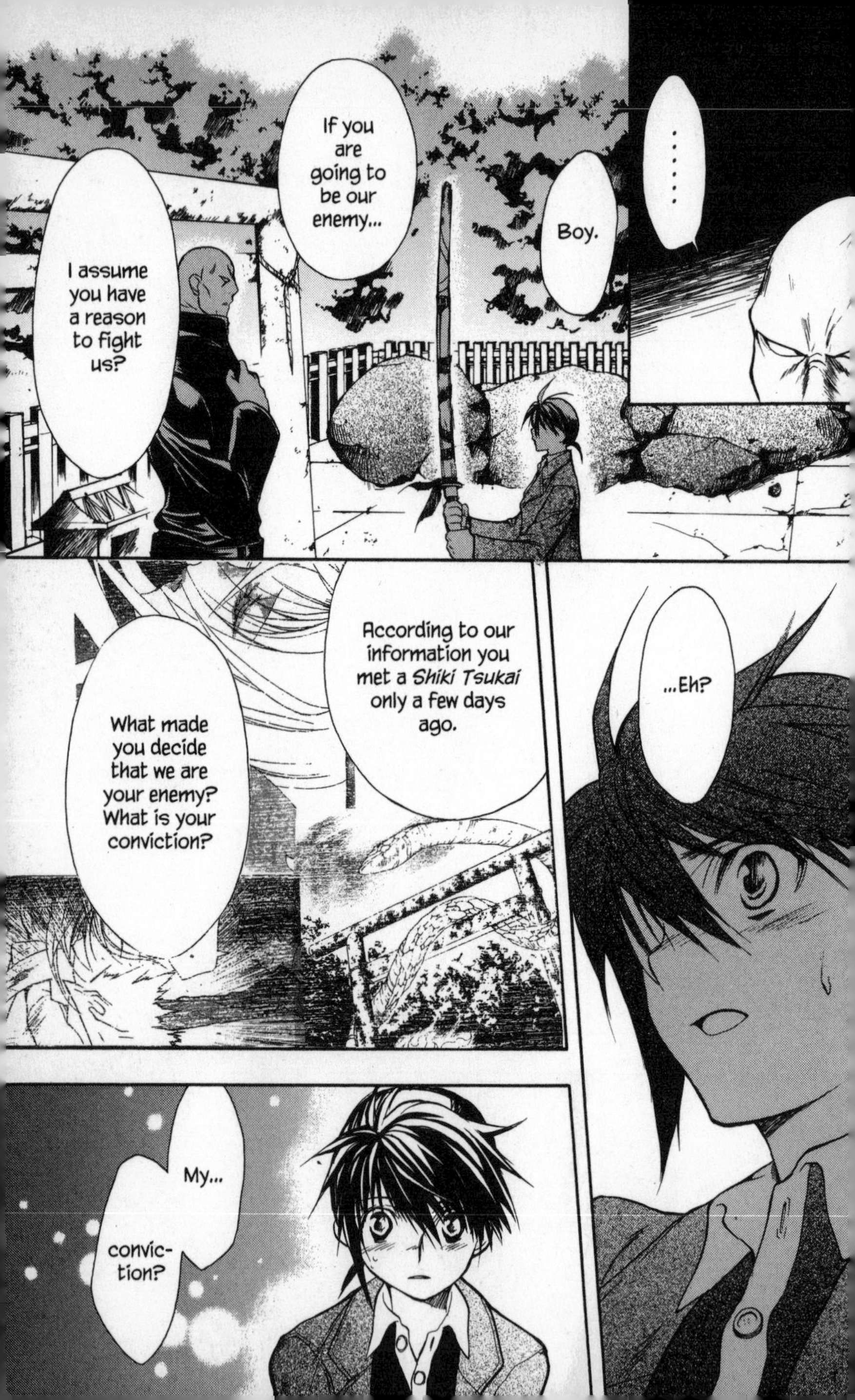
......
Boy.
If you are going to be our enemy...
I assume you have a reason to fight us?
...Eh?
According to our information you met a *Shiki Tsukai* only a few days ago.
What made you decide that we are your enemy? What is your conviction?
My...
convic-tion?

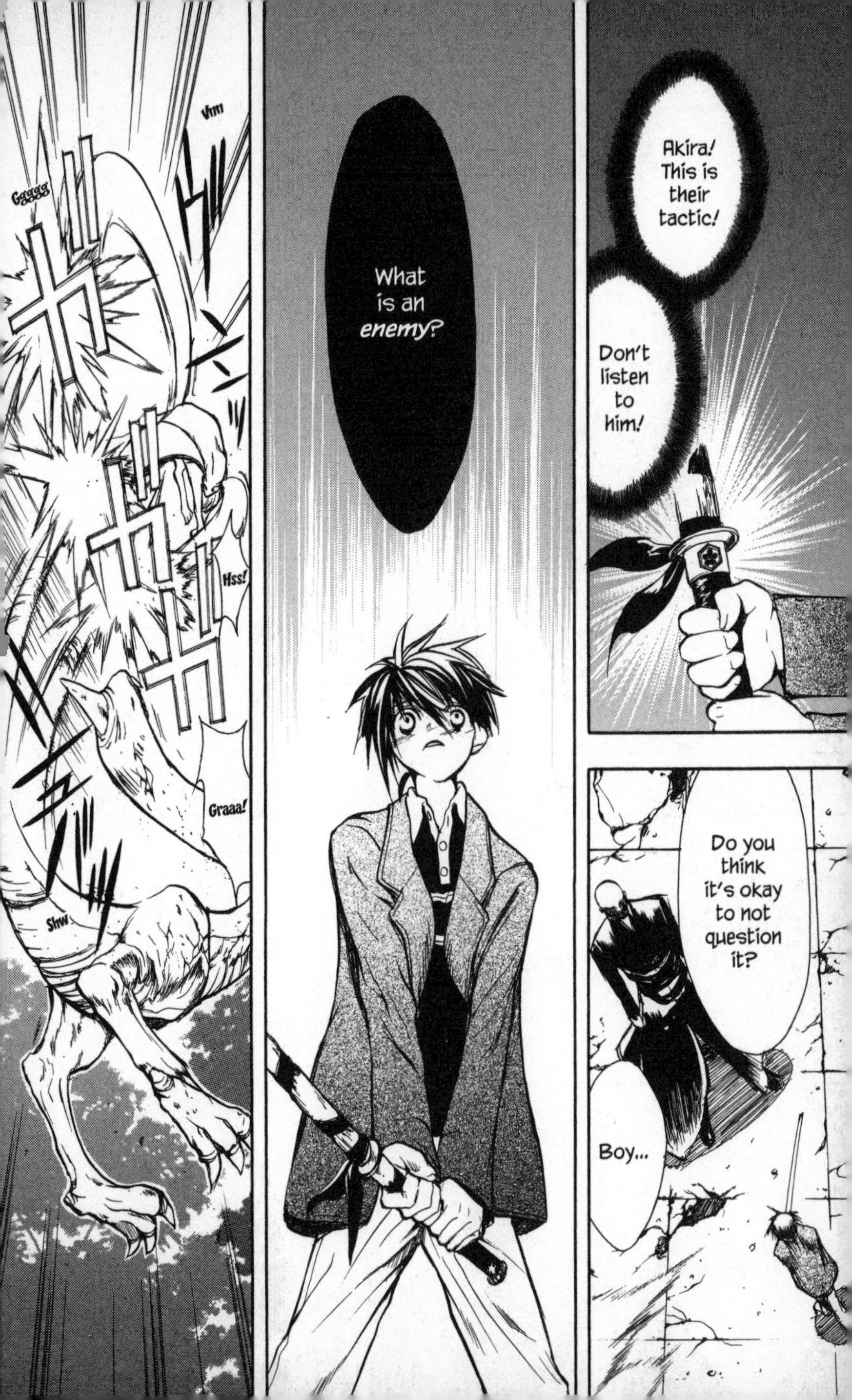
Akira! This is their tactic!
Don't listen to him!
Do you think it's okay to not question it?
Boy...
What is an *enemy?*
Vnn
Gaaaa
Hss!
Graaa!
Shw

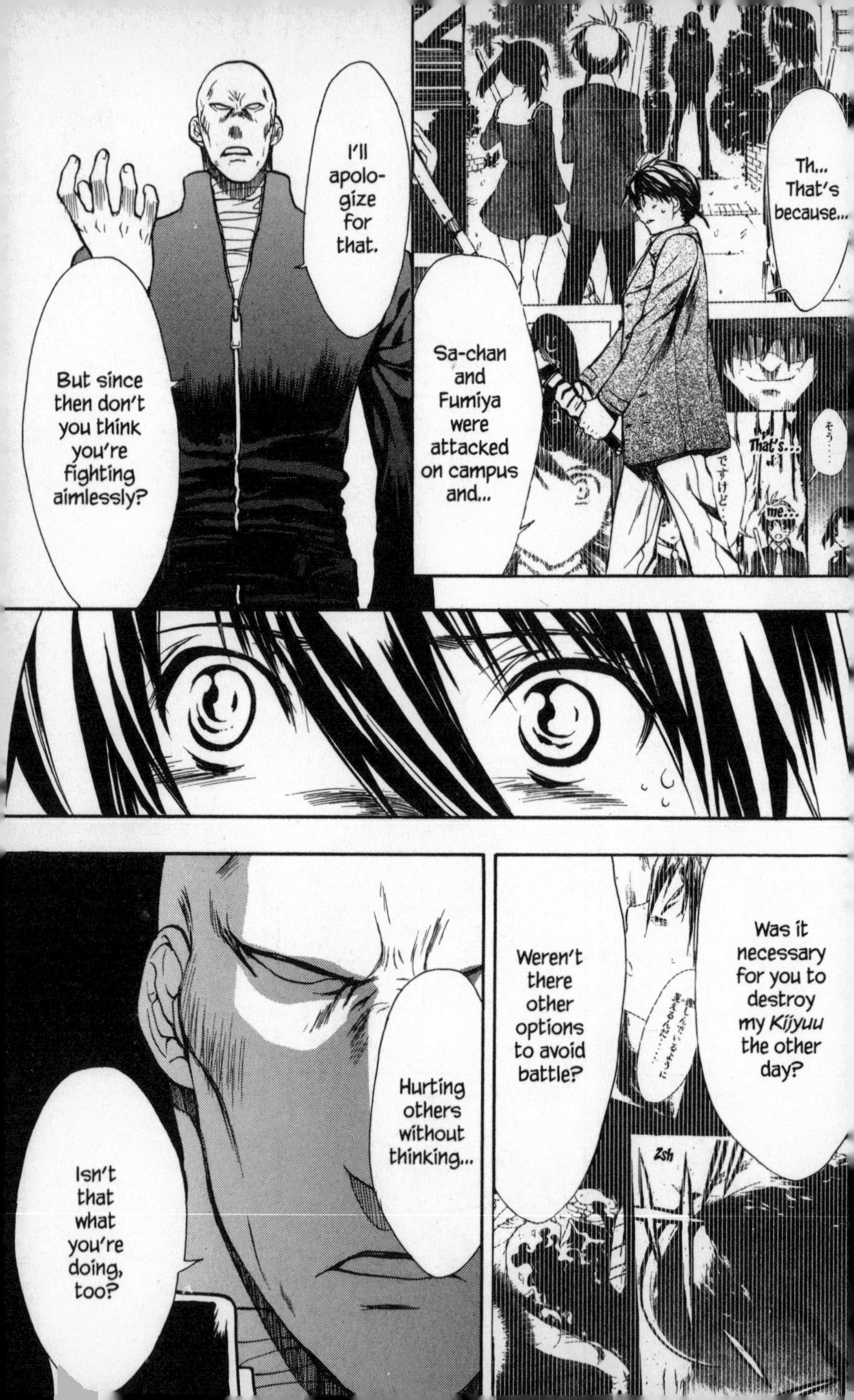

Th... That's because...
Sa-chan and Fumiya were attacked on campus and...
That's...
me...
I'll apolo-gize for that.
But since then don't you think you're fighting aimlessly?
Was it necessary for you to destroy my *Kijyuu* the other day?
Weren't there other options to avoid battle?
Zsh
Hurting others without thinking...
Isn't that what you're doing, too?

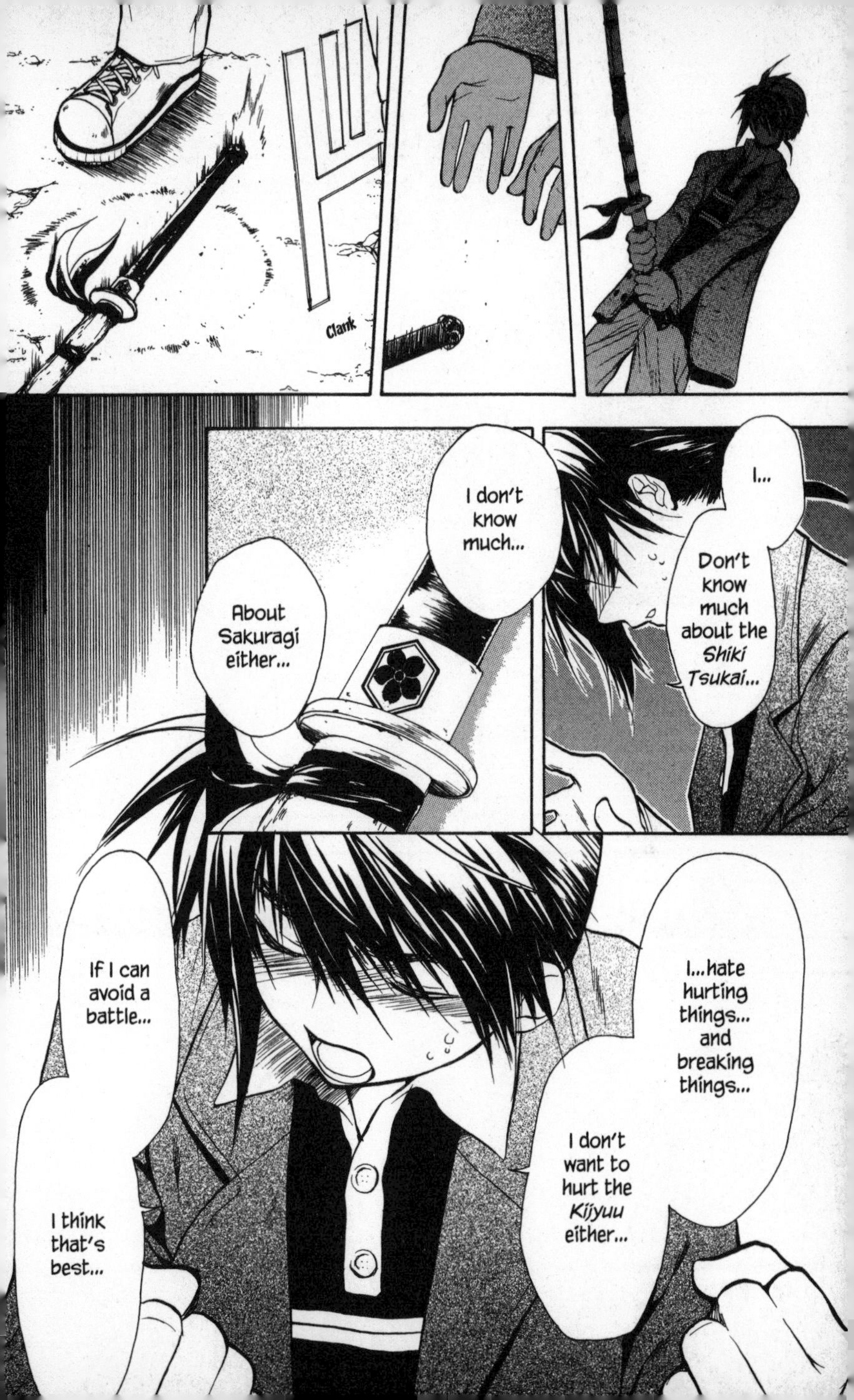
Clank
I...
Don't know much about the *Shiki Tsukai*...
I don't know much...
About Sakuragi either...
I...hate hurting things... and breaking things...
I don't want to hurt the *Kijyuu* either...
If I can avoid a battle...
I think that's best...

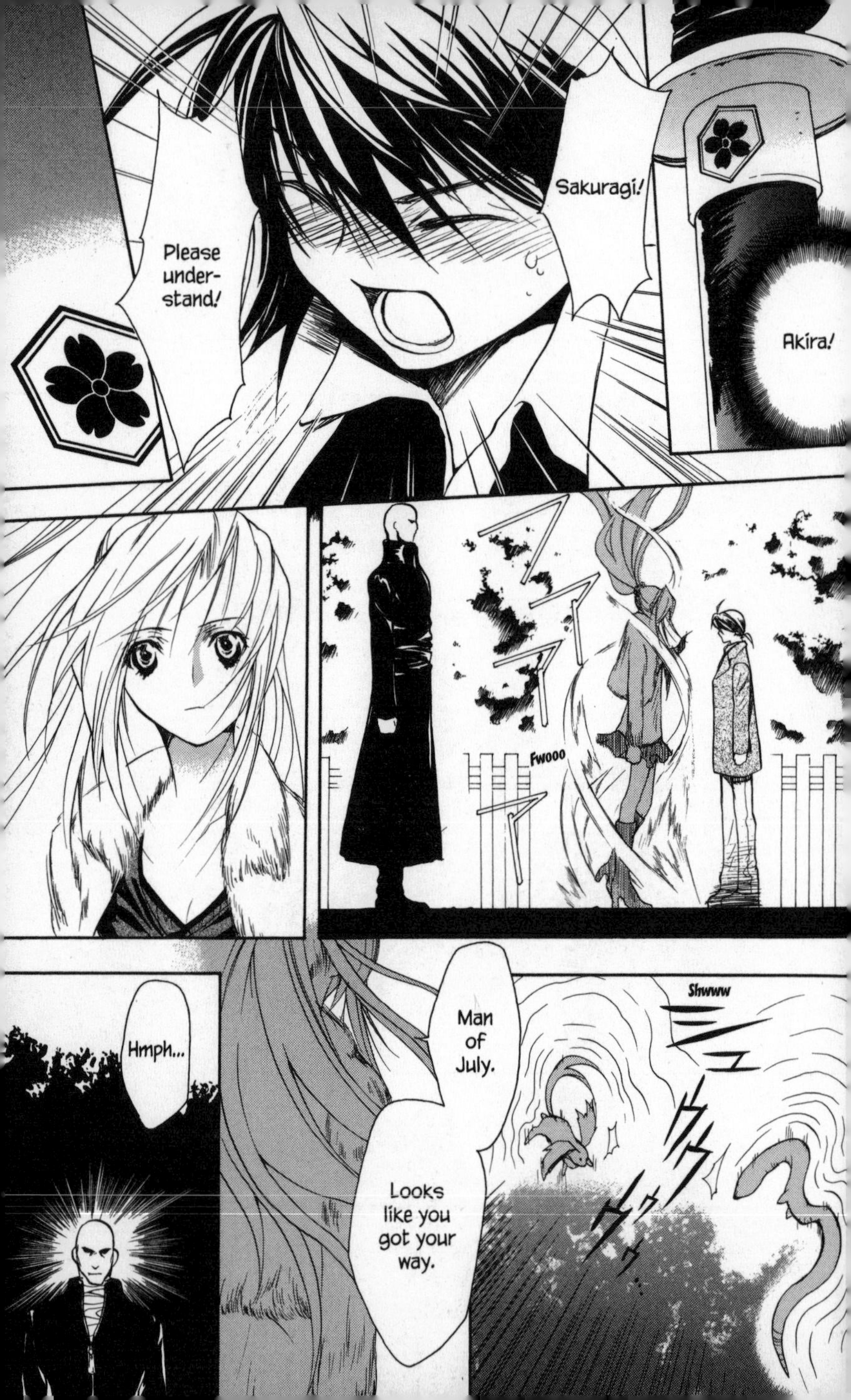
Akira!
Sakuragi!
Please under-stand!
Fwooo
Shwww
Man of July.
Looks like you got your way.
Hmph...

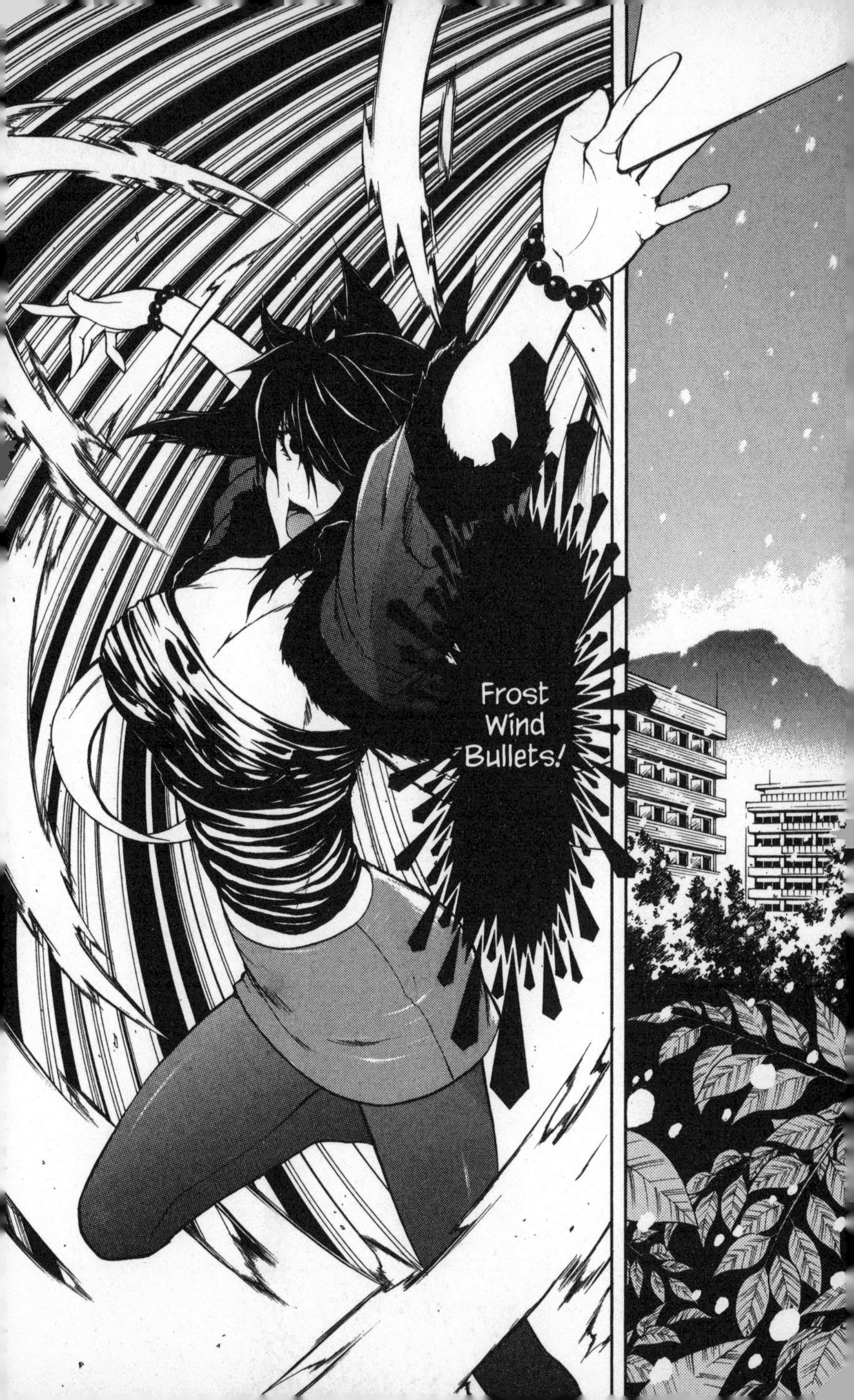
Frost Wind Bullets!

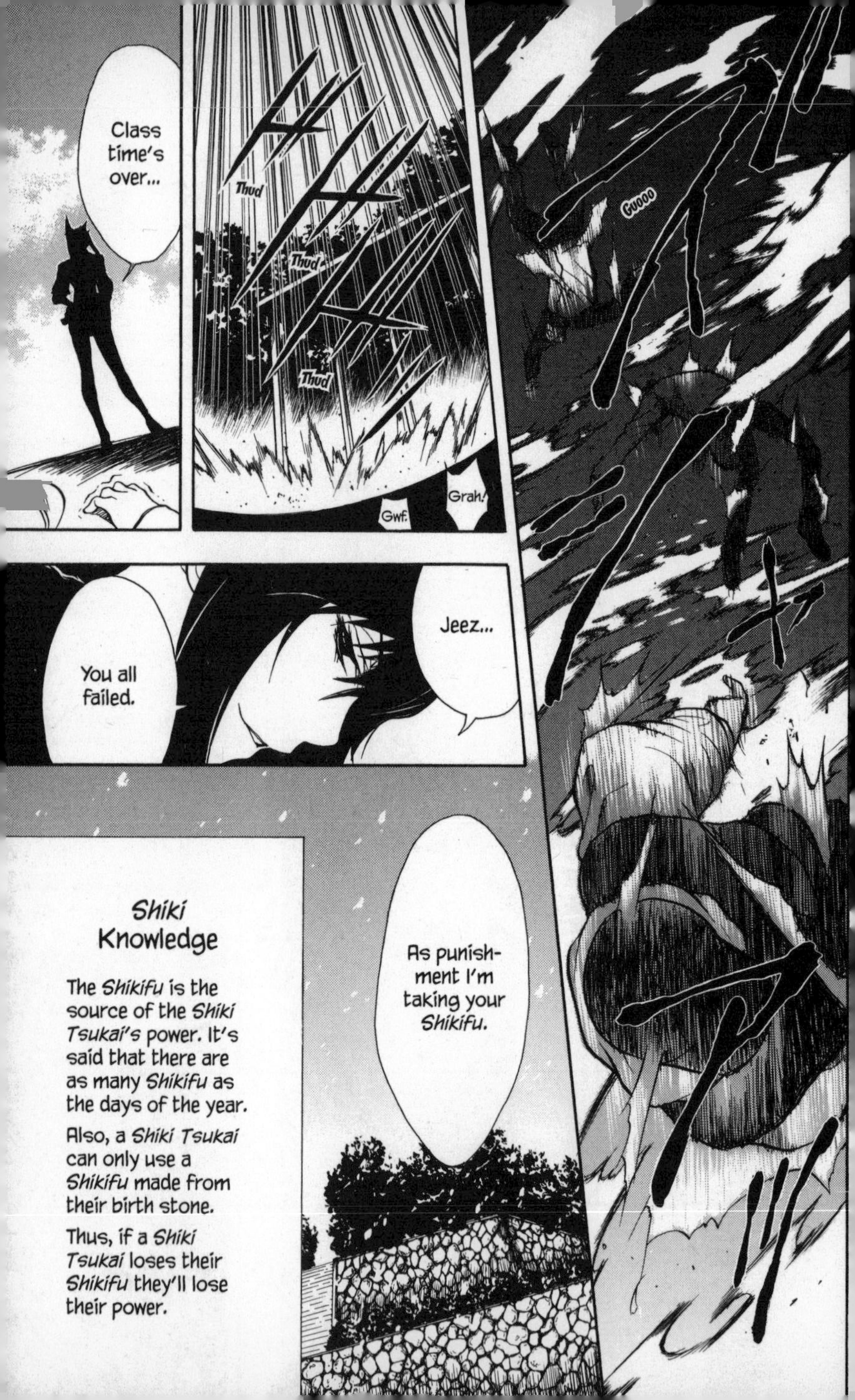
Guooo
Thud
Thud
Thud
Grah!
Gwf.
Class time's over...
Jeez...
You all failed.
As punishment I'm taking your *Shikifu*.
Shiki Knowledge
The *Shikifu* is the source of the *Shiki Tsukai's* power. It's said that there are as many *Shikifu* as the days of the year.
Also, a *Shiki Tsukai* can only use a *Shikifu* made from their birth stone.
Thus, if a *Shiki Tsukai* loses their *Shikifu* they'll lose their power.

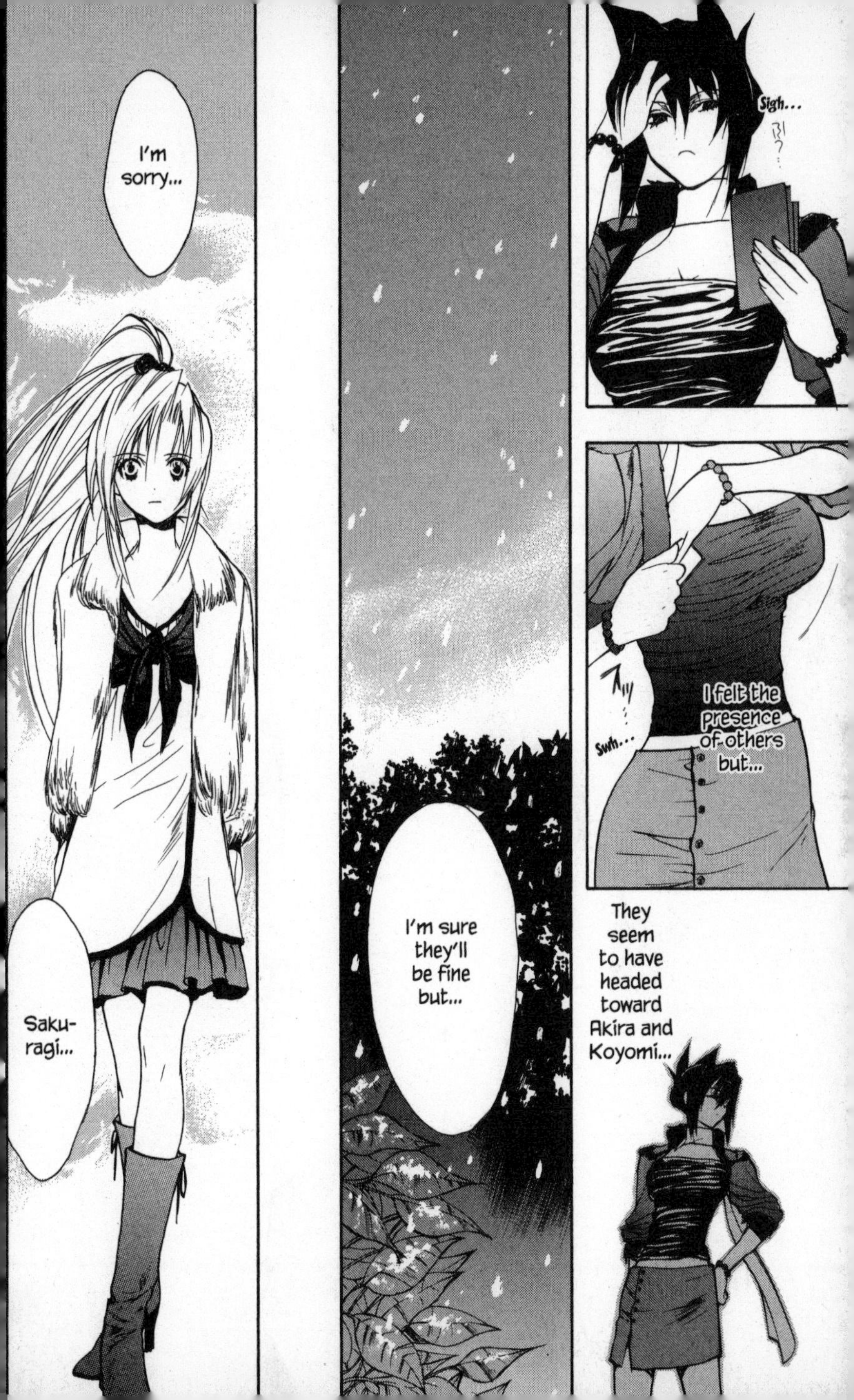
Sigh...
Swh...
I felt the presence of others but...
They seem to have headed toward Akira and Koyomi...
I'm sure they'll be fine but...
I'm sorry...
Saku-ragi...

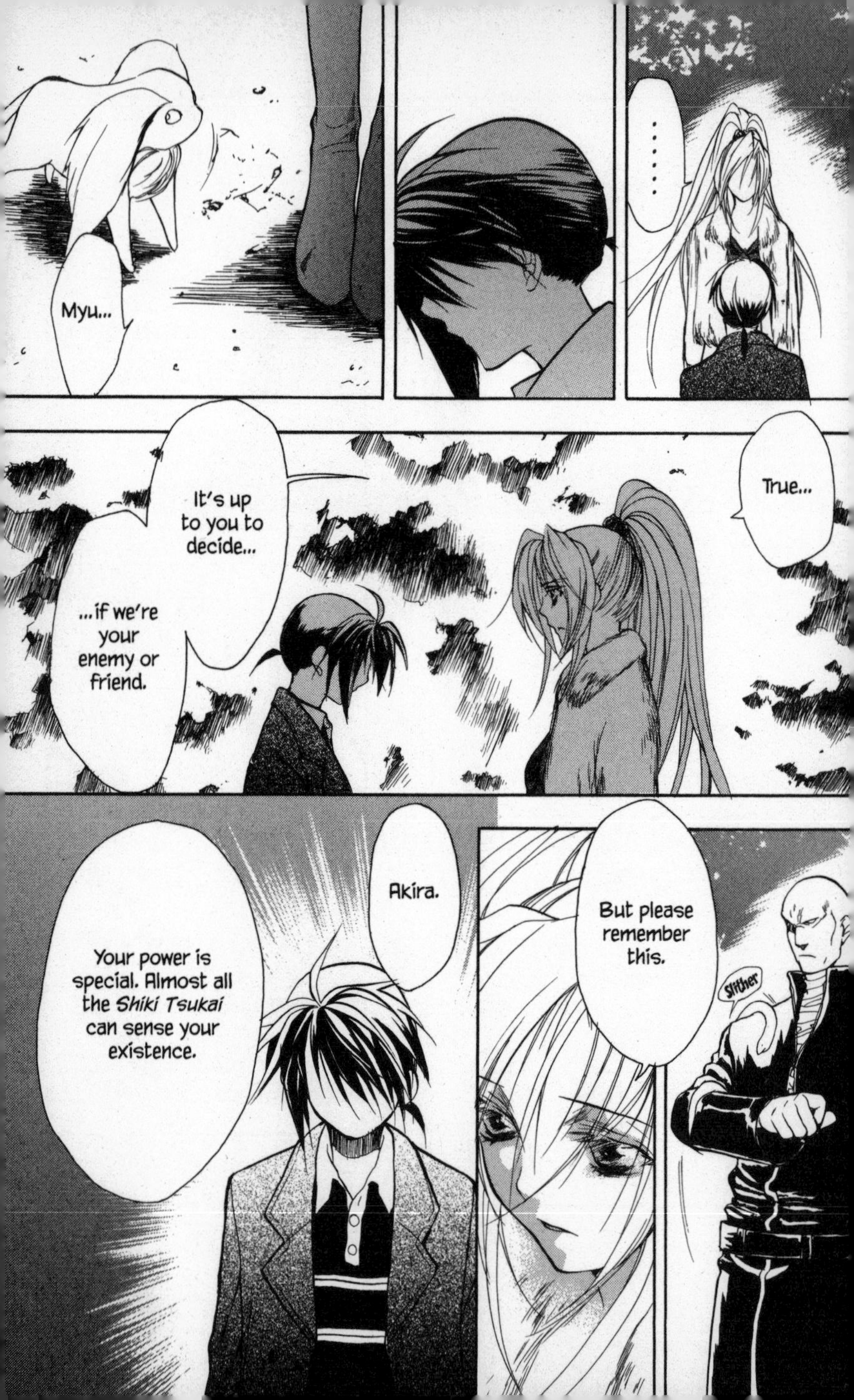
......
Myu...
True...
It's up to you to decide...
...if we're your enemy or friend.
But please remember this.
Slither
Akira.
Your power is special. Almost all the *Shiki Tsukai* can sense your existence.

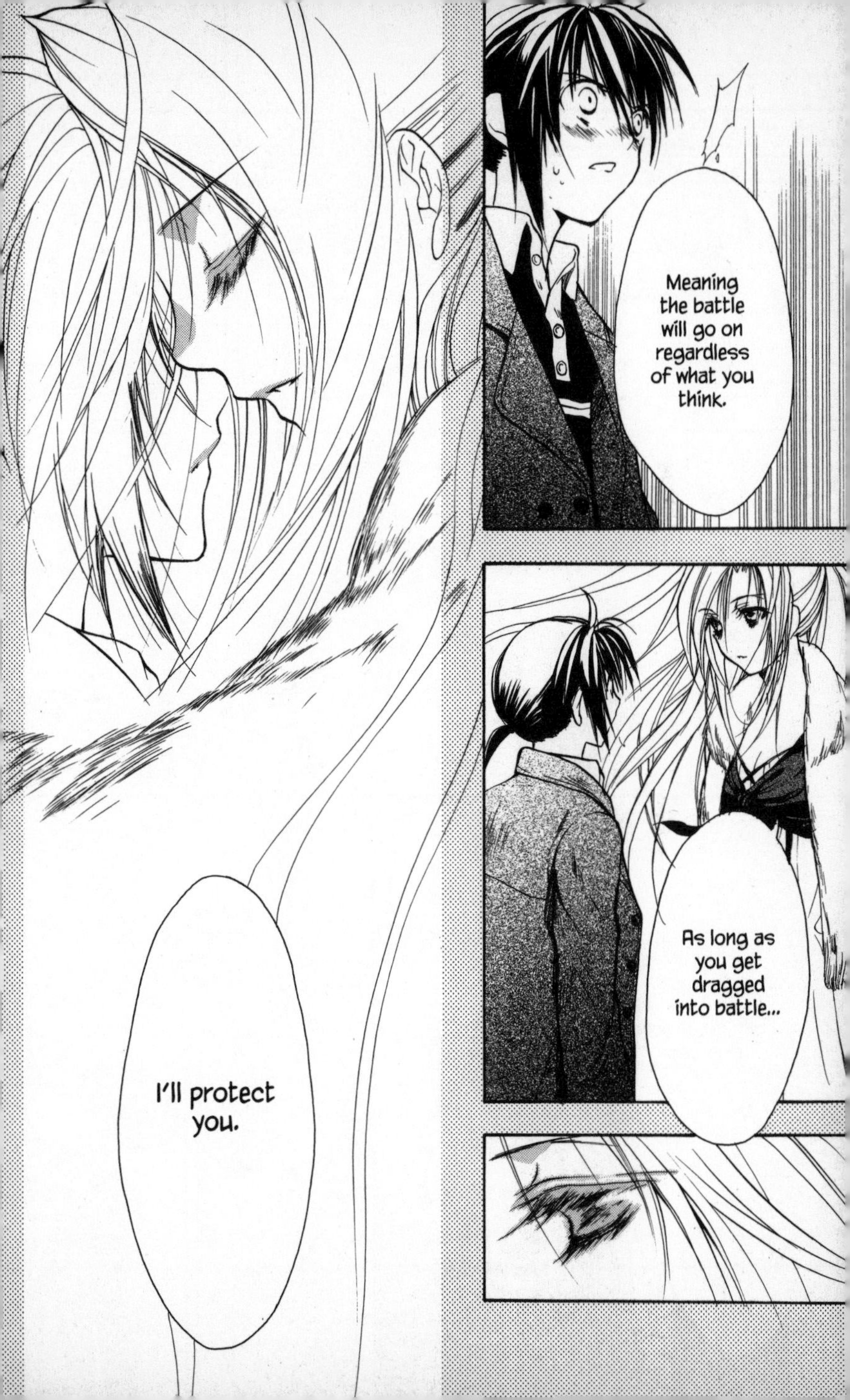
Meaning the battle will go on regardless of what you think.
As long as you get dragged into battle...
I'll protect you.

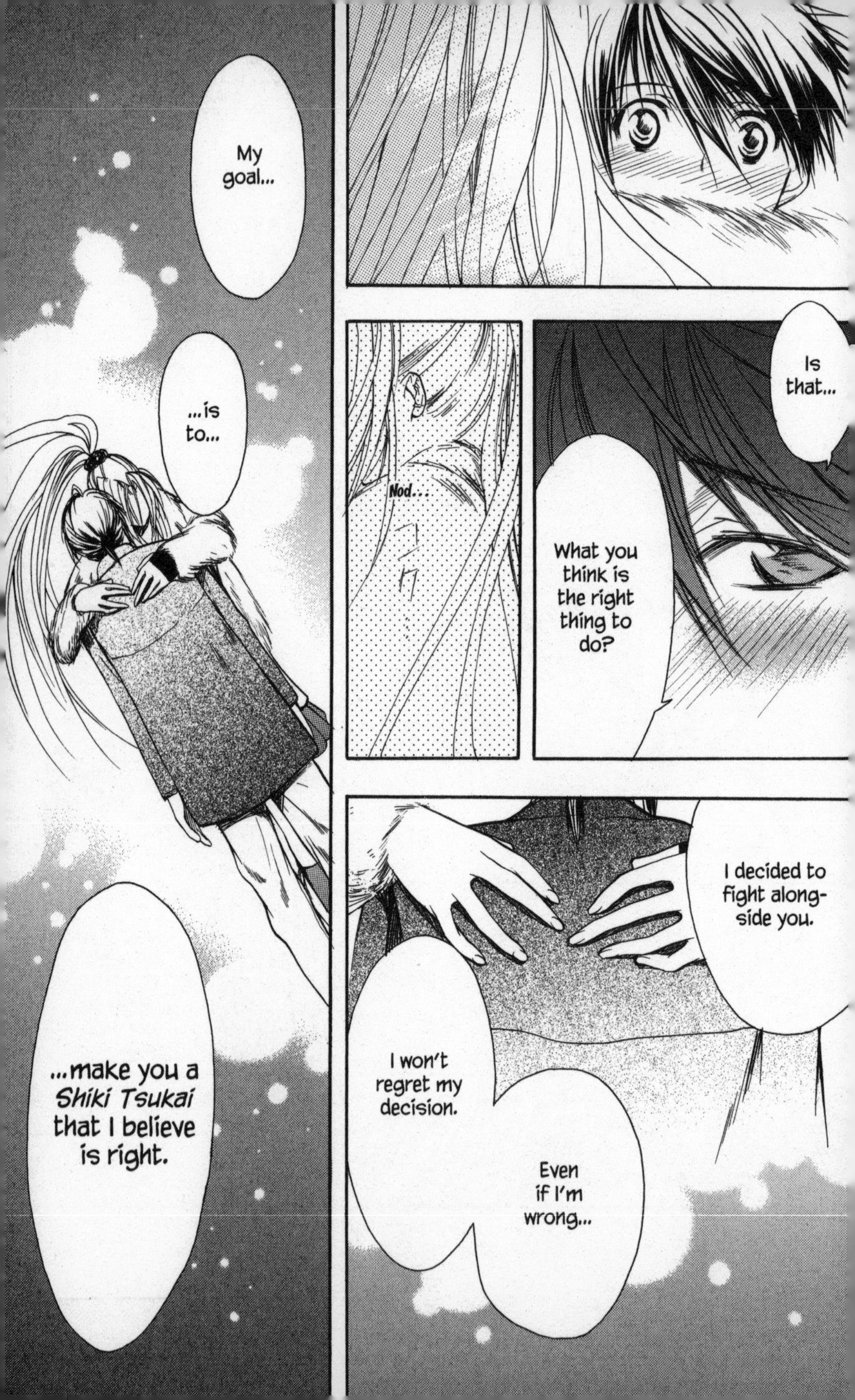

Is that...
What you think is the right thing to do?
Nod...
I decided to fight along-side you.
I won't regret my decision.
Even if I'm wrong...
My goal...
...is to...
...make you a *Shiki Tsukai* that I believe is right.

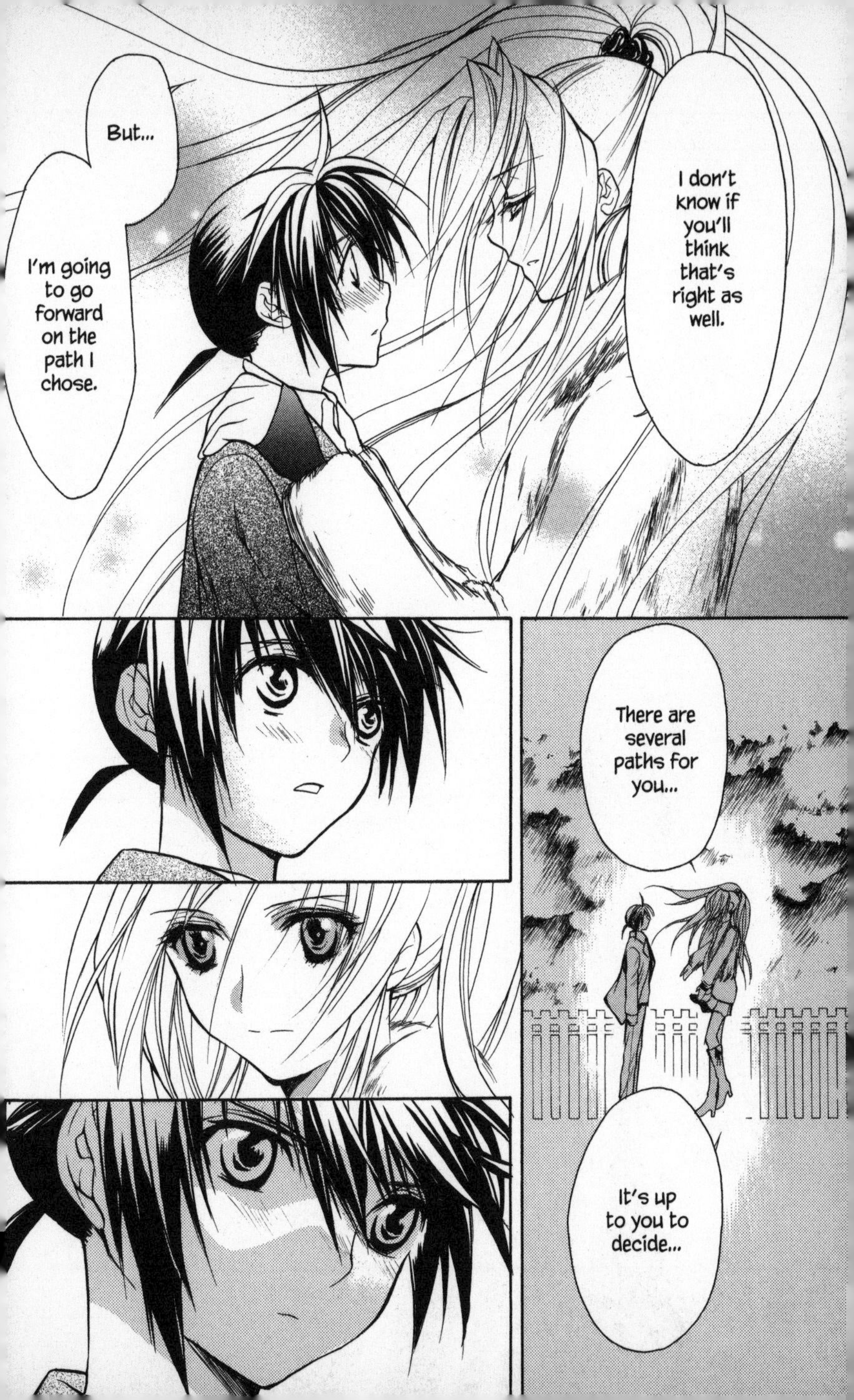
I don't know if you'll think that's right as well.
But...
I'm going to go forward on the path I chose.
There are several paths for you...
It's up to you to decide...

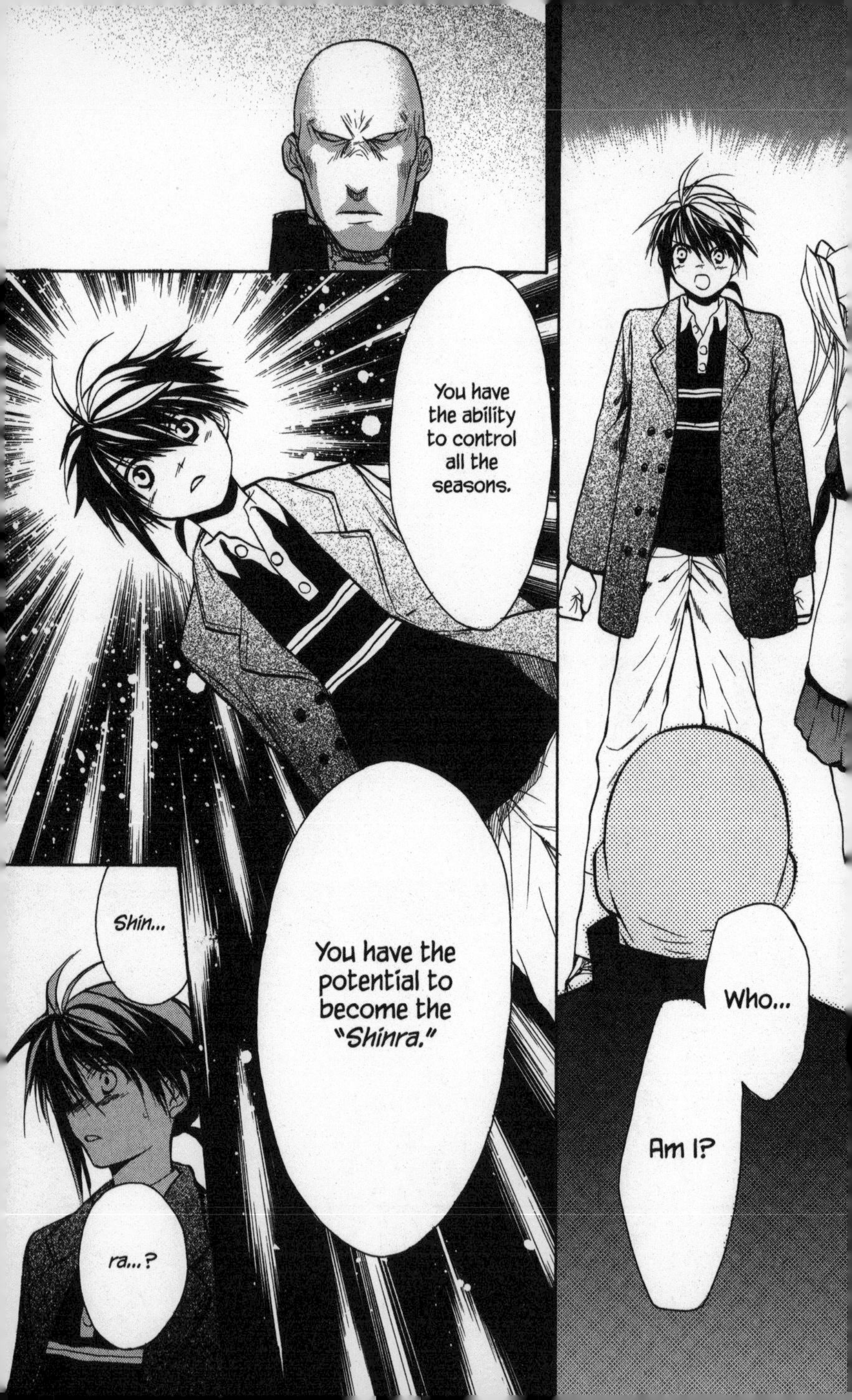
Who...
Am I?
You have the ability to control all the seasons.
You have the potential to become the "Shinra."
Shin...
ra...?

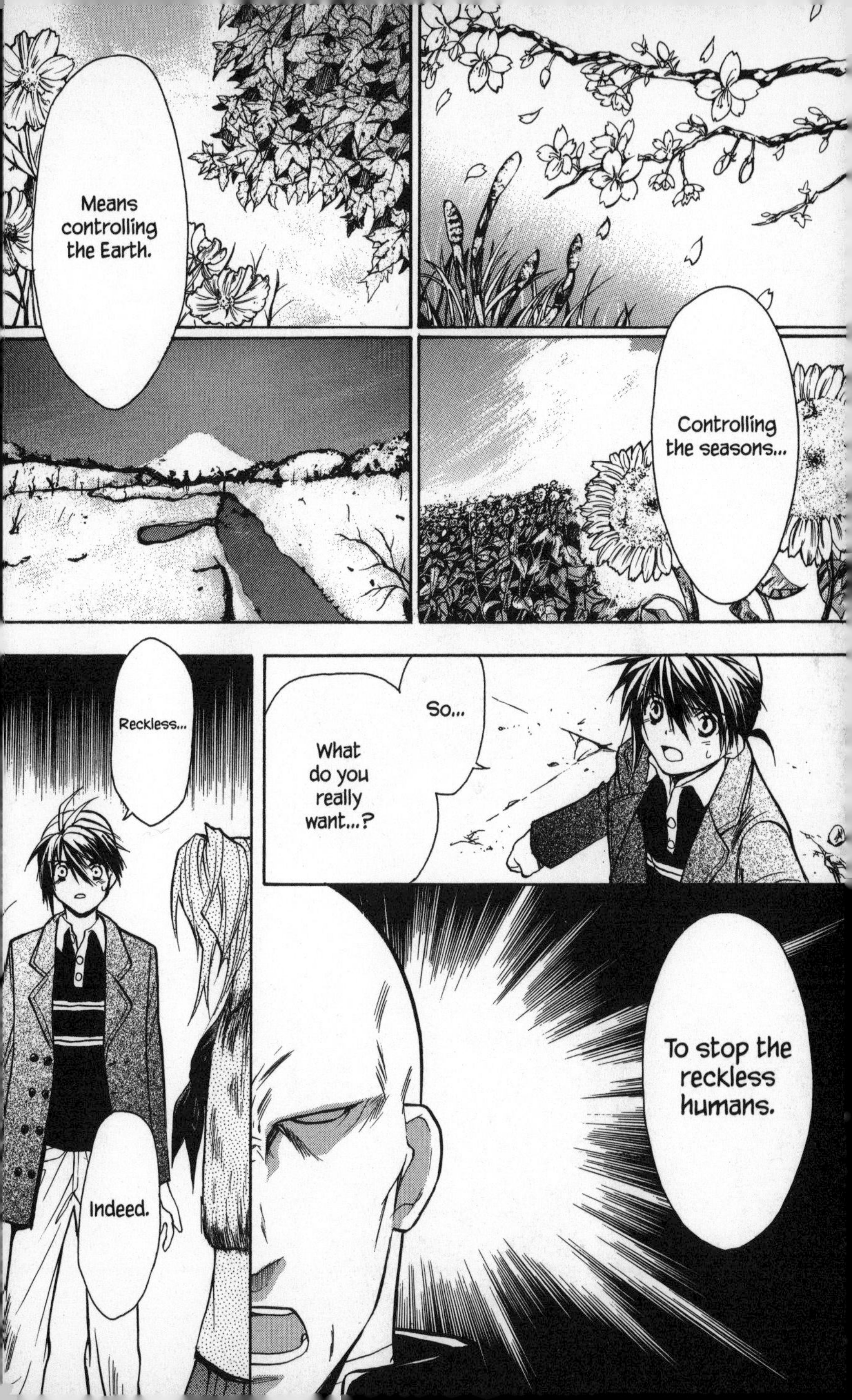
Controlling the seasons...
Means controlling the Earth.
So...
What do you really want...?
To stop the reckless humans.
Reckless...
Indeed.

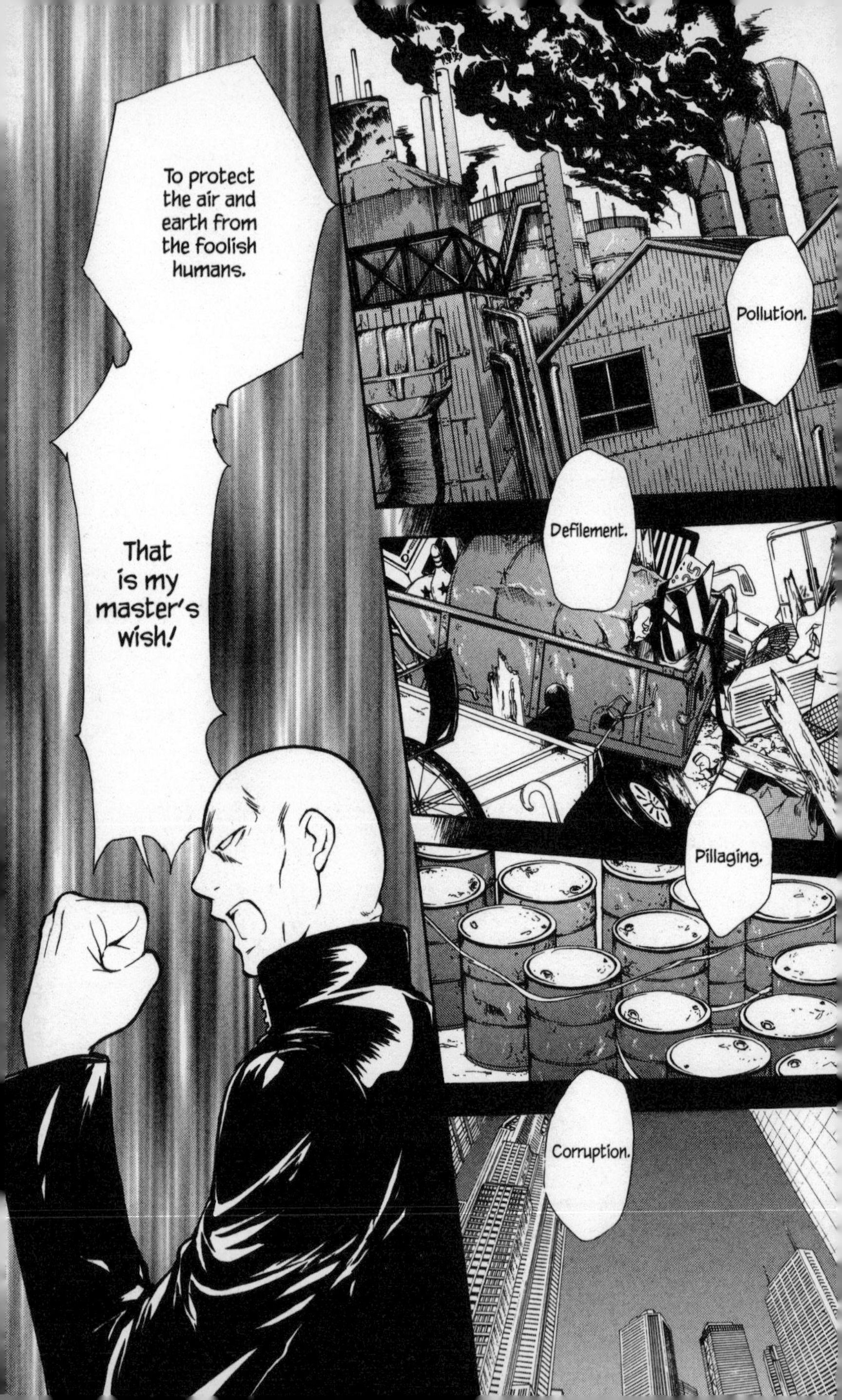
Pollution.
Defilement.
Pillaging.
Corruption.
To protect the air and earth from the foolish humans.
That is my master's wish!

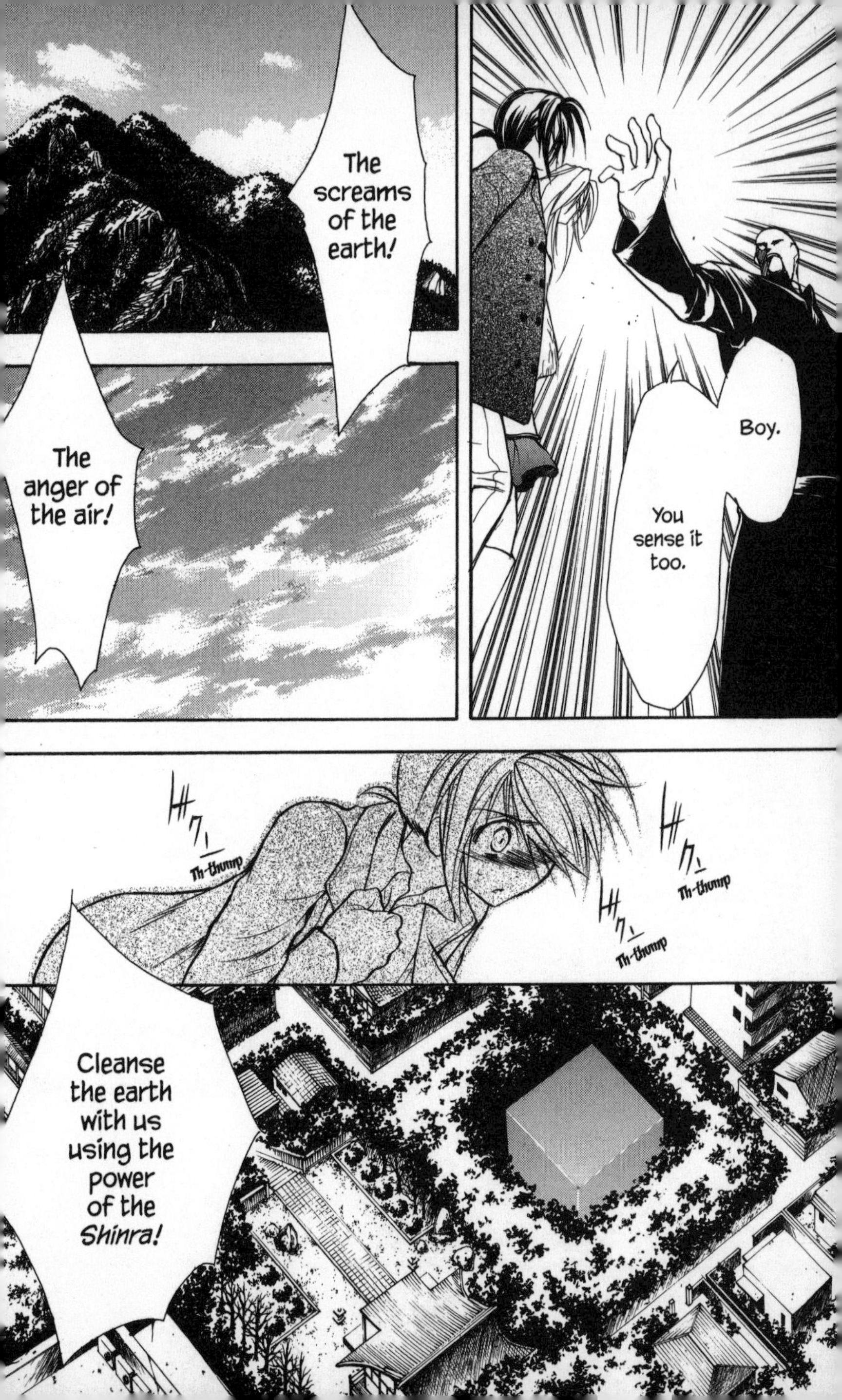
Boy.
You sense it too.
The screams of the earth!
The anger of the air!
Th-thump
Th-thump
Th-thump
Cleanse the earth with us using the power of the *Shinra*!

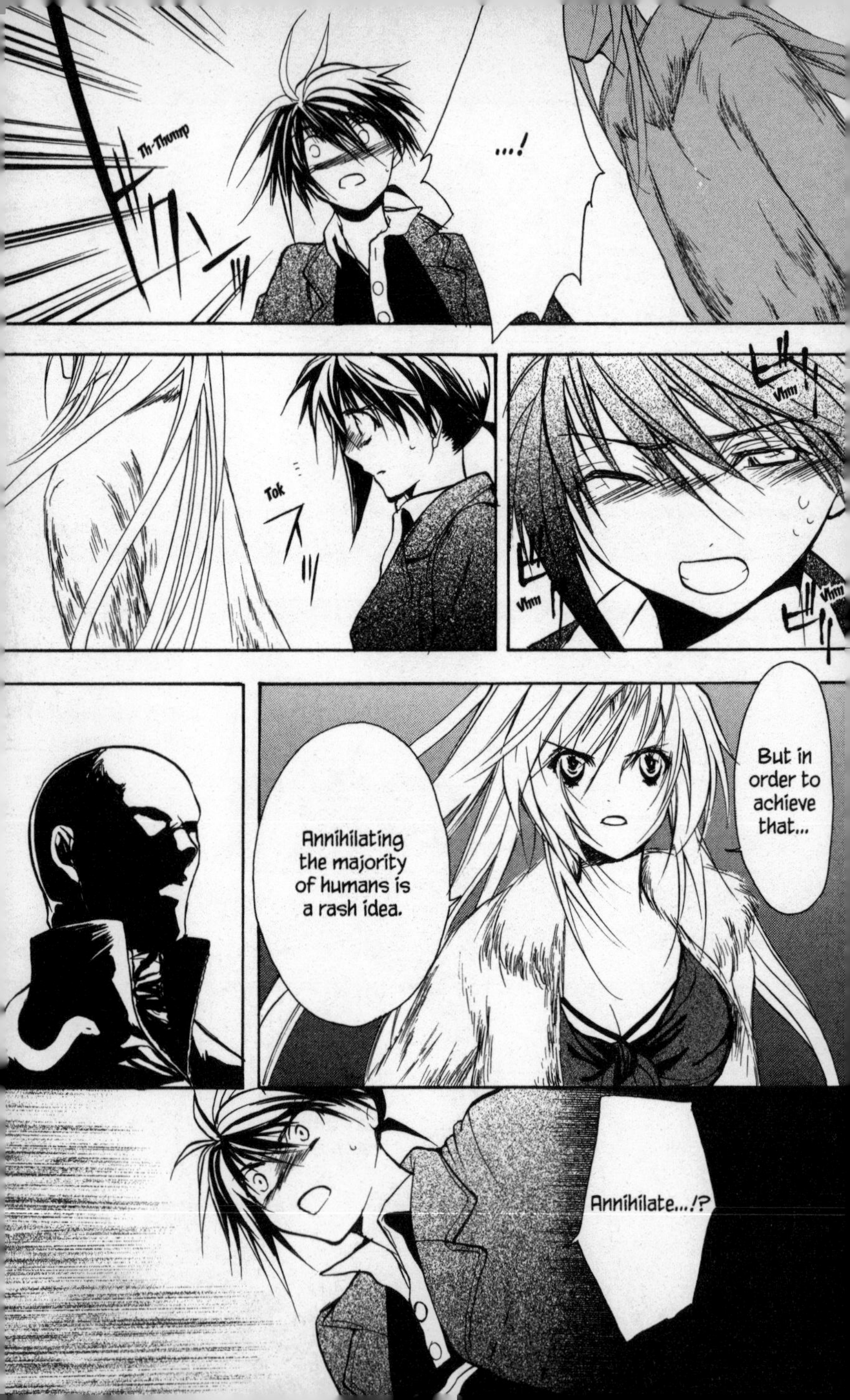
...!
Th-Thump
Vhm
Vhm
Vhm
Tok
But in order to achieve that...
Annihilating the majority of humans is a rash idea.
Annihilate...!?

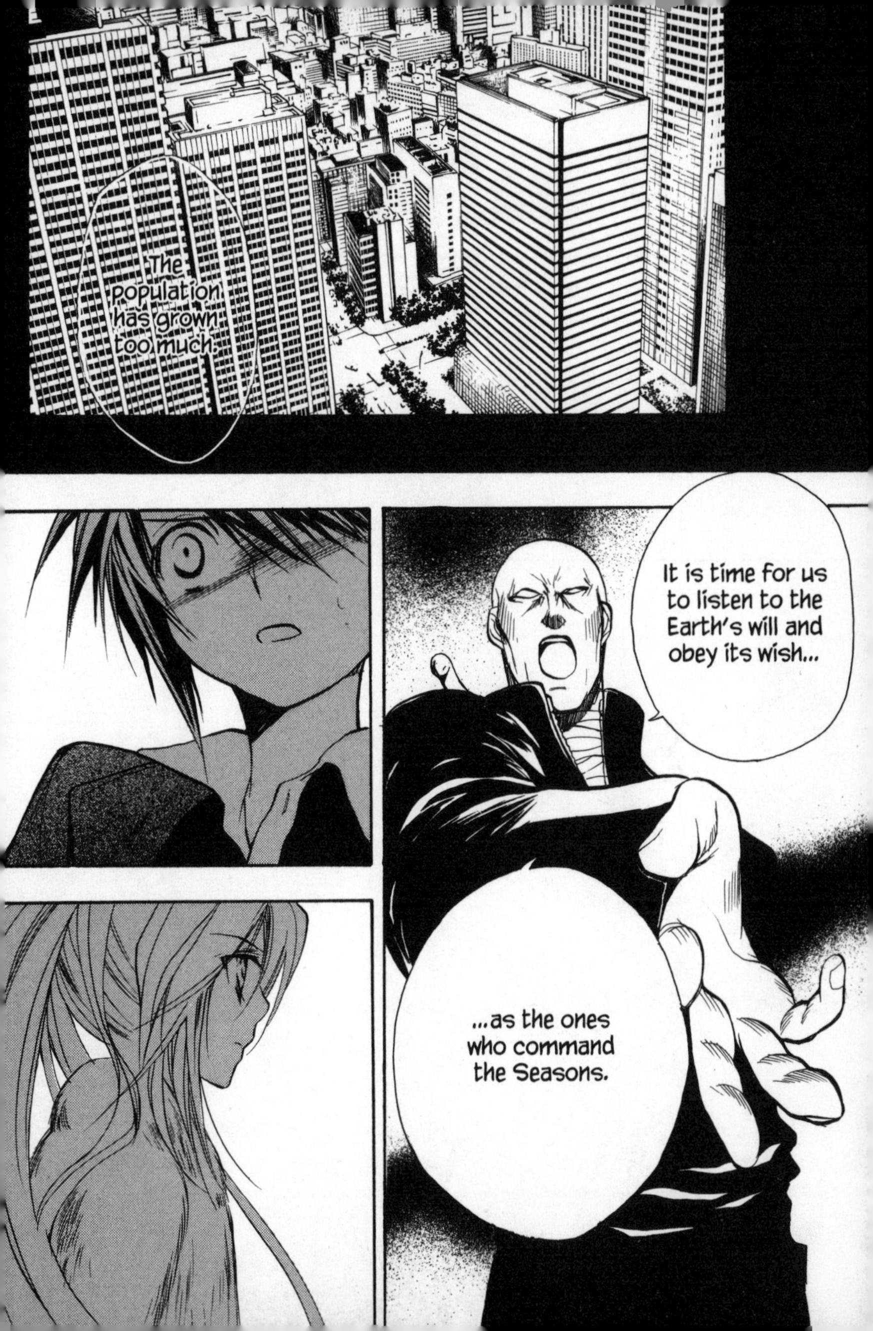
The population has grown too much.
It is time for us to listen to the Earth's will and obey its wish...
...as the ones who command the Seasons.

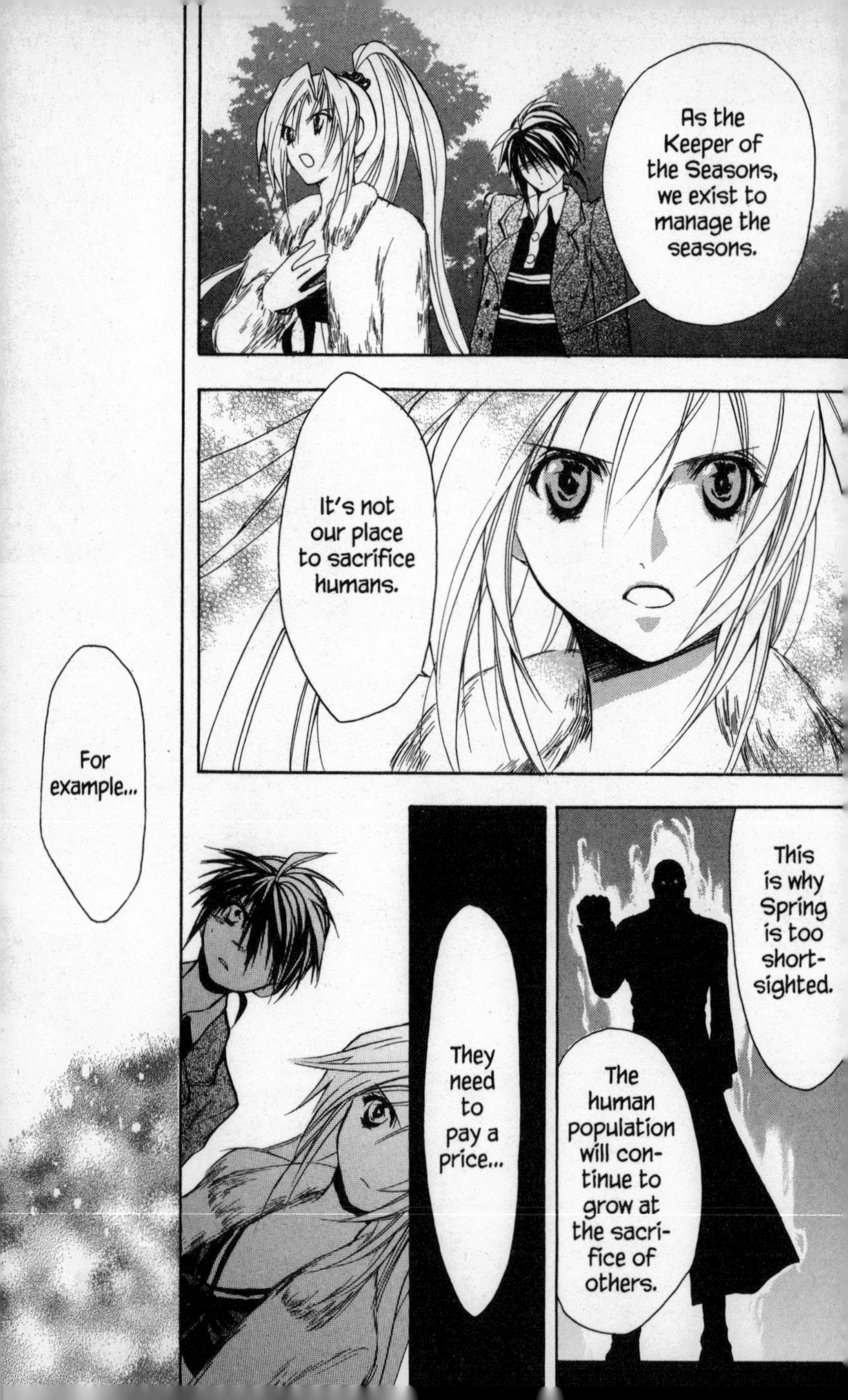
As the Keeper of the Seasons, we exist to manage the seasons.
It's not our place to sacrifice humans.
This is why Spring is too short-sighted.
The human population will continue to grow at the sacrifice of others.
They need to pay a price...
For example...

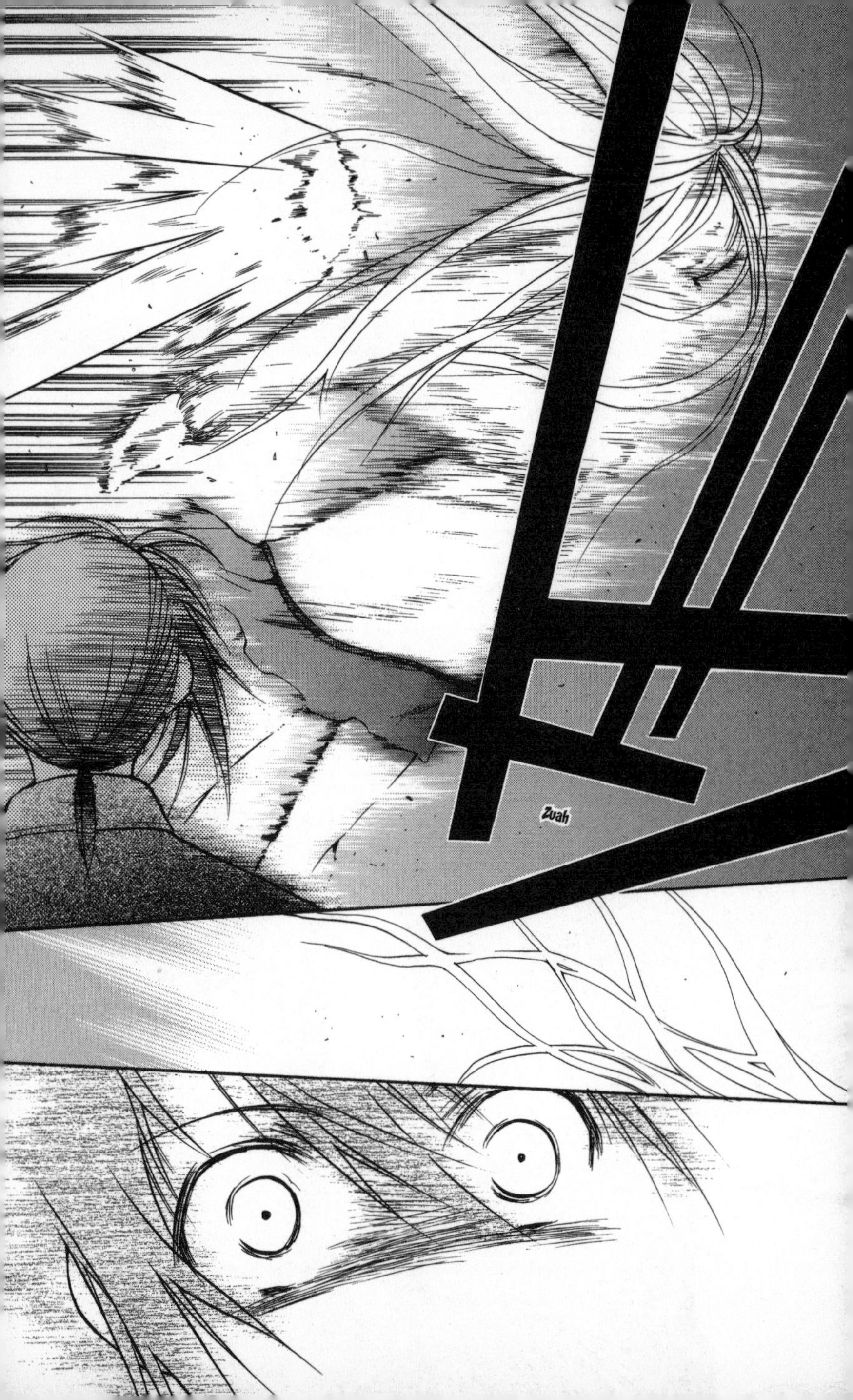
Zuah

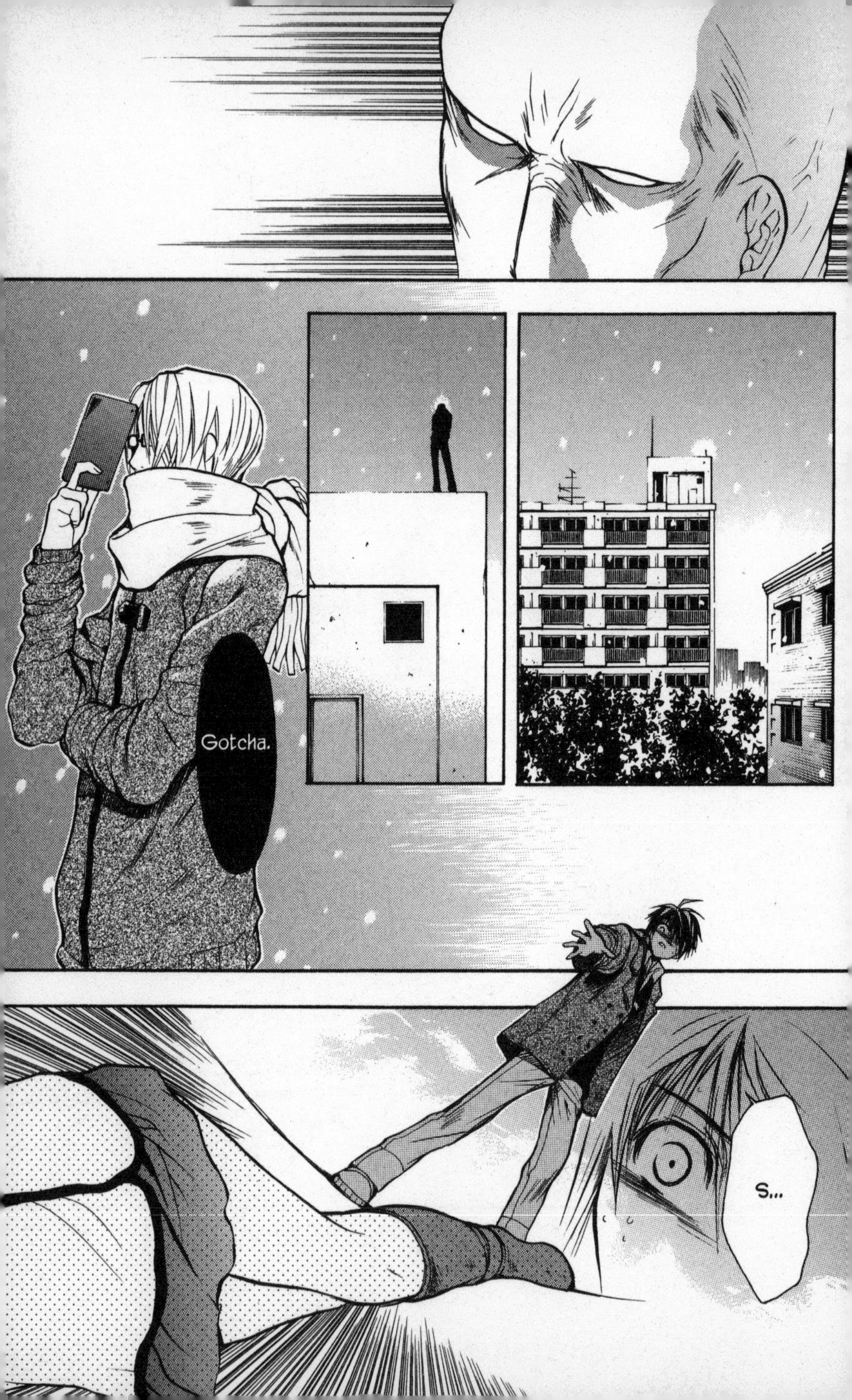
Gotcha.
S...

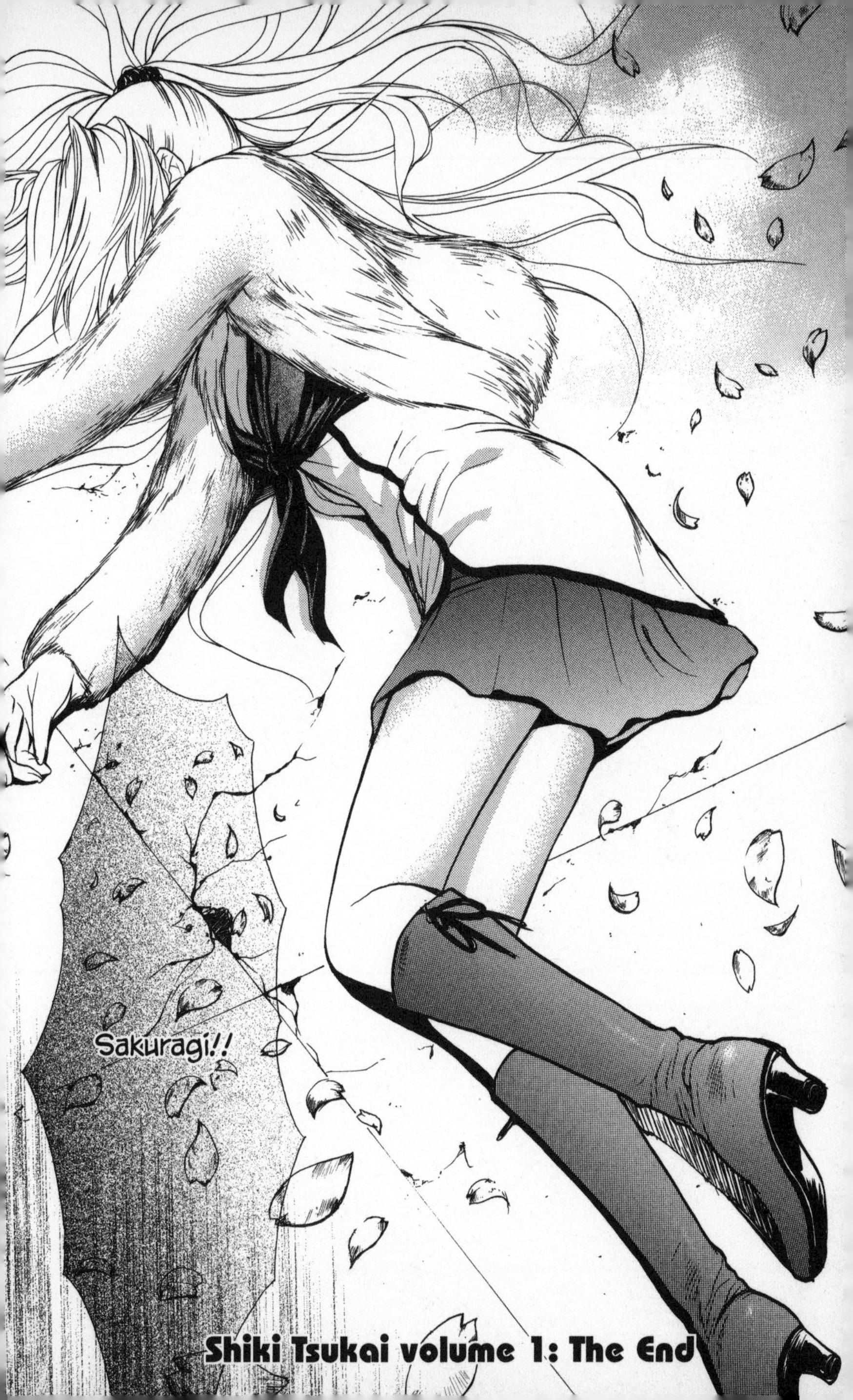
Sakuragi!!
Shiki Tsukai volume 1: The End

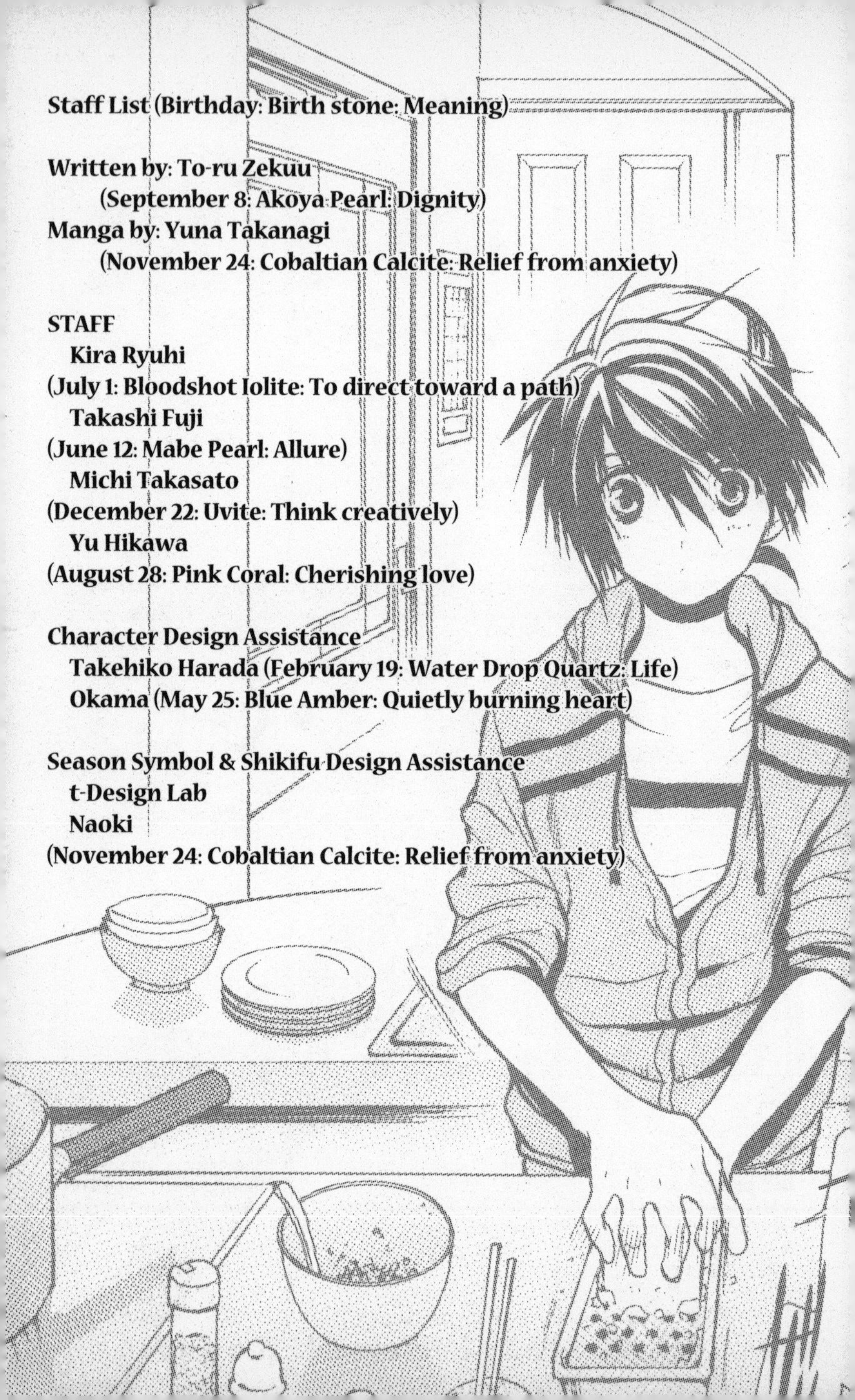

Staff List (Birthday: Birth stone: Meaning)

Written by: To-ru Zekuu
(September 8: Akoya Pearl: Dignity)
Manga by: Yuna Takanagi
(November 24: Cobaltian Calcite: Relief from anxiety)

STAFF
Kira Ryuhi
(July 1: Bloodshot Iolite: To direct toward a path)
Takashi Fuji
(June 12: Mabe Pearl: Allure)
Michi Takasato
(December 22: Uvite: Think creatively)
Yu Hikawa
(August 28: Pink Coral: Cherishing love)

Character Design Assistance
Takehiko Harada (February 19: Water Drop Quartz: Life)
Okama (May 25: Blue Amber: Quietly burning heart)

Season Symbol & Shikifu Design Assistance
t-Design Lab
Naoki
(November 24: Cobaltian Calcite: Relief from anxiety)

JANUARY

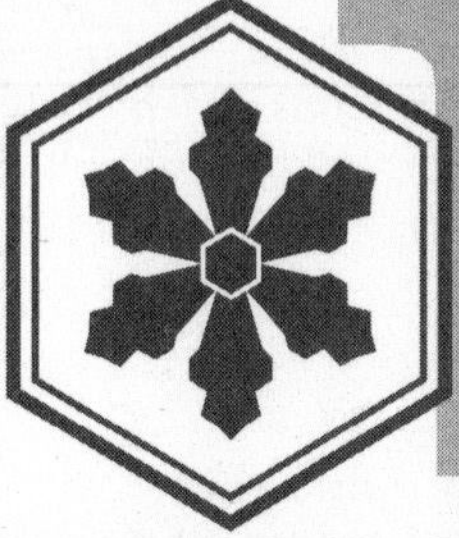

Mid-winter month and has the ability to control "Ice." Can also use lightning and illusion incantations.

Winter

FEBRUARY

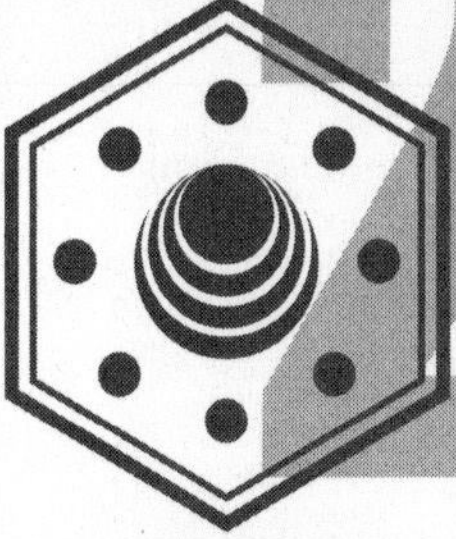

Has the ability to amplify, manipulate, and shoot "Chi." Can also use illusion incantations and has healing abilities.

Winter

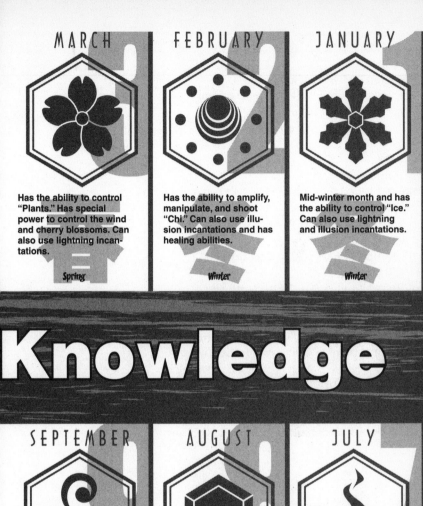

MARCH

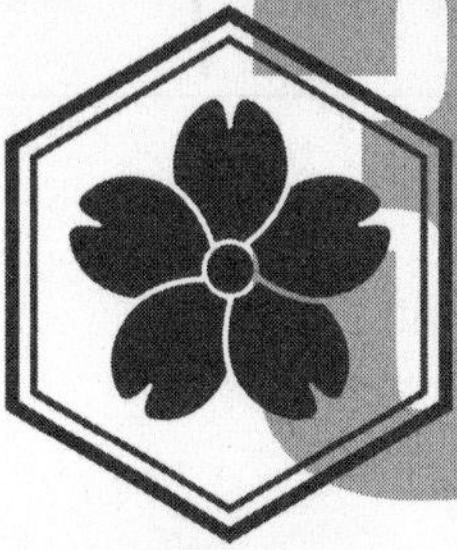

Has the ability to control "Plants." Has special power to control the wind and cherry blossoms. Can also use lightning incantations.

Spring

Knowledge

JULY

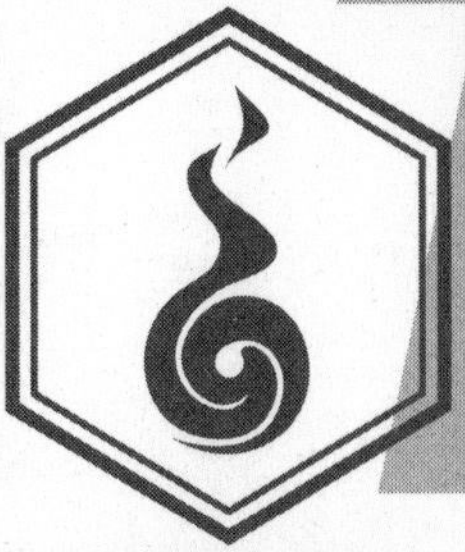

Mid-summer month and has the ability to control "Heat." Can also use lightning incantations. The opposite of January and has many similar ability incantations.

Summer

AUGUST

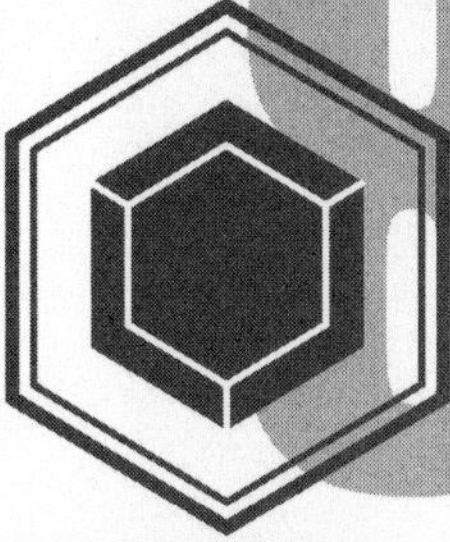

Has the ability to amplify, manipulate, and shoot "Spirit Power." Can also use healing and illusion incantations.

Summer

SEPTEMBER

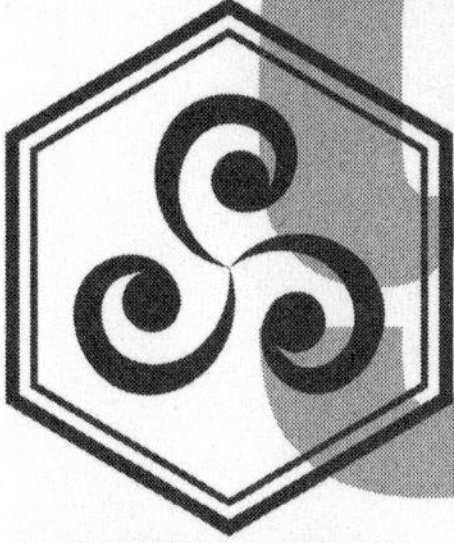

Has the ability to control "Air." Has special power to control gravity and typhoons. Can also control the wind and has strong offensive abilities.

Fall

Shiki

Twelve-month ability chart

The Shiki Tsukai are divided into 12 different groups. Here are their "abilities" and the symbol of each month.

APRIL

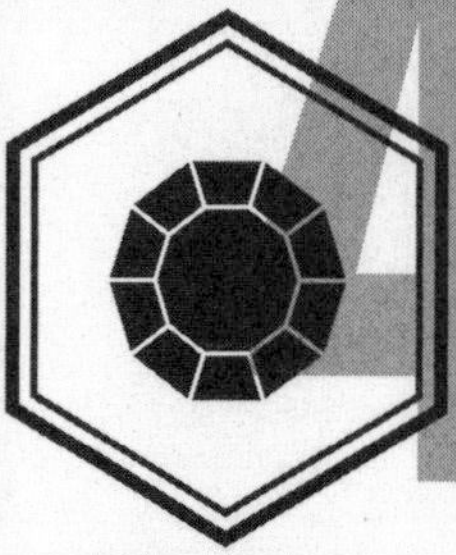

Mid-spring month and has the ability to control the "Earth." Can also use lightning, plant, and magnetic incantations.

Spring

MAY

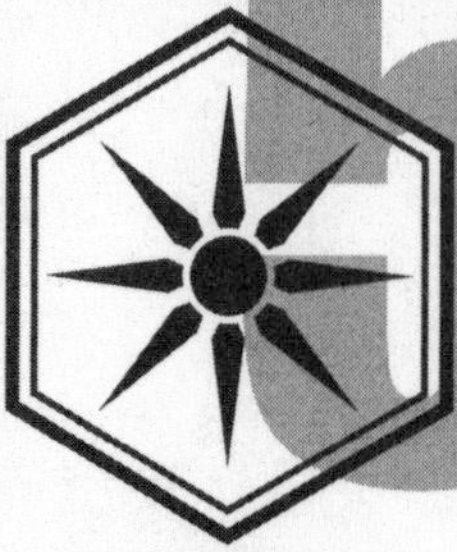

Has the ability to control "Light." Has special power to control heat. Can also use plant incantations.

Spring

JUNE

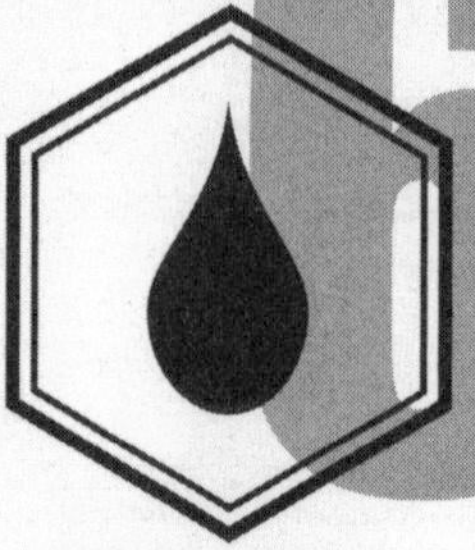

Has the ability to control "Liquids." Has special power to control decay. Can also use defense incantations.

Summer

OCTOBER

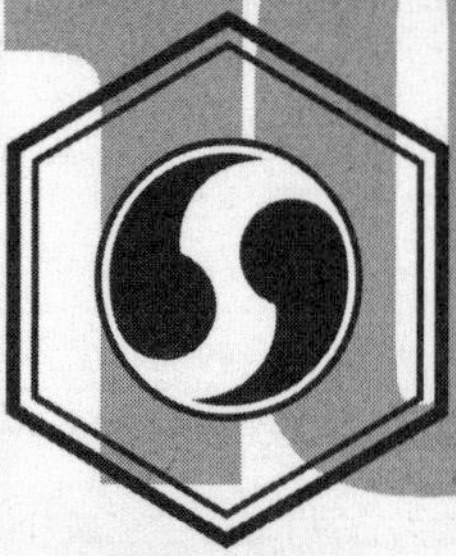

Mid-fall month and has the ability to control "Metal." Can also use lightning incantations and has special defense abilities. The opposite of April and has similar ability incantations.

Fall

NOVEMBER

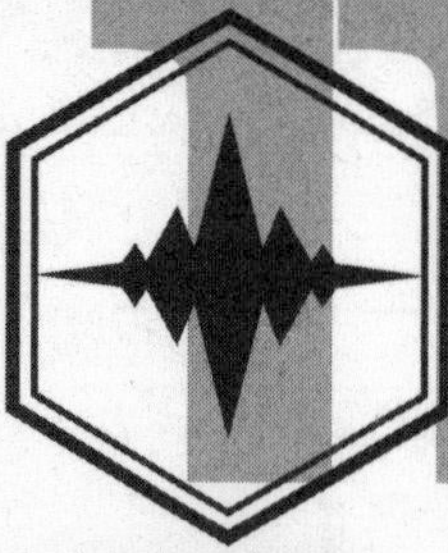

Has the ability to control "Sound." Has special power to control colors. Can use cold temperature incantations. Has many abilities that affect the senses.

Fall

DECEMBER

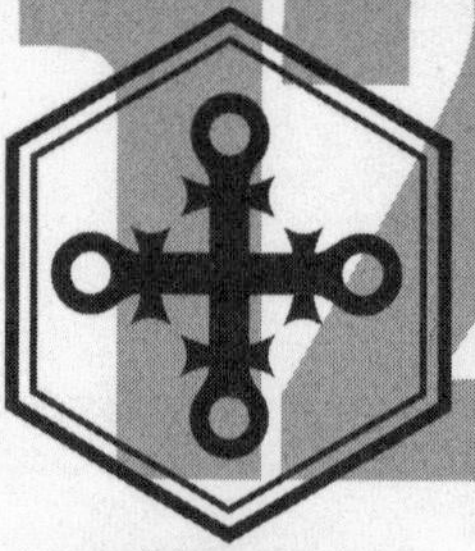

Has the ability to control and communicate with "Animals." Has incantations to arm people. Also has special abilities to control thought and has defense incantations.

Winter

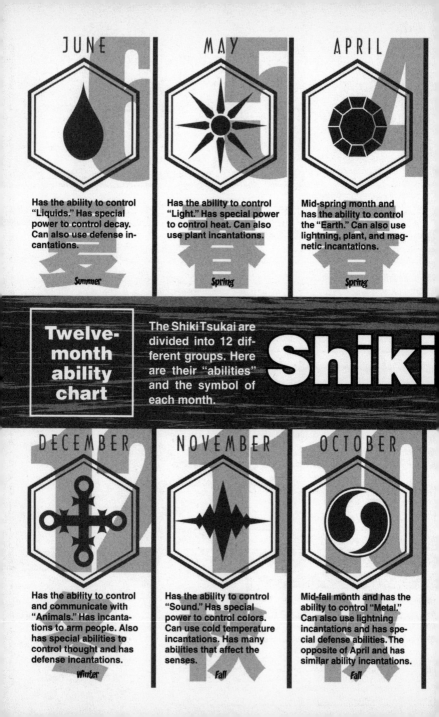

Shiki Tsukai

Season Incantation Collection

Volume 1

Here we will explain the Incantations used in this volume.

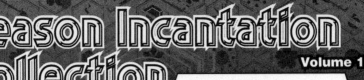

◆ Name of Incantation
▼ User
● Season Incantation and Phrases
■ Explanation

First Incantation: First Season

◆ Enou Blaze

▼ July: Man with hood

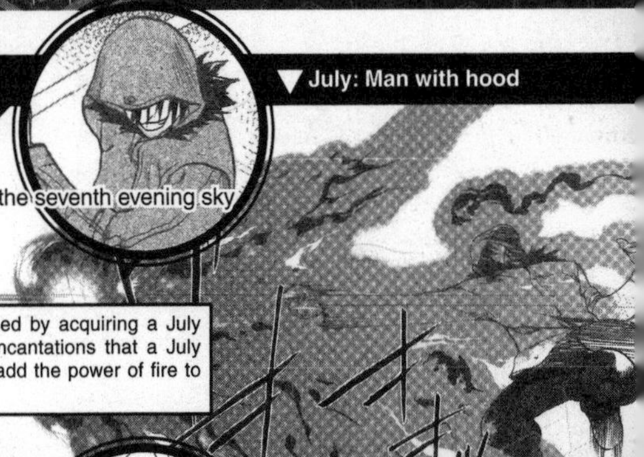

● First Phrase: Fumitsuki Shousho
● Second Phrase: Heat rises and dances in the seventh evening sky
● Third Phrase: Falcon Flight
● Enou Blaze

■ An "Offensive: Fire" incantation that can be used by acquiring a July 17–22 sigil date. It's one of the main offensive incantations that a July Shiki Tsukai uses as they control heat. They can add the power of fire to their weapon.

Second Incantation: First Season

◆ Blue Heaven Adazakura

▼ March: Koyomi Sakuragi

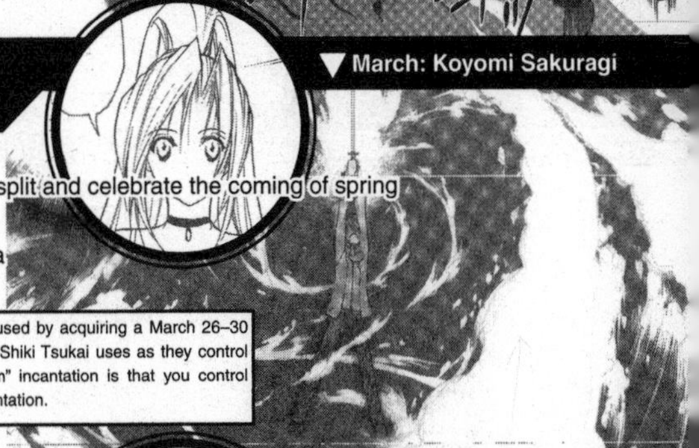

● First Phrase: Yayoi Shunbun
● Second Phrase: Days and nights have split and celebrate the coming of spring
● Third Phrase: Sakura Blossom
● Fourth Phrase: Blue Heaven Adazakura

■ A "Special: Cherry Blossom" incantation that can be used by acquiring a March 26–30 sigil date. It's one of the main incantations that a March Shiki Tsukai uses as they control plants. The characteristic of a "Special: Cherry Blossom" incantation is that you control Cherry Trees. Blue Heaven Adazakura is a defensive incantation.

Third Incantation: Third Season

◆ Tree Summon, Peach Wall

▼ March: Koyomi Sakuragi

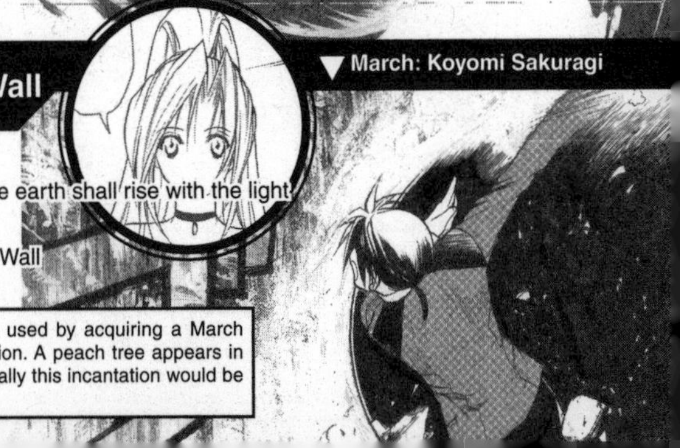

● First Phrase: Yayoi Keichitsu
● Second Phrase: Those who hide in the earth shall rise with the light
● Third Phrase: Peach Blossom
● Fourth Phrase: Tree Summon, Peach Wall

■ An "Armor: Plant" incantation that can be used by acquiring a March 11–15 sigil date. This is a defensive incantation. A peach tree appears in front of the Shiki Tsukai to shield them. Normally this incantation would be used to equip various trees.

Fourth Incantation: Third Season

◆ Ice Storm Bullets

▼ February: Rei Seichou

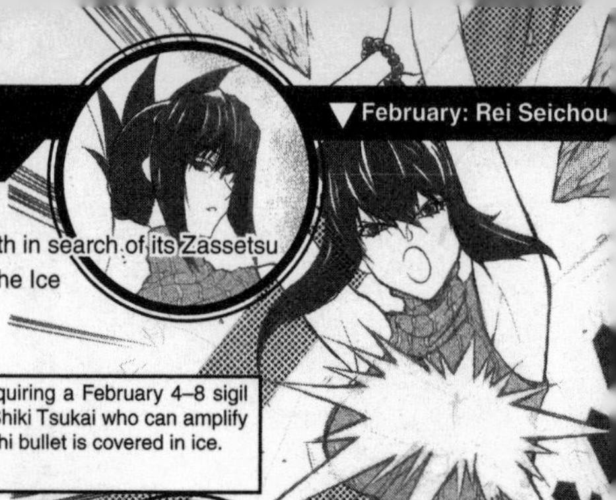

- First Phrase: Kisaragi Risshun
- Second Phrase: Spring arrives from the North in search of its Zassetsu
- Third Phrase: The Eastern Wind Shall Melt the Ice
- Fourth Phrase: Ice Storm Bullets

■ A "Bullet: Chi" incantation that can be used by acquiring a February 4–8 sigil date. It's one of the main incantations by a February Shiki Tsukai who can amplify their Chi and shoot it. As it's a winter incantation the chi bullet is covered in ice.

Fifth Incantation: Fourth Season

◆ Water Ogre Summon

▼ June: Leader (Baldy)

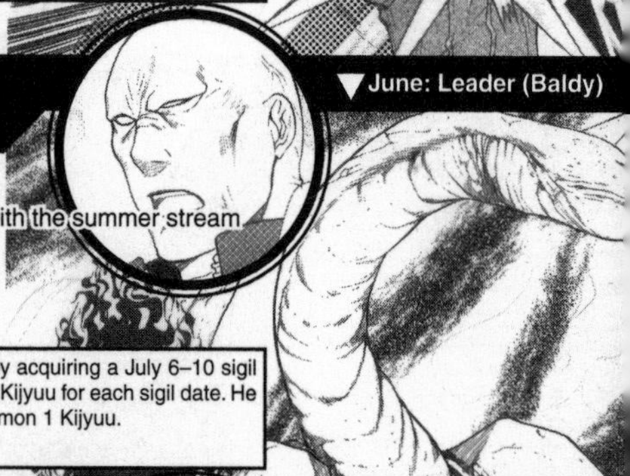

- First Phrase: Minazuki Boushu
- Second Phrase: Bearded grains shall flow with the summer stream
- Third Phrase: Mantis Birth
- Fourth Phrase: Water Ogre Summon

■ A "Summon: Kijyuu" incantation that can be used by acquiring a July 6–10 sigil date. It's a summon incantation and there is a different Kijyuu for each sigil date. He has acquired the July 9 sigil date so he is able to summon 1 Kijyuu.

Sixth Incantation: Fifth Season

◆ Tree God Summon

▼ March: Koyomi Sakura

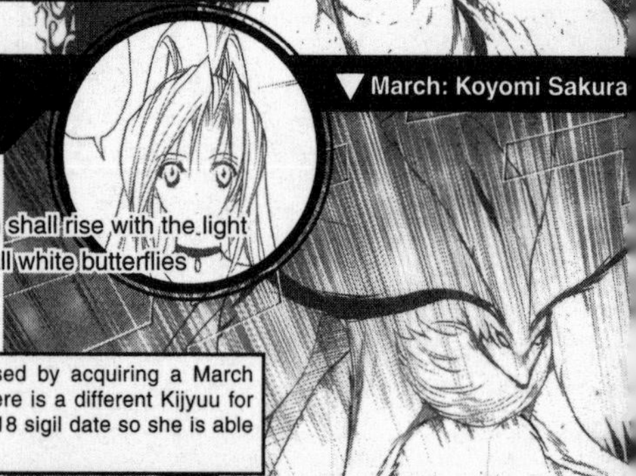

- First Phrase: Yayoi Keichitsu
- Second Phrase: Those who hide in the earth shall rise with the light
- Third Phrase: Caterpillars shall become small white butterflies
- Fourth Phrase: Tree God Summon

■ A "Summon: Kijyuu" incantation that can be used by acquiring a March 16–20 sigil date. It's a summon incantation and there is a different Kijyuu for each sigil date. Koyomi has acquired the February 18 sigil date so she is able to summon 1 Kijyuu.

Seventh Incantation: Fifth Season

◆ Frost Wind Bullets

▼ February: Rei Seichouj

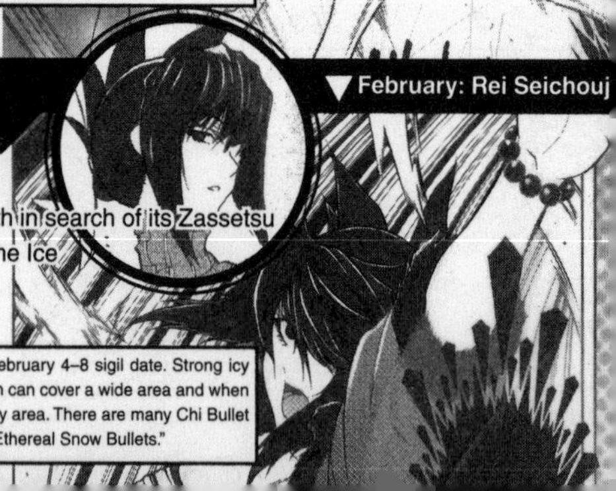

- First Phrase: Kisaragi Risshun
- Second Phrase: Spring arrives from the North in search of its Zassetsu
- Third Phrase: The Eastern Wind Shall Melt the Ice
- Fourth Phrase: Frost Wind Bullets

■ A "Bullet: Chi" incantation that can be used by acquiring a February 4–8 sigil date. Strong icy winds arise from below and blow everything away. The incantation can cover a wide area and when used inside a Formation of Winter the incantation can reach every area. There are many Chi Bullet variations such as "Ice Storm Bullets," "Frost Wind Bullets," and "Ethereal Snow Bullets."

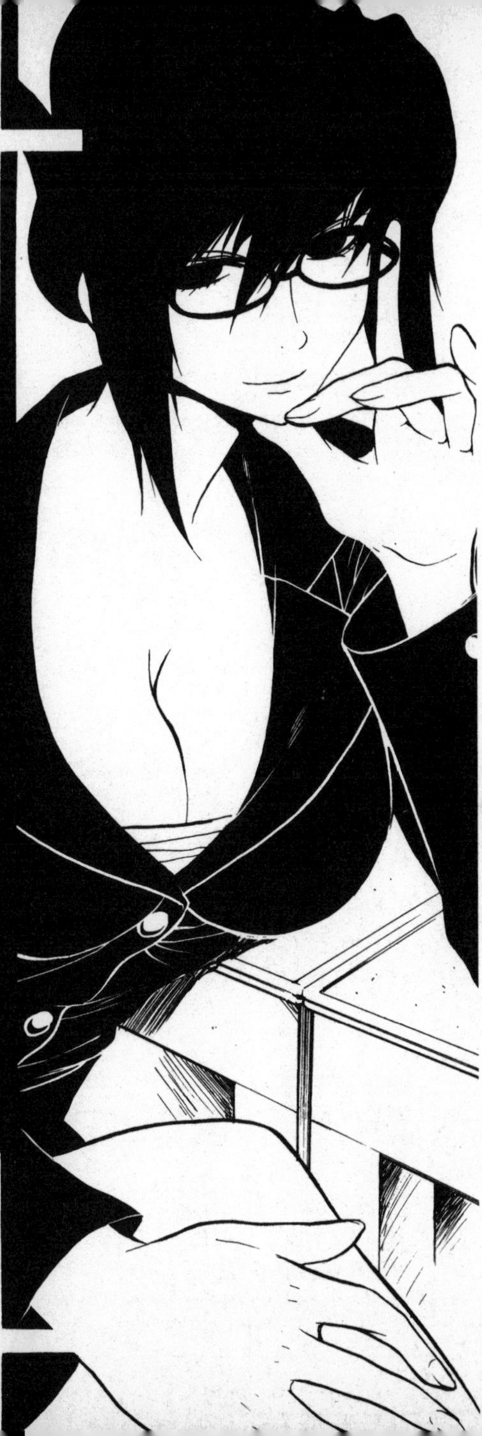

Hello, nice to meet you! This is *Shiki Tsukai* volume 1.

The story has just begun but I'm still learning how to draw as I go.

One of the things I thought when the serialization started is that I wasn't expecting to draw so many animals! (or monsters?) I personally like playing with animals but I've never had a fluffy pet so I sometimes think it must be fun to have a pet like Benjamin around. I'm jealous . . . I haven't drawn animals a lot so it takes me longer to draw them but it's fun ransacking through my research books. (I also bought a pocket-size book.) One day I'd like to see the "Red List of Threatened Animals" too. (It's a book about endangered species.) *Shiki Tsukai* makes me want to appreciate nature more. Please look forward to the next volume of *Shiki Tsukai*.

Yuna Takanagi

I think Rei Sensei is so cool. I think she's great . . .

Hello! It's *Shiki Tsukai* volume 1!

Instead of battle scenes on elemental powers I wanted to write about battles between the seasons. This story was actually conceived almost eight years ago. The idea was to get cards (*Shikifu*) from arcade machines and fight but it was ahead of its time so we couldn't do it.

But times have changed and now that I have a great partner like Yuna Takanagi, I'm so grateful!

The story has just begun and there are still a lot of mysteries but I love the seasons of Japan.

It would make me happy if you become interested in the seasons by reading this manga.

To-ru Zekuu

I'm pleasantly surprised that Koyomi ended being so mysterious.

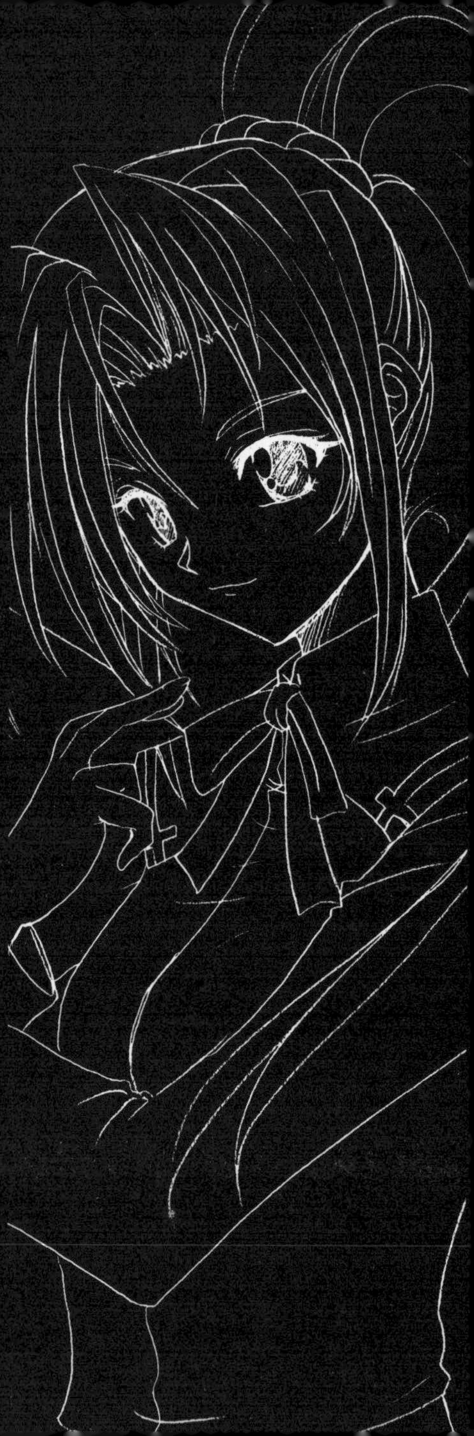

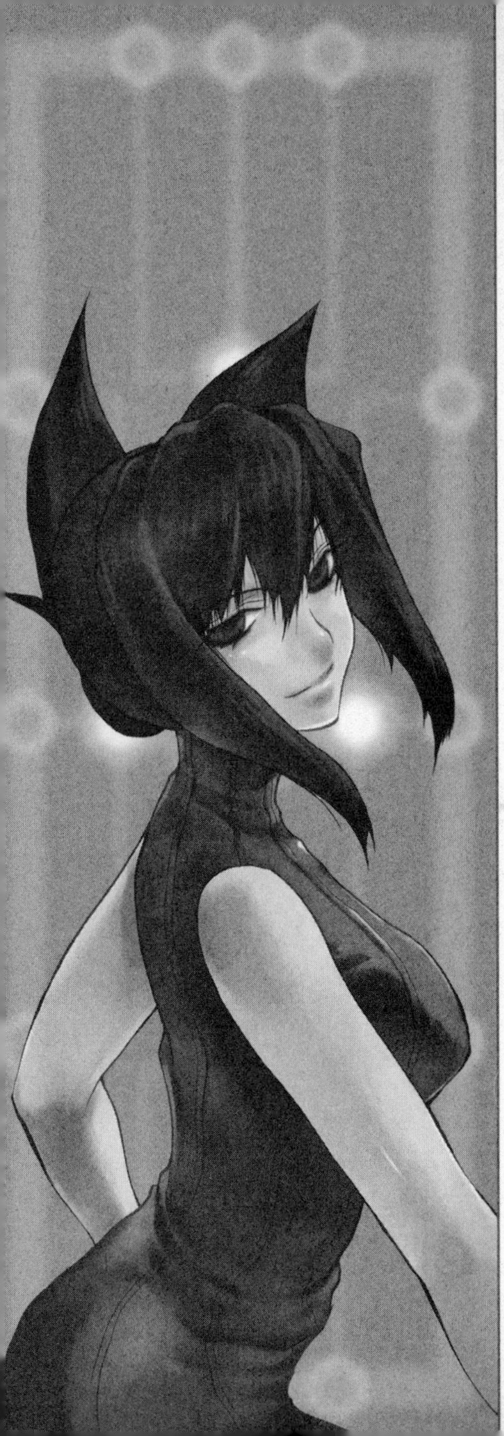

Rei Seichouji

Shikifu: Conch Pearl

Shiki Tsukai of February

Birthday: February 2, 1998
Age: Super Secret
Blood Type: O
Height: 5'7"
Weight: Secret
Measurements: Bust 36"/Waist 21"/ Hips 35"

- Akira's homeroom teacher. Teaches 2nd year, classroom A at Ouka Prefectural Middle School.
- The only daughter of the esteemed Seichouji family from Kyoto.
- Seems to be Akira's mother's rival.
- Cat lover.
- A humanitarian with a nice body.

Koyomi Sakuragi

Shikifu: Pink Beryl

Shiki Tsukai of March

Birthday: March 3, 1998
Age: 15 years old
Blood Type: Unknown
Height: 5'3"
Weight: 105 lb.
Measurements: Bust 33"/Waist 22"/ Hips 33"

- Has special ability to transform into a weapon.
- Daughter of the owner of the Sakuragi Corporation.
- Has lived overseas.
- Has great hearing.
- A realist with a straightforward personality.

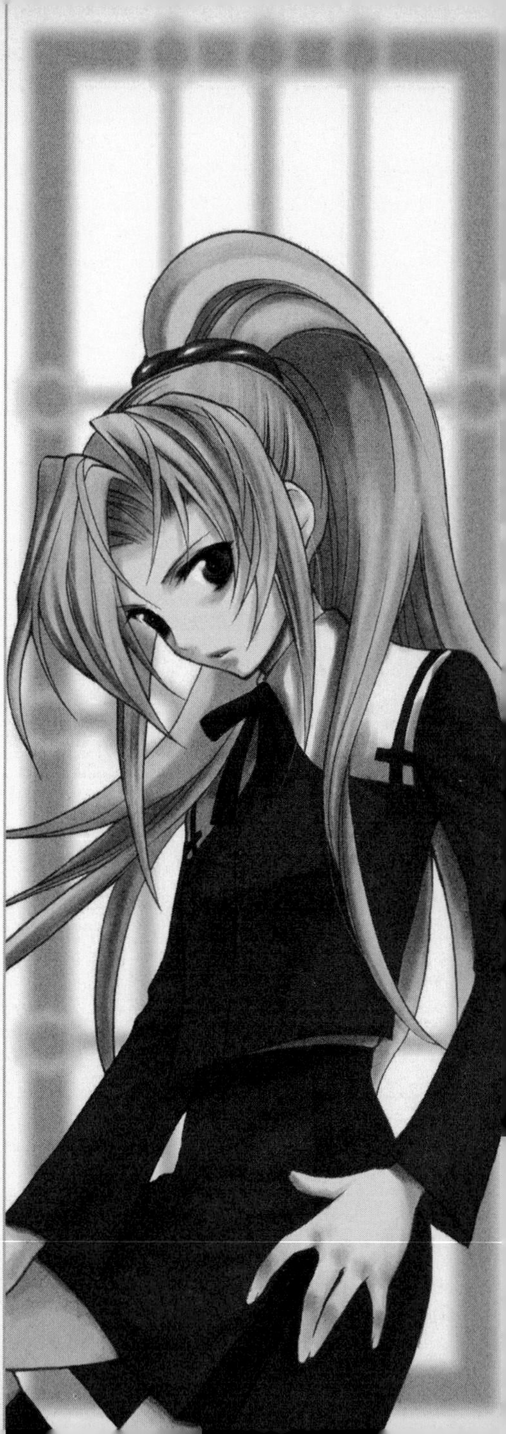

Translation Notes

Japanese is a tricky language for most Westerners, and translation is often more art than science. For your edification and reading pleasure, here are notes on some of the places where we could have gone in a different direction in our translation of the work, or where a Japanese cultural reference is used.

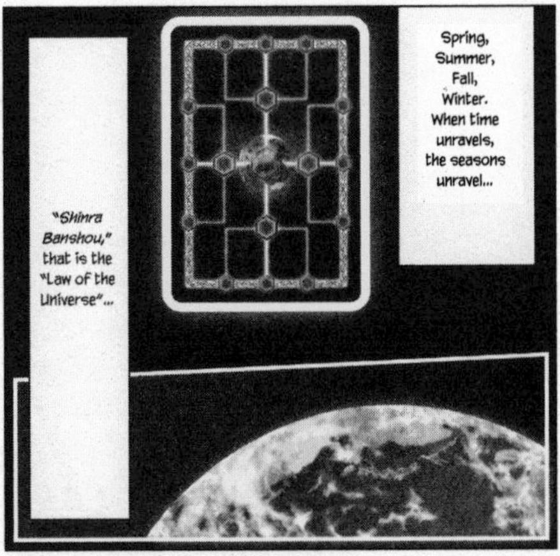
Spring, Summer, Fall, Winter. When time unravels, the seasons unravel...
"Shinra Banshou," that is the "Law of the Universe"...

Shinra Banshou, page 3

Shinra banshou means "all creation" or "the universe."

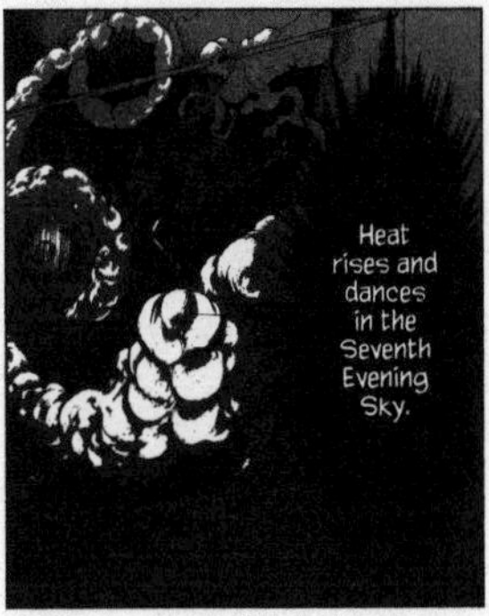
Heat rises and dances in the Seventh Evening Sky.

Seventh Evening Sky, page 11

The Seventh Evening Sky is July 7—the seventh day of the month.

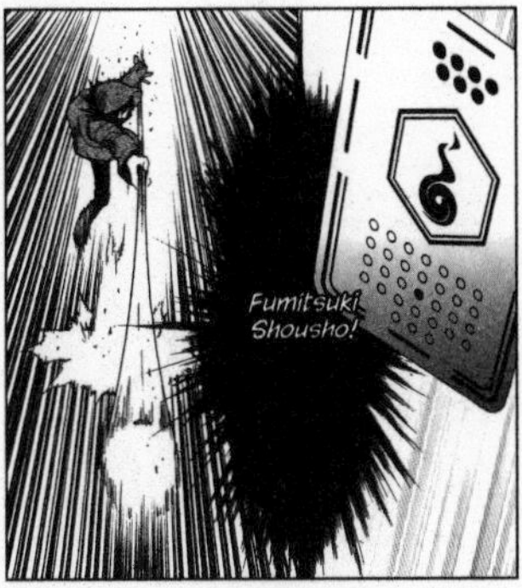
Fumitsuki Shousho!

Fumitsuki Shousho, page 10

Fumitsuki Shousho is the equivalent of July 7 under the lunisolar calendar. See the introduction for more information on the lunisolar calendar.

Take flight!

Enou Blaze!

Falcon Flight.

Falcon Flight, page 11

Wild Japanese falcons learn how to fly in July.

Enou Blaze, page 12

The Amida Buddha is also referred to as the Twelve Light Buddha. The Amida Buddha's light of compassion is divided into twelve different lights and each light has its own Buddha as well. One of them is called *enou kou* (*enou* Light), also called "the most superior light."

The days and nights have split and celebrate the coming of spring.

Yayoi Shunbun!

Yayoi Shunbun, page 13

Yayoi Shunbun is the equivalent of March 20 under the lunisolar calendar.

The days and nights have split and celebrate the coming of spring, page 13

In March the days and nights are almost split evenly. "*Shunki kourei*" ("Spring" in the spell) is the pre-war name of the modern March 21 holiday called "*Shunbun no hi.*" *Shunbun no hi* celebrates nature and the birth of living things in spring.

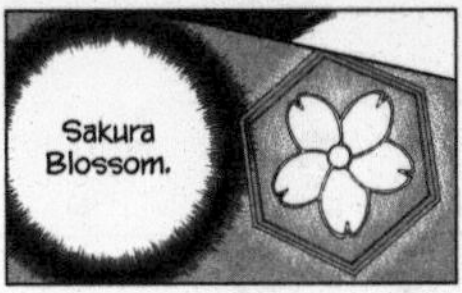
Sakura Blossom.

Sakura Blossom, page 13

In Japan, *sakura* (cherry blossoms) typically bloom in March.

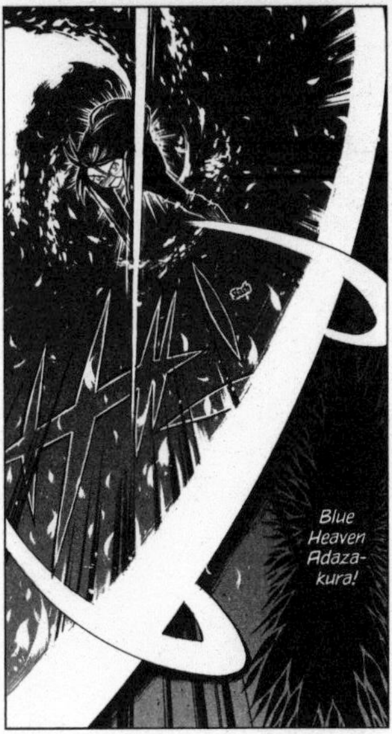
Blue Heaven Adazakura!

Blue Heaven *Adazakura*, page 14

Adazakura are *sakura* (cherry blossoms) that lose their petals fast. They are a symbol for ephemeral things.

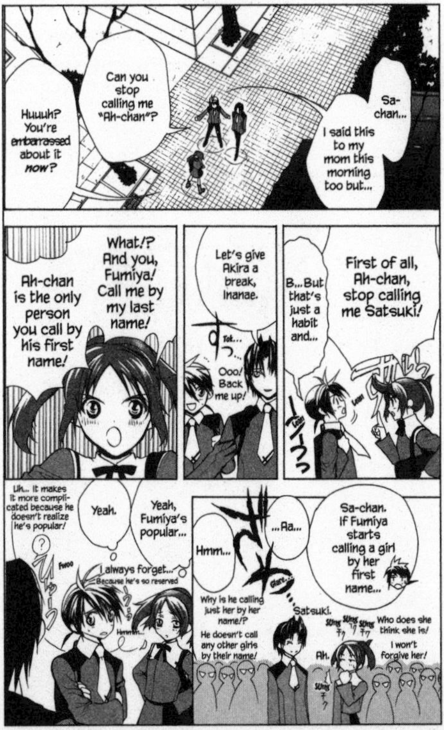
Sa-chan...
I said this to my mom this morning too but...
Can you stop calling me "Ah-chan"?
Huuuh? You're embarrassed about it *now*?
First of all, Ah-chan, stop calling me Satsuki!
B...But that's just a habit and...
Let's give Akira a break, Inanae.
Tok...
Ooo! Back me up!
What!? And you, Fumiya! Call me by my last name!
Ah-chan is the only person you call by his first name!
Sa-chan. If Fumiya starts calling a girl by her first name...
...Ra...
Hmm...
Glare...
Satsuki.
Why is he calling just her by her name!?
He doesn't call any other girls by their name!
Who does she think she is!
I won't forgive her!
Ah.
Yeah, Fumiya's popular...
Yeah.
Uh... It makes it more complicated because he doesn't realize he's popular!
?
I always forget...
Because he's so reserved
Hmmm...
Fwoo

Names, page 20

It's typically rude to call someone by his or her first name in Japanese unless you are somewhat acquainted with the person. Thus it's common for people to refer to one another other by surname. When two people call each other by their first names, it suggests they are more than acquaintances. And when members of the opposite sex call each other by their first names, it represents their closeness and could also be a sign that they are "more than friends."

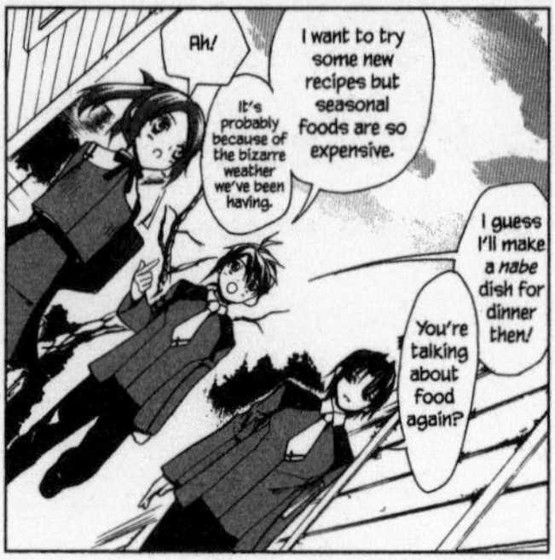
I want to try some new recipes but seasonal foods are so expensive.
Ah!
It's probably because of the bizarre weather we've been having.
I guess I'll make a *nabe* dish for dinner then!
You're talking about food again?

Nabe dish, page 21

Nabe, or a hot pot dish, is a seasonal dish typically enjoyed in winter.

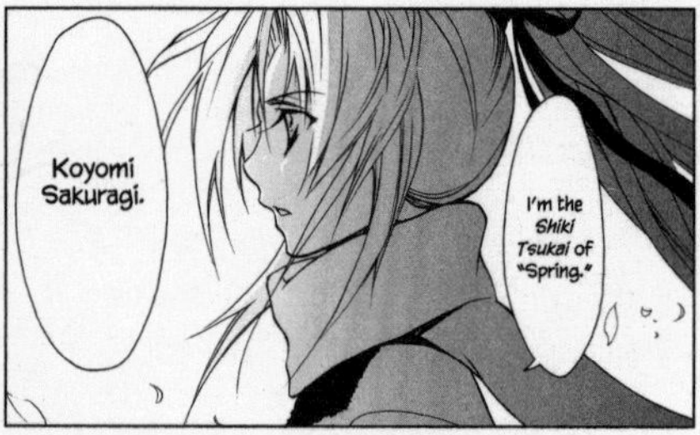
I'm the *Shiki Tsukai* of "Spring."
Koyomi Sakuragi.

Shiki Tsukai, page 34

One who possesses the power of the seasons. *Shiki* means "the four seasons" and *tsukai* literally means "one who uses" (in this case the seasons).

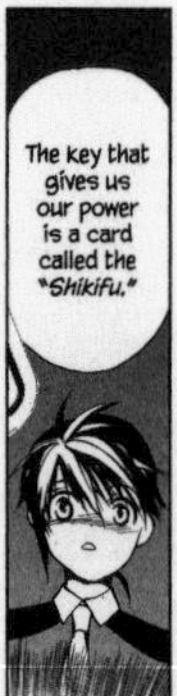
The key that gives us our power is a card called the "*Shikifu*."

Shikifu, page 65

The *Shikifu* is a magic card from which *Shiki Tsukai* derive their power. We'll learn more about *Shikifu* as the series progresses!

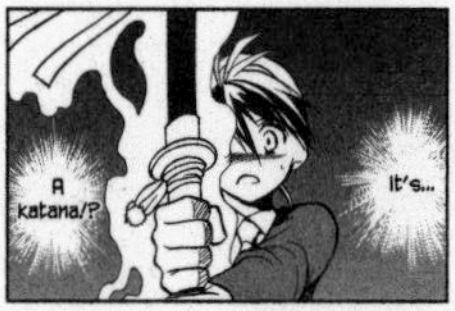
It's...
A katana!?

Katana, page 38

A *katana* is a Japanese sword, traditionally used by samurai.

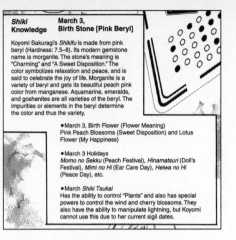

Shiki Knowledge

March 3, Birth Stone [Pink Beryl]

Koyomi Sakuragi's *Shikifu* is made from pink beryl (Hardness: 7.5–8). Its modern gemstone name is morganite. The stone's meaning is "Charming" and "A Sweet Disposition." The color symbolizes relaxation and peace, and is said to celebrate the joy of life. Morganite is a variety of beryl and gets its beautiful peach pink color from manganese. Aquamarine, emeralds, and goshenites are all varieties of the beryl. The impurities or elements in the beryl determine the color and thus the variety.

● March 3, Birth Flower (Flower Meaning)
Pink Peach Blossoms (Sweet Disposition) and Lotus Flower (My Happiness)

● March 3 Holidays
Momo no Sekku (Peach Festival), *Hinamatsuri* (Doll's Festival), *Mimi no Hi* (Ear Care Day), *Heiwa no Hi* (Peace Day), etc.

● March *Shiki Tsukai*
Has the ability to control "Plants" and also has special powers to control the wind and cherry blossoms. They also have the ability to manipulate lightning, but Koyomi cannot use this due to her current sigil dates.

Momo no Sekku, page 65

Momo no Sekku, or the Peach Festival, is celebrated when the peach blossoms begin to bloom in March.

Hinamatsuri, page 65

Hinamatsuri, also known as "Doll's Festival" or "Girls' Day" is a holiday on March 3, on which one wishes for a healthy upbringing for little girls.

Mimi no Hi, page 65

Mimi no Hi, or "Ear Care Day," is a holiday celebrated on March 3. It is meant to raise awareness of deafness.

Heiwa no Hi, page 65

Heiwa no Hi, or "Peace Day," is a holiday celebrating peace on March 3.

Yayoi Keichitsu, page 93

Yayoi Keichitsu is the equivalent of March 15 under the lunisolar calendar.

Yayoi Keichitsu

It's an elemental beast...a "Kijyuu."

Raa/ A snake/? That's...

Kijyuu, page 72

Kijyuu is an elemental beast that's born from the seasons. *Ki* means "seasons" and *jyuu* is the character for "beast."

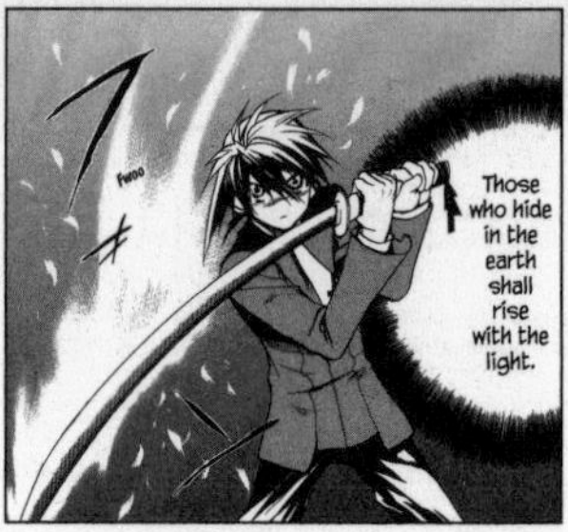
Fwoo
Those who hide in the earth shall rise with the light.

Those who hide in the earth shall rise with the light, page 93

This is a reference to the hibernating insects that emerge from the ground in spring.

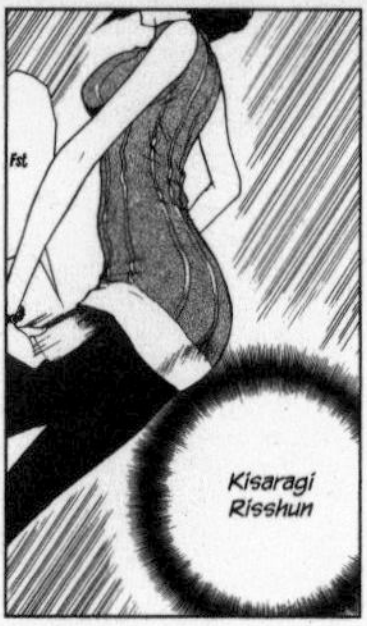
Fst
Kisaragi Risshun

Kisaragi Risshun, page 96

Kisaragi Risshun is the equivalent of February 4 under the lunisolar calendar.

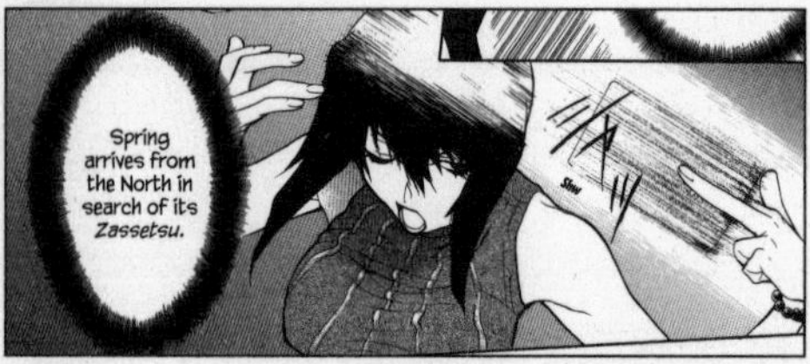
Spring arrives from the North in search of its *Zassetsu.*

Zassetsu, page 96

Zassetsu is a collective term for the seasonal days other than the *24 Sekki*.

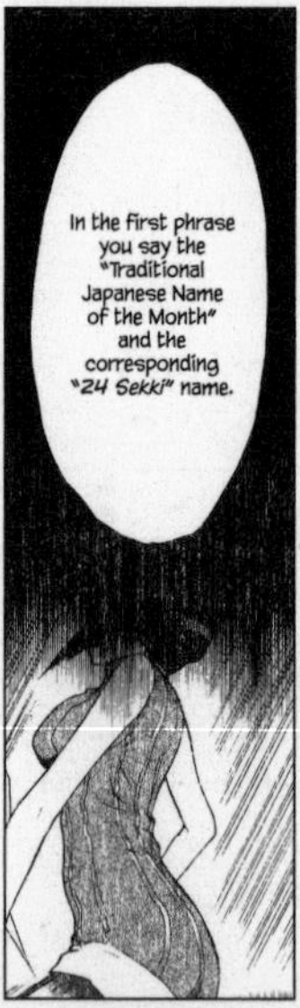
In the first phrase you say the "Traditional Japanese Name of the Month" and the corresponding "*24 Sekki*" name.

24 Sekki, page 102

24 sekki are days that divide the lunisolar calendar into 24 equal sections and have special names to mark the change in seasons. See the introduction for a complete list of the *24 sekki*.

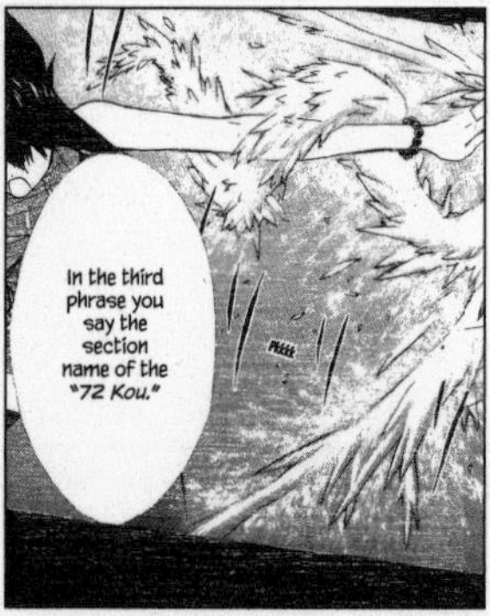
In the third phrase you say the section name of the "*72 Kou*."

72 Kou, page 103

72 kou are 72 equal sections made by dividing the *24 sekki* further into 3 sections.

Shiki Knowledge
February 2, Birth Stone [Conch Pearl]
Rei Seichiouji's *Shikifu* is made of from a Conch Pearl (Hardness: 2.5–4.5). The stone means, "My Dearest." It's a type of pearl that typically has a teardrop shape unlike a perfectly circular pearl. This pearl comes from the conch shell. Its characteristic is its pink color, similar to a coral pink, and it is very rare.
•February 2, Birth Flower (Flower Meaning) White Freesia (Innocence, Virginity), Quince (Ordinary, Fairy's Sparkle), etc.
•February 2 Holidays [Candlemas], [Married Couples Day], [Moxibustion Day], [Police Booth Installation Day], etc.
•February *Shiki Tsukai* Has the ability to amplify, manipulate, and shoot their "Chi." Also has healing abilities. They also use illusion incantations.
I, Rei

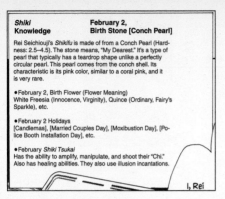

Candlemas, page 106

Candlemas, or the Feast of the Purification of the Virgin, is celebrated on February 2 and celebrates an early episode in the life of Jesus.

Married Couples Day, page 106

Married Couples Day is celebrated on February 2. It is the day on which one thanks and shows special appreciation toward one's spouse.

Moxibustion Day, page 106

It's believed burning mox would be most effective on February 2 and thus that day became a holiday.

Police Booth Installation Day, page 106

It's a holiday celebrating the installation of 7 police booths in Tokyo in 1881.

The Setsubun Festival day Shikifu...
Grab

Setsubun, page 129

Setsubun is a holiday celebrated on February 3. By throwing soybeans outdoors, one cleanses and wards off the evil and misfortunes of the previous year. Also eating the soybeans symbolically brings in good luck for the year to come.

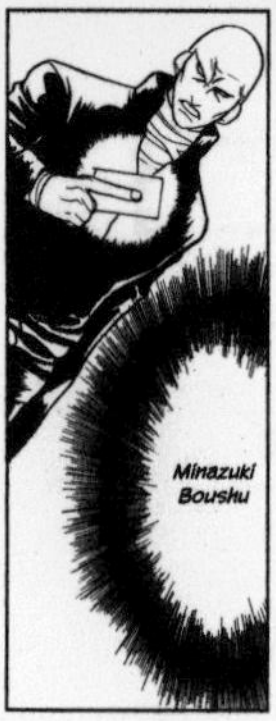
Minazuki
Boushu

Minazuki Boushu, page 140

Minazuki Boushu is the equivalent of June 6 under the lunisolar calendar.

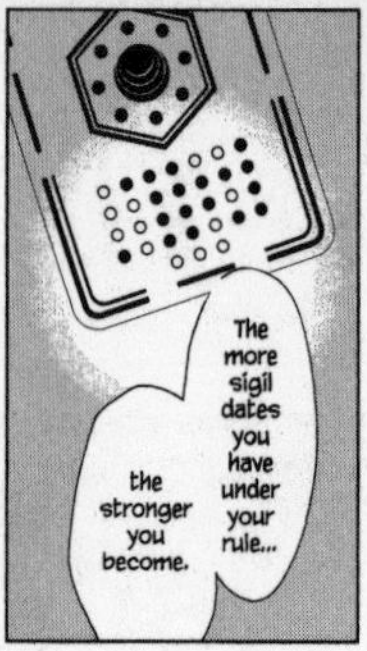
The more sigil dates you have under your rule...
the stronger you become.

Sigil dates, page 130

Sigil dates are the days that the *Shiki Tsukai* have under their rule. The sigil dates appear as black dots on their *Shikifu*.

TOMA

止まれ
[STOP!]

You're going the wrong way!

Manga is a completely different type of reading experience.

To start at the *beginning*, go to the *end*!

That's right! Authentic manga is read the traditional Japanese way—from right to left. Exactly the *opposite* of how American books are read. It's easy to follow: Just go to the other end of the book, and read each page—and each panel—from right side to left side, starting at the top right. Now you're experiencing manga as it was meant to be!